Issues in the Law of Rescission

Issues in the Law of Rescission

Edited by

JORDAN ENGLISH

Associate Professor of Law, Faculty of Law, University of Oxford, UK

JONAS ATMAZ AL-SIBAIE

Shaw Foundation Junior Research Fellow in Law, Jesus College, University of Oxford, UK

OXFORD
UNIVERSITY PRESS

OXFORD
UNIVERSITY PRESS

Great Clarendon Street, Oxford, OX2 6DP,
United Kingdom

Oxford University Press is a department of the University of Oxford.
It furthers the University's objective of excellence in research, scholarship,
and education by publishing worldwide. Oxford is a registered trade mark of
Oxford University Press in the UK and in certain other countries.

Published in the United States of America by Oxford University Press
546 Fifth Avenue, New York, NY 10036, United States of America.

British Library Cataloguing in Publication Data
Data available

Library of Congress Control Number: 2026936574

ISBN 9780198982869

DOI: 10.1093/9780198982852.001.0001

Printed and bound by
CPI Group (UK) Ltd., Croydon, CR0 4YY

MIX
Paper | Supporting responsible forestry
FSC® C013604

The manufacturer's authorized representative in the EU for product safety is
Oxford University Press España S.A. of Parque Empresarial San Fernando de Henares,
Avenida de Castilla, 2 – 28830 Madrid (www.oup.es/en or product.safety@oup.com).
OUP España S.A. also acts as importer into Spain of products made by the manufacturer.

Foreword

This splendid book seeks, by a collection of essays from a star-studded international cast of legal academics, to de-mythologise one of the most confused and uncertain areas of both Common Law and Equity. It does so by an adroit combination of legal history, precise statement of the current law, and thoughtful proposals for reform, and it leaves no stone unturned in the excavation and deployment of cases and academic writings from all over the common law world.

In the forty-five years since the general chaos caused by misusing 'rescission' also to describe termination of contracts for breach was put right in *Johnson v Agnew*,[1] judges and academic writers have continued to struggle to build a coherent uniform framework for the law of rescission. This is in part because it is par excellence an area where the Common Law and Equity have continued to use the same label to pursue their very different separate paths, with no attempt at fusion. Nor has the development of restitution and unjust enrichment provided an overall thesis for rescission, or any other unifying enlightenment. Hopeful statements from distinguished judges in the lower courts that rescission is ripe for review in the apex courts have met with little response, not out of any disinclination but because they rarely get cases which require it to be undertaken. The recent UK Supreme Court case of *Hopcraft v Close Brothers Ltd*[2] is a sad example. Rescission was on the agenda, but alas didn't have to be considered in any depth. My own judicial experience consists of participating in a couple of anodyne summaries (not tempered by any adversarial argument) and in one decision in the Court of Appeal,[3] where we were reversed 5-nil in the Supreme Court.[4]

But the book is about much more than just rescission. As a remedy, the law of rescission is, in both its common law and equitable forms, intricately linked with the legal analysis of the conduct (such as fraudulent misrepresentation and undue influence) which may bring it about. In its equitable form the still (just) live question whether and if so how far it is truly discretionary has to be, and is, addressed in the context of equitable remedies generally, and there is careful consideration of its operation and effect upon third parties and in insolvency. This book by no means shirks that necessary wider review, so as to set rescission in its proper place in the law. It will be a valuable source of legal understanding. It is also, in bite-sized chunks, a very enjoyable read.

Lord Briggs of Westbourne JSC
7 January 2026

[1] [1980] AC 367.
[2] [2025] UKSC 33, [2025] 3 WLR 423.
[3] *Hayward v Zurich Insurance Co plc* [2015] EWCA Civ 327, [2015] 1 CLC 581.
[4] *Hayward v Zurich Insurance Co plc* [2016] UKSC 48, [2017] AC 142.

Preface

This book is a collection of essays originally presented at a symposium on 'Issues in the Law of Rescission' hosted by the University of Oxford at the Weston Library on 14 March 2025. That symposium brought together judges, practitioners, academics, and students from around the world to discuss important and unresolved questions pertaining to rescission.

Rescission is a topic that straddles a number of divides in private law. The sheer breadth of legal topics it intersects with means that readers of this book will get the benefit of the full spectrum of private law scholarship touching on topics as diverse as contract, trusts, property, restitution, corporate transacting, and the intersection between private law and insolvency. Yet despite the breadth of topics dealt with in this book, the unifying feature remains the operation and conceptualisation of rescission.

We owe a great deal of thanks to many people. First and foremost, to our contributors, Elise Bant, Steven Elliott, Birke Häcker, Lusina Ho, Ben McFarlane, Magda Raczynska, Lionel Smith, Robert Stevens, William Swadling, and Man Yip, all of whose papers were presented at the symposium and all of whom undertook the work to produce the excellent chapters that are now found in this collection.

Second, we would like to thank Lord Briggs, Mr Justice Andrew Baker, Lady Justice Cockerill, and Professor Dame Sarah Worthington for chairing the sessions at which each draft chapter was presented. The authors have all benefited from the excellent comments provided by the chairs and those received from the audience, which were skilfully marshalled by the chairs. We are particularly grateful to Lord Briggs who, in addition to acting as a chair, kindly agreed to write the generous Foreword to this book.

It is also the case that symposia and books like this do not get produced without institutional support. We would therefore also like to thank the Faculty of Law at the University of Oxford for financially supporting this initiative through its Research Support Fund. That support allowed us additionally to retain Alexander Hughes, who provided excellent research and editorial support in the final stages of the book, and to whom we are also indebted. We must also thank Lionel Smith and Julius Grower (as chair of the Private Law Research Group) for extending their research budgets to further support the symposium. 'It takes a village' and we are fortunate to live in an excellent academic ecosystem here in Oxford.

Finally, we would like to thank the team at Oxford University Press, Rachel Mullaly, and Charlotte Kershaw for believing in this project and allowing it to come to fruition.

J. S. English
J. Atmaz Al-Sibaie
7 January 2026

Brief Contents

Detailed Contents

Table of Cases

AUSTRALIA

CANADA

CAYMAN ISLANDS

EUROPEAN COURT OF JUSTICE

HONG KONG

IRELAND

NEW ZEALAND

SINGAPORE

UNITED KINGDOM

UNITED STATES

Table of Legislation

ITALY

SPAIN

UNITED KINGDOM

Contributors

Jonas Atmaz Al-Sibaie is Shaw Foundation Junior Research Fellow in Law, Jesus College, Oxford, United Kingdom. https://orcid.org/0000-0003-3903-4403

Elise Bant is Professor of Private Law and Commercial Regulation, The University of Western Australia, Perth, Australia, and Professorial Fellow, University of Melbourne, Melbourne, Australia. https://orcid.org/0000-0003-2188-0521

Steven Elliott KC is Professor of Law, National University of Singapore, Singapore; Barrister, One Essex Court, London, United Kingdom.

Jordan English is Associate Professor of Law, University of Oxford, and Tutorial Fellow of Magdalen College, Oxford, United Kingdom. https://orcid.org/0000-0001-9456-1199

Birke Häcker is Schlegel Chair in Civil Law, Common Law and Comparative Law, University of Bonn, Bonn, Germany.

Lusina Ho is Harold Hsiao-Wo Lee Professor in Trust and Equity, The University of Hong Kong, Hong Kong. https://orcid.org/0000-0001-6241-4960

Ben McFarlane is Professor of English Law, University of Oxford, and Fellow of St John's College, Oxford, United Kingdom.

Magda Raczynska is Associate Professor, University College London, London, United Kingdom.

Lionel Smith is Professor of Comparative Law, University of Oxford, and Professorial Fellow of Brasenose College, Oxford, United Kingdom. https://orcid.org/0000-0001-7120-3735

Robert Stevens is Professor of English Private Law, University of Oxford, and Professorial Fellow of Lady Margaret Hall, Oxford, United Kingdom.

William Swadling is Professor of Law, University of Oxford, and Fellow of Brasenose College, Oxford, United Kingdom.

Man Yip is Professor of Law, V3 Group Professor in Family Entrepreneurship, Singapore Management University, Singapore.

1

Unravelling Rescission

Jordan English and Jonas Atmaz Al-Sibaie***

I. Introduction

Rescission is the principal mechanism by which voluntarily assumed obligations and transactions are unwound. As a result, it is of importance to a great range of commercial (and non-commercial)[1] transactions. It also cuts across various private law fields, such as contract law, trusts, property law, and the law of restitution. Yet, despite this commercial importance and the wide range of practitioners and scholars who regularly deal with it, the law on rescission remains riddled with conflicting decisions, poorly understood distinctions, and unresolved controversies. The normative foundations of rescission have also been under-analysed and theorised. Such is the state of the law that in *HMRC v IGE USA Investments Ltd*,[2] Henderson LJ remarked, in respect of one of the issues addressed in this volume,[3] that rescission is 'a notoriously difficult subject, on which the authorities are in such a state of disarray that . . . only the Supreme Court can reconcile them'.[4]

Why does a subject that attracts academic and practitioner attention[5] remain so bedevilled by unresolved issues? The reasons appear to be threefold.

First, for much of the twentieth century, the law's development has been hampered, at least in the contractual sphere, by the use of the label 'rescission' to describe two fundamentally different processes:[6] 'rescission' as a means by which to 'unwind', 'set aside', 'avoid', or 'terminate *ab initio*' a contract; and 'rescission' as a synonym for 'termination'—a means by which the parties to a contract may be relieved or discharged from further performance of their primary obligations under that contract.[7]

The difficulties caused by this have not just been semantic. Having the same label to describe two different concepts has led to substantive confusion. In *Horsler v Zorro*,[8]

* Associate Professor of Law, University of Oxford, and and Tutorial Fellow of Magdalen College, Oxford, United Kingdom.
** Shaw Foundation Junior Research Fellow in Law, Jesus College, Oxford, United Kingdom.

1 See Chapter 7 of this book (Yip Man, 'Rescission of Unconscionable Gifts').
2 [2021] EWCA Civ 534, [2021] Ch 423.
3 See Chapter 4 of this book (W Swadling, 'Rescission—The Role of the Court').
4 *HMRC v IGE USA Investments Ltd* [2021] Ch 423 [91].
5 Including the excellent monograph: D O'Sullivan, S Elliott, and R Zakrzewski, *The Law of Rescission* (3rd edn, OUP 2023).
6 See generally ibid [1.07]–[1.09]; Chapter 2 of this book (B Häcker, 'Explaining the Right to Rescind') 16–17; Swadling (n 3) 67; J O'Sullivan, 'Rescission as a Self-Help Remedy: A Critical Analysis' (2000) 58 CLJ 509, 525–28.
7 *Johnson v Agnew* [1980] AC 367, 392–93.
8 [1975] Ch 302.

for example, Megarry J held that in a contract for the sale of land, following an actual breach of contract, the innocent party could either (i) affirm the contract and claim damages or (ii) 'rescind', in which case they could not claim damages for the loss of the bargain.[9] This was because, in his words:

> [The innocent party] cannot in the same breath say that the contract should be set aside and the parties restored to their former positions and also that the contract should be treated as still being in force, and the party in breach made to pay damages for breach of the contract.[10]

This confuses the two concepts. The 'termination of a contract on accepted repudiation' does not involve 'rescission *ab initio*'[11]—that is, restoring the parties to their former positions. The decision was overruled in this respect by the House of Lords in *Johnson v Agnew*,[12] but the remnants of this confusion remain. In particular, due to other comments made by Megarry J in the case, *Horsler v Zorro* has been cited for the proposition that rescission, even in equity, is effected by an act of the party rather than an order of the court.[13] Yet as Professor William Swadling, commenting on one such instance, puts it in his contribution to this volume:

> [*Horsler v Zorro*] was concerned with termination for breach, decided shortly before the disentangling of the two concepts, rescission and termination, by the House of Lords five years later in *Johnson v Agnew* and *Photo Production Ltd v Securicor Transport Ltd*. Indeed, in light of these two decisions, it is a wonder that *Horsler v Zorro* was cited at all.[14]

A second reason is that while it is common to speak of rescission of 'contracts', this is not the only type of transaction that can be rescinded. Indeed, as Professors Birke Häcker and Lionel Smith point out in their contributions, other transactions are equally amenable to rescission.[15] Gifts of rights, as in *Allcard v Skinner*,[16] and declarations of trust, as in *Pitt v Holt*,[17] can also be rescinded. Achieving uniformity of the rules across different types of transactions is therefore difficult and may not even be desirable. Professor Yip Man argues in her contribution that the rules that have been developed for the rescission of contracts on the ground that the transaction was an 'unconscionable bargain'—rules that were 'chiefly formulated for market-related activities'[18]—cannot

[9] ibid 309.
[10] ibid.
[11] *Johnson v Agnew* [1980] AC 367, 398.
[12] ibid.
[13] See eg *Brotherton v Aseguradora Colseguros SA* [2003] EWCA Civ 705, [2003] 2 All ER (Comm) 298 [27], [45].
[14] Swadling (n 3) 87.
[15] Häcker (n 6) 18; Chapter 6 of this book (L Smith, 'Rescission in the Context of Fiduciary Relationships') 114.
[16] (1887) 36 Ch D 145.
[17] [2013] UKSC 26, [2013] 2 AC 108.
[18] Chapter 7 of this book (Yip Man, 'Rescission of Unconscionable Gifts') 137.

simply be applied to gifts without modification. This requires reflection 'on the values that underpin relationships where gifts are made and how to construct a sensible legal understanding of acceptable conduct in the social practice of gift-giving which has immense social value'.[19]

Even in the contractual sphere, it may not be accurate to speak of 'contracts' being rescinded. As Häcker explains, in German law '"rescission" is not something that operates directly on the contract itself, but instead on the affected party's "declaration of intent"'.[20] The position in English law is unclear. Smith, in his contribution, suggests '[i]t may be correct that rescission is always of unilateral legal acts'.[21] On this view, when a party exercises a power to rescind they are rescinding their legal act—that is, the offer or acceptance (as the case may be)—with the result that the contract falls away. Professor Robert Stevens, who more definitively adopts this view, argues in his chapter:

> 'Rescission' describes the exercise of a form of legal power: the power to set aside a juridical act, such as entering into a contract, making a will, declaring a trust, accepting a gift, or, in principle, an earlier act of rescission.[22]

The third reason the law of rescission gives rise to a great number of conflicting decisions and overlooked distinctions is that it spans so many divides in private law. Those who study it in detail must be 'able and energetic disciples'.[23] It spans the divide between contract and unjust enrichment,[24] personal and proprietary rights,[25] substantive and remedial law,[26] and statute and common law.[27] It also spans the divide between common law and equity. Thus, as Swadling explains in his chapter, '[t]he orthodoxy is that at common law rescission is a self-help remedy, while in equity it is effected by the issuance of a court order'.[28] The distinction between common law and

[19] ibid 137.
[20] Häcker (n 6) 18.
[21] Smith (n 15) 114 fn 5.
[22] Chapter 8 of this book (R Stevens, 'The Scope of Rescission for Duress') 163.
[23] As Francis Rose once said of restitution scholars for the same reason: F Rose, 'The Evolution of the Species' in A Burrows and A Rodger (eds), *Mapping the Law: Essays in Memory of Peter Birks* (OUP 2006) 13, 21.
[24] Where a contract (or a deed) creates an obligation to confer a benefit on the defendant, this will usually preclude an action in restitution even where an 'unjust factor' is present: *Dargamo Holdings Ltd v Avonwick Holdings Ltd* [2021] EWCA Civ 1149, [2022] 1 All ER (Comm) 1244 [70]. But once a party 'exercises his right of rescission . . . the obligation to make restitution may follow': *Portman Building Society v Hamlyn Taylor Neck* [1998] 4 All ER 202, 208. On whether rescission itself should be seen as a response to unjust enrichment, see Häcker (n 6) and compare Chapter 3 in this book (B McFarlane, 'Understanding Powers to Rescind: Property, Equity, and Unjust Enrichment') 63–64.
[25] On which, see McFarlane (n 24). As for whether rescission gives rise to personal or proprietary consequences, see Chapter 11 of this book (L Ho, 'The Proprietary Consequences of Rescission in Equity').
[26] If remedial law (ie the law of remedies) is understood to comprise the law of court orders, or court rulings (as is argued in S Smith, *Rights, Wrongs, Injustices: The Structure of Remedial Law* (OUP 2019) 3) then common law rescission—which, on the orthodox account, is effected by an act of the party alone—forms part of substantive law while equitable rescission—which, on the orthodox account, is effected by a court order—forms part of remedial law. On whether rescission is effected by the party or the court, see Swadling (n 3).
[27] In particular, see Chapter 9 of this book (S Elliott, 'The Power to Prevent Disproportionate Relief') on the interplay between the law of rescission and the Misrepresentation Act 1967, and Chapter 10 of this book (M Raczynska, 'Third-Party Rights and Insolvency as Bars to Rescission') on the interplay between rescission and the statutory schemes for personal and corporate insolvency.
[28] Swadling (n 3) 67. See also Ho (n 25) 243.

equitable rescission, aside from being relevant to when,[29] and by whose action, rescission takes effect, is also said to give rise to a further consequence: that when ordering rescission in equity 'there is a residual discretion in the court to refuse relief, even beyond the bars'.[30]

Both the proposition that rescission in equity is court-ordered and the proposition that it is subject to a residual discretion beyond the well-established bars have provoked strong reactions.[31] Insofar as these distinctions between common law and equitable rescission are a product of history, it has been said that 'there can be no justification for retaining historical categories for the sake only of history: no rational legal system should treat closely related vitiating factors differently merely because of the accident of their historical development'.[32] But while history alone is never an adequate justification, there is a concomitant danger in assuming that just because rescission at common law and in equity travel under the same label they are, in fact, fulfilling the same function. As Professor Ben McFarlane reminds us in his contribution:

> There are many contexts in which equity, at first glance, appears to have rules which mimic the effect of certain legal rules . . . It can be argued, however, that, in such cases, it is a serious mistake to think that the equitable rules are in fact answering the same question as their common law counterparts . . . The same care must be taken in relation to rescission in equity.[33]

This may not seem a promising start for a book on issues in the law of rescission. The risk of mistakes is high and the possibility that some context has been overlooked significant. But if anything, these difficulties demonstrate the clear need for continued scholarly attention on and engagement with the issues that arise in the context of rescission. That is what this book aims to provide.

II. The Issues

This book, let alone this introduction, cannot resolve the myriad of issues that arise in the law of rescission. They persist precisely because they are difficult. Instead, the aim of this volume is to shed light on these continuing controversies and to showcase the various different ways in which they could be resolved. There are six issues that deserve mention.

[29] A matter addressed by Professor Lusina Ho in her chapter: see Ho (n 25) 242–245.
[30] Swadling (n 3) 87. See also Ho (n 25) 243–245.
[31] On rescission in equity being court-ordered, see Swadling (n 3); S Elliott, 'The Basic Structure of Rescission' in B McFarlane and S Elliott (eds), *Equity Today: 150 Years after the Judicature Reforms* (Hart 2023) 167; O'Sullivan (n 6). On rescission in equity being subject to a residual discretion, see J English, 'Bribery and Secret Commissions: A Common Law-Equity Divide?' [2025] LMCLQ 158, 172–75.
[32] O'Sullivan (n 6) 528.
[33] McFarlane (n 24) 56–56.

A. Rescission: The Parties or the Court?

The first such issue has already been considered: whether rescission is always effected by the act of the parties or whether, at least when rescinding in equity, rescission is effected by a court order. As has been seen, Swadling, in his contribution, firmly takes the view that rescission in equity takes place by way of court order:

> [I]t is difficult to see how it could be otherwise. Given that the claimant in equity often wants some form of consequential relief, there is clearly a need to obtain a court order, for they will require the contempt jurisdiction of the court should the defendant refuse to comply.[34]

By contrast, Professor Steven Elliott, whose contribution to this volume concerns awards of damages in lieu of rescission,[35] has elsewhere taken the contrary view. In particular, he has argued forcefully that 'the Supreme Court should hold that rescission is effected in every case by the election of the rescinding party, rather than the eventual order of the court'.[36]

B. Justifying the Power to Rescind

Another uncertainty concerns the very justification for the right (or power) to rescind. Again, the contributors to this volume take different approaches. Häcker, in her contribution, argues that 'rescission is not merely "restitutionary" in the sense of potentially reversing already executed transactions, but that the *right to rescind* is itself based on unjust(ified) enrichment, even where it relates to a purely executory contract'.[37] In this respect, Häcker goes further than leading commentators, such as the editors of *Goff & Jones on Unjust Enrichment*.[38] She argues:

> [I]f a system chooses not simply to disregard a transaction beset by defects of consent, but to treat it as valid unless and until rescinded, then it has thereby moved the problem into the realm of restitution for unjustified enrichment. It is in the realm of restitution because the technique is one of reversal rather than automatic ineffectiveness, and it is in the realm of unjustified enrichment because the very reason for the reversal is the lack of justificatory basis (or *causa*).[39]

[34] Swadling (n 3) 88.
[35] Chapter 9 of this book (S Elliott, 'The Power to Prevent Disproportionate Relief').
[36] Elliott, 'The Basic Structure of Rescission' (n 31) 185.
[37] Häcker (n 6) 15.
[38] C Mitchell, P Mitchell, and S Watterson, *Goff & Jones on Unjust Enrichment* (10th edn, Sweet & Maxwell 2022) [40-16]–[40-17].
[39] Häcker (n 6) 38.

But this explanation of the power to rescind as being justified by unjust enrichment is controversial and is resisted by various other contributors. Professor Lusina Ho, for example, in her contribution, notes that one difficulty with the unjust-enrichment analysis is that although the counterparty to the contract acquires a right, '[a] right does not necessarily involve an enrichment in value, and treating a mere receipt of a right as enrichment begs the very question why this should be so'.[40]

McFarlane, similarly, in his chapter, notes that while 'there is some correspondence between the grounds that may give rise to rescission and the "unjust factors" that are relevant under such an analysis', there are, nonetheless, 'good grounds for scepticism as to the usefulness of such an approach'.[41] But while rejecting the utility of a general unjust enrichment analysis, he concedes that there is a sense in which the core case in which rescission operates—'where A holds a right and then exercises a power to transfer that right to B'[42]—can be analogised to what is sometimes said to be the core case of unjust enrichment—a mistaken payment (as in *Kelly v Solari*):[43]

> In each case, a primary legal event has occurred (in *Kelly*, a payment; in our case, the transfer of a right) and then a secondary set of rules operates to regulate the impact on A of the operation of the primary set of rules. Importantly, in each case, those secondary rules do not deny the validity of those primary set of rules: in *Kelly*, it is recognised that a payment has been made; in our case, it is accepted that a right *was* transferred. Nonetheless, something has gone wrong: A has exercised a power, conferred by the law to increase A's options, in circumstances where some flaw in A's consent compromises the value of A's choice to exercise the power. It is then possible for secondary rules to mitigate the impact on A of that flaw. Indeed, having such a secondary set of rules forms part of the justification for the content of those primary rules.[44]

C. The Grounds of Rescission

An important question in this volume is whether anything connects the various grounds of rescission. The grounds include misrepresentation (whether fraudulent or innocent), duress, undue influence, unconscionable bargains, 'breach' of fiduciary duty,[45] and bribery. Smith and Ho both argue that there is something that unites these various different grounds, albeit they differ on precisely what. Smith argues that '[i]n all of its manifestations, the rescission of a legal act is possible because the [claimant's] legal act is in some way defective when measured against the rules for the performance

40 Ho (n 25) 231.
41 McFarlane (n 24) 63.
42 ibid 43.
43 (1841) 9 M&W 54, 152 ER 24.
44 McFarlane (n 24) 64.
45 For the difficulty with the language of breach, see Smith (n 15) 114, 119.

of the act'—'wrongdoing [by the defendant] is not the direct foundation of rescission'.[46] In his view, although the law may insist on some conduct by the defendant, this is only because of a concern, in some cases, to take account of the interests of both parties.[47] In all cases, rescission is because of a defect in the *claimant*'s legal act.

Ho, however, argues that 'impaired consent alone does not render a transfer voidable save in limited circumstances'.[48] Instead, she locates the feature that unites the different grounds of rescission in *both* the claimant's defective consent and the conduct of the defendant. Powers to rescind are justified on the basis that 'those who coerce, mislead, or knowingly exploit the constraints affecting the other party's autonomy should not be allowed to rely on the impaired consent to assert their rights against the transferors'.[49] Given this justification, all the grounds for rescission must involve some coercion, misleading, or knowing exploitation on behalf of the defendant.

Altogether different is Stevens' account. Stevens rejects any unity to the grounds for rescission.[50] The 'central claim' of his chapter 'is that rescission is justified by a number of different reasons'.[51] What unifies rescission is not the justification of the right but rather the *form* of the right; the right to rescind is 'the power to set aside a juridical act'.[52] And '[j]ust as with other forms of right, such as subrogation, it should not be surprising that such a power arises for more than one reason.'[53]

Controversially, and contrary to the view taken by Smith above, this leads Stevens to argue that one such reason for rescission is the commission of a wrong:

> The (only) explanation for some cases of rescission is that a right against another has been acquired through wrongdoing, a breach of a duty owed to the promisor . . . Placing the parties as near as possible in the position they would have been in had the contract not been wrongfully procured may therefore mandate rescission, just as much as wrongdoing commonly requires compensation for consequential loss suffered.[54]

The view one takes on the grounds of rescission also leads to certain issues 'downstream'. In particular, if rescission is in some (or all) cases justified by a defect in the claimant's consent, then difficulties arise when the claimant is not a natural person but a legal person, such as a corporation. This is the subject of Professor Elise Bant's contribution.[55] As she demonstrates, determining the state of mind of a corporation is rarely straightforward.[56] One difficulty is that corporations do not have minds in the way

[46] ibid 114.
[47] ibid.
[48] Ho (n 25) 231.
[49] ibid 232.
[50] Stevens (n 22) 163.
[51] ibid 163.
[52] ibid.
[53] ibid. See also McFarlane (n 24) 64.
[54] Stevens (n 22) 172. Compare Smith (n 15) 114.
[55] Chapter 5 in this book (E Bant, 'Corporate Rescission and Director Fraud').
[56] ibid.

natural persons do. As such, the traditional approach to determining the state of mind of a corporation involves attributing the state of mind of some individual in the corporation to the corporation itself.[57] A second difficulty, which stems from this first, is that the traditional rules for attribution have held that when a director of a corporation acts fraudulently, and particularly contrary to the corporation's interests, the act or state of mind of that director is usually not attributed to the company.[58] Where the relevant act is contracting, this means that the contract is void, and not just voidable. The problem, as Bant points out, is that where the fraud has become a part of the corporation's business practices, holding that any resultant contract is 'void' allows the corporation to escape responsibility.

Bant seeks to resolve these difficulties by developing her model of 'Systems Intentionality'.[59] 'Systems Intentionality posits that corporations manifest (in the dual senses of reveal and instantiate) their states of mind through their adopted or deployed systems of conduct, policies, and practices.'[60] This means that, in finding that a corporation had some intention or acted, it is not always necessary to find a specific individual in the corporation who held that intention or acted, and whose intentions or acts can be attributed to the corporation in the traditional way. Accordingly, 'where the corporation acted with intention through some system of conduct in which the director played a part, it is prima facie responsible for that conduct.'[61] The result is that, if the act was the making of a contract, the contract should not be void as is sometimes thought, but it may still be voidable.

D. The Relevance of Discretion

Another important issue addressed by the contributors to this volume is the relevance of discretion to rescission. We have already seen one way in which discretion is addressed in this volume, namely, the extent to which courts have a discretion to refuse rescission beyond the applicable bars. Swadling, in his contribution, adopts the view that such a discretion exists.[62]

There is, however, a further way in which discretion is relevant to the law of rescission. If rescission is in principle available, the court has, under s 2(2) of the Misrepresentation Act 1967, a discretion to award damages in lieu of rescission. Elliott's contribution to this volume concerns the principles underpinning this discretion.[63] In his view, the purpose of s 2(2) of the 1967 Act is to empower courts to prevent rescission from giving the claimant disproportionate relief. Consequently, the power should be available 'wherever the consequences of rescission would be out of all proportion

[57] *Meridian Global Funds Management Asia Ltd v Securities Commission* [1995] 2 AC 500, 506–07.
[58] Bant (n 55) 102.
[59] Explored in detail in E Bant (ed), *The Culpable Corporate Mind* (Hart 2023).
[60] Bant (n 55) 92.
[61] ibid 102.
[62] Swadling (n 3) 87–88. Compare English, 'Bribery and Secret Commissions' (n 31) 172–75.
[63] Elliott, 'The Power to Prevent Disproportionate Relief' (n 35) 185–186.

to the injury suffered by the plaintiff'.[64] It is said to follow from this that the discretion should be exercised where 'the losses the misrepresenting party would suffer if the contract were rescinded'[65] would be disproportionate to 'the losses the aggrieved party will suffer by reason of the misrepresentation if the adjudicator upholds the contract'.[66] Once the discretion to award damages in lieu of rescission has been exercised, Elliott argues that the damages should be measured according to the ordinary compensatory measure in tort. In particular, he rejects the suggestions that the measure of damages should reflect some form of 'pecuniary rescission' or indeed that damages under s 2(2) should be based on the contract measure.[67]

How this discretion to award damages in lieu of rescission interacts with the supposed discretion in equity to refuse rescission beyond the applicable bars is another difficult issue. On one view, the very existence of the discretion to award damages in lieu of rescission under s 2(2), which only applies for non-fraudulent misrepresentations (usually the province of equitable rescission), suggests that Parliament did not think there was a residual discretion to refuse rescission in equity and is at least a good indication that courts should not be creating such a discretion outside of the s 2(2) power.[68]

E. Effect of Third-Party Rights

A further issue identified by contributors to this volume is the effect of third-party rights on the availability of rescission. As conventionally understood, 'the option to void the contract is barred where innocent third parties have, in reliance on the fraudulent contract, acquired rights which would be defeated by its rescission'.[69] The bar is 'concerned to protect the rights of third parties'.[70] Dr Magda Raczynska, in her contribution, joins a number of scholars[71] who have attacked this formulation of the third-party-rights bar.[72] In her words, as a total bar to rescission, 'the bar protects the third party while leaving the fraudster with an unwarranted windfall'.[73] Raczynska argues that the better view is that, at least in equity, 'the acquisition of property rights by a third party does not bar rescission . . . but only precludes rescission having restitutionary effects as against third parties'.[74]

[64] ibid 185, quoting Law Reform Committee, *Innocent Misrepresentation (Tenth Report)* (Cmnd 1782, 1962) [13].
[65] ibid 188.
[66] ibid 188.
[67] ibid 191–202.
[68] Elliott, 'The Basic Structure of Rescission' (n 31) 180; English, 'Bribery and Secret Commissions' (n 31) 174.
[69] *Tennent v City of Glasgow Bank (in liq)* (1879) 4 App Cas 615, 620–21.
[70] *Moses v Moses* [2022] UKPC 42 [90].
[71] B Häcker, 'Rescission and Third Party Rights' (2006) 14 RLR 21; B Häcker, *Consequences of Impaired Consent Transfers: A Structural Comparison of English and German Law* (Hart 2013) ch VII; S Zogg, *Proprietary Consequences in Defective Transfers of Ownership* (Intersentia 2020) 191–201; O'Sullivan, Elliott, and Zakrzewski (n 5) ch 20; J English, 'Deeds, Rescission and Restitution' (2023) 139 LQR 363, 368.
[72] Chapter 11 in this book (M Raczynska, 'Third-Party Rights and Insolvency as Bars to Rescission').
[73] ibid 205.
[74] ibid.

In a particularly novel contribution, Raczynska extends this analysis to the so-called insolvency bar to rescission, which is sometimes analysed as a third-party rights issue.[75] While again, the orthodox analysis is that the insolvency of the fraudster acts as a bar to rescission since it would prejudice the rights of the fraudster's creditors, Raczynska argues that 'the "insolvency bar" rests on some misconceptions and weak authority'.[76] Properly understood, 'the defrauded party is not generally precluded from rescinding the contract on the insolvency of the fraudster'.[77] The exception is in relation to contracts to take up shares in a company, in respect of which, upon insolvency, a bar on rescinding is justifiable.[78]

F. The Consequences of Rescission

The final controversy concerns the consequences of rescission. Following rescission, should the claimant get merely a personal right to restitution of benefits conferred pursuant to the transaction or do they acquire legal proprietary rights, or equitable proprietary rights in respect of the rights, to the assets that have been conveyed to the defendant pursuant to the transaction being rescinded? Swadling, in other writing, has argued that the claimant never obtains a power unilaterally to revest a right at law[79] and that the defendant is never a trustee for the claimant; all the claimant should have is 'a power in the court of equity . . . to order specific reconveyance'.[80] Ho, in her contribution to this volume, takes a different view:

> The availability of a purely personal remedy gives rise to a vulnerable period during the interval between the initial transfer and the court's final restorative order. The disputed right may be dissipated or sold to third parties, or the transferee may become insolvent . . . To leave the transferor exposed to these risks, especially after they have elected to rescind, would render meaningless the fundamental interest in transactional autonomy that the law seeks to protect.[81]

Beyond just suggesting that the power to rescind should be binding on third parties and that its exercise should give rise to a trust,[82] Ho also suggests that the claimant should be entitled to proprietary injunctions, remedies against those who dishonestly assist in dissipating the assets, and claims against recipients of the assets.

[75] For the reasons why this is not quite accurate, see ibid 205.
[76] ibid.
[77] ibid 213.
[78] ibid 213.
[79] W Swadling, 'Rescission, Property, and the Common Law' (2005) 121 LQR 123.
[80] W Swadling, 'The Proprietary Consequences of Fraud' in P Davies and H Tijo (eds), *Fraud and Risk in Commercial Law* (Hart 2024) 170.
[81] Ho (n 25) 233.
[82] ibid 236–239.

III. Why It Matters

It would be wrong to consider the resolution of these issues in the law of rescission as being of theoretical interest only. Even the most theoretical issues, such as the justifications for the power to rescind, have important, practical, consequences. In the final section of this introduction, we highlight three examples where the issues addressed in this volume have arisen before the courts and been relevant to the determination of the dispute.

A. *Zurich Insurance Co plc v Hayward*

The first is *Zurich Insurance Co plc v Hayward*.[83] In 1998, Hayward suffered an accident at work. In 2001, he commenced proceedings against his employer claiming approximately £420,000 in compensation for the injury. His employers admitted liability but disputed the amount recoverable. They did not believe that Hayward was as injured as he claimed to be. But given concerns about their ability to prove this in court, they entered into an agreement to settle Hayward's claim for £134,973.

Two years later, Hayward's neighbours approached Zurich Insurance, who had conducted the litigation on behalf of Hayward's employers, with evidence that Hayward was not as injured as he purported to be. With this evidence in hand, Zurich Insurance sought to rescind the settlement agreement with Hayward.[84]

The Court of Appeal (Underhill, Briggs, and King LJJ) had held that Zurich was not entitled to rescind. Briggs LJ (as his Lordship then was) said that '[f]or a misstatement to be the basis for a claim to rescind a contract, the claimant must have given some credit to its truth, and been induced into making the contract by a perception that it was true rather than false'.[85] But here, because Zurich knew full well that Hayward was not as injured as he claimed to be, they were not in any way mistaken.

The Supreme Court allowed Zurich's appeal. Differing from the Court of Appeal, Lord Clarke (with whom Lord Neuberger, Baroness Hale, Lord Reed, and Lord Toulson agreed) said, at least in the context of deceit, that 'it is not necessary, as a matter of law, to prove that the representee believed that the representation was true'.[86]

The dispute in *Zurich* and the difference between the Court of Appeal and the Supreme Court go to the heart of the issue discussed in Section II.C above, namely, whether there is anything that unites the various grounds of rescission. On the view that all grounds of rescission involve some impairment in the claimant's consent,[87] the result in the Supreme Court looks difficult to defend. And indeed, *Zurich* has been

[83] [2016] UKSC 48, [2017] AC 142.
[84] Zurich Insurance also brought claims in the tort of deceit.
[85] *Hayward v Zurich Insurance Co plc* [2015] EWCA Civ 327, [2015] 1 CLC 581 [28].
[86] *Zurich Insurance Co plc v Hayward* [2017] AC 142 [18].
[87] See Smith (n 15) 114; J Edelman and E Bant, *Unjust Enrichment* (2nd edn, Hart 2016) 125.

strongly criticised on the basis that it is inconsistent with the 'long-standing view that the basis of rescission for fraudulent (or indeed any form of) misrepresentation lies in the representee's induced mistake.'[88]

But on the view put forward by Stevens in his contribution to this volume, namely, that the power to rescind can arise for a variety of different reasons, *Zurich* is defensible. This is because one of the reasons that gives rise to the power to rescind is where the contract or other transaction is procured by a wrong. As Stevens argues:

> [I]f the misrepresentation constitutes deceit, it suffices that it contributed to the entering into of the contract, regardless of whether it is believed or not. Rescission is then justified by the wrong committed in acquiring the right, rather than by any defect in the promisee's consent.[89]

B. *Patarkatsishvili v Woodward-Fisher*

We have already seen that one consequence of the distinction between common law and equitable rescission, highlighted in Swadling's and Ho's contributions,[90] is that when seeking rescission in equity 'there is a residual discretion in the court to refuse relief, even beyond the bars.'[91] This 'broad discretion' is controversial[92] and has led to creative arguments being made by litigants to persuade the court to refuse relief.

One such case is *Patarkatsishvili v Woodward-Fisher*,[93] discussed in Ho's contribution.[94] In that case, the claimants were induced by fraudulent misrepresentations of the defendant to purchase a house for £32.5 million. The misrepresentations concerned a severe moth infestation in the insulation of the house. After discovering the infestation, and undertaking remedial work, the claimants sought to rescind the contract of sale on the ground of the defendant's fraudulent misrepresentations.

It was accepted by the parties that rescission was only available in equity.[95] Although fraud is a ground of rescission at law, title to the house was registered and therefore could not revest without the assistance of the court.[96] The defendant argued that because rescission was taking effect in equity, the court had a discretion to refuse relief if 'practical justice' could not be achieved by rescission.[97] In particular, the defendant (unmeritoriously) argued that practical justice could not be achieved because *he* did not have £32.5 million to effect restitution of the purchase price. He also argued that

[88] Mitchell, Mitchell, and Waterson (n 38) [9-63] fn 161. See also the criticism in P Davies and W Day, 'A Mistaken Turn in the Law of Misrepresentation' [2019] LMCLQ 390.
[89] Stevens (n 22) 172.
[90] Swadling (n 3) 87; Ho (n 25) 243–245.
[91] Swadling (n 3) 87.
[92] See Ho (n 25) 243–245; English, 'Bribery and Secret Commissions' (n 31) 172–75.
[93] [2025] EWHC 265 (Ch).
[94] Ho (n 25) 244.
[95] *Patarkatsishvili v Woodward-Fisher* [2025] EWHC 265 (Ch) [173].
[96] ibid.
[97] ibid.

the works undertaken by the claimants and the fact that they had lived in it meant that restitution could not be made by the claimants of the property sold. The Court rejected these arguments and ordered rescission.

Fancourt J, in particular, rejected the suggestion that even where there was no bar to a claim for rescission, the Court retained a broad discretion to refuse rescission where it would be 'unjust' or deny 'practical justice' to the parties.[98] He said:

> I therefore reject the Defendant's argument that, where fraud is established, the court retains a discretion to refuse rescission in equity. The authorities establish that there may be bars to a claim for rescission, which include inability of a claimant to make counter restitution; but if counter restitution can be given and there is no bar, there is no residual discretion that the Court can exercise on the basis that it appears fairer to leave a claimant to recover damages at law.[99]

The rejection of this broad discretion in *Woodward-Fisher* runs contrary to the line of authority, which suggests that such a discretion does exist.[100] As Ho argues in her contribution, '[u]ntil the Supreme Court provides guidance, these conflicting judicial opinions mean that the availability of rescission will remain unpredictable'.[101]

C. *Moses v Moses*

The final case to mention is the decision of the Privy Council on appeal from Trinidad and Tobago in *Moses v Moses*.[102] The claimant was the executor of the will of her husband and had, by mistake,[103] executed a deed transferring title to 3.5 acres of land to her son who was not entitled to it under the terms of the will. The Privy Council agreed with the Court of Appeal of Trinidad and Tobago's assessment that the deed had been executed under a serious mistake such as would entitle the claimant to rescind. But in the meantime, title to the land had been sold for $300,000 to a bona fide purchaser for value without notice of any interest of the claimant, who subsequently developed and subdivided the land, selling on those plots to various purchasers. Five of the plots were sold back to the defendant who, after on-selling them, had made a further profit of $320,000.

The Privy Council proceeded on the basis—which, as we have seen, is challenged by Raczynska in this volume[104]—that the intervention of third-party rights precluded

[98] ibid [187].
[99] ibid.
[100] See eg *Johnson v EBS Pensioner Trustees Ltd* [2002] EWCA Civ 164, [2002] Lloyd's Rep PN 309 [78]–[79]; *Hurstanger Ltd v Wilson* [2007] EWCA Civ 299, [2007] 1 WLR 2351 [45]; *UBS AG (London Branch) v Kommunale Wasserwerke Leipzig GmbH* [2017] EWCA Civ 1567, [2017] 2 Lloyd's Rep 621 [157], [370]–[371].
[101] Ho (n 25) 244.
[102] [2022] UKPC 42.
[103] Albeit this point was disputed, and part of the case concerned whether the Court of Appeal should have interfered with findings of the primary judge that there had been no mistake: see ibid [56]–[57]; English, 'Deeds, Rescission and Restitution' (n 71) 364–65.
[104] Raczynska (n 72).

rescission of the deed of conveyance. Lord Sales (with whom Lord Kitchin and Lord Lloyd-Jones agreed) noted the possibility that rescission might not be precluded,[105] but ultimately said that the Board had heard no argument on the question.[106] By contrast, Lord Burrows and Lady Rose (in dissent, but only due to a disagreement about whether the Court of Appeal should have interfered with the findings of fact of the primary judge) went further and expressed the more definitive view that rescission was barred. They said there are 'well-established bars to rescission and, at least normally, one such bar is concerned to protect the rights of third parties'.[107] Ultimately, the Privy Council allowed a claim in restitution of unjust enrichment to succeed on the basis that the defendant had been enriched by the claimant's mistake in the amount of $300,000, but not the further profit of $320,000.[108]

Had it been argued, as Raczynska does in this volume, that the third-party rights bar is not a total bar to rescission in equity but rather simply prevents rescission having third-party effects, then the result may have been different.[109] On this analysis, the claimant *would* have been entitled to rescind in equity as against the defendant but not the bona fide purchaser. The effect of rescinding, as discussed in Ho's contribution to this volume,[110] would then be to give the claimant retrospectively[111] a trust over the title to the land, which would then have enabled the claimant to trace into the $300,000 obtained by the defendant in exchange. And if that original $300,000 was used to repurchase the five plots, which were then sold on, the claimant could have traced into these proceeds of sale too.

IV. Conclusion

The aim of this introduction has been to set the scene for the chapters that follow. Rescission is a topic that straddles a number of divides in private law. For that reason, it is difficult and various issues remain contested. But it is also for that reason that it is of great interest. Moreover, as this introduction has sought to show, the arguments advanced in this book are by no means of theoretical interest only. They are relevant to the determination of disputes before courts at all levels.

[105] Citing D O'Sullivan, S Elliott, and R Zakrzewski, *The Law of Rescission* (2nd edn, OUP 2014) [20.23].
[106] *Moses v Moses* [2022] UKPC 42 [66].
[107] ibid [90].
[108] ibid [73], citing *Investment Trust Companies v HMRC* [2017] UKSC 29, [2018] AC 275; *Prudential Assurance Co Ltd v HMRC* [2018] UKSC 39, [2019] AC 929.
[109] See the discussion in English, 'Deeds, Rescission and Restitution' (n 71) 368.
[110] Ho (n 25).
[111] Although see the discussion in ibid 240–242.

2

Explaining the Right to Rescind

*Birke Häcker**

I. Setting the Scene

Consider the following scenario: in an effort to force herself to walk at least ten thousand steps a day, academic A decides to do away with her car. She advertises it on social media. B, introducing himself as a student at A's university, shows an interest and tells A that he has the requisite funds available at his disposition. A thereupon agrees to sell the car to B for a price of £8,000. Since B promises to transfer the money the same day, A lets him take away the car immediately. The bank transfer fails to materialise, however, and it transpires that B is a fraudster who has no funds whatsoever. The law gives A the ability to rescind the agreement(s) with B, but why?

The aim of this chapter is to explore the conceptual foundations of the law of rescission. What explains and justifies a party's right to rescind a contract or other transaction? How do we account for a mechanism that treats a transaction as neither fully valid nor automatically invalid or void, but 'voidable' at the behest of one party? And what exactly is the relationship between rescission and restitution, given that restitution is often described as an effect of rescission? These kinds of questions are obviously far too 'big' to be answered comprehensively and definitively in the space allocated. Yet it is nonetheless helpful to view them side-by-side since they are closely connected. It is also instructive to take a step back and to consider the issues from a wider perspective than can be gained by focusing just on the position at common law and/or in equity. Such a broader vista need not entail abstract pontifications of principle, devoid of 'black-letter' substantive content, but instead encourages the adoption of a comparative approach with the concomitant historical awareness. A good comparator for present purposes is the civilian tradition of continental Europe, as exemplified by German and French law.

It will be seen that a given system's justifications for rescission are intimately intertwined with its conception of contract and with what makes contracts binding. This in fact explains why the recognised grounds for rescission diverge more strongly between the common law and the civilian tradition than other aspects of contract law. That conclusion should hopefully emerge from the chapter as beyond contention. With regard to the relationship of rescission with restitution, however, the claim here is bolder and

* Schlegel Chair in Civil Law, Common Law and Comparative Law, University of Bonn, Bonn, Germany.

at the same time more experimental. Building on the link between rescission and the binding effect of contracting, the contribution also seeks to explore and defend a suggestion which has been floated for some time (yet which has also been met with strong resistance), namely that rescission is not merely 'restitutionary', in the sense of potentially reversing already executed transactions, but that the *right to rescind* is itself based on unjust(ified) enrichment, even where it relates to a purely executory contract.

II. Preliminaries: The Mechanism of 'Rescission' and its Reach

Oliver Wendell Holmes Jr once observed that '[r]escission, or avoidance properly so called, annihilates the contract, and puts the parties in the same position as if the contract had never existed'.[1] While this statement might at first sight appear to be a perfectly plausible definition of rescission and thus a good starting point for the present discussion, it was in fact made in the context of a repudiation case.[2] Holmes J held that 'notice that a party will not perform his contract has the same effect as a breach'.[3] His statement is nonetheless a useful starting point for the exercise to be undertaken in this chapter since it raises a number of issues which will help delineate 'rescission' properly so called and its scope with greater precision. Four key preliminaries ought to be borne in mind when pondering what follows.

A. Rescission versus Termination

First, we are here dealing with rescission for misrepresentation, undue pressure, and, depending on the system and the context, some instances of spontaneous mistake.[4] We are distinctly *not* dealing with what in the common law world used to be called (and sometimes still is) 'rescission for breach'. The preferred modern terminology for the latter is 'termination'.[5] The distinction between the two scenarios was famously highlighted in *Johnson v Agnew*[6] and in *Photo Production Ltd v Securicor Transport Ltd*.[7] As Lord Wilberforce said in the former case:

> [I]t is important to dissipate a fertile source of confusion and to make clear that although the vendor is sometimes referred to in the [case of an accepted repudiation] as

[1] *Ballou v Billings*, 136 Mass 307, 309 (1884).

[2] The mixing up of the two categories, at least linguistically, is not at all uncommon in this area of the law: cf eg *Boomer v Muir*, 24 P.2d 570 (1933).

[3] *Ballou v Billings*, 136 Mass 307, 309 (1884).

[4] In the common law tradition, breach of fiduciary duty is frequently also counted as a ground for rescission, but this has no direct civilian counterpart and it is not explored here. For a critical assessment, see Chapter 6 of this book (L Smith, 'Rescission in the Context of Fiduciary Relationships'). For rescission in the bribery context, see J English, 'Bribery and Secret Commissions: A Common Law–Equity Divide?' [2025] LMCLQ 159, esp 171–75.

[5] See eg J Cartwright, *Misrepresentation, Mistake and Non-Disclosure* (7th edn, Sweet & Maxwell 2025) [8-41]–[8-43].

[6] [1980] AC 367.

[7] [1980] AC 827, esp 844, 850.

'rescinding' the contract, this so-called 'rescission' is quite different from rescission ab initio, such as may arise for example in cases of mistake, fraud or lack of consent. In those cases, the contract is treated in law as never having come into existence ... In the case of an accepted repudiatory breach the contract has come into existence but has been put an end to or discharged. Whatever contrary indications may be disinterred from old authorities, it is now quite clear, under the general law of contract, that acceptance of a repudiatory breach does not bring about rescission ab initio.[8]

The difference between 'rescission' in this narrower sense and 'termination' lies in the fact that the former annihilates the contract with retroactive effect, wiping it out completely. The latter, by contrast, typically discharges only the parties' primary obligations, leaving secondary obligations (such as the duty to pay damages for breach) as well as ancillary arrangements (such as arbitration clauses) in place. In our original example, there is a clear conceptual difference between the seller A 'terminating' the sale contract with the buyer B on account of B's failure to pay, and A 'rescinding' the contract on account of B's fraudulent misrepresentation concerning the availability of funds.

B. The Right to Rescind as an Option

The second point is that, regardless of how precisely discharge following 'termination' operates,[9] there is no doubt that 'rescission' in the sense considered here is something that has to be initiated by the party entitled to raise the matter. This is the person whose agreement to the transaction was adversely affected through whatever factor the legal system recognises as relevant. 'Rescission' is then the mechanism by which the 'mistake, fraud or lack of consent' (to use Lord Wilberforce's words for the time being) is asserted. It does not matter for present purposes whether the mechanism is one of self-help or requires a court order.[10] The crucial characteristic of the right to rescind—a 'remedy' to the common law mind—is that the holder has an option whether or not to exercise it. This is effectively a choice between leaving the affected transaction in place, treating it as fully valid, and avoiding it *ab initio*. If, in our original example, A as the defrauded seller decides to hold onto the bargain despite B's misrepresentation, and if she tells B so, she will have affirmed the contract. If A instead elects to exercise her right to rescind, the contract of sale will, for all intents and purposes, be annihilated. Properly rephrased, we should be speaking not of a 'right to rescind', but of an 'option' or 'power' to rescind.

[8] *Johnson v Agnew* [1980] AC 367, 392–93.

[9] See the recent contribution by J English, *Discharge of Contractual Obligations* (OUP 2025).

[10] Different legal systems adopt different approaches here. German law treats rescission as a self-help remedy (see s 143(1) of the Bürgerliches Gesetzbuch (BGB)), while French law follows the court-order model (see arts 1131, 1178, 1181 of the *Code Civil*). In the common law tradition, the matter is more complicated and heavily disputed: see eg Chapter 4 of this book (W Swadling, 'Rescission—The Role of the Court'), and contrast S Elliott, 'The Basic Structure of Rescission' in B McFarlane and S Elliott (eds), *Equity Today: 150 Years after the Judicature Reforms* (Hart 2023) 167.

C. The Object on which Rescission Operates

Third, while—like Holmes—lawyers all over the world tend to think of rescission in connection with 'contracts', it is worth examining the remit of the mechanism a little more closely. One of the best-known rescission cases in English law is *Allcard v Skinner*,[11] yet that case involved a gift rather than a contract. It is therefore clear that transactions other than 'contracts' are potentially also amenable to rescission as far as common law systems are concerned. In fact, we know from *Pitt v Holt*[12] that 'voluntary dispositions' such as gifts can be 'set aside' more readily than contractual bargains.[13] Civilian jurisdictions without a doctrine of consideration do not need to enter a corresponding proviso about gratuitous transactions also being amendable to rescission since, for them, gifts simply constitute a special type of contract.[14] The French Civil Code (*Code Civil*) thus squarely places its equivalent to the law of rescission into the section dealing with the 'validity requirements' of contracts,[15] namely under the heading 'defects in consent' (*les vices du consentement*).[16]

German law has an even wider notion of contract, encompassing not merely 'obligatory' transactions such as sale or gift agreements, but also transactions with purely proprietary effect (so-called 'real agreements'). For German lawyers, any legal transaction brought about by the corresponding declarations of two or more parties (offer and acceptance where the agreement comes about in consecutive steps) is technically a 'contract'. Contracts can be either of an 'obligational' or a 'dispositive' nature. Obligational contracts are used to create an obligatory relationship between the parties, thereby generating inter-party personal claims, especially claims to performance. Dispositive contracts are transactions that transfer, extinguish, burden, or reconfigure an existing right (personal or proprietary: hence the term 'real agreements'). They often play a role in the discharge of personal claims, such as when the seller of goods (in our example, A) transfers ownership to the buyer (B) in performance of the

11 (1887) 36 Ch D 145.

12 [2013] UKSC 26, [2013] 2 AC 108.

13 It was held in this case that a purely unilateral 'causative mistake of sufficient gravity' counted, although such a mistake would not have justified the rescission of a reciprocal contract. For a discussion, see B Häcker, 'Mistaken Gifts after Pitt v Holt' (2014) 67 CLP 333.

14 This does not in and of itself mean that gifts are—or ought to be—necessarily subject to the same rules on rescission as reciprocal contracts. There is an argument to be made for operating a more generous regime for setting aside gratuitous transactions. Broadly speaking, this is indeed the approach of French law (see *Code Civil*, art 1135(2)), whereas German law makes no similar concession. For a discussion, see B Häcker, '*La Troisième Jeunesse du Code Civil*: A German Lawyer Looks at the Reform of French Contract Law' in J Cartwright and S Whittaker (eds), *The Code Napoléon Rewritten: French Contract Law after the 2016 Reforms* (Hart 2017) 387, 404–06.

15 *Code Civil*, art 1128 (as reformed in 2016/2018) in the English translation by J Cartwright, B Fauvarque-Cosson, and S Whittaker (from which all further translations of the reformed Code are also taken):

> 'The following are necessary for the validity of a contract:
> 1. the consent of the parties;
> 2. their capacity to contract;
> 3. content which is lawful and certain.'

16 *Code Civil*, arts 1130–44.

vendor's obligations under the contract of sale. The thing to note about German law is that, formally speaking, 'rescission' is not something that operates directly on the contract itself, but instead on the affected party's 'declaration of intent'.[17] But since 'declarations of intent' are the elementary building blocks from which all legal transactions are constructed, the retroactive annihilation of one party's consent (or 'declaration of intent') to a legal transaction makes the whole transaction collapse with retroactive effect.[18] In this way, the remit of rescission is comparatively broad under German law. It applies not merely to reciprocal contracts and gratuitous gift contracts but also to unilateral transactions such as the making of a will, and potentially even to purely dispositive transactions such as conveyances of rights *in rem*. All that matters is whether the rescinding party's consent to a *specific* transaction was impaired in a relevant way, so that the avoidance of the *specific* declaration of intent can be justified by one of the recognised grounds for rescission.

D. Rescission *Ab Initio* and Restitution

Finally, as a fourth preliminary, a word on Holmes' observation that rescission 'puts the parties in the same position as if the contract had never existed'. This can be read in two different ways. Subject to the proviso that one is talking about rescission *ab initio* rather than termination,[19] it could be read as saying something quite unremarkable. Of course, a contract that has been completely annihilated with retroactive effect is, as far as the parties are concerned, a contract that never actually existed.[20] Yet many common lawyers pondering Holmes' statement will understand it as saying something more. It can also be read to mean that the rescission of a contract automatically *effects* restitution of all performances that have been exchanged in pursuance of it. In our initial example, it would mean that title to the car that was the subject matter of the sale would automatically revert to A if and when A rescinds the contract of sale on account of B's fraudulent misrepresentation. That appears to be the case under English law, as illustrated by well-known decisions such as *Car & Universal Finance Co Ltd v Caldwell*.[21] Some caveats are warranted to nuance the picture, however.[22]

[17] As evidenced by the place where the grounds of rescission are set out in the Code: BGB, ss 119–24.

[18] See BGB, s 142(1).

[19] See text to and following nn 5–8.

[20] It is sometimes said that the retroactive annihilation of a contract is not possible under English law where third-party rights have intervened (so-called 'third-party rights bar to rescission'), yet this qualification is neither warranted nor necessary as far as the relationship between the contracting parties is concerned: see B Häcker, 'Rescission and Third Party Rights' [2006] RLR 21 as well as Chapter 10 of this book (M Raczynska, 'Third-Party Rights and Insolvency as Bars to Rescission').

[21] [1965] 1 QB 525.

[22] For background information in connection with the discussion which follows, see B Häcker, 'Contract and Conveyance: The Further Repercussions of Different Transfer Systems' in J Cartwright and AM López y López (eds), *Property and Contract: Comparative Reflections on English and Spanish Law* (Hart 2021) 89, esp 92–101, 114–18.

First, if rescission does indeed effect restitution in the context of the sale of goods under English law,[23] that may be down to no more than the fact that the contract of sale was the vehicle for passing title. Systems treating obligatory contracts as vehicles of conveyance in the way the Sale of Goods Act 1979 does must expect restitution to follow from the rescission of such obligatory contracts.[24] This is the position in France, for instance. In fact, under the French *Code Civil*, the pure consensual principle in property transfers goes far beyond the sale of goods.

Second, what about legal regimes which treat contract and conveyance as distinct, namely systems (or areas of the law) where the conveyance requires a delivery or some other public manifestation of the transfer, such as registration? How far does the rescission of the contract then impact the conveyance? The answer depends on whether or not one regards the existence and validity of a personal claim to performance as essential to the validity of a transfer of ownership or title made in pursuance of it. It is perfectly coherent for a legal system to link the conveyance to the underlying contract in this way. Systems adopting such an approach are known as 'causal'. If, for instance, our case were to play out under Austrian law, A's rescission of the contract of sale for B's fraud would mean that ownership of the car could not have passed to B upon delivery, simply because the purported transfer lacked a recognised legal basis (*iusta causa traditionis*). Any common lawyer who thinks that rescission of an obligatory contract automatically leads both parties' performances to be reversed, irrespective of the mode of transfer used,[25] must be impliedly assuming the entire common law to be, in principle, 'causal'.

The alternative is to maintain that conveyances are not merely separate transactions from the obligatory contract in pursuance of which they are made, but that the validity of the former is entirely independent of the existence and validity of the latter. This is how 'abstract' transfer systems approach the matter. German law is (in)famous for its firm commitment to the so-called principle of abstraction. Under the German Civil Code—the *Bürgerliches Gesetzbuch* (BGB)—the 'dispositive' contract forming part of the conveyance will entail an unimpeachable property transfer whether or not there is a valid legal basis, and therefore irrespective of whether an underlying 'obligatory' contract has been rescinded. Where the 'abstract' approach is adopted, the task of 'rectifying'—in appropriate cases—what ultimately becomes a normative mismatch between the (valid) conveyance and the (rescinded) obligatory transaction falls entirely to the law of unjustified enrichment. By contrast with the English law governing the sale of goods, abstraction clearly pervades English land law. A conveyance of realty

[23] Questioned by W Swadling, 'Rescission, Property, and the Common Law' (2005) 121 LQR 123.

[24] See eg B Häcker, 'Rescission of Contract and Revesting of Title: A Reply to Mr Swadling' [2006] RLR 106.

[25] The following quite general statement may serve as just one example: H Beale, 'Misrepresentation' in H Beale (ed), *Chitty on Contracts*, vol 1 (36th edn, Sweet & Maxwell 2026) [10-133]: 'When a contract is rescinded it has the effect of revesting any property transferred in the transferor, so far as no formal steps are required for the retransfer.' This view then has to contend with the question why, in a case where the buyer of goods has already paid for them, rescission of the contract of sale does not in and of itself effect restitution of the purchase price, regardless of whether it was the seller or buyer rescinding and regardless of whether the money was still identifiable in the seller's hands.

does not fail at common law merely because the contract for the sale of land lacks formality or happens to be rescinded.[26]

Third, and further to the original sale of goods example, there is another puzzle in the common law. Quite irrespective of whether the outcome of sale cases such as *Caldwell* is explicable solely by the fact that the contract itself operated as a vehicle of conveyance (the preferable explanation) or whether a more general 'causal' principle of property transfer accounts for it (the significantly broader alternative explanation), it is not entirely clear why common lawyers routinely speak of title to goods sold 'revesting' when the contract of sale is rescinded *ab initio*, as though title literally 'came back' to the seller upon rescission—when one might otherwise be tempted to say that, in retrospect, title never actually passed to the buyer at all.

III. What Makes a Contract or Other Transaction Binding?

In light of these preliminaries, the first issue to be examined a little more closely is what exactly accounts for the binding force of some transactions, but not others. At a general level, all legal systems have to make choices on issues such as the protagonists' capacity, the confines of legality (and possibly morality), as well as—in some situations—formal requirements. Such choices will directly impact what parties can and cannot validly do and thus be in play when it comes to bindingness. What we are primarily interested in, however, is *consent* as it manifests itself in someone who in principle has full capacity, and in *any other element* that may additionally explain why and how such a person is held to their word.

Looking at the long-term historical development, it is undeniable that the binding nature of a number of transactions was originally rooted in pure ceremony and form. The Roman 'verbal' contract of *stipulatio* and conveyances by *mancipatio* or *in iure cessio* immediately come to mind.[27] A similar point could be made with respect to the old English action of covenant and conveyances by livery of seisin.[28] In archaic law, form was often able to work its magic regardless of full and free consent. This has changed. We are today living in legal systems where form may occasionally be required to *manifest* consent (eg in contracts for the sale of land), and where form may sometimes even 'replace' some other element—beside consent—that would otherwise be essential to validity or enforceability (eg when a promise not supported by consideration is enshrined in a deed under English law). But today form alone is typically no conclusive answer to the question of when parties will be held to their word, or at any rate no

[26] Common lawyers who assume their system to be wholly 'causal' might try to put this down to the formality of the transfer and the operation of the land register: cf the passage quoted in the immediately preceding footnote.

[27] See only the account in Gaius' *Institutes* (second century AD): G.3.92 et seq (on verbal contracts), G.1.119, G.2.14a et seq (on formal conveyances).

[28] See eg J Baker, *An Introduction to English Legal History* (5th edn, OUP 2019) 339–42 (on the action of covenant), 250, 275–77 (on livery of seisin).

final answer. We will therefore try to leave formality rules as far as possible to one side in the analysis that follows.

For exposition purposes, we can subdivide the analysis of what makes contracts and other transactions binding into two parts: 'obligatory transactions', with reciprocal contracts such as sale as the central case, and (where applicable) 'dispositive transactions' entered into for the purposes of discharging contractual or other obligations. We then need to look more closely at what legal systems actually mean by 'agreement' and 'consent'.

A. Obligatory Transactions: Consideration, *Causa Contractus*, and Consent

In a reciprocal contract, where each party promises the other some performance in return for the expected counter-performance, the key question from a modern perspective is whether the binding nature of the parties' agreement is rooted in the fact alone that it has been concluded, or whether some additional factor is indispensable to explaining its validity and/or enforceability.[29]

The comparative picture is relatively straightforward, at least on a basic level.[30] It is well known that the common law requires promises to be supported by consideration if they are to be enforceable. Mere acceptance of a promise is not enough. The consideration provided by the promisee must be 'sufficient' but need not be adequate.[31] This means that a degree of reciprocity is inherent in every fully-fledged contract as far as English law is concerned.[32] Where a contract is wholly executory, the parties' mutual promises each constitute the consideration for the other.

If there is such a thing as a civilian equivalent to the common law doctrine of consideration, it is the doctrine of *causa contractus*. That developed at a time when the Roman law governing a miscellany of various different types of *contracts* was slowly being fashioned by medieval scholars into a more coherent civilian law of *contract*.[33] Broadly speaking, *causa* was a shorthand reflecting the reason why a particular contract was being entered into, or, looking more narrowly at the individual protagonists and their motivations, the purpose pursued by each of its parties. While the English doctrine

[29] I do not here wish to enter into the debate over the exact line between validity and enforceability, where that line might be drawn in a particular case, and its relevant repercussions for the use of legal terminology. These issues are all very tricky, both in respect of domestic law and from a comparative perspective.

[30] For a more detailed discussion of some of the points that follow, see B Häcker, 'Causa, Consideration and Unjust(ified) Enrichment' in A Legerén Molina, B Rodríguez-Rosado, and R Caro Gándara (eds), *Cause and Consideration: Exploring the Foundations of Contract Law* (Hart 2025) 243, 244–50.

[31] See *Chappell & Co Ltd v Nestlé Co Ltd* [1960] AC 87.

[32] See eg M Chen-Wishart, 'In Defence of Consideration' (2013) 13 OUCLJ 209, but query whether, on closer analysis, the orthodoxy holds true in all cases. Interest-free loans are not reciprocal bargains (economically speaking, they are a form of gratuitous transaction), yet the lender's payment to the borrower is conventionally identified as the consideration for the borrower's promise to repay the loan.

[33] For an overview with further references, see G Albers, 'History of a Notion' in G Albers, FP Patti, and D Perrouin-Verbe (eds), *Causa contractus. Auf der Suche nach den Bedingungen der Wirksamkeit des vertraglichen Willens / Alla ricerca delle condizioni dell'efficacia della volontà contrattuale / À la recherche des conditions de l'éfficacité de la volonté contractuelle* (Mohr Siebeck 2022) 19, esp 24–26, 33–35.

of consideration can be said to explain why the *promisee* can enforce a promise given by another, the doctrine of *causa* (at the obligatory level) explains why the *promisor* should be held to their word.[34] In a contract for the sale of goods, for instance, the seller undertakes to deliver the goods and to 'transfer the property in [them]'[35] to the buyer in order to receive the purchase price in return. The buyer, on the other hand, agrees to pay the agreed price in order to obtain the goods.

Up until the early modern period, the civilian notion of *causa* had thus been shaped into a helpful 'analytical tool . . . applicable to all contracts', a tool of 'common European [civilian] heritage'.[36] Thereafter, the further doctrinal fine-tuning of the notion of *causa contractus*, and the purposes to which the doctrine was put in different European states and traditions, began to diverge.[37] In 1804, the French *Code Civil* firmly enshrined *causa* as an essential validity requirement of every contract.[38] The same happened in many other countries, including Italy and Spain.[39] Germany, however, went down a different route, partly perhaps because political circumstances delayed large-scale codification efforts until the end of the nineteenth century. By that time, the will theory of contracting had become so prominent—and dominant—in legal thinking that it seemed neither necessary nor appropriate to insist on anything more[40] than that the parties should have given their full and free consent to the transaction.[41] Why, after all, should the law inquire into the reasons driving the parties to contract when these are either obvious[42] or based on highly personal choices which ought to be respected for their own sake? So long as no relevant defect of consent has impaired the decision-making process and so long as there is no illegality or the like, an autonomous individual's will alone justifies treating the expressed intentions as legally valid and binding. In a sense, the rise of the will theory, taken extremely seriously by nineteenth-century Pandectists, accounts for the decline of the obligational *causa* in German legal thinking. The obligational *causa* does not therefore feature in the BGB.

Remarkably, France as the once leading advocate of the doctrine of *la cause du contrat* (or *la cause de l'obligation*), has—after over 200 years—recently arrived at a

34 On this aspect, see B Häcker, 'A Comparative Journey Through the Life of a Contract' in C Kennefick, B Häcker, and M Dyson (eds), *Comparing Contract Laws: Essays in Honour of John Cartwright* (forthcoming).

35 Wording borrowed from the Sale of Goods Act 1979, s 2.

36 Albers (n 33) 26.

37 For an overview with further references, see ibid 26–32.

38 In addition to the requirements of consent, capacity, and a 'definite object forming the subject matter of the undertaking', the former art 1108 of the *Code Civil* (1804) also required the parties' obligations to have 'a lawful cause' (*une cause licite*). There was always an unresolved ambiguity here between the contract viewed as a whole (*cause du contrat*) and the parties' mutual obligations viewed individually (*cause de l'obligation*).

39 See art 1325 of the Italian *Codice Civile* and art 1261 of the Spanish *Código Civil*.

40 For gift promises as well as undertakings of suretyship, the German Code requires special formalities to protect the promisor against rash decision-making (BGB, ss 518, 766), but other gratuitous undertakings, such as contracts of mandate or loan, are binding without any form.

41 Indeed, the centrality of the promisor's will was so dominant in legal thinking that the doctrine of *causa contractus* received no more than fleeing attention by the draftsmen, namely in connection with its converse: the deliberate establishment of expressly and wholly 'abstract obligatory promises' in BGB, s 780 (*abstrakte Schuldversprechen*). For a summary and further references, see Albers (n 33) 30.

42 Even though a *causa contractus* may not be an express validity requirement, reciprocal contracts other than 'abstract obligatory promises' (cf n 41) typically have an 'inbuilt' *causa*—in that every party undertakes to perform in order to obtain or keep the other party's counter-performance.

similar position. A fundamental review first initiated by French scholars on the bicentenary of the enactment of the *Code Civil* led to a large-scale reform of the French law of obligations and contracts in particular.[43] In 2016, in an effort to increase the 'attractiveness of French law',[44] a Presidential Ordinance formally abandoned recourse to the notion of *la cause* and assigned the various residual functions it had come to perform in practice[45] to a series of new, designated provisions targeting these issues individually.[46] The Presidential reform was subsequently (in 2018) ratified by statute. As a result, the French doctrine of *la cause* is now also firmly submerged or 'suppressed'.[47]

If we look closely at English law, we can see hints of a comparable shift of emphasis away from consideration and towards consent in the evolving case law concerning contract variation. There is a long-standing debate over whether consideration should only be required at the inception of a contract or also when the parties subsequently agree to change the rights and duties they have incurred. Ever since the doctrine of duress emerged as a powerful control mechanism for cases where one party pressures the other into accepting a one-sided variation of terms, consideration looked to some like the fifth wheel on the coach. The acceptance of 'practical benefit' as consideration in cases such as *Williams v Roffey Bros & Nicholls (Contractors) Ltd*[48] or, more recently, *MWB Business Exchange Centres Ltd v Rock Advertising Ltd*[49] reinforces this impression, but that is another story. For present purposes, it suffices to note that most (and in some jurisdictions all) of the justificatory weight of the binding force of obligatory transactions is today borne by the parties' consent and the agreement they have concluded.

B. Dispositive Transactions: Causality, Abstraction, and *Causa Traditionis*

At this point, a word needs to be said on dispositive transactions.[50] It concerns mainly those legal systems—or fields within a given system—where a sharp distinction is drawn between contract and conveyance. The question is whether or not the affected parties' consent to the conveyance, when coupled with any additional act or formality that may be required, brings about the desired result (eg a transfer of ownership or title). If so, as explained above,[51] the system is 'abstract'; if not, it is a 'causal' system. In

[43] See the contributions in Cartwright and Whittaker (n 14).

[44] Thus expressly stated in the preceding Report to the President of the Republic (Rapport au Président de la République relatif à l'ordonnance n° 2016-131 du 10 février 2016 portant réforme du droit des contrats, du régime général et de la preuve des obligations).

[45] Such as policing the legality of a contract for unlawful purposes, explaining the interdependence of the parties' mutual performances in reciprocal contracts, ensuring a minimum level of reciprocity at the inception of non-gratuitous contracts, or invalidating certain particularly onerous standard terms.

[46] See esp *Code Civil*, arts 1162–63, 1168–70, 1219–20.

[47] This is the language that seems to have established itself in order to avoid speaking of the doctrine having been abolished.

[48] [1991] 1 QB 1.

[49] [2016] EWCA Civ 553, [2017] QB 604; overturned on other grounds by *MWB Business Exchange Centres Ltd v Rock Advertising Ltd* [2018] UKSC 24, [2019] AC 119.

[50] For a more detailed discussion, see Häcker, 'Causa, Consideration and Unjust(ified) Enrichment' (n 30) esp 250–55.

[51] In Section II.D of the present chapter.

a 'causal' system, a disposition effected to discharge a particular obligation will not be valid unless the envisaged obligation actually exists (*causa traditionis*). But we have already seen that 'abstract' systems, too, cannot ultimately dispense with an underlying basis. For them, the juncture is simply further 'downstream'. Although a disposition made without a valid legal basis will be fully effective in 'abstract' transfer systems, the law of unjustified enrichment there orders its subsequent reversal (by requiring the recipient of the transfer to retransfer the right acquired or at least its value).[52]

The notion of *causa* or 'legal basis' operating here, at the dispositive level, is in fact quite closely related to the (now widely 'suppressed') notion of *causa* we have just seen operating at the obligatory level.[53] In both cases, *causa* ultimately points to the reason *why* a transaction is entered and thus helps to account for its binding nature. It has, moreover, in both contexts always been open to either a subjective or an objective understanding.[54] *Causa* can either be viewed as a party's subjective purpose for entering a transaction or as a more objective criterion. In the context of a performance being rendered in order to discharge an obligation which turns out not to exist, such as the typical 'mistaken payment' case, the subjective understanding has been all but replaced by the objective understanding of *causa*. Lawyers tend not to invoke the frustrated purpose of the person who performed *causa solvendi*, but instead directly equate the obligation to be discharged with the *causa traditionis* for the disposition. That (supposed) obligation is then—objectively viewed—the 'juristic reason' or 'legal basis' for the transfer, and where it does not exist, there is an 'absence of basis'.

C. The Meaning of 'Agreement' and 'Consent': Subjective or Objective?

While agreement and consent are clearly central to the bindingness of legal transactions, and while 'rescission' operates in precisely this sphere, nothing has so far been said about the exact meaning of these terms. In particular, not unlike the notion of *causa*, agreement and consent can be understood in a subjective and a more objective sense. In the realm of consent-based causative events, does a legal effect (the creation of an obligation or the disposition over some right) come about because a party subjectively *intends* and desires it, or is the effect down to the *outward expression* of such an intention, objectively determined? Put differently, where two or more parties transact, is it truly their 'meeting of the minds' that counts, or is the outward manifestation of their agreement determinative?

As might be expected, approaches once again differ. The opposite ends of the spectrum are conventionally described as the 'will theory' (subjective approach) and the

[52] The retransfer is then underpinned by a legal basis in the shape of the original transferor's personal claim to restitution, securing the permanence of restitution.

[53] A common lawyer will immediately recognise that a similar observation can be made with respect to consideration, albeit that the conceptual link is much less strong there: Häcker, 'Causa, Consideration and Unjust(ified) Enrichment' (n 30) 255–57.

[54] On the following, see Albers (n 33) 35; Häcker, 'Causa, Consideration and Unjust(ified) Enrichment' (n 30) 252–53.

'declaratory theory' (objective approach). The common law famously adopts the objective approach, while civilian systems tend to adopt the subjective approach, at least as a starting point.[55] This is because, true to Enlightenment ideals, civilians see a person's ability to bind themselves as rooted in their 'private autonomy', and the latter as resting on the autonomous will, guided by reason. In order to be genuinely autonomous, that will has to be formed free of heteronomous influences and must not be impaired by mistake.

Recalling what was said above about the different perspectives of the common law and the civilian tradition with respect to consideration and *causa*,[56] one could here make a similar point with respect to the objective and subjective understanding of 'agreement' and 'consent'. Since the common law asks primarily why the *promisee* should be able to enforce the promisor's promise, it has good reason to determine the content of that promise purely objectively, by reference to a reasonable person in the promisee's position. Civilian systems such as French or German law, on the other hand, will be looking primarily at the *promisor*'s position. From the vantage point of private autonomy, the latter should in principle only be held to promises they genuinely intended to undertake and/or dispositions they genuinely intended to bring about.

IV. Asserting the Absence of Operative Consent Through Rescission

The different perspectives just outlined help explain why the grounds for rescission accepted by the common law (including equity) overlap no more than partially with the grounds for rescission accepted by civilian systems. Let us first explore these divergences and then consider the reasons why the absence of the kind of consent the individual legal system regards as operative generates an option to rescind, rather than leading to the impaired consent simply not being recognised.

A. Explaining the Diverging Grounds for Rescission

Broadly speaking, the grounds of rescission in common law systems are what I have described elsewhere as 'process-orientated', while the grounds for rescission in civilian systems are mixed: primarily 'substantive' or 'content-orientated', yet with significant concessions to process thrown into the mix.[57] This statement needs some unpicking.

English law allows rescission for fraud and duress at common law (in the narrower sense) and for non-fraudulent misrepresentation as well as undue influence in equity.[58] There is arguably also a doctrine of 'unconscionable bargains' warranting

[55] It will be seen below (in the text accompanying nn 73–75 and nn 81–88) that this starting point is modified in various respects and thus in practice absorbs some elements of the more objective approach.

[56] See the text accompanying n 34.

[57] For the terminology and an overview, see B Häcker, *Consequences of Impaired Consent Transfers: A Structural Comparison of English and German Law* (Mohr Siebeck 2009, republished by Hart 2013) 22–24, 165–70.

[58] On rescission for breach of fiduciary duty and in the bribery context, see n 4.

rescission,[59] but that will be left to one side for present purposes. The point about 'process-orientated' grounds of rescission is that they explain why the promisee cannot insist on enforcing the other party's promise. It is because, in the typical case,[60] the promisee has brought about the promisor's agreement to the transaction in a way the legal order disapproves of, namely by making a misrepresentation, or by exerting some form of improper pressure or influence over the promisor. It matters not that the misrepresentation may be entirely innocent or the exercise of the influence inadvertent. The promisee will still be denied the benefit of the promise once the promisor raises the matter. That it is the promisee's conduct[61] rather than the promisor's impairment of consent as such that justifies rescission is easily visible when we ponder the law of misrepresentation, which is actually a law of induced mistakes (but tellingly always referred to as the former rather than the latter). English law is concerned with the promisor's mistake only insofar as the mistake constitutes the causal nexus between the misrepresentation and the resulting contract. All induced mistakes potentially count, regardless of the exact nature of the misapprehension. By contrast, spontaneous mistakes are, under English law, typically[62] the promisor's own problem: *caveat promisor.*

The picture is entirely different in civilian systems, here represented by France and Germany. They recognise a narrower range of 'process-orientated' grounds for rescission than English law, but at the same time begin their analysis by paying particular attention to the *quality* of the parties' consent—thus accepting certain purely 'content-orientated' or 'substantive' grounds for rescission in the realm of mistake. A good place to see the civilian 'mix' is the newly drafted French provision introducing the section dealing with 'defects of consent' in the *Code Civil*:

> Mistake, fraud and duress vitiate consent where they are of such a nature that, without them, one of the parties would not have contracted or would have contracted on substantially different terms.[63]

If there is a mistake of the relevant kind, one that by its nature calls into question the quality of the mistaken parties' (apparent) consent, then that alone undermines the requisite private autonomy. The existence of such a mistake justifies *not* holding the mistaken party to their word, even in the absence of outside interference with the process through which the parties' will is formed. Fraud and duress are on this account

[59] *Fry v Lane* (1888) 40 Ch D 312; *Creswell v Potter* [1978] 1 WLR 255. See also the contribution in Chapter 7 of this book (Yip Man, 'Rescission of Unconscionable Gifts').

[60] Cases of duress or undue influence exerted by third parties—rather than the promisee—are atypical, but many can be explained either on the basis that the third party acted as an agent for the promisee (and was therefore in their 'camp') or on the basis of the promisee having notice of the third party's conduct.

[61] Or, in third-party cases, possibly knowledge/notice: see the comment in the immediately preceding footnote.

[62] Again, there are certain mistakes which, if known to the other party, may enable the promisor to argue that the contract either failed to be concluded in the first place (because offer and acceptance never objectively matched: offer and acceptance mistakes) or that the resulting contract ought to be rectified on account of a recognised unilateral mistake as to terms. Neither theme can be pursued further here. For an overview with critical comparative assessment, see the discussion in Häcker, 'A Comparative Journey' (n 34) under the heading 'Falsa demonstratio non nocet?'.

[63] *Code Civil*, art 1130(1).

additional or alternative factors which, for entirely different reasons, also undermine the private autonomy of the party subjected to them.

Yet not all causative mistakes undermine private autonomy, or at least not sufficiently for the law to intervene. The French *Code Civil*, for instance, normally regards as relevant '[m]istake[s] of law or of fact . . . bear[ing] on the essential qualities of the act of performance owed or of the other contracting party'.[64] The line between operative mistakes and those considered irrelevant is in even plainer sight under German law, where the former—the operative—category comprises the following: (i) misapprehensions as to the content of the affected parties' declaration of intent (ie mismatches between what was subjectively intended and what was outwardly declared when interpreted from the perspective of a reasonable person);[65] (ii) mistakes made in the process of declaring the intention to the outside world (eg typographical errors or slips of the tongue);[66] and (iii) as in French law, mistakes relating to an essential quality of a person or a thing, namely qualities that are generally regarded as significant to the transaction at hand (eg mistakenly believing a piece of jewellery to be made of cheap brass when in fact it consists of gold, or vice versa).[67] By contrast, mere 'motivational' mistakes made in the process leading up to the intention being formed are typically irrelevant on this scheme.[68] They pertain to the *reasons* why someone consents to a transaction, but they do not affect the inherent *quality* of the consent per se. It is only where a motivational mistake is induced by the other party's fraud[69] that the proverbial coin flips and rescission becomes possible even for mere motivational mistakes,[70] such as misapprehensions regarding the need for the object acquired or (arguably) its market value.[71]

There are, inevitably, a number of differences in the detail between the grounds of rescission recognised by French and German law.[72] Yet in both jurisdictions the grounds for rescission ultimately reflect impairments or defects of the promisor's consent which justify *not* holding the promisor to their word despite their (apparent) agreement to the terms of a transaction. This explains why some spontaneous mistakes warrant

[64] *Code Civil*, art 1132. The provision outlines what mistakes normally count as operative *vices du consentement*. There is also a (smaller) category known as *erreur obstacle*, where the mistake in question prevents the parties' minds meeting in the first place. Common lawyers can think of the latter as a French version of offer and acceptance mistakes (cf n 62). It may well be that some of the German grounds for rescission discussed in what follows (nn 65–67 and the accompanying text) would in French law be categorised as cases of *erreur obstacle*.

[65] BGB, s 119(1), alt 1.

[66] BGB, s 119(1), alt 2.

[67] BGB, s 119(2). While an object's 'essential qualities' will typically impact its value, the value of an object *in and of itself* does not count as an 'essential quality' in either German or French law: see *Code Civil*, art 1136.

[68] Expressly stated by *Code Civil*, art 1135(1). But see the exception for gifts mentioned in n 72.

[69] Fraud committed by third parties is a special case regulated in BGB, s 123(2).

[70] BGB, s 123(1); *Code Civil*, art 1139.

[71] A fascinating question, which cannot be pursued further here, is whether, when, and how far a deliberate misrepresentation concerning the (pure) market value of the subject matter of a contract can count as a 'white lie'. There is, in a sense, no 'true' and 'objective' market value for goods, services, or any other element of a bargain.

[72] In particular, French law requires ordinary mistakes of the kind mentioned in art 1132 of the *Code Civil* (see n 64 and text thereto) to be 'excusable' (or, more precisely, 'not inexcusable'), while German law only requires that mistakes of the kind outlined in s 119 of the BGB should be genuine and causative. French law exceptionally allows gifts and other *liberalités* to be rescinded for mere motivational mistake, while German law does not: see *Code Civil*, art 1135(2) and cf n 14 above. Moreover, French law now features a ground of rescission looking remarkably like the English doctrine of undue influence (*Code Civil*, art 1143), without there being any direct counterpart in the German law of rescission.

rescission in the civilian tradition, while the common law tradition would treat them as immaterial.

B. Explaining the Optional Nature of Rescission

If there are factors militating against holding the promisor to their word or against allowing the promisee to enforce the promise given by the promisor, then why should the legal system not automatically treat the promise—and any contract/transaction based on it—as wholly ineffective? From an economic point of view, indeed from a pragmatic point of view, the answer is obvious. Given that it is the promisor whose decision-making autonomy is being protected in one way or another (through insisting on full and free consent or through guarding against misrepresentations and pressure emanating from the promisee), it makes sense to afford the promisor the opportunity to let the transaction stand. In theory, this could also be achieved by giving the affected party an option to ratify an otherwise ineffective transaction, much as a principal can ratify the acts of an agent acting without the principal's authority.

Historically, and from a comparative point of view, the fine-grained lines and distinctions between transactions which are 'non-existent', 'void', 'invalid', 'ineffective', 'unenforceable', or 'voidable' are in fact not always easy to make out. Suffice it to say that all three of the legal systems considered here ultimately arrived at the conclusion that relevant problems with consent should not be 'rectified' automatically by operation of law, but ought instead to be left to the affected party to raise.[73] The original French *Code Civil* of 1804 (also called *Code Napoléon* on account of the Emperor's initiative and involvement in its drafting) spelt this out in express terms. Although agreements entered into as the result of some operative mistake, duress, or deception were described as 'null' (*nul*), the nullity did not follow automatically, but depended on it being asserted by the party concerned.[74] The reformed French Code now expressly classifies this as 'relative nullity'—as opposed to 'absolute nullity', which can be asserted by anyone.[75]

The backstory of English law, with its mixture of grounds for rescission recognised at common law and in equity, all playing out within the corresponding procedural frameworks, is far too complicated to be recounted here.[76] Only two points merit attention for present purposes. First, given that the equitable doctrine of rescission always required some form of court intervention at the instance of the aggrieved party,[77] it was quite naturally 'optional' in nature. Second, as far as the common law is concerned, it

[73] It is always tricky to try to rationalise historical 'choices' made by legal systems, not least in view of the linguistic variance just outlined, but one may observe in general terms that 'validity subject to avoidance' will in most cases be more conducive to the stability of legal relationships than the alternative of holding impaired transactions 'void subject to ratification'.

[74] *Code Civil*, art 1117 (original 1804 version).

[75] *Code Civil*, arts 1131, 1178–85.

[76] The reader may instead be referred to the detailed account in D O'Sullivan, S Elliott, and R Zakrzewski, *The Law of Rescission* (3rd edn, OUP 2023) ch 3.

[77] As O'Sullivan, Elliott, and Zakrzewski (n 76) [11.62] point out, the need for a court decree to effect rescission in equity was beyond contention until about 1870. Doubts only started to arise later: see ibid [11.67]–[11.112].

appears that contracts procured by fraud were until the mid-nineteenth century routinely described (and treated) as 'void'.[78] The notion that they might be no more than 'voidable' has been traced back to Parke B's decision in *Load v Green*,[79] and it is perfectly plausible that the shift of terminology and approach could be owed to the strong influence of French contract theory on the evolution of English contract law during this period.[80]

Much easier to trace is the way German law arrived at the current position.[81] In cases of fraud and duress, transactions had long been treated as voidable by rescission. Yet the will theory seemed to dictate that where (what was above described as) a 'content-orientated' defect of consent was in play,[82] there was strictly speaking no valid declaration of intent at all. Any declaration based on a mistake as to the nature or content of the transaction, a typographical error or slip of the tongue, or a mistake as to an essential quality of the subject matter or the other contracting party, was a mere chimera because it was not underpinned by the declaring party's genuine consent.[83] Accordingly, the first draft of the BGB provided for such a declaration to be, in principle, automatically void.[84] This approach, however, created a remarkable mismatch in the treatment of different types of defective consent. Moreover, the will theory of contracting had a contemporary rival in the declaratory theory, which put greater store on the impression outwardly created, in an effort to protect the legitimate expectations of the declaring party's counterparts.[85] It is, for instance, reflected in the fact that declarations of intent addressed to another are not necessarily to be given the interpretation subjectively intended by the declaring party, but need to be construed in light of how a reasonable person in the recipient's position would understand them.[86] The second BGB drafting commission in the end found a compromise. Observing that neither the will theory nor the declaratory theory were viable in their pure form, and declining to express a preference for one or the other, the draftsmen agreed that 'voidability' was the pragmatic and equitable solution to defective consent, doing justice to all relevant interests at stake.[87] The blow that a rescission for spontaneous mistake might nevertheless deal an innocent contract partner was further softened by providing that, following a

[78] See, with further references, ibid [3.05].

[79] (1846) 15 M & W 216, 153 ER 828.

[80] O'Sullivan, Elliott, and Zakrzewski (n 76) [3.05], speculating that Robert Joseph Pothier's writings may have been the source, while stressing that firm evidence has yet to be found.

[81] For an overview with further references on what follows, see M Schmoeckel, J Rückert, and R Zimmermann (eds), *Historisch-kritischer Kommentar zum BGB. Bd. I: Allgemeiner Teil, §§ 1–240* (Mohr Siebeck 2003) §§ 142–144 [1]–[6] at 800–05 (MJ Schermaier).

[82] The terminology is explained in the text accompanying and following n 57.

[83] See FC von Savigny, *System des heutigen römischen Rechts*, vol 3 (Veit & Co 1840) 263–307 (esp under § 135) and 440–47.

[84] BGB E-I (1888), s 98. Exceptionally, the declaration was to be treated as valid where the affected party's spontaneous mistake rested on his own gross negligence, with a counter-exception being made for the case where the other party knew or ought to have known of the mistake: BGB E-I (1888), s 99 sub-ss (1), (3).

[85] For an account and discussion, see W Flume, *Allgemeiner Teil des Bürgerlichen Rechts, Bd. 2: Das Rechtsgeschäft* (4th edn, Springer 1992) 54–56.

[86] See BGB, s 157, modifying BGB, s 133 in this respect.

[87] A Achilles, H Gebhard, and P Spahn (eds), *Protokolle der Kommission für die zweite Lesung des Entwurfs des Bürgerlichen Gesetzbuchs*, vol 1 (Guttentag 1897) 105–07. The commission was evidently also impressed by the argument that the French *Code Civil* as well as the Prussian Code of 1794 were already successfully operating a 'voidability' model.

successful avoidance, the rescinding party should be strictly liable for losses suffered by the other as a result of relying on the validity of the declaration of intent.[88]

V. Distinguishing the Effects of Rescission from the Basis of the Right to Rescind

What does all this tell us about the right to rescind and its relationship with the law of restitution and/or unjust(ified) enrichment? To what extent does rescission accomplish restitution in the sense suggested by Holmes' quote,[89] and where it does, can we draw any inferences on what generates the right to rescind? The most important point for present purposes is that we need to distinguish quite clearly between the *effect* of rescission and the *basis* of the right to rescind. The former is the concern of the present section, while an argument pertaining to the latter will be presented in the next—final—part of the chapter.

It has been seen that rescission is a mechanism allowing a party to 'recall' or 'wipe out' their (apparent) consent to a transaction and thereby to avoid it retroactively. This may be because the consent has been obtained in a way the legal order regards as procedurally flawed or, in civilian systems, because the consent is beset by some 'substantive' defect, making it inherently flawed. Depending on what exactly hinged on the presence of consent to the transaction, rescission may well entail proprietary consequences. This is where the three legal systems considered here diverge significantly.[90]

If an obligatory contract and the dispositive transaction it envisages are conceptually rolled into one, and if the contract in fact functioned as a vehicle of conveyance, then—subject to the right thus transferred having meanwhile been lost or destroyed—rescission of the contract will automatically lead to restitution of the right conveyed under it. The same result also pertains in those 'causal' transfer systems which draw a conceptual distinction between contract and conveyance. Because such systems require valid conveyances to have a valid legal basis, namely a *iusta causa traditionis* in the form of an obligation (or reason) to make the disposition, the conveyance cannot stand once the underlying contract has been avoided.

Even 'abstract' transfer systems such as the German system will occasionally experience acts of rescission having proprietary effects. This can happen for different reasons. First is a simple scenario. It will be recalled that German lawyers treat all dispositive transactions as involving contracts in the form of 'real agreements' (not entailing any obligations whatsoever).[91] If, in a given scenario, contracting parties decide to make the validity of a disposition *expressly* conditional on the existence and validity of an

[88] Achilles, Gebhard, and Spahn, *Protokolle I* (n 87) 107–08. A similar provision had already been contained in the first draft, but was there made dependent on the rescinding party having been negligent in making the mistaken declaration: BGB E-I (1888), s 99(2). The liability of the rescinding party imposed by BGB, s 122 as enacted is discussed further in Section VI.B below (in the text to and following n 116).

[89] Set out in the text accompanying n 1.

[90] The following account builds on Sections II.C and II.D.

[91] Where a disposition involves only one party (such as the dereliction of ownership), a unilateral declaration of intent takes the place of the 'real agreement'.

underlying obligation in pursuance of which the 'real agreement' is concluded, then it lies within their private autonomy to do so. In effect, they have then achieved 'causality' by means of the incorporated condition precedent, and their conveyance will automatically fail if the underlying obligatory basis is later avoided *ab initio*. The second scenario is different and slightly more complicated. It arises where *both* an underlying contract *and* the real agreement can be rescinded—typically for the same defect of consent, but notionally through separate acts of rescission. The case posited in the introduction is a good example. Since the buyer B's fraud has induced the seller A both to enter the contract of sale and to agree to the ensuing transfer of ownership by delivery, A can avoid both the obligatory and the dispositive transaction on the ground of the deception practised by B. Though this may look like an abandonment of the principle of 'abstraction', it is in fact a merely apparent exception.[92]

Although in all of the above cases rescission clearly *effects restitution* (in the sense of returning[93] to one or both parties a right they would, but for the rescission, have lost), none of the cases strictly necessitates there being any *claim to restitution* aimed at the reversal of the original performance(s).[94] A personal claim to restitution is only required where—and only as far as—the act of rescission does *not* automatically restore the parties to the position they were in, or would be in, had the 'defective' transaction never been concluded. In particular, it is needed where, in an 'abstract' system, a disposition is made in order to discharge some (supposed) obligation and where it later turns out that the obligation has been retroactively avoided through rescission or never existed in the first place. Its role then is to rectify the 'normative mismatch' mentioned earlier between where a right has ended up and where it is actually meant to be. As Barry Nicholas once astutely observed:

> [T]he more readily a system gives abstract effect to a conveyance or other transaction (ie allows it to be effective although its accompanying cause is vitiated by mistake or other defect), the more prominent will be the need for a remedy in terms of unjust enrichment.[95]

One main role of the law of unjust(ified) enrichment[96] is therefore to reverse performances rendered without a legal basis, or *causa*, in situations where the legal system itself does not or cannot automatically invalidate such 'unfounded' performances.[97]

92 See Häcker, *Consequences of Impaired Consent Transfers* (n 57) 60–63.

93 That word is not intended to say anything about prospectivity or retrospectivity. While common lawyers tend to think of title literally 're-vesting' (see comment in the text after n 26), it is equally possible to think of 'restitution' happening with retroactive effect in the sense of undoing relevant transfers *ab initio*.

94 Such a claim could only take the form of a *condictio possessionis* to ensure that the transferor 'recovers' not merely ownership or title but also possession of any object they have already delivered to the transferee.

95 B Nicholas, 'Unjustified Enrichment in the Civil Law and Louisiana Law, Part 1' (1962) 36 Tul L Rev 605, 608.

96 As English and German lawyers would think of it. The categorisation and nomenclature of unjust(ified) enrichment in French law is different: see comment and references in n 104 below.

97 I do not mean to say that an abstract disposition lacking a *causa* is the only scenario where a personal claim to restitution will be a useful and indeed necessary legal device. It is just as essential to recover, for instance, the actual possession of a chattel or the value of services rendered without a concomitant transfer of rights.

In other words, whereas in 'causal' systems a disposition without an underlying *causa* cannot take effect, in 'abstract' systems, where dispositions are effective regardless of any underlying *causa*, the law of unjust(ified) enrichment provides the requisite corrective counterbalance to the principle of abstraction. It ensures that rights transferred and obtained without a valid legal basis cannot be kept by the transferee. Abstract systems differ from causal systems in that they leave it up to the performing party to reclaim what has been rendered without a *causa*.

VI. Conceiving of the Right to Rescind as Generated by Unjust(ified) Enrichment

To say that rescission may effect restitution and hence automatically reverse or—if retroactivity is taken seriously at the proprietary as well as the obligatory level—prevent the recipient's unjust(ified) enrichment at the transferor's expense is one thing. It is quite another to argue that the very *right to rescind* itself is based on the unjust(ified) enrichment of the party who would, but for a potential rescission, have obtained a right through the transaction now liable to be set aside. Yet the writings of a number of common lawyers seem to suggest just that, by describing rescission as a 'proprietary remedy' for unjust enrichment and the right to rescind as a form of 'proprietary restitution'.[98] The difficulty is that not all of these writings draw the requisite distinction between the *effects* of rescission on the one hand and the *basis* of the right to rescind on the other.[99] Logically, the question whether a particular right to rescind is itself generated by unjust(ified) enrichment is prior to any question of how an unjust(ified) enrichment coming about as a result of rescission is reversed in a given system.

I, too, have long toyed with the idea that rights—or, better, powers—to rescind could be responding to an unjust(ified) enrichment, quite irrespective of whether their exercise merely divests the counterparty of personal rights or entails proprietary consequences,[100] and I am now convinced that this is indeed the best account.[101] One aim of the present contribution is to place this argument centre-stage rather than merely touching on it tangentially. It will be seen that much of the ground has already been prepared in the preceding sections.

[98] An overview with further references is provided by C Mitchell, P Mitchell, and S Watterson, *Goff & Jones On Unjust Enrichment* (10th edn, Sweet & Maxwell 2022) ch 40, esp at [40-6]–[40-32]. See also J Edelman and E Bant, *Unjust Enrichment* (2nd edn, Hart 2016) 38–42, 45, containing hints of the unjust enrichment analysis of rights to rescind, without however fully developing it.

[99] The author-editors of *Goff & Jones* (n 98) themselves are exceptionally clear in making the distinction, but do not ultimately commit to one view or the other: see [40-16]–[40-17].

[100] See already Häcker, *Consequences of Impaired Consent Transfers* (n 57) 171–74; B Häcker, 'Fog on the Channel? Six Comparative Lessons in Unjust(ified) Enrichment' [2017] RLR 61, 75–76; Häcker, 'Contract and Conveyance' (n 22) 122–23.

[101] Most recently Häcker, 'Causa, Consideration and Unjust(ified) Enrichment' (n 30) 266–68.

A. Clearing the Ground: Countering Objections to the Argument's Premises

Having looked earlier at *when* different legal systems allow parties to disavow transactions they have entered into on account of there being some recognised deficiency of consent, and having then considered *how* the optional mechanism of rescission works, we must now ask *why* the affected party should have the power to bring about (with or without the help of a court) the retroactive avoidance of the transaction. If the unjust(ified) enrichment explanation propagated here is correct, then the answer must be that the power to rescind arises because any person who has obtained a right under the 'deficient' transaction has obtained that right 'unjustly' or, depending on the theory, without a valid legal basis, at the expense of the party now entitled to rescind.

Although the argument would (have to) pertain to all instances of rescission for 'deficient' consent, the best example to use in order to make it with the greatest possible clarity is that of an executory contract being rescinded, where the parties have not yet exchanged any performances. As far as executed contracts go, the most helpful case example might be one where the obligatory contract is first concluded, then performed by means of a separate transaction (such as payment or delivery), and subsequently rescinded by the transferor. Those who deny that the right to rescind is based on unjust(ified) enrichment would argue that, in the first case, no unjust(ified) enrichment ever arises, and in the second case, that it arises only once the contract has been rescinded, thereby causing the performance to have been obtained unjustly and/or without a valid legal basis.[102]

It will be useful to dispense with the potential objections first. Three related reasons may come to mind for why the right to rescind should not itself be seen as generated by unjust(ified) enrichment. First, one could regard the right to rescind as exclusively a matter of contract law and as responding to a vitiation of consent rather than any unjust(ified) enrichment. Second, restitution for unjust(ified) enrichment is conventionally thought to involve a process of 'giving' or 'claiming back', leading to the recovery of some right or value by the party at whose expense the enrichment was obtained. It is not usually understood more broadly to include processes such as rescission in the first (executory contract) example, where one party unilaterally strips the other of a right which thereupon effectively disappears into thin air. The third potential objection is closely connected. Conceptually, it is often assumed that unjust(ified) enrichment in performance cases is confined to the realm of *dispositions* lacking an obligatory basis or some other recognised purpose, but that it never has a role to play at the pure *obligatory* level.

[102] These objections are, for example, implicit in R Stevens, *The Laws of Restitution* (OUP 2023) esp 83–84. On this issue at least, Stevens' approach nicely typifies the objectors' view. He writes: 'The rescission of a wholly executory contract involves the reversal of no performance, it is simply the setting aside of otherwise binding legal obligations' (at 38); 'After rescission, the basis for performance that once exists has been retrospectively invalidated, or nullified. Restitution of the performance rendered under the contract then follows' (at 75).

None of these concerns are compelling, however. The fact that rescission is indeed a tool employed by contract law says nothing about the causative event to which the right owes its existence.[103] And while 'consent' can be a causative event, a 'vitiation of consent' alone has no explanatory value. The very thing we are here trying to account for is *why* the party who has (ostensibly) given their consent and thereby bestowed a right on the other party can now unilaterally and retroactively revoke consent, thereby undoing the legal consequences which the deficient consent had temporarily brought about. Regarding the second potential objection, it is simply an assertion that restitution for unjust(ified) enrichment necessarily involves the retransfer or recovery of some right or value. Yet there is no good reason why a personal claim based on another party's enforceable promise (contractual or otherwise) should not count as a relevant enrichment, or why one party stripping the other of such a claim should not be a form of restitution. There can be no doubt the exercise of the right to rescind restores the rescinding promisor to their pre-promise position. Third, the fact that both common lawyers and many[104] civilians are accustomed—and indeed conditioned through their textbooks and Codes—to think of the black-letter law of unjust(ified) performances as dealing first and foremost with mistaken payments and other dispositions made without a legal basis and/or for a purpose which fails, does not mean that, on a deeper level, the principle against unjust(ified) enrichments cannot be much more broadly conceived.

B. Structural Parallels Exposed: The Argument Itself

The idea that one party's right to rescind could be based on the other's unjust(ified) enrichment at the former's expense appears today to fall on more fertile ground in the common law world than amongst civilian lawyers. This is probably because, not having a Code formally restricting the law called 'unjustified enrichment' to a particular set of cases or provisions (such as sections 812–22 of the BGB), common lawyers are in a better position to understand the potential for a wider remit of the field. For instance, they routinely envisage not merely personal claims to restitution for unjust enrichment but also various forms of 'proprietary restitution'.[105] If unjust enrichment can generate proprietary powers and full-blown property rights, then why should it not also be able to generate powers to avoid a purely executory contract? Yet although common lawyers seem more open-minded to the basic idea, interestingly, the argument itself may

[103] A similar point is made by W Swadling, 'Property' in J Atmaz Al-Sibaie and J English (eds), 'The Laws of Restitution' [2024] LMCLQ 353, 367: 'If the law gives the defrauded party the power to rescind, it must come from somewhere, and a species of unjust enrichment (or wrongs) seems at least a plausible source.'

[104] An express caveat is here warranted as far as French law is concerned. When French lawyers speak of *l'enrichissement injustifié* (previously *l'enrichissement sans cause*), they actually have a different scenario in mind. The law of restitution for unjust(ified) enrichment, as English and German lawyers think of it, is in the French *Code Civil* to be found in the rules on 'undue payment' and in the judicial 'annulment' of contracts, with the ensuing restitutionary regime. For an explanation and further details, see Häcker, 'Contract and Conveyance' (n 22) 118–19; Häcker, 'Causa, Consideration and Unjust(ified) Enrichment' (n 30) 253–55, 262–64.

[105] See eg *Goff & Jones* (n 98) chs 37–40 for an overview.

actually be easier to make and see from the civilian perspective. As far as the common law is concerned, the view is obstructed by two factors. First, the causative event we are dealing with is traditionally thought of as 'unjust'—not 'unjustified'—enrichment. Second, the relevant grounds for rescission of contract—namely, misrepresentation, duress, and undue influence—look as if they could potentially also be responding to wrongs (albeit not necessarily all leading to a compensation claim) rather than unjust enrichments. So let us take a step back and consider the civilian structures.

Put in abstract terms, we have established the following:

1. All transactions—whether obligatory or dispositive—are entered into for a particular purpose, which in the civilian tradition came to be known as *causa*. The *causa* has always been part of the traditional explanation for why a transaction is binding. Another part of the explanation is that the party or parties entering the transaction have consented to it.
2. As far as conventional 'obligatory' contract law is concerned, the justificatory weight has now clearly shifted from *causa* to consent. So long as a party fully and freely agrees to undertake an obligation, that alone is enough to account for why the law, at the behest of the other contracting party, holds them to their word.
3. Although the will theory of contracting explains why certain spontaneous mistakes are enough to undermine the binding force of a promise in civilian systems, these systems have chosen not to declare the affected contract automatically void but to give the party concerned an option to rescind it.
4. As far as dispositive transactions are concerned, such as performances by way of conveyance, the notion of *causa* has become largely 'objectivised', in the sense that we tend today to understand *causa* to refer not to the performing party's aim of discharging a debt, but rather as referring to the very existence of the underlying obligation.
5. In a 'causal' transfer system, such as French law or Austrian law, a disposition *sine iusta causa traditionis*—that is, a disposition lacking a legal basis—is automatically invalidated. In an 'abstract' transfer system, such as under the German BGB, the disposition is typically[106] valid and effective in the first instance, but at the same time the legal system generates a personal claim to restitution through the law of unjustified enrichment (in the form of a *condictio indebiti*). The transaction's effects are therefore not permanently in place, but can subsequently be reversed at the behest of the party who has rendered performance without a valid legal basis.

Although the above observations are somewhat simplified for expository purposes,[107] the reader will hopefully see the distinct structural parallel between the

[106] Subject to the exceptional cases discussed in the text to nn 91–92 above.

[107] In actual fact, the matter is slightly more complicated. It is, for instance, possible to undertake an obligation in order to discharge a debt, hence *solvendi causa*. If, in such a case, there is in fact no debt to discharge, the promisor will have a personal claim in unjustified enrichment to be released from the obligation they have undertaken (just as described in the text for a disposition case). Despite this caveat, the present simplification does not impinge on the key aspects of the argument made here.

obligatory and the dispositive levels. There are, in general terms, two possible approaches to tackling a problem with the normative underpinnings of a given transaction. One is for the law simply to deny its validity outright, as the full-blown will theory of contracting would have had it for operative content-mistakes when the German BGB was being drafted, and as 'causal' transfer systems do when they hold transfers without a legal basis invalid at the dispositive level.[108] The other is for the law to let the transaction stand in the first instance, but to make provision for its subsequent reversal. This is how 'abstract' transfer systems connect dispositions to their underlying *causa*, and it is also how all three legal systems we have looked at approach the grounds of rescission: by giving the affected party an option to undo the transaction.[109] That option takes the shape of a right to rescind. Structurally, the 'right'—or power—to rescind resembles a *condictio*; that is to say, it is similar to the grant of a claim or action to achieve the reversal of the transaction. The similarity with the *condictio* exists even though the power to rescind does not depend on the cooperation of the other party.

Remarkably, these structural parallels between the *condictio* and the power to rescind transactions were already clearly spelt out in some of the nineteenth-century literature preceding the German BGB. The great jurist Friedrich Carl von Savigny himself said that there were (only) two situations in which a party's motivational mistake was sufficient for a transaction to be 'rescinded as invalid', namely rescission of a contract for fraud[110] and the various *condictiones*, where a transaction which is 'in principle valid' is subsequently 'invalidated' by means of a special action.[111] Writing over fifty years after Savigny, just before the BGB was enacted, a much less well-known jurist by the name of Leonard Jacobi sought to analyse the implications of the drafting commission's decision to subject all mistakes, even those which undermine the declaring party's will, to the rescission regime. He astutely observed that this was not merely a matter of technique but that it represented a decisive conceptual shift:

> If a particular factor—eg, a defect in the declarative intent resulting from mistake—is not treated in law as a nullity or as a reason for invalidity, but instead as a ground for rescission, then this involves the recognition that this factor does not constitute a defect in the declaration itself, but [that it] can only be *relevant as a ground for restitution (ex aequitate) external to the declaration.*[112]

[108] See text to nn 81–87 and text to and following n 51, respectively.

[109] It is here worth footnoting an interesting development of the 'old' (pre-reform) French law that applied until 2016. Even though the *Code Civil* at the time still required all obligatory contracts to be based on a lawful *causa* (*cause licite*), French courts had already taken the step of holding that a lack of *cause* should not normally result in 'absolute nullity' but only entail the contract's 'relative nullity'—meaning that the lack of *cause* would have to be actively asserted by the disadvantaged party (cf n 75). For an account of this development, see J Bell, S Boyron, and S Whittaker, *Principles of French Law* (2nd edn, OUP 2008) 321.

[110] It will be recalled that Savigny's adherence to the will theory meant that he would have held transactions beset by operative content mistakes as automatically invalid: see n 83 and text thereto. That explains why he is here only speaking of rescission for fraudulently induced motivational mistakes.

[111] Savigny (n 83) 358–61. In Savigny's day, both rescission for fraud and the *condictiones* involved actions which needed to be brought in court. Today's out-of-court rules are their direct successors.

[112] L Jacobi, 'Die fehlerhaften Rechtsgeschäfte: Ein Beitrag zur Begriffslehre des deutschen bürgerlichen Rechts' [1896] 86 Archiv für die civilistische Praxis (AcP) 51, 76 (my translation, emphasis added).

In other words, if a system chooses not simply to disregard a transaction beset by defects of consent, but to treat it as valid unless and until rescinded, then it has thereby moved the problem into the realm of restitution for unjustified enrichment. It is in the realm of restitution because the technique is one of reversal rather than automatic ineffectiveness, and it is in the realm of unjustified enrichment because the very reason for the reversal is the lack of justificatory basis (or *causa*).

The juncture is comparable to the one legal systems face when deciding whether a dispositive transfer made without a legal basis should be automatically invalid—as a 'causal' approach would have it—or merely generate rights in unjust enrichment. Common law critics of (the crude version of) Samuel Stoljar's so-called 'proprietary theory'[113] will know that a transaction *not* happening cannot, and need not, be justified by reference to the theory of unjust enrichment; but where, despite some recognised deficiency, the transaction *does* happen in law, the right or ability to have it reversed is a response to unjust enrichment.[114]

Accepting this structural argument no doubt challenges conventional preconceptions about the function and remit of the law of restitution for unjust(ified) enrichment. Yet the moment one is willing to let go of the conviction that 'restitution' is only ever about reversing transfers of value or rights *which previously resided in the transferor*, and that the transferee cannot be 'enriched' at the transferor's expense unless they have obtained just such a transfer of value or rights from the latter, the idea of powers to rescind being responses to unjust(ified) enrichment becomes more than a tantalising possibility—it becomes, in my view, almost a conceptual inevitability.

C. Explanatory Value

What is the explanatory value of all this, other than conceptual precision (which is, of course, a great value in itself)? It is submitted that *if* we understand a recognised defect of consent to a given transaction as tantamount to the absence of a normative basis for whatever rights the affected transaction may have created or transferred, and *if* the right to rescind therefore responds to an unjust(ified) enrichment, then this in turn explains some otherwise puzzling features of the law of rescission.

In particular, it explains why common law treats the ability to restore the other party to the pre-contractual position (requirement of *restitutio in integrum*) as a precondition to rescission. Any counter-performance which the other party has rendered to the now rescinding party counts as a relevant disenrichment *even before* rescission has occurred. The promisee-enrichee has obtained a right, and in order to be able to enforce that right in a typical reciprocal contract (and/or subsequently to keep what they are hoping to receive), the promisee has to abide by their side of the

[113] SJ Stoljar, *The Law of Quasi-Contract* (2nd edn, Law Book Co 1989) 5–10, 13, 250; SJ Stoljar, 'Unjust Enrichment and Unjust Sacrifice' (1987) 50 MLR 603.

[114] See also the discussion of the 'proprietary theory' and its relationship with so-called 'proprietary restitution' in Häcker, 'Causa, Consideration and Unjust(ified) Enrichment' (n 30) 264–65.

bargain. The promisee's enrichment (by receipt of the promisor-enrichor's promise) and disenrichment (through rendering counter-performance) are directly related. The promisor cannot unilaterally strip the promisee of the enrichment without ensuring that counter-restitution also follows.[115] Other acts of reliance, such as the promisee foregoing a contract with a third party, do not count as relevant disenrichments in the common law tradition. This is because the promisee is, *ex hypothesi*, in some way 'responsible' for causing the promisor to enter the transaction: by making a misrepresentation or exerting the improper pressure. At the very least, in the world of 'process-orientated' grounds for rescission, the promisee will know or have notice of the underlying problem (as eg in the case of third-party duress).

It will be recalled that civilian systems incorporate various 'substantive' grounds for rescission, allowing the promisor to escape from a transaction even where their mistake was entirely spontaneous.[116] It will also be recalled that, in order to accommodate the concerns of the declaratory theory and to protect the reliance of the other contracting party, German law coupled the mistaken party's right to rescind with an obligation to compensate the other for any reliance losses. The relevant damages clause is today found in s 122 of the BGB:

> (1) If a declaration of intention ... has been avoided on the basis of [sections] 119, 120, then, if the declaration was one addressed to another party, the person making it must compensate the other ... for any loss suffered as a result of relying on the validity of the declaration, but not beyond the amount of the interest which the other ... has in the validity of the declaration.
> (2) The liability to compensate does not arise if the party suffering the loss knew of the ground for avoidance or would have known of it but for his negligence (ought to have known).

Academics have over the years produced a number of different justifications for this form of strict liability. Famously, and very influentially, Claus-Wilhelm Canaris identified s122 of the BGB as an emanation of a more general principle of 'reliance liability' (*Vertrauenshaftung*) which he saw as underpinning certain parts of the BGB.[117] Yet imposing strict liability is actually quite uncharacteristic of German law, where damages claims are otherwise mostly fault-based, in the realms of both tort and contract.[118]

[115] This might suggest that *actual* counter-restitution—rather than merely the rescinding promisor's *ability* to render it—should be the precondition of rescission. As the law stands, it is not entirely clear what the 'bar' actually hinges on. Yet even the mere *ability* to make counter-restitution would be a defensible criterion. Given the promisee's involvement with the factor that provides the 'process-orientated' ground of rescission (cf text surrounding n 60), the hurdle for the rescinding promisor ought not to be put too high. A legal system can plausibly let it suffice that, following rescission, there is a realistic prospect of the promisee's disenrichment being made good by subsequent counter-restitution.

[116] See the text accompanying nn 63–68.

[117] CW Canaris, *Die Vertrauenshaftung im deutschen Privatrecht* (CH Beck 1971) 423; CW Canaris, 'Die Vertrauenshaftung im Lichte der Rechtsprechung des Bundesgerichtshofs' in CW Canaris and others (eds), *50 Jahre Bundesgerichtshof: Festgabe aus der Wissenschaft*, vol 1 (CH Beck 2000) 129, 171–72.

[118] See BGB, ss 280–84 (contractual claims) and ss 823–39 (delictual claims, where genuinely strict liability is confined to a single special case in s 833 of the BGB, namely damage caused by animals maintained by their keeper for 'luxury' purposes other than earning a living).

This is why other authors have tried to explain s 122 of the BGB as an instance of liability for *culpa in contrahendo* ('fault in contracting'), by arguing that the promisor making a spontaneous mistake would not be in the position of having to rescind the transaction if he had paid proper attention at the point of contracting.[119]

The argument here is that there is a third explanation, which is at least as strong a contender. The strict nature of the liability, its focus on reliance losses, and the fact that the claim is capped at the performance interest, are all entirely plausible if the right to rescind is generated by unjustified enrichment as suggested above. On this view, s 122 of the BGB is a version of the disenrichment defence. The performance interest delineates the maximum amount of the claimant-promisee's enrichment at the rescinding promisor's expense, and hence the maximum amount of any potential disenrichment. Since, in a rescission case, the promisee is simply divested of his rights and is not 'returning' anything to the promisor from which a relevant disenrichment could be deducted (as in a normal restitution case), the only way of accounting for it is by imposing on the rescinding party a strict liability to make good the promisee's reliance losses. Admittedly, the disqualification threshold in s 122(2) of the BGB, namely knowledge or ignorance as a result of negligence, is lower than in the 'normal' law of unjustified enrichment, where the disenrichment or change of position defence is said to be unavailable only where the enrichee is positively aware of the enrichor's claim to restitution.[120] However, if this is indeed a 'mismatch' between the two sets of provisions, it is not one which should obscure the fundamental structural parallels outlined above.

The explanatory value of regarding rights to rescind for defective or 'vitiated' consent as based on the promisee's unjust(ified) enrichment at the promisor's expense thus lies in allowing us to see in a different light certain rules with which a given system's law of rescission is hedged about. This, in turn, puts us in a better position to ask and answer tricky questions we may not hitherto have got a proper handle on. For instance, it would bolster the already popular argument that English law need not require *restitutio in integrum* to be precise when it comes to rescission, so long as the other party is not thereby left out of pocket (so-called 'pecuniary rescission').[121] It would moreover challenge us to consider whether some parties—fraudsters in particular—ought themselves to bear the risk of counter-restitution becoming impossible, at least in certain defined circumstances.[122] For German lawyers, it opens fresh opportunities for re-evaluating the liability rule in s 122 of the BGB and working out whether (and, if so, when and how far) its disqualification threshold merits adjustment.[123] In short, understanding rights

[119] T Lobinger, *Rechtsgeschäftliche Verpflichtung und autonome Bindung* (Mohr Siebeck 1999) 207–17.

[120] This is generally inferred from reading s 818(3) of the BGB in conjunction with ss 819(1) and 818(4).

[121] That term appears to have been coined about thirty years ago, when the idea was first prominently expressed: see P Birks, 'Unjust Factors and Wrongs: Pecuniary Rescission for Undue Influence' [1997] RLR 72; NY Nahan, 'Rescission: A Case for Rejecting the Classical Model?' (1997) 26 UWAL Rev 66, esp 66–67, 82–85.

[122] Such as when confronted with a rescinding minor: see (albeit outside the context of rescission) B Häcker, 'Minority and Unjust Enrichment Defences' in A Dyson, J Goudkamp, and F Wilmot-Smith (eds), *Defences in Unjust Enrichment* (Hart 2016) 195, 209–15.

[123] It has, for instance, been suggested that reliance losses are not recoverable by parties who are themselves responsible for inducing the rescinding party's mistake under BGB, s 119 (even outside the case of deceit): see eg Flume (n 85) 424. This is interesting from a comparative point of view as it would remove the liability stipulated by

to rescind as responses to unjust(ified) enrichment makes pieces of the puzzle, which were hitherto thought of as distinct, line up and fit together nicely.[124]

VII. Conclusion

The present chapter has sought to excavate the conceptual foundations of the law of rescission using a comparative approach informed by the historical evolution of both the English common law tradition and, on the civilian side, French and German law.

It explained how different conceptions of what a contract is, and what makes transactions legally binding, ultimately account for the systems' divergences when it comes to the recognised grounds for rescission. If the key question is why the *promisee* should be entitled to enforce the promisor's promise, as in the common law tradition, it follows quite naturally that rescission should be by and large confined to instances where the promisee is in some way responsible for the promisor's consent being defective. If, on the other hand, the *promisor*'s private autonomy lies at the heart of the matter, then this dictates that the promisor should only be held to their word where the outward appearance of their will coincided with what they actually wanted.

For reasons of principle and pragmatism, all three legal systems have decided that what they individually regard as defective consent is best treated as a ground for avoidance of the affected transaction. Consent is 'vitiated', not wholly absent. Voidable transactions are thus valid unless and until they are rescinded by the affected party.

There is a remarkable structural parallel with the doctrine of *causa* to be observed. Though historically no less significant in the realm of obligatory contracts than in the realm of dispositive transactions, that doctrine is today discussed almost exclusively in connection with the latter. A transfer lacking a valid *causa traditionis* or legal basis is automatically ineffective in 'causal' transfer systems. In 'abstract' systems, the absence of a *causa* does not itself prevent the transaction happening. Yet this is not the end of the matter in 'abstract' systems: the law of unjust(ified) enrichment steps in and ensures that the transfer lacking a normative basis can subsequently be undone at the behest of the disadvantaged party.

In connection with obligatory transactions, the doctrine of *causa* has been all but replaced by consent as the determinative factor of bindingness in both Germany and France. As far as the English common law is concerned, the focus of the inquiry has at

BGB, s 122 in situations where the otherwise 'content-orientated' ground for rescission has a 'process-orientated' overlay. As in the common law tradition, the mistake-inducing party would then be confined to seeking counter-restitution, but could not hope to recover any reliance expenditure beyond that.

124 Whether one or the other grounds of rescission (such as fraud or duress by means of threats) can be subjected to an alternative analysis in the sense of being a form of restitution for wrongs is a question that hinges on the exact relationship between unjust(ified) enrichment, restitution, and the law of wrongs. It cannot be pursued further here. It suffices to note that, on one approach at least, restitution and unjust(ified) enrichment do square, and an enrichment may count as unjust(ified) precisely because it has been obtained by an infringement of or interference with another's rights. This could easily be extended to another's decision-making autonomy.

any rate shifted away from consideration and towards the quality of the parties' agreement. In all three systems, consent is essential to the legal effects of transacting. Where that consent is defective by the standards of a given system, but where it nevertheless counts as valid unless and until the transaction is avoided, we are on closer inspection dealing with a type of 'abstraction'. The very way rescission operates resembles the 'abstract' approach: leave in place for the time being, but provide the option to unwind later. The existence of the option to rescind is best accounted for through the law of unjust(ified) enrichment.

The analysis of the right to rescind presented here applies quite regardless of whether rescission occurs in relation to a purely obligatory transaction (such as an executory contract) or a full-blown disposition (such as a consensual transfer of title) or a mixture of both. Put in general terms, the proposition is as follows: a party whose consent is impaired in a way a given legal system regards as relevant, but whose consent is nonetheless treated by that system as temporarily valid, with the effect of bestowing some legal right on another, be it personal and/or proprietary, has enriched that other in a manner the system regards as normatively unjust(ified). The disadvantaged party who is then provided with a power (with or without the help of a court) to avoid the consequences of the consensual transaction, and thus to divest the other party of whatever rights were acquired by virtue of it, is thereby afforded a restitutionary remedy based on the other's unjust(ified) enrichment. This is the core essence of the so-called 'right to rescind'.

3

Understanding Powers to Rescind

Property, Equity, and Unjust Enrichment

*Ben McFarlane**

I. Three Points of Introduction and Three Sources of Confusion

This chapter focuses on a particular aspect of the third-party effect of the law of rescission. The core case considered is where A holds a right and then exercises a power to transfer that right to B. The transfer is effective but there is a ground for rescission, either at common law or in equity. If rescission occurs whilst B still holds the transferred right, then it is possible that the right will immediately revest in A, or that B will hold the right on trust for A. What if, however, *before* the transfer has been rescinded, B passed the right on to a third party, C? What is the best way to analyse the difficult question of the effect on C of the fact that, because of some flaw in the transaction between A and B, there was the possibility of A's regaining, either directly or through a trust, the right which is now held by C? In other words, as the question is often put,[1] what is the effect of A's power to rescind, either at common law or in equity, on C?

The first introductory point is that, even where C acquires C's right prior to rescission, there are nonetheless circumstances in which the flaw in the transaction between A and B may have an impact on C. As far as the grounds of rescission recognised at common law are concerned, this is evident in *Car and Universal Finance Ltd v Caldwell*.[2] A transferred A's title to a car to B under a contract of sale but, as a result of B's fraud, A had a power to rescind and revest title to the car. B had quickly sold the car to C1 (Motabella) who had very soon sold the car to C2 (G & C Ltd). It was conceded that, given the circumstances of the sale to C1, and C1's prior dealings with B, C1 had 'notice of the defect of title'.[3] It was accepted therefore that the flaw in the transaction between A and B had an impact on C1: A had the power to rescind and revest title to the car even after the transfer to C1. The focus at first instance and the Court of Appeal

* Professor of English Law, University of Oxford, and Fellow of St John's College, Oxford, United Kingdom. I am grateful to the editors for their suggestions, for comments received at the conference that led to the volume, and to Dr John Macleod for discussion of Scots law. All errors are mine alone.

[1] On the approach adopted in this chapter, there are important differences between rescission at common law and in equity, and so care must be taken when grouping the two together by using the term 'power to rescind': see further Section III.B below.

[2] [1965] 1 QB 525.

[3] ibid 556. In the original action (*Caldwell v Motabella Co Ltd*), A had obtained judgment by default against C1, and C1 had been ordered to return the car to A.

was on the position of C2. The Court of Appeal upheld Lord Denning MR's finding that, prior to C2's acquisition of title to the car, A had rescinded A's contract with B, and legal title to the car had revested in A. On that analysis, as regards the position of C2, *Caldwell* is not an example of the core case considered here: C2's acquisition occurred after, rather than before, rescission. However, Lord Denning MR also held that, even if rescission had not occurred before C2's acquisition, C2 'did not acquire a good title to the goods because they were affected by the notice which their agents [C1] had of the defect of title and so they themselves did not get a good title'.[4] That finding was rejected by the Court of Appeal, on the basis that C1 could not be regarded as C2's agents and so C1's knowledge or notice of B's fraud could not be attributed to C2. It was accepted, however, that, if C2 did have such knowledge or notice of the defect in title, the flaw in the sale from A to B would have an impact on C2, even if rescission had not occurred before C2's acquisition of title to the car.

The possibility of a ground of rescission recognised only in equity having an impact on C can be demonstrated by *Latec Investments Ltd v Hotel Terrigal Pty Ltd*.[5] A had registered title to a hotel and, to secure a loan, granted B a legal mortgage. When A fell into arrears, B had the power to sell A's title. However, B misused that power by transferring title to C1, its subsidiary: 'there was a lack of that kind of good faith which in the eyes of a court of equity is essential to the validity of a mortgagee's sale'.[6] As B and C1 were found to have collaborated in this misuse of the power, it was recognised that, if A had at that point asked for relief, this would 'necessarily have led to a decree setting aside the sale as against [B] and [C1] and granting consequential relief'.[7] The difficulty arose as, before any such application had been made, C1 had given an equitable charge in relation to the land to C2, and C2 had acquired that charge for value and without notice of any defect in C1's acquisition of title. The High Court of Australia held, in effect, that A's claim to have the sale and transfer from B to C1 set aside should succeed only against B and C1, and not against C2.[8]

The second introductory point is that there is currently uncertainty as to the best way to understand how, and why, it is that a flaw in the transaction between A and B may have an impact on C. As to the how, one question is as to the nature of A's right, or power, in relation to the right transferred to B, before rescission. In a case such as *Caldwell*, it might be said that A has a power to rescind, arising at common law, and that this is a form of legal property right in the car, prima facie binding on C. In a case such as *Latec*, it might be said that A's power to rescind, arising in equity, gives A a form of equitable property right in relation to the land, which is then prima facie binding on C. These rights, however, take an unusual form. If A has a legal property right in *Caldwell*, it is, unusually for such rights, subject to a bona fide purchaser for value defence. Similarly, if A has an equitable property right in *Latec*, it is, unusually for such

[4] ibid 534.
[5] (1965) 113 CLR 265.
[6] ibid [5].
[7] ibid [7].
[8] ibid [10].

rights, incapable of binding a third party that later acquires, for value and in good faith, its own *equitable* interest in relation to the land: that is why, in *Latec* itself, C2's equitable charge was protected. This quirk is often indicated by referring to A's interest as a 'mere equity', rather than as a fully fledged equitable property right. The terminology is somewhat unhelpful; after all, as Professor William Swadling has memorably noted, it would be 'both silly and unhelpful' to refer to A's right in *Caldwell*, before rescission, as a 'mere common law'.[9] There is also the question as to whether, in the case of equitable rescission, A really does have a power to rescind, rather than a power to apply to the court so that the court can effect rescission.[10] Such questions as to the form of A's right are related to the justifications for A's ability to make a claim that can have an impact on C. Swadling, for example, doubts that such justifications exist, arguing that, in a case such as *Caldwell*, B's fraud does not in itself justify allowing A to make a claim against a third party[11] and, in a case such as *Latec*, it is 'surprising' that A's ability to petition a court for relief 'has any third-party effect at all'.[12]

The third and final point to make by way of introduction is that understanding our core case, where C acquires a right before rescission occurs, has both practical and conceptual importance. Practically, C, when acquiring a right from B, needs to have the ability to know if and in what circumstances a flaw in the earlier transaction between A and B may have an impact on C's position. Debates as to the nature of A's position before rescission can affect, for example, the location of the burden of proof:[13] is C prima facie bound by A's pre-existing power to rescind, subject to C's making out a bona fide purchaser, or other, defence; or is it for A to establish that C's notice of the flaw in the A–B transaction is such that A should be able to make a claim against C? Further, understanding A's position in relation to the right transferred to B is important not only when considering the position of C but also when considering the position of B. For example, in *Bainbridge v Bainbridge*,[14] A, as a result of a unilateral mistake, transferred rights to land to trustees (B) to hold on a discretionary trust. B, acting with authority under that trust, sold part of the land to C. The sale proceeds were then used by B to buy new land, and A sought an order that title to the new land should be transferred by the trustees to A. It was accepted that no claim could be brought against C, who had acquired rights from the trustees in good faith and without notice of A's mistake, but, as will be discussed in Section III, the analysis of A's position at the point when B sold the land to C was crucial in the court's decision to grant A the order sought.

In conceptual terms, the debate as to the core case forms part of a number of broader questions, both in and beyond the law of rescission. For example, if it is the case that, in each of *Caldwell* and *Latec*, A, having transferred a right to B, nonetheless acquired a

[9] W Swadling, 'Property, Rescission, and the Common Law' (2005) 121 LQR 123, 133.

[10] For discussion of that question in this volume, see Chapter 4 (W Swadling, 'Rescission—The Role of the Court') and Chapter 11 (L Ho, 'The Proprietary Consequences of Rescission in Equity') of this book. See also D O'Sullivan, S Elliott, and R Zakrzewski (eds), *The Law of Rescission* (3rd edn, OUP 2023) ch 16.

[11] See eg Swadling, 'Property, Rescission, and the Common Law' (n 9).

[12] W Swadling, 'The Proprietary Consequences of Fraud' in P Davies and H Tijo (eds), *Fraud and Risk in Commercial Law* (Hart 2024) 169, 178.

[13] See eg *Barclays Bank v Boulter* [1999] 1 WLR 1919, 1924–25, discussed in Section II.C below.

[14] [2016] EWHC 898.

form of proprietary interest, this may be seen as evidence that, in at least some cases, the need to prevent B's unjust enrichment at A's expense may justify a proprietary response. If such analysis is accepted, these cases may then be used as part of a broader argument in favour of recognising that other cases of unjust enrichment, unrelated to rescission, may also give rise to proprietary rights.[15] Indeed, an analogy can be drawn between *Caldwell* and the well-known decision of the House of Lords in *Lipkin Gorman v Karpnale Ltd*.[16] In the latter case, there is a puzzle as to the nature of the proprietary interest that the claimant partners were said to have in the cash, withdrawn from the partnership bank account, with which the rogue partner gambled at the defendant casino. It has been argued, for example, that the partners had a 'power *in rem*', arising at common law, in relation to the money: the same type of right that A, in *Caldwell*, had prior to rescission.[17]

This chapter does not purport to provide a definitive answer to the contested questions of how, and why, the flaw in the A–B transaction that permits rescission may have an impact on C. It does however aim to make progress by tackling three 'fertile sources of confusion'[18] and by locating the questions within a wider set of legal rules that aim to mitigate the impact on A of a flawed exercise of a power given to A by common law or equity. The first source of confusion is the use of what may generally be called 'property terms'. The second is the divide between common law and equity. The third is as to the application of principles of unjust enrichment. As will be seen, there are links between these three issues: they are certainly not watertight compartments.

Section II of the chapter focuses on rescission at common law, and hence on cases such as *Caldwell*. It takes as given the position that where A has transferred A's title to goods to B under a contract of sale procured by B's fraud, A's exercise of a choice to rescind operates immediately to revest title to the goods in A. It will be argued here that it is dangerous to assume that, because rescission thus operates to give A a right that is prima facie binding on the rest of the world, A must be seen as having such a right *before* rescission. A's power to rescind need not have the same sort of third-party effect as the title A re-acquires upon rescission. Indeed, there is a sense, expressed in passing by Lord Hoffmann in *Barclays Bank v Boulter*,[19] in which A's power is not even prima facie binding on a third party such as C who acquires rights from B. If this argument is accepted, it removes one element of support for the view that, in *Lipkin Gorman*, a common law power to acquire a property right had a third-party effect on an innocent recipient.[20]

Section III of the chapter focuses on rescission in equity and argues that in this area, as in so many others, it is a mistake to see equitable rules as simply replicating the effects

[15] For such an argument, see eg R Chambers, *Resulting Trusts* (OUP 1997).

[16] [1991] 2 AC 548.

[17] See eg B Häcker, *Consequences of Impaired Consent Transfers* (Hart 2013) 241–43.

[18] To borrow the term used by Lord Wilberforce in *Johnson v Agnew* [1980] AC 367, 392–93, when noting the difference between the power to 'rescind' a contract following a significantly serious breach by a counterparty and the different power, discussed in this chapter, to rescind *ab initio* in cases of 'mistake, fraud, or lack of consent'.

[19] [1999] 1 WLR 1919, 1924–25. See too the convincing analysis of A Reilly, 'Voidable Title in the Sale of Goods: One Power to Rescind, or Two?' (2024) 35 King's Law J 177.

[20] See the discussion in Section II.C of *Lipkin Gorman v Karpnale Ltd* [1991] 2 AC 548.

of seemingly equivalent legal rules. If, as confirmed by *Caldwell*, rescission at common law can revest legal title in A, it is tempting to see rescission in equity as revesting 'equitable title'.[21] It will be argued that it is a mistake to think of there being one set of circumstances in which a transfer may be voidable at common law, and a different set of circumstances in which a transfer may be voidable in equity. This is because, where A exercises a choice to avoid an exercise of a power, avoidance means that the power is regarded as never having been exercised. That can be the case where, as in *Caldwell*, A's legal right revests; it cannot be the case where, following a transfer of a legal right, rescission in equity is available. This is because the effect of rescission in equity is *not* to revest the legal right in A: it is rather, at its highest, to impose a duty on B to return the right to A. Nor does rescission operate to *re*-vest an equitable title in A: prior to the transaction with B, if A simply held A's right outright, then A had no such distinct equitable title which could return to A. As a result of this difference in the effect of rescission, a closer analogy can be drawn in equity, rather than at common law, between A's position before rescission and A's position after it. It will be argued that this is important when understanding the effect on third parties, such as C in our example, who acquire rights from B before equitable rescission occurs.

Section IV focuses on the argument that, in understanding both rescission and the nature of A's position prior to rescission, it is useful to consider the four-stage unjust enrichment analysis set out in cases such as *Banque Financière de la Cité SA v Westgate Insurance Co*.[22] Consistently with some recent commentary sceptical of such an approach,[23] it will be argued here that our core case provides another example where such an analysis confuses rather than clarifies. This is significant as it means that cases of rescission cannot then be used to support arguments as to the circumstances in which the unjust enrichment of B at A's expense gives rise to a legal property right or equitable interest of A.

The argument in Section IV does not mean, however, that cases said to provide clear examples of unjust enrichment, such as A's making a payment to B in the mistaken belief that A is under a duty to make that payment,[24] have nothing significant in common with rescission. On the contrary, the positive argument made here is that, to understand the core case where a flaw in the A–B transaction can have an impact on C, it is necessary to draw a link to the mistaken payment case. The claim in the mistaken payment case, like the possibility of rescission, provides A with a form of protection against the inherent danger that powers given to A, by common law or equity, to increase the useful choices available to A, may sometimes be validly exercised in cases where A's consent to their exercise is in some sense flawed. Rescission thus takes its place alongside a set of doctrines, including those allowing the claim in the mistaken payment

[21] For clear judicial adoption of such an analysis, see eg Potter LJ in *Twinsectra v Yardley* [1999] Lloyd's Rep Bank 438 [99]; Dixon CJ, Webb, Kitto, and Taylor JJ in *Alati v Kruger* (1955) 94 CLR 216, 223–24.

[22] [1991] 2 AC 249.

[23] See eg R Stevens, *The Laws of Restitution* (OUP 2023). Although for a partial defence of the utility of unjust enrichment analysis in this context, see Chapter 2 of this book (B Häcker, 'Explaining the Right to Rescind').

[24] See eg *Kelly v Solari* (1841) 9 M&W 54, 152 ER 24; *Barclays Bank Ltd v WJ Simms & Son Ltd* [1980] QB 677.

case, which are secondary in the particular sense that they respond to a problem which arises through the operation of primary legal rules, without denying the operation of those primary rules.[25] So, whilst the wider principle of unjust enrichment, as set out in a case such as *Banque Financière*, does not in fact illuminate the law of rescission, our understanding of both the law of rescission, and of cases said to fall within that wider principle, can be improved if those case are analysed together.

In the core case considered here, then, the notorious complexity of the law of rescission can be seen as a corollary of the fact that, were it clear that the flaw in relation to A's power is such that A should be protected, the law would most likely respond by simply saying that A's purported exercise of a power was never effective.[26] Equally, if it were clear that A should not be protected, then A would have no claim at all, whether a personal claim against B or otherwise.[27] Rescission, in its two distinct forms of common law and equitable rescission, necessarily occupies a delicate position between these extremes, but in doing so it provides the law with valuable additional means of performing the very difficult role of resolving disputes such as those between A and C. The complexity of the law is the price paid for such nuance, and it can be managed successfully if care is taken when considering key ideas such as property, equity, and unjust enrichment.

II. The Role of Property

A. The Meanings of 'Property'

The core case considered here is where A has transferred a right to B, and, before rescission occurs, B transfers that right to C, or otherwise exercises a power in relation to that right in favour of C. In considering A's position prior to rescission there are a variety of different questions which we might pose in asking if A has 'property'. It is important, of course, to distinguish the different senses in which the term 'property' is used. For example, one question is whether A has a right that is capable of being assigned to, or assumed by, a third party.[28] A different question is whether A has a right that is capable of forming the subject matter of a trust.[29] A further, still different question—the one with which this chapter is concerned—is whether A has a right which is capable of having an effect not only on B, but also on third parties. In addressing this question it is useful to distinguish between two different types of liability to which third parties may be

[25] See further B McFarlane, 'Equitable Estoppel and Restitution as Interstitial Causes of Action' in S Bray and others (eds), *Interstitial Private Law* (OUP 2024).

[26] This occurs in cases such as *Cundy v Lindsay* (1878) 3 App Cas 459 and *R v Ashwell* (1885) 16 QBD 190.

[27] See eg *Smith v Hughes* (1871) LR 6 QB 597.

[28] See eg *Melbourne Banking Corp v Brougham (No 2)* (1882) 7 App Cas 307, holding that A's equity to set aside the release of an equity of redemption had passed to A's successor under a general conveyance without needing to be specifically assigned.

[29] For the (puzzling) use of the term 'property' to determine such a question, see eg *AA v Persons Unknown* [2019] EWHC 3556 (Comm) and *Ruscoe and Moore v Cryptopia Ltd* [2020] NZHC 728. For criticism of the approach taken in those cases, see K Low, 'Trusts of Cryptocurrency' (2021) 34 TLI 191.

subject: trespassory liability, which arises where there is interference with a resource by the third party; and successor liability, which arises only where the third party acquires a particular type of right.[30]

It is very common, in English law at least, to run together these two different types of third-party liability, and to regard the possibility of successor liability as sufficing to justify a description of A's pre-existing right as proprietary, or '*in rem*'. A clear example of this tendency is provided by Lord Sumption's analysis, in *Akers v Samba Financial Group*,[31] of A's position where B holds a right on trust for A. Lord Sumption states there that A's right 'possesses the essential hallmark of any right in rem' because it is capable of binding successors in title to B,[32] although he later makes clear that such parties are bound only if their 'conscience is affected'.[33] A civil lawyer, for example, would be reluctant to accept that a right is '*in rem*' simply because it can give rise to successor liability, not least where this liability does not even affect all successors in title to B but depends on whether 'the conscience of the transferee is affected'.[34] Indeed, it might be thought that ownership is a core example of a right *in rem*, and it is hard to apply the concept of binding successors in title where A simply has ownership.

The distinction between a right which prima facie binds all parties who may interfere with a resource, and one which instead affects only the particular class of third parties who have acquired a right from a specific party, and are thus subject to successor liability, is not merely technical. It has been argued that it is crucial to understanding the different effects of legal property rights on the one hand and equitable interests on the other.[35] For example, where O has ownership of goods, the rest of the world is under a prima facie duty to O not to interfere, deliberately or carelessly, with those goods. So if, for example, O were to allow B to take possession of the goods, and B, purporting to pass the best title to the goods to C, transferred B's title to the goods to C, then O's ability to bring a claim against C does not depend at all on C's being a successor in title to B: C is liable for the same tort, and in the same way, as X would be if X had simply stolen the goods directly from O. C's acquisition of any rights plays no part in explaining C's liability to O. In contrast, if B instead has ownership of the goods, and holds that right on trust for A, then the rest of the world owes no such prima facie duty to A. If B, acting without authority under the trust, transfers B's title to the goods to C, then, if A brings a claim against C that C must give up that title, and restore it to B, or a replacement trustee, A's claim *does* depend on C's having acquired a right from B. So it can be said, and indeed overwhelmingly often is said, that A, like O, has a property

[30] See J Penner, 'Duty and Liability in Respect of Funds' in J Lowry and L Mistelis (eds), *Commercial Law: Perspectives and Practice* (LexisNexis Butterworths 2006).

[31] [2017] UKSC 6, [2017] AC 424.

[32] ibid [82].

[33] ibid [89].

[34] Note eg the finding of the European Court of Justice (agreeing with the decision of Paul Baker QC, sitting as a deputy judge, on this point) in *Webb v Webb* [1994] QB 696, holding that A's claim that title to French land was held on trust by B for A was not a proceeding which had as its object a right *in rem* and so did not fall within what is now art 24 of the Recast Brussels I Regulation.

[35] See eg B McFarlane, *The Structure of Property Law* (Hart 2008), and B McFarlane and R Stevens, 'The Nature of Equitable Property' (2010) 4 J Eq 1.

right; but it must be appreciated that, if this is the case, then 'property right' has two quite different meanings.

B. The Effect of Rescission at Common Law

The '*in rem*' nature of a title to goods is amply demonstrated by *Car and Universal Finance Ltd v Caldwell*.[36] As common law rescission had occurred, revesting title to the car in A, before C2 had acquired any right, C2 was, absent any defence,[37] liable to A in conversion for C2's dealing with that car. C2's good faith or otherwise was irrelevant given conversion's nature as a strict liability tort. A comparison can be drawn with *Cundy v Lindsay*.[38] In that case, B's fraud had a different effect: the fraud went to B's identity and meant that B was unable to accept A's offer to enter a contract of sale, as that offer was not in fact made to B. It was held that, as there had never been a contract of sale between A and B, A's title to the goods had not passed to B, even though A had delivered the goods to B. As a result, after B purported to sell the goods to C, C was strictly liable to A for C's dealing with the goods: it did not matter that C had acquired possession of the goods, in good faith, from B. The difference between the two cases, of course, is the effect of the problem affecting the initial dealings between A and B. In *Cundy*, the problem meant that the conditions necessary for the transfer of A's right to B had simply not been met and so, whilst possession of the goods may have moved to B, A's title to them remained with A. Given the nature of the problem was as to B's identity, it was not reasonable for B to believe that A had intended to transfer A's title to B, and so no transfer occurred. This is the strongest form of protection that can be given to A's pre-existing right: a claimed dealing with the right is void and so has not in fact occurred. In *Caldwell*, the problem was of a different nature: it *was* reasonable for B to believe that A had intended to transfer A's right to B, but B's fraud had played a role in A's decision to enter into that transaction.

The first question to consider in a case such as *Caldwell* is whether, as in *Cundy*, the fraud should mean that no transfer of A's right to B has occurred. This is a question as to the legal conditions necessary for the transfer of the right. The modern view,[39] following *Load v Green*,[40] and applied in, for example, *Shogun Finance v Hudson*,[41] is that,

[36] [1965] 1 QB 525.

[37] For a case where a defence was available to C, under s 9 of the Factors Act 1889, see *Newtons of Wembley Ltd v Williams* [1965] 1 QB 560, discussed by Häcker, *Consequences of Impaired Consent Transfers* (n 17) 231–33.

[38] (1878) 3 App Cas 459.

[39] In some earlier cases, it had been thought that fraud would prevent A's right passing to B: see eg *Earl of Bristol v Wilsmore* (1823) 1 B & C 514, discussed by Swadling, 'Property, Rescission, and the Common Law' (n 9) 149. Similarly, it had in some cases been said that duress imposed by B on A would suffice to prevent title passing from A to B: *Duke de Cadaval v Collins* (1836) 4 Ad & El 858, 864–65; 111 ER 1006, 1009 (where Lord Denman CJ stated that the effect of the compulsion was that 'property in the money, therefore, never passed from the plaintiff, who parted with it only to relieve himself from the hardship and inconvenience of a fraudulent arrest'); *Grainger v Hill* (1838) 4 Bing NC 212, 221; 132 ER 769, 773 (where A purported to transfer his title to a ship's register to B under compulsion of a fraudulent arrest—Tindal CJ analysed the case as a 'taking the property of [A] without his consent').

[40] (1846) 15 M & W 216, 153 ER 828.

[41] [2003] UKHL 62, [2004] 1 AC 919.

as long as there is consensus between A and B as to the right to be transferred, and the identity of the transferee, then the conditions for the transfer of title from A to B have been met, and the transfer is voidable rather than void. Dr John MacLeod shows how Scots law reached the same conclusion, by moving away from a model in which fraud would mean that an apparent transaction had not occurred to a model in which fraud, by itself, instead made the transfer 'reducible': that is liable to be set aside by an act of A.[42] No less a thinker than Hume, for example, justified this shift, and the validity of a transfer resulting from fraud, by distinguishing between situations such as theft, when there is no consent by A, and hence no transfer, and fraud, where there is consent, and so the transfer occurs but is liable to be set aside.[43] Certainly, the approach taken in *Load v Green* is foreshadowed not only by some English cases[44] but also by some commentators on Scots law. MacLeod, for example, notes that Mungo Brown, writing on the sale of goods in 1821, stated that, even if procured by threats of violence, where there is actual agreement then 'although such a contract is clearly *voidable*, on the head of force and fear, *it is not ipso jure void*, and the property is, in the first instance, transferred so as to enable the wrongdoer to give a good title to a *bona fide purchaser*'.[45]

The modern approach, that fraud, by itself, does not prevent the transfer of A's right to B, can be justified. It can be argued that the essential justification for such a transfer, whether by sale or gift, lies in the agreement of A and B.[46] If, notwithstanding the fraud, there is such an agreement as to the identity of the transferee and the identity of the right to be transferred, then the relevant legal event has occurred, and there is a transfer even if that agreement was procured by fraud. There are good reasons for having relatively simple and clear tests as to when a right has been transferred and, as implied by Brown's analysis above, the protection of third parties is one such reason.[47] Nonetheless, the presence of fraud, even if it does not prevent agreement as to the identity of the transferee or the right transferred, is a significant concern. It involves not only deception by B, but also reliance by A, such that B's deception makes a contribution to A's decision-making process. It can therefore be argued that fraud involves manipulation by B, by deception, of A's decision-making process.[48]

There are at least two concerns where A's decision-making process relates to A's power to transfer a right. First, as Nicholas McBride notes,[49] the law endows A with that power so as to allow certain benefits to be realised by A, and the interference with

[42] J MacLeod, *Fraud and Voidable Transfer* (Edinburgh Legal Education Trust 2020) ch 2. Note also the discussion by Häcker, 'Explaining the Right to Rescind' (n 23) of a similar shift in German law.

[43] *Baron David Hume's Lectures 1786–1822* (ed G Paton, Stair Society, vols 5, 13, 15, and 17–19, 1939–1958) *I*, 316.

[44] As noted by Häcker, *Consequences of Impaired Consent Transfers* (n 17) 131: see *Ferguson v Carrington* (1829) 9 Barn & Cress 57, 109 ER 22 and *Strutt v Smith* (1834) 1 Cromp M & R 312, 149 ER 1099.

[45] M Brown, *A Treatise on the Law of Sale* (1821) [563] (italics in original), discussed by MacLeod (n 42) [2-79].

[46] On the importance of agreement to gifts, see eg Stevens, *The Laws of Restitution* (n 23) 197–98.

[47] Indeed, the minority in *Shogun Finance v Hudson* [2004] 1 AC 919 (Lords Nicholls and Millett) would have gone further and found that the contract is formed, and the transfer valid, even if the fraud is such as to mean there is no agreement as to the identity of the transferee. For problems with the minority's view, see eg R Stevens, 'Objectivity, Mistake, and the Parol Evidence Rule' in A Burrows and E Peel (eds), *Contract Terms* (OUP 2007).

[48] See C Cox, 'This is a Chapter about Deception' in Bray and others, *Interstitial Private Law* (n 25).

[49] N McBride, 'Rescission' in G Virgo and S Worthington (eds), *Commercial Remedies: Resolving Controversies* (CUP 2017).

A's decision-making process creates a real risk that those benefits will not be realised. Second, where A transfers a right to B, and B's manipulation of A has made a contribution to A's decision to transfer, it seems that B is taking advantage of the legal rules relating to transfer by an illegitimate means. As McBride has powerfully argued more generally,[50] an important concern of private law is to prevent respect for the primary rules of private law (which confer, for example, powers to transfer rights) being undermined by such abuse. As demonstrated by *Caldwell*, rescission at common law is drastic, but the possibility of its occurring provides an important means both to limit the impact on A of the primary legal rules that allow for the transfer of a right notwithstanding B's fraud, and to limit B's ability to benefit from an abuse of those rules. Whilst the English courts' recognition of a common law power to rescind in cases of fraud has been challenged,[51] English law is far from being an outlier in giving such protection to A,[52] and the presence of such a power can be justified. Note too that, on this analysis, a power to revest legal title to goods should arise in relation to a gift procured by fraud as in relation to a contract of sale. As McBride has noted,[53] it would be strange if the law provided less protection to a deceived donor than to a deceived contracting party, and there is no reason why the concept of rescission, as allowing the cancellation of a legal event, should apply only in relation to contracts.[54]

C. The Position Before Rescission at Common Law

The core case for this chapter involves understanding A's position, in a case such as *Caldwell*, *before* the exercise of A's common law power to rescind. Professor Birke Häcker has argued that, in such a case, A has a 'legal power *in rem*'.[55] It will be argued here, however, that this is not the best way to understand A's position prior to rescission. This is not to deny that, in our core case, the possibility of rescission may have an impact on C. The argument, rather, is that the means by which such impact occurs, and the justifications for such impact, differ from those that apply in the standard case where one party asserts a legal property right against another. In a case such as

[50] N McBride, *The Humanity of Private Law, Part I: Explanation* (Hart 2018) ch 6.

[51] See eg Swadling, 'Property, Rescission, and the Common Law' (n 9).

[52] In addition to the position in Scots law, discussed above, note that in German law, notwithstanding the general abstraction principle, an exception is made where the transfer of a right is based on fraud: see Häcker, *Consequences of Impaired Consent Transfers* (n 17) 60–63. See also *Anderson v Ryan* [1967] IR 34 confirming that, in Ireland, A also has a power to revest title following a voidable transfer but cannot assert that power where title has passed to a bona fide purchaser.

[53] McBride (n 50) 188–94.

[54] See too Häcker, *Consequences of Impaired Consent Transfers* (n 17) 141, noting that in *Moynes v Cooper* [1956] 1 QB 439, 445, Lord Goddard CJ stated that '[w]here a transfer of property is obtained by fraud, there is no doubt but that the property does pass, subject ... to the right of the defrauded party on discovering the fraud to disaffirm the transaction and resume his property'. Stevens, *The Laws of Restitution* (n 23) 198 also suggests that it is possible for A to revest title to a gift procured by fraud or duress, although the cases cited there (*Duke de Cadaval v Collins* (1836) 4 Ad & El 858, 111 ER 1006 and *Grainger v Hill* (1838) 4 Bing NC 212, 132 ER 769) rather seem to involve a court finding that an apparent transfer was void.

[55] See eg Häcker, *Consequences of Impaired Consent Transfers* (n 17) 129. See also S Zogg, *Proprietary Consequences in Defective Transfers of Ownership* (CUP 2020) chs 4 and 5.

Caldwell, it is true, as seen in Section II.B, that the effect of rescission is to give A a legal property right. That does not mean, however, that A must be regarded as having such a proprietary interest *before* rescission.

We have seen that A's exercise of the power, by revesting title to the goods, gives A a right that is prima facie binding on all third parties. It is true then that, for as long as A can exercise the power, A does have the ability to change A's legal relations with the rest of the world. That would still be the case, however, even if A's power could be exercised only for so long as B has title, and so would cease to operate if B transferred that title to C. This suggests that care must be taken in describing A's power as *in rem*. The *effect* of the power (ie the fact that, if exercised, it changes A's legal relations with the rest of the world) need not determine its *durability* (ie whether or not the power continues to exist after C acquires a right to the goods). Further, immediately after the transfer to B, A's power as regards B operates differently from A's power as regards all third parties. A has a power to regain the title that B currently holds, and thus B's liability to A (which consists in losing that title) is different from any other party's liability to A. This is significant as, when considering legal rights *in rem*, it is usually the case that all third parties are under the same duties to the holder of the legal right: for example, a duty not to deliberately or carelessly interfere with a particular physical thing. In contrast, prior to A's exercise of the legal power to revest title, it cannot be said that *all* third parties are under the same liability to A, as only B is liable to lose B's title to goods. Moreover, if A's power to rescind a transfer at common law is said to be a 'power *in rem*', then, as with Lord Sumption's use of the term '*in rem*' in *Akers v Samba Financial Group*,[56] the focus is on successor liability rather than trespassory liability, and so the term differs in a significant way from its use when applied to legal property rights more generally.

It is therefore important to separate out the '*in rem*' aspect of A's power that relates to the specific question of durability: whether A can exercise the power to revest title even when that title is no longer held by B. There is a sense in which, where B has transferred title to C, and A seeks nonetheless to revest title, there appears to be a priority dispute between A and C. In a case such as *Parker v Patrick*,[57] for example, A had regained possession of goods following a transfer of title from A to B induced by B's fraud. Prior to rescission, C had given value to acquire a legal property right from B, without notice of A's fraud. C was successful in suing A in trover and so it might be said that C had priority over A's pre-existing 'power *in rem*'.[58] However, where A has a pre-existing legal property right, such priority disputes usually have a different structure. The prima facie effect of A's right is that all third parties owe a duty of non-interference to A. This means that C is under a duty to A *before* C acquires any right in relation to the goods. Priority rules, such as the so-called exceptions to *nemo dat* set out in the Sale of Goods Act 1979, make exceptions to that general position: they give C a liberty whereas, in the absence of such an exception, C would have a duty to A. In contrast, where A has a

[56] [2017] UKSC 6, [2017] AC 424 [82]. See Section II.A above.
[57] (1793) 5 TR 175.
[58] See too *Anderson v Ryan* [1967] IR 34, where, following a transfer to B induced by fraud, A was unable to revest title after A's title had been passed to C.

pre-existing but unexercised power to rescind then, as we have seen, there is no general duty of non-interference on third parties and so no need for C to seek an exception in C's favour.

Moreover, consider a case where, rather than transferring title to C, B instead allows C to acquire some lesser right in relation to the goods. In *Whitehorn Bros v Davison*,[59] for example, after B had fraudulently induced A to transfer A's title to a necklace, B created a pledge of the goods in favour of C to secure a loan of £875. A's claim against C for the return of the necklace failed, with Vaughan Williams LJ stating that the contract of sale between A and B (and hence the transfer of title from A to B) 'cannot be avoided as against' C where C is an 'innocent third person who has given value and has accepted the transfer without either knowledge of anything wrong, or any knowledge of such circumstances as might lead him to wish not to make any further inquiry lest he should find that there was something wrong'.[60] The term 'transfer' is inapt when considering the creation of a pledge, but the important point for present purposes is that the court's analysis is not the same as would apply if C sought priority in the standard sense. If the pledge were to take priority to A's pre-existing legal property right, then presumably A could assert that right by paying C the sum secured and thus removing the pledge. The analysis in *Whitehorn* is different—it is not that A's pre-existing legal property right is subject to C's right, but rather, it seems, C's intervention has extinguished A's pre-existing power to revest title.

Indeed, in *Barclays Bank v Boulter*,[61] Lord Hoffmann drew on *Whitehorn* to reject a priorities-based analysis of the possible impact of A's power to revest title on third parties. On a priorities-based analysis, A's power is prima facie binding on C, unless C can show a defence: a reason why, exceptionally, C has priority to A's power *in rem*. Such an analysis may apply, for example, to the operation of the rules, protecting C against a pre-existing title to goods, now set out in ss 24 and 25 of the Sale of Goods Act 1979. In such cases, then, it is clearly the task of C to show why A's legal property right is not in fact binding on C. In contrast, on Lord Hoffmann's view, where A instead has an initial power to revest title, A 'retains no proprietary interest in the chattel and it is therefore not for the purchaser [C] to establish a defence which would defeat it. Instead, it is for the owner [A] to prove that the purchaser had actual or constructive knowledge of the fraud.'[62] This is consistent with the approach of Lord Denning MR at first instance in *Caldwell*, when considering the position of C2 if rescission had not occurred prior to C2's acquisition of a title. As noted above, Lord Denning MR there stated that C2 'did not acquire a good title to the goods because they were affected by the notice which their agents [C1] had of the defect of title'.[63] It seems that, in contrast to other cases where A asserts a pre-existing legal property right against C, the existence of notice plays a positive role in justifying C's liability, rather than the absence of notice forming

[59] [1911] 1 KB 463. See too Reilly (n 19) at 190.
[60] ibid 476.
[61] [1999] 1 WLR 1919, 1924–25.
[62] ibid 1926.
[63] [1965] 1 QB 525, 534.

part of a defence to a prima facie, strict liability of C. If notice operates in this positive way, it is also inconsistent with an explanation of A's ability to assert a power to revest against C as based on a *nemo dat* analysis,[64] in which B can give C only a title burdened by A's power to revest title.

Swadling, writing in 2005, objected to Lord Hoffmann's analysis on the basis that 'it cannot be true to say that the owner [A] "retains no proprietary interest" in the chattel, for, if that were the case, how are we to explain the fact that third parties can be bound by his right to rescind?'.[65] One aim of this chapter, however, is to defend Lord Hoffmann's view. That view does not deny the ability of A to exercise A's power against *certain* third parties, including volunteers, or a party administering B's rights on B's insolvency. As MacLeod has argued in relation to Scots law,[66] it is possible to argue that A's power to revest title can be exercisable notwithstanding some third-party intervention, without regarding that power as a legal property right, or as a prima facie binding right *in rem*. Indeed, Lord Hoffmann's analysis gains some support from the justification for A's power to revest title suggested in this chapter. If, in relation to fraud as in relation to other grounds of rescission at common law, A's power to revest title arises as a result of B's actual or threatened wrongdoing against A, then it might be surprising to think that A can prima facie exercise that power in a way which can prejudice a third party who is in no sense implicated in that wrongdoing. As MacLeod does in relation to Scots law,[67] it may be possible to explain the persistence of A's power to revest title against those with a relevant degree of knowledge or notice of B's fraud, and against volunteers, on the basis that those parties are either, in some sense, implicated in the fraud or are now seeking to profit from it.[68]

If Lord Hoffmann's analysis is accepted, and A is not regarded as having, prior to rescission, a legal power *in rem*, this does then remove one piece of support for the view that, in *Lipkin Gorman*, A (the partners) had a legal power *in rem* in relation to the cash which B (the rogue partner) used to place bets with C, the defendant casino. It has been suggested that, instead of having a legal power *in rem* in relation to the cash, the partners instead had an interest under a trust of B's title to the money.[69] This is consistent, for example, with the assumption that no claim would have been possible against C if C had been a bona fide purchaser for value of B's title to the money. In cases where B has acquired a right essentially by an unauthorised taking from A, rather than through

[64] See too Reilly (n 19) who rejects the view that A has a power in rem and considers (at 197–201) how this should affect the position in B's insolvency.

[65] Swadling, 'Property, Rescission, and the Common Law' (n 9) 132. It is unlikely however that Swadling would now make the point in quite the same way, given his analysis in 2024 in Swadling, 'The Proprietary Consequences of Fraud' (n 12).

[66] MacLeod (n 42) chs 2 and 7.

[67] ibid [1-10], [7-93]–[7-95]. MacLeod also invokes C's unjustified enrichment to explain the ability to exercise the power against a volunteer, but this is difficult to square with the fact that C acquires C's right from B, not from A, so that C's enrichment is at the expense of B, not of A.

[68] As to volunteers, an analogy can be drawn to the approach in *Bridgeman v Green* (1757) Wilmot 58, 97 ER 22 and *Huguenin v Baseley* (1807) 14 Ves Jun 273, 33 ER 526 to cases where A makes a gift directly to C as a result of B's undue influence.

[69] See B McFarlane, 'Unjust Enrichment, Property Rights and Indirect Recipients' [2009] RLR 37, also applying that analysis to *Banque Belge pour l'Etranger v Hambrouck* [1921] 1 KB 321; L Smith, 'Simplifying Claims to Traceable Proceeds' (2009) 125 LQR 338.

any exercise of a power by A, then a trust analysis may be appropriate.[70] Where such a trust exists, this can justify claims that A may have in relation to substitutes for the right initially acquired by B, without calling in aid the rather flimsy apparatus of common law tracing.

Indeed, it has been suggested that, in a case such as *Caldwell*, the position prior to A's exercise of a power to revest title is best understood as A's having a right under a trust.[71] There is clearly an analogy: for example, it has been argued that rights which relate to other rights are characteristic of equitable interests,[72] and A's power to revest does relate specifically to the title to the goods, rather than to the goods themselves. Moreover, the possibility of rescission at common law can be seen as mitigating the effects on A of the primary legal rules which regulate the transfer of legal rights. It is significant that such a role is more commonly associated with equitable principles, which can be seen to have a 'supplemental',[73] 'meta-law',[74] or 'secondary'[75] nature. The analogy to the case of a trust may therefore be relevant in explaining why A is permitted to exercise that power where title has been acquired by C, a volunteer. If, however, a trust is understood as involving a case where B has a right, and holds that right subject to duties to A which relate to the benefit of that right,[76] then the mere fact of voidability does not give rise to a trust. That is because, prior to the exercise of the power to rescind, B is under a liability to A, rather than any duty.

III. The Relationship between Common Law and Equity

A. Avoiding Contradiction between Common Law and Equity

There are many contexts in which equity, at first glance, appears to have rules which mimic the effect of certain legal rules: equitable assignment, for example, might be thought of as recognising situations in which equity allows for the transfer of rights; equitable estoppel might be seen as involving cases where equity, rather than common law, prevents a party from asserting a particular matter of fact or law. It can be argued, however, that, in such cases, it is a serious mistake to think that the equitable rules are

[70] See eg *Westdeutsche Landesbank Girozentrale v Islington LBC* [1996] AC 669, 716; *Nasrullah v Rashid* [2018] EWCA Civ 2685, [2020] Ch 37 [52]–[58]. See also *Black v S Freedman & Co* (1910) 12 CLR 105.

[71] McFarlane, *The Structure of Property Law* (n 35) 300–03. Indeed, where fraud is present, the circumstances fall within Lord Browne-Wilkinson's general statement in *Westdeutsche Landesbank Girozentrale v Islington LBC* [1996] AC 669, 716, as to when a trust may arise.

[72] See eg McFarlane, *The Structure of Property Law* (n 35); McFarlane and Stevens, 'The Nature of Equitable Property' (n 35).

[73] FW Maitland, *Equity: A Course of Lectures* (AH Chaytor and WJ Whittaker eds, revised by J Brunyate, 2nd edn, CUP 1936) 17.

[74] H Smith, 'Equity as Meta-Law' (2021) 130 Yale LJ 1050.

[75] B McFarlane and R Stevens, 'What's Special about Equity? Rights about Rights' in S Degeling and others (eds), *Philosophical Foundations of the Law of Equity* (OUP 2022).

[76] See eg McFarlane and Stevens, 'The Nature of Equitable Property' and 'What's Special about Equity?' (nn 35 and 75), although for criticism of this view, see W Swadling, 'Unjust Enrichment: Value, Rights, and Trusts' (2021) 137 LQR 56.

in fact answering the same question as their common law counterparts.[77] As Maitland memorably observed, it would, for example, be misleading to think that, in identifying one party as a beneficiary of a trust of an estate in land, equity is contradicting the common law on the fundamental question of who is owner of the land.[78]

The same care must be taken in relation to rescission in equity. If, as in *Caldwell*, rescission at common law revests legal title in A, it is tempting to see rescission in equity as revesting an 'equitable title'. In *Alati v Kruger*,[79] for example, it was said by Dixon CJ, Webb, Kitto, and Taylor JJ that 'a rescission which the common law courts would not accept as valid cannot of its own force revest the legal title to property which had passed, but if a court of equity would treat it as effectual the equitable title to such property revests upon the rescission'.[80] There are similarly references throughout the case law to rescission in equity allowing A to recover or revest, in equity, A's initial right.[81] However, if applied in cases where A's initial right is a common law right, such statements are misleading. In a case such as *Caldwell*, the immediate effect of rescission is for A to recover the very right, title to the car, which A held prior to the transfer to B. If, instead, the transfer was procured by an innocent misrepresentation of B, so that rescission is available only in equity, then it would not be the case that rescission allows A to revest A's initial equitable title to the car. A had no such initial equitable title—A held title to the car outright, free from any obligation in relation to the benefit of that right, so there was no equitable title to the car at the start of the story. Whilst courts have often used the language of revesting in equity, it is generally[82] true that, when precision is required, the courts have made clear that, where A simply holds a right free from any duty, A has no equitable title which can revest.[83] If A is to acquire an equitable right following rescission, that right will be a new one, not one which A previously held.

In a recent analysis,[84] Swadling makes this important point very clearly: the outcome of rescission in equity may be that B is under a duty to transfer a right back to A, and so it is a means towards an eventual goal in which a right is revested in A. In contrast to the position at common law, however, the rescission is not self-executing: a further step is required before A regains A's initial right. This is consistent with the view that, where rescission is available on a ground that sounds in equity only (such as undue influence or an innocent misrepresentation), it does not occur immediately upon A's exercising A's choice, but rather requires an order by the court.[85] As Swadling also notes in relation

[77] See eg McFarlane and Stevens, 'The Nature of Equitable Property' and 'What's Special about Equity?' (nn 35 and 75). In relation to assignment, see the analysis in CH Tham, *Understanding the Law of Assignment* (CUP 2021).

[78] Maitland (n 73).

[79] (1955) 94 CLR 216.

[80] ibid 223–24.

[81] See eg Potter LJ in *Twinsectra v Yardley* [1999] Lloyd's Rep Bank 438 [99]; Rimer J in *Shalson v Russo* [2003] EWHC 1637 (Ch), [2005] Ch 281 [122], [136].

[82] For missteps, see *Chase Manhattan v Israel-British Bank* [1981] Ch 105 and *Malory Enterprises Ltd v Cheshire Homes (UK) Ltd* [2002] Ch 216.

[83] *Westdeutsche Landesbank Girozentrale v Islington LBC* [1996] AC 669; *Swift 1st v Chief Land Registrar* [2015] EWCA Civ 330, [2015] Ch 602.

[84] Swadling, 'The Proprietary Consequences of Fraud' (n 12).

[85] For thorough discussion of this point, see eg O'Sullivan, Elliott, and Zakrzewski (n 10) ch 11, and Swadling, 'Rescission—The Role of the Court' (n 10).

to contracts,[86] it is therefore unhelpful, in this context, to think that a transfer may be either voidable at common law or voidable in equity. Where, as in *Caldwell*, A has a legal right, and transfers that right to B, voidability means that A has a power to revest that right: that is a consequence of common law rescission, but it is not the immediate effect of rescission in equity. It may be possible to think of an *obligation* being voidable either at common law or in equity, as the question there is simply whether there is a ground on which, either directly or following a court order, the obligation can be avoided. However, to say that a *transfer* of a legal right is voidable in equity leads to confusion, as it implies the incorrect position that the effect of rescission is to revest an equitable title.

B. The Effect of Rescission in Equity

What then is the effect, in our context, of rescission in equity? One way to answer this is to consider the possible outcomes, in a case where A transfers a legal right to B, if there were no possibility of rescission in equity. The first possible outcome is that the transfer is simply void, so that A retains the right.[87] The second possible outcome, discussed above, is that the transfer is voidable, so that A can exercise a power to regain the right.[88] As A's initial right is a legal one, those two possibilities are available only at common law. The third outcome, introduced by equity, is that, either on receipt of the right from A,[89] or at some later point (eg later acquisition of knowledge of the problem relating to A's initial transfer)[90] B comes under a duty to A in relation to the benefit of that right, and so holds it on trust for A, thus giving A a new equitable interest. In *Westdeutsche Landesbank Girozentrale v Islington LBC*,[91] Lord Browne-Wilkinson considered that such a trust could arise, for example, where B's fraud led to the transfer of A's right to B, or where the transfer was caused by a mistake of A, and B learned of that mistake whilst still holding the transferred right or its traceable proceeds.[92] The possibility of rescission in equity seems to add a further set of circumstances in which that third outcome can arise, and B can be said to hold on trust for A: where a court, following A's choice to rescind, orders B to transfer the right back to A.

One problem concerns the relationship between the circumstances in which A has a power to rescind at common law and the circumstances in which a trust can arise in favour of A. That problem was considered by Rimer J in *Shalson v Russo*,[93] when considering a case where A advanced money to B under a contract of loan procured by fraud. On the general analysis of Lord Browne-Wilkinson in *Westdeutsche*, it could be

[86] Swadling, 'The Proprietary Consequences of Fraud' (n 12) 176.
[87] See eg *Cundy v Lindsay* (1878) 3 App Cas 459, discussed in Section II.B above.
[88] See eg *Caldwell* [1965] 1 QB 525, discussed in Section II above.
[89] As in eg *Nasrullah v Rashid* [2018] EWCA Civ 2685.
[90] See eg Lord Browne-Wilkinson's analysis in *Westdeutsche Landesbank Girozentrale v Islington LBC* [1996] AC 669 of the trust arising in *Chase Manhattan Bank v Israel-British Bank* [1981] Ch 105.
[91] [1996] AC 669.
[92] ibid 704–05.
[93] [2005] Ch 281.

argued that, as a result of B's fraud, a trust arose in favour of A as soon as B received the payment. That argument was, however, rejected by Rimer J on the basis that the contract between A and B in such a case 'is voidable, not void, and that it is and remains a valid contract until set aside by [A]'.[94] Once A exercised a power to rescind, however, A 'had revested in him the property in the money which he advanced to [B] entitling him at least to trace it into assets into which it was subsequently applied'.[95] One way of understanding the position is as follows. The presence of a valid contract between A and B, under which A was obliged to advance a sum to B, prevents A from showing that B holds any rights acquired by A under that contract on trust for A: unless and until rescission occurs, B is free to use those rights for B's own benefit. In other words, as Lord Goff put it in *Guinness plc v Saunders*,[96] A 'cannot short circuit an unrescinded contract simply by alleging a constructive trust'.[97] However, as the contract was procured by fraud, it is voidable, and A's exercise of the power to rescind means the contract is treated as though it had never been made, and so the obstacle to applying Lord Browne-Wilkinson's analysis disappears, and a trust may arise. It is the presence of that trust which may then support a claim in relation to traceable proceeds. In such a case, A's exercise of the power to rescind can be effective outside of court, as the power arises at common law in the case of fraud. Rimer J's use of the term 'revesting' is nonetheless inapt: it is clear that, as a result of exercising the power to rescind, A does not regain any rights which A formerly held. Rather, A removes an obstacle to the finding of a trust and thus acquires new rights under that trust.[98]

One complication then, in a case such as *Shalson v Russo*, is as to the interaction of common law and equitable grounds for rescission. Such complications can be limited if the courts bear in mind the different nature and effects of rescission at common law and in equity. Where a transaction is procured by fraud, A has a power to rescind that transaction through A's own act, even if, for example because of the nature of the right which B has acquired in the parties' transaction, that act by itself is not capable of revesting any specific right in A. That is the case, for example, where the right transferred is a legal

[94] ibid [108].

[95] ibid [127].

[96] [1990] 2 AC 663.

[97] ibid 697. The contract there was between A (a company) and B (one of its directors), and rescission was available as B had breached his duty of disclosure. For further consideration of the interaction of rescission and constructive trusts in this context, see *Hotel Portfolio II v Ruhan* [2023] EWCA Civ 1120, [2024] 2 All ER (Comm) 297 [23]–[40]. The Court of Appeal held there that the first instance judge had been wrong to suggest that, where a director (B), acting in breach of self-dealing rules, sold properties belonging to the company (A) to a party related to B (C), those properties were immediately subject to a constructive trust in favour of A. Such a trust could not arise before rescission of the sale to C. The issue was not examined by the Supreme Court when allowing an appeal ([2025] UKSC 28, [2025] 3 WLR 293—although the point is noted at [117] by Lord Burrows in his dissent) as it was by then common ground that B held the profits received from the sale of the properties on constructive trust for A. That trust could arise without the need for rescission of any contract.

[98] In such cases, those new rights of A are nonetheless seen as arising retrospectively, from the moment of the transfer to B, at least as far as is necessary to allow A to trace into substitute assets acquired by B using the right originally transferred: see eg *Shalson v Russo* [2005] Ch 281 [122]; *Independent Trustee Services Ltd v GP Noble Trustees Ltd* [2012] EWCA Civ 195, [2013] Ch 91 [53]; *RnD Funding Pty Ltd v Roncane Pty Ltd* [2023] FCAFC 28, (2023) 297 FCR 91 [109]. For discussion of possible justifications for this approach, see MJ Hafeez-Baig and J English, *The Law of Tracing* (Federation Press 2021) [5.24]–[5.26] and Ho (n 10). As Ho notes there in relation to the availability of proprietary injunctions in such cases, the 'legal fiction of retrospectivity obscures the policy grounds' justifying A's protection.

estate in land, which is now registered in the name of B. A's exercise of a power to rescind, in such a case, cannot revest title to the land in A—that occurs only with a change to the register. To that extent both the first and second possible outcomes set out above are precluded: even if A rescinds on account of B's fraud, A can at most hope that B will be found to hold B's registered legal estate on trust for A. In that specific sense, the effect of rescission will take place in equity. If, however, the transfer to B was procured by B's fraud, then there is no need to say that A is unable to exercise a power to rescind a relevant contract out of court, or that any rescission must be subject to a general discretion of the court to refuse to permit rescission. Rather, as the specific problem consists of B's fraud then, even if A is not able to revest title by simply exercising a power to rescind, A should still be able to rescind the contract, and remove an obstacle to B's holding that title on trust, without being subject to any general equitable discretion of the court to deny a specific remedy.[99] The same analysis applies where A seeks rescission on the grounds of B's having committed the tort of bribery: it would be a mistake to say that, simply because revesting of a legal right in A is not possible, and so A seeks to impose an equitable duty on B, rescission now depends on a general discretion of the court, which can refuse rescission where it would be 'unfair and disproportionate'.[100]

The analysis in the preceding paragraph is, however, limited to cases in which the ground of rescission is one which is recognised at common law. It can be dangerous to draw analogies between the operation of rescission in such cases and in those where the ground is a purely equitable one. In *Bainbridge v Bainbridge*,[101] for example, the ground for setting aside a transfer of land into a discretionary trust was a significant mistake made by A, the settlor of the trust. Part of the land had been sold by the trustees to C, and no claim was made against C, who was assumed to have been a bona fide purchaser with no knowledge of A's mistake. The sale proceeds had been used by the trustees to buy new land, and A sought an order that the new land should be transferred to A. Master Matthews (as he then was) held that the involvement of C did not prevent the grant of the order sought. The reasoning, however, proceeded on an analogy with *Shalson v Russo*, and the impact of fraud. It was said that A could trace into the new land as, following rescission, the land transferred into the trust was to be regarded in equity as having belonged throughout to A, thus establishing the basis for tracing into substitute assets: 'the consequence of the rescission is the same whether it takes place because of fraud . . . or because of causative and basic unilateral mistake.'[102] If, however, the role of fraud in a case such as *Shalson* is to allow A to remove an obstacle to B's holding on trust, with such a trust arising because of B's knowledge of the relevant problem with the transfer, then the analogy does not hold in a case where B has no such knowledge, as the defect is instead a unilateral mistake of A. A more convincing explanation for the

[99] This analysis is consistent with the view of Fancourt J in *Patarkatsishvili v Woodward-Fisher* [2025] EWHC 265 (Ch) [187].

[100] This analysis therefore casts doubt on the approach taken in *Hurstanger Ltd v Wilson* [2007] EWCA Civ 299, [2007] 1 WLR 2351, which is also questioned on similar grounds by J English, 'Bribery and Secret Commissions: A Common Law–Equity Divide?' [2025] LMCLQ 158.

[101] [2016] EWHC 898. See Section I above.

[102] ibid [30].

result in *Bainbridge* is simply that the requested order was the most effective means, on the facts, to protect A from the mistaken exercise of A's legal power to establish the trust. Rules of tracing, in this context, can be seen as identifying those new rights that B acquired through the use of the legal powers associated with holding a specific initial right; if, at the time when those new rights were acquired, B was under a liability to be ordered to return that initial right to A, then the aim of rescission—protecting A in A's dealing with the initial right—is furthered by allowing A's claim to extend to the substitute assets.[103]

C. The Position Before Rescission in Equity

If it is said that, where the ground of rescission sounds at common law, A has a legal power *in rem*, it might then be said that, where the ground is equitable only (such as undue influence or innocent misrepresentation), A has an equitable power *in rem*.[104] This is another tempting analogy between common law and equity which should, in fact, be resisted. The first difficulty is that the analysis assumes, contrary to the view expressed above, that rescission in equity is simply a different means to the same end of revesting a right in A. The second difficulty with such an analysis is that, if the arguments made in Section II above are accepted, the concept of a 'legal power *in rem*' should, in any case, be rejected.

The argument made in Section II.C contrasted A's position before and after the power to rescind is exercised. The same contrast can be drawn in cases where the grounds of rescission sound only in equity. Consider a case where a transfer is made by B to C after rescission has occurred on a ground recognised only in equity. As argued above, the effect of rescission is that B now holds the transferred right on trust for A. In making a claim against C, A is not attempting to enforce a duty that C was under prior to C's acquisition of the right from B. As noted in Section II.A above, A's equitable interest is not prima facie binding on the rest of the world in the same way as a legal property right. Rather, following the analysis of Lord Sumption in *Akers v Samba Financial Group*, A may assert a claim against a particular class of third parties (successors in title to B), if the conscience of such a party is affected. Where C is a volunteer, it is not necessary to show that C's conscience was affected, through knowledge of the trust, at the time of C's acquisition of the right: rather, such knowledge must merely coincide with C's holding the right or its traceable proceeds.[105] In a case where C has acquired the very right held by B on trust for A as a bona fide purchaser for value without notice, C will be

[103] This explanation is close to that given by Hafeez-Baig and English (n 98) where the ability to trace, in cases of rescission for fraud at least, is explained as based on a principle of 'next-based compliance', but it differs from that explanation as it does not require B to have been under an initial duty to A, and so can apply beyond cases of fraud.

[104] See eg Häcker, *Consequences of Impaired Consent Transfers* (n 17) 132: 'The position must therefore be that a legal right to rescind a contract of sale entails a legal power in rem, whilst an equitable right to rescind entails an equitable power in rem'. See too Zogg (n 55) ch 5.

[105] See further S Agnew and B McFarlane, 'The Paradox of the Equitable Proprietary Claim' in B McFarlane and S Agnew (eds), *Modern Studies in Property Law*, vol 10 (Hart 2019).

immune from any claim by A.[106] Such a case is sometimes said to present an exception to the principle of *nemo dat quod non habet*.[107] That analysis is mistaken, however,[108] as, where B holds a right on trust for A, B does have that right, and so has the power to transfer it to C, who thus does not need to invoke any exception to *nemo dat*.[109] As noted by the Supreme Court in *Akers v Samba Financial Group*, where B transfers trust property to C, even where C takes the right free from any claim of A, it is B's own right that is transferred to C: B does not give *A*'s right to C, and so no exception from *nemo dat* is required.[110] Where B holds on trust for A, and makes an unauthorised disposition to C, the priority dispute between A and C therefore comes down to whether the circumstances of C's acquisition are such that C comes under the same core duty to A which B owed to A: a duty in relation to the benefit of the specific right that B held, and which was then transferred to C.

Now consider the position where there is an equitable ground for rescission and, *prior* to rescission having occurred, B transfers to C the right that B acquired from A. Prior to the transfer to C, B was under a liability in relation to a particular right: a liability to come under a duty to A in relation to the right transferred by A to B. Such a duty would arise upon rescission, and thus on the making of a court order giving effect to A's request for relief. The question is then whether C, on acquiring the right from B, should be under that same liability. C's acquisition of the right from B is clearly an important part of C's potential liability, just as it is in the case where B holds on trust for A and then transfers the right to C. It is therefore no surprise that, whether C acquires the right from B before or after rescission has occurred, the circumstances in which C acquired that right, in particular whether C was a bona fide purchaser for value, will be relevant.

In equity, therefore, as opposed to common law, there is a much stronger similarity between the position where C acquires a right *after* rescission and the position where C acquires a right *before* rescission. This is reflected in the fact that the courts' approach to deciding if rescission is available, on equitable grounds, against C is very similar to the approach when deciding if A's pre-existing interest under a trust can be asserted against C. The difference between B's being under a pre-existing duty to A in relation to a specific right and B's being under a liability to come under such a duty to A is relatively small. It is seen in the case where C is a bona fide purchaser of an *equitable* interest and so can be subject to a claim by a holder of a pre-existing equitable interest, but is immune from A's claim where A only has a 'mere equity': that is, where there is a ground of rescission but rescission has not yet occurred.[111] That is why, in *Latec Investments Ltd v*

[106] *Pilcher v Rawlins* (1872) LR 7 Ch App 259.

[107] P Birks, 'Notice and Onus in *O'Brien*' (1998) 12 TLI 2.

[108] B McFarlane and A Televantos, 'As Complex as ABC? Bona Fide Purchasers of Equitable Interests' in P Davies and T Cheng-Han (eds), *Intermediaries in Commercial Law* (Hart 2022).

[109] See eg Browne-Wilkinson LJ in *Rolled Steel Products Ltd v British Steel Corp* [1986] Ch 246, 303.

[110] *Akers v Samba Financial Group* [2017] AC 424 [51].

[111] See eg *Phillips v Phillips* (1861) 4 De G F & J 208, 45 ER 1164; *Latec Investments Ltd v Hotel Terrigal Pty Ltd* (1965) 113 CLR 265. For full discussion, see D O'Sullivan, 'The Rule in *Phillips v Phillips*' (2002) 118 LQR 296; A Reilly, 'What Were Lord Westbury's Intentions in *Phillips v Phillips*? Bona Fide Purchase of an Equitable Interest' (2021) 80 CLJ 156; McFarlane and Televantos, 'As Complex as ABC?' (n 108).

Hotel Terrigal Pty Ltd,[112] it mattered that rescission had not occurred at the point when C2 acquired its equitable charge: as C2 had acquired that equitable interest from C1 as a bona fide purchaser, without notice of the problem affecting the sale from B to C1, it was not possible to give A relief which would compromise C2's position. In *Latec*, C2's additional protection reflects the difference between C2's position and the position of A: the existence of C2's equitable interest means that C1 is under a *duty* to C2; the fact that recission has not yet occurred means that C1 is only under a *liability* to A. As a result, the case is not one in which the equities, in the sense of the positions of A and of C2, are equal, and so the fact that A's equity arose first is not decisive.

A final point in relation to A's position prior to rescission in equity concerns the suggestion, raised by Lord Millett extrajudicially,[113] and more recently endorsed by Swadling,[114] that it is helpful to think of such rescission as 'specific unperformance'. This would mean that, when considering the suitability of an order requiring a right to be returned to A, the court should draw on rules about the availability of specific performance. On that view if, for example, the right related to non-unique property, monetary relief, rather than specific relief, would be appropriate. Such a suggestion of course gains some support from the view, supported in this chapter, that rescission on purely equitable grounds requires an order of the court. Nonetheless, the suggestion should be resisted. There is no reason why specific performance principles, which govern when A should be allowed to have the assistance of the court to acquire a wholly new right, or other benefit, should apply in the quite different situation where A instead seeks protection in relation to a right which A previously held, and has lost only through the exercise of a power which was, in some way, flawed. This means, for example, that the current law is correct in not limiting orders for the return of a right to A to cases in which that right is in some way unique.

IV. The Role of Unjust Enrichment

It has been argued[115] that, in considering our core case, it is useful to consider A's power to rescind as arising on the grounds of unjust enrichment and thus as subject to the four-stage analysis set out in cases such as *Banque Financière de la Cité SA v Westgate Insurance Co*.[116] One reason for doing so is to attempt to explain certain features of the law of rescission;[117] another is to use such cases to support a more general argument that unjust enrichment can give rise to proprietary rights. Certainly, there is some correspondence between the grounds which may give rise to rescission and the 'unjust

[112] (1965) 113 CLR 265: see Section I above.

[113] P Millett, 'Restitution and Constructive Trusts' (1998) 114 LQR 399, 416.

[114] Swadling, 'The Proprietary Consequences of Fraud' (n 12) 173–75. See also Swadling, 'Rescission—The Role of the Court' (n 10).

[115] See eg C Mitchell, P Mitchell, and S Watterson, *Goff & Jones On Unjust Enrichment* (10th edn, Sweet & Maxwell 2022) ch 40.

[116] [1991] 2 AC 249.

[117] See the discussion in Häcker, 'Explaining the Right to Rescind' (n 23).

factors' that are relevant under such an analysis. There is also a weight of academic commentary that links those grounds to defects in the consent of A.[118] However, there are good grounds for scepticism as to the usefulness of such an approach.

First, in our core case, it is clear that there are a number of different ways in which English law deals with problems in relation to A's consent and, as we have seen, allowing rescission is just one of those responses.[119] Second, as pointed out by, for example, Professor Robert Stevens,[120] it is not clear that a single approach, based on defects in consent, reflects the current law, which applies different tests in relation to setting aside different types of transaction.[121] Third, and perhaps most importantly for present purposes, the availability of rescission does not depend on B in fact being better off at A's expense as a result of the flaw in A's consent. As Professor Robert Chambers has pointed out,[122] it may be that, notwithstanding the flaw, the transaction is one which objectively leaves A better off, as value overall flows from B to A: this is not, however, a bar to rescission if a ground for rescission, such as a misrepresentation by B, exists. Chambers deals with this point by arguing that, within a single law of unjust enrichment, there are two types of enrichment: by value and by rights. On Chambers' view, where, as in our core case, there is a transfer of a right from A to B, an enrichment of B at A's expense can thus be found, even if, overall, the transaction leaves B better off than A.

Chambers' division can, however, be developed in a different way, arising from the fact that B's simply becoming better off at A's expense, coupled with a presence of an unjust factor such as mistake, does not suffice for a restitutionary claim. The now-classic hypothetical example is where A, by mistakenly destroying A's valuable stamp, increases the value of B's similar valuable stamp.[123] Similarly, if A mistakenly performs a service that benefits B, that, by itself, does not give rise to a claim. In *Blue Haven Enterprises Ltd v Tully*,[124] for example, where A improved B's land in the mistaken belief that the land belonged to A, Lord Scott took the view that some specific conduct of B (such as encouragement of A's mistaken belief) would be required for a claim to arise.[125] The facts of A's mistake and B's benefit do not suffice to impose a strict liability on B, even if the benefit is one which B would have been willing to pay for.[126] Birks, for example, took a mistaken payment case such as *Kelly v Solari* as the core case of a restitutionary claim, and sought to generalise from its facts to the four-stage unjust enrichment analysis,

[118] See eg Häcker, *Consequences of Impaired Consent Transfers* (n 17); Häcker, 'Explaining the Right to Rescind' (n 23); E Bant, 'Reconsidering the Role of Election in Rescission' (2012) OJLS 467.

[119] See J Mee, 'The Past, Present, and Future of Resulting Trusts' [2017] CLP 189, making the same point in response to the argument that resulting trusts can be seen as proprietary responses to unjust enrichment.

[120] Stevens, *The Laws of Restitution* (n 23) chs 5 and 6.

[121] The rules on recovery on the grounds of mistake, for example, vary according to whether or not a transfer occurred subject to a contractual duty: compare *Barclays Bank Ltd v WJ Simms & Son Ltd* [1980] QB 677 and *Bell v Lever Bros Ltd* [1932] AC 161.

[122] R Chambers, 'Two Kinds of Enrichment' in R Chambers and others (eds), *Philosophical Foundations of the Law of Unjust Enrichment* (OUP 2009)

[123] This is based on an example first given by D Friedmann, 'Restitution of Benefits Obtained Through the Appropriation of Property or the Commission of a Wrong' (1980) 80 Colum L Rev 504, 532 fn 144.

[124] [2006] UKPC 17.

[125] ibid [20]–[28].

[126] In *Blue Haven Enterprises Ltd v Tully* [2006] UKPC 17, A worked to develop the land as a coffee plantation, which was precisely the use B wished to make of the land.

identifying B's acquisition of value at A's expense as a crucial factor. Instead, however, the relevant fact in *Kelly* could be seen as the particular legal event of A's payment to B.[127] Notwithstanding A's mistake, that legal event did occur, and a rule allowing A to recover the value of the payment, in certain circumstances, from B can be seen as mitigating the practical impact on A of the operation of that primary legal rule. There are good reasons for allowing the legal event to occur, notwithstanding A's mistake, but that does not preclude recognising a liability of B to A. For example, in *Cressman v Coys of Kensington (Sales) Ltd*,[128] B argued that, because he had acquired a valuable car registration mark under the terms of the relevant statutory scheme, A, the former holder of that mark, who had lost it as a result of a mistake, should have no restitutionary claim against B. As Mance LJ noted,[129] however, B's acquisition of the mark was in fact vital to A's claim. This can be understood as showing that (in contrast to the general position where A mistakenly performs a service for B which benefits B) a legal event had occurred, linking A and B together. It is then possible for a restitutionary claim to mitigate the impact on A of that legal event, and hence of the primary legal rules under which it occurred.

On this view, then, it is not helpful to analyse the type of claim exemplified by *Kelly v Solari* as depending on a four-stage test which asks whether B has, in a general sense, been enriched at A's expense. Nonetheless, that type of claim *can* usefully be linked to our core case. In each case, a primary legal event has occurred (in *Kelly*, a payment; in our case, the transfer of a right) and then a secondary set of rules operates to regulate the impact on A of the operation of the primary set of rules.[130] Importantly, in each case, those secondary rules do not deny the validity of those primary set of rules: in *Kelly*, it is recognised that a payment has been made; in our case, it is accepted that a right *was* transferred. Nonetheless, something has gone wrong: A has exercised a power, conferred by the law to increase A's options, in circumstances where some flaw in A's consent compromises the value of A's choice to exercise the power. It is then possible for secondary rules to mitigate the impact on A of that flaw. Indeed, having such a secondary set of rules forms part of the justification for the content of those primary rules:[131] so, for example, the rule that says that A's right is transferred to B even if B's fraud contributed to A's entry into the transaction may seem harsh, but is easier to defend if powerful options, such as rescission, are available to protect A. Certainly, a vital aspect of rescission is that, even if, as with rescission in equity, it provides A with a new right, it, along with the strict liability personal restitutionary claim, provides protection to a pre-existing entitlement of A. As noted in Section III.C, this is why it is

[127] B McFarlane, 'Unjust Enrichment, Rights and Value' in D Nolan and A Robertson (eds), *Rights and Private Law* (Hart 2011).

[128] [2004] EWCA Civ 47, [2004] 1 WLR 2775.

[129] ibid [24].

[130] The argument here is thus similar to that of Häcker, 'Explaining the Right to Rescind' (n 23), although the idea of unjustified enrichment developed there may vary from the principle suggested here. For example, Häcker suggests that the defect in A's consent is 'tantamount to the absence of a normative basis for whatever rights the affected transaction may have created or transferred', whereas this seems too strong, as it would call for the invalidity of the transaction, rather than for the possibility of rescission.

[131] See eg McFarlane, 'Equitable Estoppel and Restitution' (n 25).

misleading to compare rescission with specific performance, which instead carries new benefits to A.

V. Conclusion

The thesis of this chapter is a negative one as far as each of its main parts casts doubt on the usefulness of a particular analogy: (i) between A's position after exercising a common law power to rescind and revest legal title, and A's position before it; (ii) between the effect of rescission at common law and in equity; and (iii) between a four-stage unjust enrichment analysis and the basis for rescission. The argument is nonetheless positive to the extent that it aims to place rescission within a broader context in which the law seeks to mitigate the impact on A of a flawed exercise of a legal power, even where the flaw is not such as to render the purported exercise of the power immediately ineffective. Rescission thus takes its place alongside a set of doctrines, including those allowing the claim in a case such as *Kelly v Solari*, which are secondary in the particular sense that they respond to a problem which arises through the operation of primary legal rules, without denying the operation of those primary rules.

4

Rescission—The Role of the Court

*William Swadling**

I. Introduction

Is rescission the act of the party or dependent on an order of the court? The orthodoxy is that at common law rescission is a self-help remedy, while in equity it is effected by the issuance of a court order.[1] This has been recently challenged by Professor Steven Elliott KC, who argues that rescission, both at law and in equity, is a self-help remedy.[2] The purpose of this chapter is to argue that though that may be true at law, rescission in equity is an act of the court.

II. Rescission at Law

A. What is Rescission?

Rescission at law, seemingly confined to contracts rather than any other transaction, for example, gifts, is the setting aside of that contract. This is allowed where there is an initially valid contract in the sense of there being offer and acceptance, intention to create legal relations, and consideration, but where there is a problem with the agreement, such that the common law allows for it to be set aside or avoided. The two most prominent examples of rescission at common law are that the contract was entered into because of either fraudulent misrepresentation or duress. Rescission operates with retrospective effect so that, once the contract is rescinded, there will be no obligation to perform in the future on either side, nor any liability for non-performance in the past. Benefits conferred by the rescinding party may also be recovered, though this will require court action. In limited circumstances, there will also be proprietary effects; these are discussed below.

At the outset, we must be careful to distinguish this form of rescission from so-called 'rescission for breach', a different thing altogether. In 'rescission for breach' cases, the

* Professor of Law, University of Oxford, and Fellow of Brasenose College, Oxford, United Kingdom.

[1] The most recent statement to this effect is that of the United Kingdom Supreme Court in *Hopcraft v Close Brothers Ltd* [2025] UKSC 33, [2025] 3 WLR 423 [77], [238].

[2] S Elliott, 'The Basic Structure of Rescission' in B McFarlane and S Elliott (eds), *Equity Today: 150 Years After the Judicature Reforms* (Hart 2023) ch 9.

validity of the contract is not impugned. Instead, one party claims the power to be discharged from future obligations to perform on the ground of a breach on the part of the other. If I contract with you to paint my house but you fail to perform, I can either sue you for damages for my loss or terminate the contract for breach; the reason I might do the latter is because I can then recover any prepayments made in a claim in unjust enrichment, which, for various reasons, may be preferable to claiming damages. Until relatively recently, both travelled under the label of 'rescission', causing no end of confusion.[3] The difference was only pointed out in the late twentieth century, in two decisions of the House of Lords, *Johnson v Agnew*[4] and *Photo Production Ltd v Securicor Transport Ltd*.[5] Since then, the language of 'termination' rather than 'rescission' is generally used for breach cases, and 'rescission' reserved for the setting aside of contracts *ab initio* because of problems with the agreement itself.

B. What Acts Amount to Rescission?

Generally speaking, rescission involves the intimation to the other party to the contract that the innocent party no longer intends to be bound by the contract. However, there will not always be a need for communication. We see this in two well-known cases, *Re Eastgate, ex parte Ward*[6] and *Car & Universal Finance Co Ltd v Caldwell*.[7]

In *Re Eastgate, ex parte Ward*, a debtor fraudulently induced a tradesman to sell him his title to furniture on credit. The debtor then committed an act of bankruptcy by absconding, leaving behind the furniture in a rented house. Five days later, and with the consent of the landlord, the tradesman broke in and repossessed the furniture. The debtor's trustee in bankruptcy's sued the tradesman in conversion but lost. The reception of the goods was held to be sufficient to rescind the contract of sale, thereby revesting title in the tradesman. Consequently, as Bingham J put it, the tradesman 'was only taking . . . that which was his own'.[8]

In *Car & Universal Finance Co Ltd v Caldwell*, a rogue fraudulently induced the holder of a title to a Jaguar car to sell it to him in return for a cheque. When the cheque was later dishonoured, the victim of the fraud informed the police and the Automobile Association that he wanted the car back. The Court of Appeal held that, though there was no communication with the rogue, this was a sufficient act of rescission of the contract of sale, its effect being to revest the vendor's title to the car so that persons subsequently receiving from the rogue committed the tort of conversion. Sellars LJ held that the issue was whether the victim of fraudulent misrepresentation took 'all possible

[3] A particularly difficult example in this respect is *Rowland v Divall* [1923] 2 KB 500, a breach case, but framed throughout in terms of rescission.
[4] [1980] AC 367.
[5] [1980] AC 827.
[6] [1905] 1 KB 465.
[7] [1965] 1 QB 525.
[8] *Re Eastgate, ex p Ward* [1905] 1 KB 465, 467.

steps to regain the goods even though he cannot find the rogue nor communicate with him'.[9] On the facts, he found that he did. Upjohn LJ likewise held that there was a rescission because the victim 'did everything he reasonably could to avoid the contract of sale, short of communicating his intention so to do to [the rogue]'.[10]

C. Grounds of Rescission

The grounds of rescission—that is, the reasons why the making of the contract can be avoided from the start—are quite limited at common law, at least in comparison to equity. There are four. First are misrepresentations of various hues which cause the other party to enter into the contract. These must generally be fraudulent, though non-fraudulent ones will suffice where the contract is one of guarantee or where there is a duty to disclose a relevant fact which was not disclosed, the non-disclosure thereby amounting to a misrepresentation.[11] The second is where the contract is induced by duress, while the third is where it is brought about by bribery.[12] Fourth and finally, contracts induced by breach of a duty in an agency relationship can be set aside at common law.[13]

D. Right or Power

Of course, the innocent party does not have to rescind the contract. Despite the presence of the misrepresentation, duress, or other ground of rescission, there is still a perfectly valid contract, all the requirements thereof being present. The contract is thus voidable, not void. The innocent party's ability to avoid the contract is often described in terms of a 'right' to rescind, but it is not a right, at least in the Hohfeldian sense of a claim-right,[14] because there is no correlative duty on anyone else. Indeed, until the contract is avoided, the party with the ability to rescind will be subject to duties under the contract. Only on avoidance will they be relieved of their duty to perform. Given that the innocent party can avoid the contract without a court order, rescission is properly termed a power in the Hohfeldian sense of their being enabled unilaterally to alter the legal relations of others.[15]

[9] *Car & Universal Finance Co Ltd v Caldwell* [1965] 1 QB 525, 551, adopting the words of Lord Denning MR, sitting at first instance.

[10] ibid 554.

[11] Of course, a misrepresentation which causes the representee to act is a species of mistake, an induced mistake. Spontaneous mistakes, by contrast, do not generate powers to rescind. If a mistake is sufficiently serious, whether induced or spontaneous, it will have the effect of preventing a contract coming into existence at all: *Shogun Finance Ltd v Hudson* [2003] UKHL 62, [2004] 1 AC 919.

[12] *Hopcraft v Close Brothers Ltd* [2025] UKSC 33, [2025] 3 WLR 423.

[13] *Armstrong v Jackson* [1917] 2 KB 822.

[14] WN Hohfeld, 'Some Fundamental Legal Conceptions as Applied in Judicial Reasoning' (1913) 23 Yale LJ 16, 30–32.

[15] ibid.

E. Relief

As seen, the orthodoxy is that the rescinding party avoids the contract by their own act and so is not seeking any relief from the court. However, if they want consequential relief, for example, an order that the defendant restore the value of performances received under the now avoided contract,[16] or damages in conversion against third parties who have dealt with chattels after title has revested on rescission,[17] they will need to become a claimant and obtain a court order to that effect. Such money awards are available at common law. However, if the rescinding party needs some other relief, for example, an order for a reconveyance of rights transferred pursuant to the contract, which will be the case in every instance save where titles to goods have been transferred pursuant to a now avoided contract of sale, they will have to become claimants and seek orders from the court of equity, the common law having no power generally to award anything other than monetary relief.[18]

F. Bars

Though a power to avoid a contract may have arisen, certain later events can bring that power to an end. The 'bars' to rescission are fourfold.

1. Affirmation

As seen, the starting point is that, despite the presence of a ground of rescission, the contract is still valid. What the ground of rescission provides, however, is the ability of one party to set the contract aside. Precisely how we might describe the juridical basis of such grounds is difficult, though they would seem, in the main at least, to be cognates of the 'unjust factors' driving the common law to allow restitution of unjust enrichments such as mistaken payments and payments by duress.[19] In those cases, though the transfer is perfectly valid, transferors can obtain orders from common law courts that the recipient pay them a sum of money equivalent to the value of the rights received.[20] It is arguably the same with rescission of the contract in these cases.[21]

Since rescission is the disaffirmation of the contract, the power will be lost if the contract has been previously affirmed. Thus, in *Clough v London & North Western*

[16] As in *Clarke v Dickson* (1858) El Bl & El 148, 120 ER 463 (claim to recover purchase price where sale of shares induced by fraud), discussed below, text to n 36.

[17] As eg in *Car & Universal Finance Ltd v Caldwell* [1965] 1 QB 525.

[18] The exception is orders for possession of land.

[19] Bribery presents a difficulty in terms of analysis. We are told by the United Kingdom Supreme Court in *Hopcraft v Close Brothers Ltd* [2025] UKSC 33, [2025] 3 WLR 423 [110]–[240] that it is a species of wrongdoing, though this does not seem to have been the thinking beforehand.

[20] It has become increasingly common to describe such cases as involving 'defective transfers', but this is a misnomer, for if the transfer really was defective, the right would not pass, as is the case with incompletely constituted trusts (*Milroy v Lord* (1862) 4 De GF & J 264, 45 ER 1185) and imperfect gifts (*Richards v Delbridge* (1874) LR 18 Eq 11).

[21] A fraudulent misrepresentation which causes a person to enter into a contract is of course a species of mistake.

Railway Co,[22] a contract for the sale of titles to pianos was induced by a down-payment of £68 and a fraudulent misrepresentation that the purchaser intended to pay the balance. Mellor J, giving the judgment of the court, which comprised himself, Byles, Blackburn, and Lush JJ, said:

> [I]f it can be shewn that the London Pianoforte Company have at any time after knowledge of the fraud, either by express words or by unequivocal acts, affirmed the contract, their election has been determined for ever.[23]

In the case of misrepresentation, affirmation requires knowledge of the misrepresentation on the part of the representee,[24] knowledge that there was a power to rescind (probably),[25] and some express words or unequivocal act of affirmation.[26] In the case of duress, knowledge of the ground will *ex hypothesi* be present, but affirmation will only occur where the victim is both free of the duress and knows of their ability to rescind, and, once again, there are some express words or an unequivocal act of affirmation.[27] Similar rules apply to the other grounds of rescission.

An example of affirmation is *Selway v Fogg*,[28] where the parties contracted for the clearance of rubbish under a fraudulent misrepresentation by one as to the amount of rubbish involved. Despite knowledge of the fraud, the innocent party performed and was held bound by the terms of the contract, with no ability to go beyond it to claim payment for the extra work involved. Abinger CJ said that once the plaintiff 'had full knowledge of all that constituted the fraud . . . he should have discontinued the work and repudiated the contract, or he must be bound by its terms'.[29]

2. Delay

Given that rescission at law is the act of the party and not a claim for court-ordered relief, then, as Henderson LJ said in *IGA USA v HMRC*,[30] common law rescission is not subject to any period of limitation under the Limitation Act 1980. Though he does later describe the position as surprising and anomalous, it was, he said, 'perhaps tempered by the strict approach which the [common law] court normally adopts to restitutio in integrum in such cases',[31] a bar discussed immediately below. Of course, if some legal or equitable relief is sought, such claims will be subject to statutory time limits.

[22] (1871) LR 7 Ex 26.
[23] ibid 34.
[24] *Glencore Grain Ltd v Flacker Shipping Ltd (The Happy Day)* [2002] EWCA Civ 1068, [2002] 2 All ER (Comm) 896.
[25] *Peyman v Lanjani* [1985] Ch 457.
[26] ibid.
[27] So, eg in *North Ocean Shipping Co Ltd v Hyundai Construction Co* [1979] QB 705, recovery of monies paid under a contract otherwise voidable for duress was denied because the threat was no longer operative.
[28] (1839) 5 M & W 83, 151 ER 36.
[29] *Selway v Fogg* (1839) 5 M & W 83, 85–86; 151 ER 36, 37.
[30] [2021] EWCA Civ 534, [2021] Ch 423 [20].
[31] ibid [93].

Delay may, however, amount to affirmation. As Mellor J said in *Clough v London & North Western Railway Co*:[32] 'lapse of time without rescinding will furnish evidence that [the innocent party] has determined to affirm the contract; and when the lapse of time is great, it probably would in practice be treated as conclusive evidence to shew that he has so determined.'[33] What is not entirely clear, however, is whether, at common law at least, there is a separate ground of delay. Though there are *dicta* to that effect,[34] there seems to be no authoritative decision either way.

3. Counter-restitution Impossible

Where the innocent party rescinds, they are trying to unwind the deal and be restored to the position they were in before the contract was made. It is a condition of their being able to do so that the other party must likewise be restored, that counter-restitution is made. In Latin, this is the requirement of *restitutio in integrum*, or in English, full restitution. So, where the other party has transferred benefits pursuant to the contract but counter-restitution cannot be made, rescission will be barred. As Parke B said: '[t]here can be no rescission of the contract, unless the parties can be placed in statu quo.'[35]

Thus, in *Clarke v Dickson*,[36] the plaintiff was induced by a fraudulent misrepresentation to buy some shares. He later sought to rescind the contract at law and recover the purchase price. His claim failed, the Court holding that his only option was to sue for damages for deceit. The partnership in which the shares had originally been purchased had since been incorporated, thus making *restitutio in integrum* impossible. Erle J said: '[T]he plaintiff cannot avoid the contract under which he took the shares, because he cannot restore them in the same state as when he took them.'[37] As Crompton J colourfully put it in argument, '[i]f you are fraudulently induced to buy a cake you may return it and get back the price; but you cannot both eat your cake and return your cake.'[38]

It is important to note that the counter-restitution rule at common law requires restitution *in specie*; a money equivalent will not suffice. The obvious reason for this is that since rescission is the act of the party, there is no-one capable of putting a definitive monetary value on the defendant's performance. As will be seen, since rescission in equity requires an order of the court, counter-restitution in money is possible.

4. Third-Party Rights Have Intervened

If third-party rights have intervened, the power to rescind is lost. As Pollock CB explained in *Kingsford v Merry*:

[32] (1871) LR 7 Ex 26.
[33] ibid 35. There are parallels here to the doctrine of 'laches and acquiescence' in equity.
[34] eg Upjohn LJ in *Car & Universal Finance Ltd v Caldwell* [1965] 1 QB 525, 554 ('Where one party to a contract has an option unilaterally to rescind or disaffirm it by reason of the fraud or misrepresentation of the other party, he must elect to do so within a reasonable time').
[35] *Blackburn v Smith* (1848) 2 Ex 783, 790; 154 ER 707, 710.
[36] (1858) El Bl & El 148, 120 ER 463.
[37] ibid 153.
[38] ibid 152.

> When a vendee obtains possession of a chattel, with the intention by the vendor to transfer both the property and possession, although the vendee has committed a false and fraudulent misrepresentation in order to effect the contract or obtain the possession, the property vests in the vendee until the vendor has done some act to disaffirm the transaction; and the legal consequence is, that if, before the disaffirmance, the fraudulent vendee has transferred either the whole or a partial interest in the chattel to an innocent transferee, the title of such transferee is good against the vendor.[39]

We will return to the revesting of property below. On the assumption that it is correct to say that on rescission of a contract for the sale of goods, title to the goods revests in the vendor, rescission will be barred if it happens after a third party has received that title.

Examples of the power to rescind being lost because of the intervention of third-party rights are *White v Garden*[40] and *Lewis v Avery*.[41] In the former, the defendant sold his title to some iron to one Parker, the latter paying by means of £83 in cash and £113 by bill of exchange. The defendant delivered the iron to Parker, who immediately sold his title to the plaintiff, a purchaser for value in good faith. When the supposed acceptor of the bill turned out to be fictitious, the defendant seized the iron from the plaintiff, who successfully sued him in trover. The defendant's power to rescind had been lost on the sale to the plaintiff, with the result that his seizure was unlawful.

In *Lewis v Averay*, Lewis sold his title to a car to a rogue, who paid by cheque. Worried that the cheque might be dishonoured, Lewis asked for identification. The rogue said he was the well-known television actor, Richard Green, and produced a Pinewood Studios' pass bearing an official stamp and photograph. Needless to say, the cheque was not met, but in the meantime the rogue had sold his title to the car to Averay, an innocent purchaser. The Court of Appeal held that the plaintiff's power to rescind had thereby been lost. Phillimore LJ said:

> True, the contract had been induced by fraud, and Mr Lewis, when he discovered that he had been defrauded, was entitled to avoid it; but in the meanwhile the rogue had parted with the property in this motor car which he had obtained to Mr Averay, who bought it bona fide without any notice of the fraud, and accordingly he thereby, as I think, acquired a good title.[42]

The power would have also been lost in *Car & Universal Finance Co Ltd v Caldwell* had the defrauded vendor not rescinded before any sale on by the rogue.

Things are very different where the contract is void from the start, as, for example, in the well-known case of *Cundy v Lindsay*.[43] The contract being seen as void *ab initio*, Lord Cairns LC held there was no initial passing of property, so no property to revest.

[39] (1856) 11 Ex 577, 579; 156 ER 960, 961.
[40] (1851) 10 CB 919, 138 ER 364.
[41] [1972] 1 QB 198.
[42] ibid 208.
[43] (1878) 3 App Cas 459. See also *Shogun Finance Ltd v Hudson* [2004] 1 AC 919.

He formulated the question thus: 'Was there any contract which, with regard to the goods in question in this case, had passed the property in the goods from the Messrs Lindsay to Alfred Blenkarn?' He said: 'If the property in the goods in question passed, it could only pass by way of contract; there is nothing else which could have passed the property.' Since there was no contract, there could be no passing of title to the goods. It was 'idle', therefore, 'to speak of property passing'.[44]

Third-party rights intervening is sometimes said to be an example of the operation of the bona fide purchase defence. That is certainly how it is presented in the Sale of Goods Acts 1893 and 1979, where, in s 23,[45] it sits alongside the (now repealed) *market overt* rule and the rules for sales by buyers and sellers in possession.[46] However, any such analysis would confine its operation to the situation where value is given in exchange for the very title received as a result of the fraudulent misrepresentation or other ground. This is inconsistent with the case law in at least two respects.

First, there are decisions where the third-party rights which intervene and thereby bar rescission have nothing to do with the right received by the defendant. An example is *Society of Lloyd's v Leighs*,[47] where the Court of Appeal held that a contract between a Lloyd's Name and certain Lloyd's companies authorising the companies to make settlements on behalf of the Name could not be rescinded for fraudulent misrepresentation because rescission would affect third parties with whom other settlements had been made, essentially forcing them to pay more under their own settlements. Those third parties did not, however, receive any rights passed from claimant to defendant.

Second, if operating as a bona fide purchase defence, though it would work for a mortgage of a title to goods, it could not do so for a pledge, for pledges involve bailments rather than transfers of title. Yet the law is that it works for pledges. Thus, in *Whitehorn Brothers v Davison*,[48] simplifying the facts somewhat, the claimant was fraudulently induced by a third party to part with his title to a pearl necklace for a promise to pay £1,400. The third party immediately pledged the necklace with the defendant to secure a loan of £875. The claimant later demanded the return of the necklace from the defendant. On his refusal so to do, the claimant sued in detinue. He failed. According to Vaughan Williams LJ:

> when you have a contract of sale which is voidable on the ground of fraud, or for any other reason, and, before it is avoided by the seller, the buyer, as against whom it could have been avoided, has transferred the subject-matter of the contract to an innocent third person who has given value and has accepted the transfer without either knowledge of anything wrong, or any knowledge of such circumstances as might lead him

[44] ibid 466. The two other judges were more equivocal, deciding not on the ground of mistake but holding instead that there had been no delivery to the rogue with intent to pass title.

[45] Sale of Goods Act 1979, s 23 ('When the seller of goods has a voidable title to them, but his title has not been avoided at the time of the sale, the buyer acquires a good title to the goods, provided he buys them in good faith and without notice of the seller's defect of title').

[46] Sale of Goods Act 1979, ss 24 and 25.

[47] [1997] CLC 1398.

[48] [1911] 1 KB 463.

> to wish not to make any further inquiry lest he should find that there was something wrong, the contract cannot be avoided as against that person.[49]

Because of the intervention of the pledge, the power to rescind was lost, so that there was no revesting of title.

The better view, therefore, is that the third-party rights intervening rule is exactly that, a bar to rescission, not a limit on the exigibility of the power to rescind. Consequently, once third-party rights have intervened, the contract can no longer be rescinded between the parties to the contract themselves. As a result, there is no possibility of title revesting, so no possibility of wrongs claims against third parties who have subsequently dealt with the goods.

G. Is Rescission the Act of the Party?

As seen, the orthodoxy is that rescission at law is the act of the party, that there is no need to obtain a court order. This is amply demonstrated by two of the cases already discussed, *Re Eastgate, ex parte Ward*,[50] and *Car & Universal Finance Co Ltd v Caldwell*,[51] in both of which, since third-party property rights were involved, the result would have been different had a court order been needed. More recently, in *Hopcraft v Close Brothers Ltd*, Lords Reed, Hodge, Lloyd-Jones, Briggs, and Hamblen described rescission at law as a 'self-help remedy that does not depend on there being an order of the court or on any discretionary considerations'.[52] There are many other statements to similar effect.

H. Consequences of Rescission

As seen, the effect of exercising the power to rescind at law is to wipe out the contract *ab initio*, so that the contract previously 'voidable' is now 'void'. Several consequences then flow. First, as noted, there will no longer be any duty on either party to perform and any so-far unperformed duty arising in the past will be extinguished. Thus, if the other party sues for breach of contract, the claim will fail. Also opened up are the possibilities of claims in unjust enrichment in respect of performances made under the now avoided contract, for example, the return of the purchase price of the shares in *Clarke v Dickson*.[53]

However, if rights have been granted or passed pursuant to the contract, these will, with one narrow exception, not revest. Typical is *Feret v Hill*,[54] where the defendant

49 ibid 476.
50 [1905] 1 KB 465.
51 [1965] 1 QB 525.
52 *Hopcraft v Close Brothers Ltd* [2025] UKSC 33; [2025] 3 WLR 423 [238].
53 (1858) El Bl & El 148, 120 ER 463.
54 (1854) 15 CB 207, 139 ER 400.

was fraudulently induced to grant a lease to the claimant, who had represented he would use the premises as a perfumery, when all along he intended it as a common brothel. The defendant ejected the claimant, who sued for wrongful ejectment. Fraud notwithstanding, the Court of Common Pleas allowed the claim. Jervis CJ said that the defendant intended to and did in fact grant the claimant a lease and delivered possession of the premises to him. What was there to avoid that or divest the claimant of the lease?[55] Maule J said that the defendant landlord's 'proper remedy' was 'in a court of equity'.[56] In other words, the defendant should have petitioned the court of equity for an order that the tenant surrender the lease and in the meantime seek an injunction restraining him from suing at law for wrongful ejectment or enforcing the judgment; only then could he lawfully eject the plaintiff.

The same thinking applies where the rights transferred are shares, the benefit of debts, patents, copyrights, and trade marks. There is, however, the exception already encountered in relation to titles to goods, though only where transferred pursuant to a contract of sale. In these cases, title revests on rescission of the contract, as demonstrated by the already discussed cases of *Re Eastgate, ex parte Ward*[57] and *Car & Universal Finance Co Ltd v Caldwell*.[58] However, on the assumption that the sale of goods special rule does not apply to barter,[59] so that a deed or delivery is required, there would be no revesting of title if a contract of barter was rescinded for fraud or duress or on some other ground. *A fortiori*, it is seemingly not possible to rescind a transfer at law made pursuant to a gift, even though induced by fraud or duress.

I. Role of the Court

Finally, the question arises as to the role of the court in cases of rescission at law. It should be clear by now that the orthodoxy is that it is the act of the party, that it is not dependent on any order of the court, something starkly illustrated by *Car & Universal Finance Co Ltd v Caldwell*,[60] where, as seen, an innocent third party became liable for wrongdoing after the act of party rescission. If the defrauded vendor had needed to go to court to obtain rescission and the consequent revesting title, it would have come too late to make the other party a wrongdoer.

It might be thought that the notion of rescission at law as the act of the party does not work, that the many contestable issues of fact which potentially arise in any purported rescission require the adjudication of a court. It may, for example, not be clear that one of the grounds of rescission was present. In cases of misrepresentation, for example, was it in fact fraudulent? It may have been only negligent or even innocent, in which

[55] *Feret v Hill* (1854) 15 CB 207, 223; 139 ER 400, 407.
[56] ibid 226 and 408.
[57] [1905] 1 KB 465.
[58] [1965] 1 QB 525.
[59] *Flynn v Mackin* [1974] IR 101. cf J Atmaz Al-Sibaie, 'Contractual Transfers of Title' (2025) 84 CLJ 527.
[60] [1965] 1 QB 525.

case rescission at law will not generally be available. Likewise, it may be a contentious question whether there was sufficient communication of the intention to rescind to the other party or, if a situation where communication is excused, the taking of reasonable steps. The same goes for any possible affirmation of the contract by subsequent conduct; whether the power was exercised without delay; whether the innocent party was able to make counter-restitution; and whether third-party rights had intervened, something generally outside the knowledge of the innocent party, as, for example, in *Society of Lloyd's v Leighs*.[61] The answer given is that the court can determine retrospectively whether the conditions of rescission were met should a challenge arise. As Megarry J said in *Horsler v Zorro*:

> [T]he process of rescission is essentially the act of the party rescinding, and not of the court. Of course, if matters are disputed, the dispute may have to be determined by the court, and until the decision is given it will not be known whether or not there has been a proper and effectual rescission: but that does not mean that there is no rescission until the court speaks.[62]

As we will see, the orthodoxy for equity is the exact opposite.

III. Rescission in Equity

There are a number of reasons why claimants might seek rescission in equity. As seen, common law rescission, when available, does nothing more than bring a duty of further performance of a contract to an end and excuse prior non-performance. Rights transferred pursuant to that contract do not revest, save in the exceptional case of titles to goods transferred by a contract of sale. In all other cases, if a claimant wants a reconveyance of rights, they will need to obtain a court order to that effect. And given that only equity has the jurisdiction to make such orders, the claim to rescind must be brought there. Claimants will also need to turn to equity if some other form of non-monetary relief, such as a declaration that a contract has been validly rescinded at law,[63] the delivery up of title deeds, or the rectification of a share register, is required. It may also be the case that the claimant cannot make restitution *in specie*, so that common law rescission is barred.

Resort to equity might also be made because equity has its own, more generous, grounds for rescission. Here, contracts can be rescinded for non-fraudulent misrepresentations, undue influence, breach of fiduciary duty, and, in parallel with the common

[61] [1997] CLC 1398.

[62] [1975] Ch 302, 310. As will be noted below, the case in fact concerned termination for breach rather than rescission properly so called, but the thinking is the same for both, though perhaps only because of their previous assimilation.

[63] As eg in *Brotherton v Aseguradora Colseguros SA* [2003] EWCA Civ 705, [2003] 2 All ER (Comm) 298 and *IGE USA v HMRC* [2021] EWCA Civ 534, [2021] Ch 423.

law, for bribery. Moreover, rescission in equity is not confined, as is the case at common law, to the setting aside of contracts. It is also possible to set aside, among other things, gifts[64] and trusts. Indeed, in the context of trusts, it was held by the Supreme Court in *Pitt v Holt*[65] that they can even be set aside for unilateral mistake, provided that the mistake is of sufficient gravity to make it 'unconscionable' for the court to refuse relief.[66] There are also the cases on 'fraud on a power', for example, that of trustees buying the trust rights from themselves,[67] by which the beneficiaries can bring actions for rescission.

In all cases, the question is whether rescission is, as at common law, the act of the party or instead contingent on an order of the court. As was noted above, it has recently been argued by Elliott that it is the former.[68] It will be seen from what follows that such a position is untenable.

A. Relief

As seen, one reason why claimants might seek relief in equity is to obtain an order that the defendant reconvey to them or surrender a right. Where this is the case, the order granted by the court is analogous to one of specific performance of contracts, though now an order to unwind a transaction rather than perform it. It was accordingly described extrajudicially by the then Sir Peter Millett as one for 'specific unperformance'.[69] In addition, the court has the power to order money payments, for example, an account of profits, as well as giving relief 'on terms', essentially ensuring non-specific counter-restitution,[70] something, as seen, not available at common law, where rescission is the act of the party.

Examples of orders for specific relief are legion. In *Clark v Malpas*,[71] a title to land was conveyed pursuant to a contract of sale which was grossly unfair, the vendor being poor and illiterate. At first instance, the Master of the Rolls declared the conveyance void and directed that it be cancelled, though refusing to direct a reconveyance on the ground that this was unnecessary. On appeal, Mr Selwyn[72] and Mr Jessel[73] (as they then were) for the plaintiff argued that this course was 'against the previous understanding of the profession, and it is important that it should be determined what is the correct form'.[74] The Court held that the proper form of decree was not to declare the deed void, but to direct it to be set aside and to order a reconveyance. Knight-Bruce

[64] As eg in *Allcard v Skinner* (1887) 36 Ch D 145.
[65] [2013] UKSC 26, [2013] 2 AC 108.
[66] ibid [121]–[122].
[67] *Tito v Waddell (No 2)* [1970] Ch 106, 223–25 (Megarry V-C). This would be a case of 'self-dealing'. Sales by beneficiaries of their interest under trusts to trustees may also be set aside under the doctrine of 'fair-dealing'. See Chapter 6 (L Smith, 'Rescission in the Context of Fiduciary Relationships').
[68] Elliott (n 2).
[69] Sir P Millett, 'Restitution and Constructive Trusts' (1998) 114 LQR 399, 416.
[70] As eg in *O'Sullivan v Management Agency and Music Ltd* [1985] 1 QB 428.
[71] (1862) 4 De GF & J 401, 45 ER 1238.
[72] Later Lord Justice of Appeal in Chancery.
[73] Later Master of the Rolls.
[74] *Clark v Malpas* (1862) 4 De GF & J 401, 403; 45 ER 1238, 1239.

LJ said that though he agreed that the transaction could not stand, the wording of the declaration that the conveyance was void was 'too strong an expression, for the deed is not legally but only equitably void'. He therefore granted an order for the execution of a reconveyance.[75] Turner LJ likewise held that the decree be framed instead as an 'order in the usual way that it be set aside and that the Defendant do reconvey the property'.[76]

Two well-known decisions concerning orders for the reconveyance of rights are *Allcard v Skinner*[77] and *Newbigging v Adam*.[78] In *Allcard v Skinner*, the relief sought was 'a declaration that the Plaintiff was induced to make over the property by the undue influence of the Defendant Skinner and repayment of the moneys and re-transfers of the railway stock'.[79] Lindley LJ described the defendant's 'equitable title' as 'imperfect by reason of the influence',[80] and would have granted the order but for the plaintiff's subsequent laches and acquiescence. Cotton LJ, dissenting, held that the plaintiff could recover 'on the ground that it was property the beneficial interest in which she had never effectually parted with'.[81] Because, in his view, this gave rise to an immediate trust, he disagreed that the claim was barred by laches.[82] However, Lindley LJ said that the conveyance was not void, merely voidable: 'Gifts liable to be set aside by the Court on the ground of undue influence have always been treated as voidable and not void'.[83] In *Newbigging v Adam*, a contract to become a partner in a business was set aside on the ground of innocent misrepresentation. The Court of Appeal decreed that the defendants were liable to repay the amount paid by the plaintiff with interest at four per cent per annum after deducting sums drawn out by the plaintiff with interest, and that the defendant should indemnify the plaintiff against all debts of the partnership to which he had become liable.[84]

Three points can be made about the orders just described. First, the remedy is clearly that of the court. Just as there is no ability in a claimant to order a contracting party to perform and invoke the contempt jurisdiction of equity if the order is disobeyed, so too there is no possibility of the 'equity to rescind' being exercisable by the innocent party alone. To attract the sanction of the court for non-performance, the order can only be that of the court. Second, as *Clarke v Malpas* demonstrates, the order of the court is not self-executing. Just as an order that the defendant perform a contract does not ipso facto mean that the contract is performed, so too an order for 'specific unperformance' will not by itself revest rights: there still needs to be a conveyance by the defendant.[85]

[75] *Clark v Malpas* (1862) 4 De GF & J 401, 405; 45 ER 1238, 1240. This, as we shall see, is not accurate. It was also equitably voidable, as his Lordship himself later stated in *Allcard v Skinner* (1887) 36 Ch D 145, 186.
[76] (1862) 4 De GF & J 401, 405; 45 ER 1238, 1240.
[77] (1887) 36 Ch D 145.
[78] (1886) 34 Ch D 582.
[79] (1887) 36 Ch D 145, 149.
[80] ibid 185.
[81] ibid 172.
[82] ibid 175.
[83] ibid 186. Bowen LJ also held that the claim was barred by laches and acquiescence.
[84] *Newbigging v Adam* (1886) 34 Ch D 582, 585; affd by the House of Lords: (1888) 13 App Cas 308.
[85] *O'Sullivan v Management Agency and Music Ltd* [1985] QB 428, citing *Leech v Leech* (1674) 2 Ch Rep 100; *Lady Hudson's Case* (1704) 2 Eq Cas Abr 52; *Clavering v Clavering* (1704) Prec Chan 235, 24 ER 114; *Harrison v Owen* (1738) 1 Atk 520, 26 ER 328; *Re Way's Trust* (1864) 2 De G, J & S 365, 46 ER 416.

Third, the orders are often both complex and conditional, as in *Newbigging v Adam*, with fine adjustments being made between the rights of both parties, backed by the coercive powers of the court, again something only consistent with rescission in equity being the order of the court.

B. Bars

Like the common law, equity also has bars to rescission; they are essentially the same.

1. Affirmation

Affirmation of the transfer or contract will mean the loss of the equity to rescind. So, for example, in *Re Hop and Malt Exchange and Warehouse Co*,[86] the claimant was induced to take shares in a company on the faith of fraudulent misrepresentations contained in the prospectus. He subsequently instructed his broker to sell the shares. Lord Romilly MR held that he had thereby affirmed the contract and refused an application for an order that the company remove him from the share register.

2. Delay

There is a general defence in equity of 'laches', whereby undue delay prejudicial to the defendant bars any claim. We saw its operation in *Allcard v Skinner*, where the claim to rescind the transfer of shares failed because brought too late. Unlike statutory periods of limitation, there is no fixed point at which laches takes effect, thus necessitating an exercise of judgment by the court. As Lord Blackburn said in *Erlanger v New Sombrero Phosphate Co*: 'The determination of such a question must largely depend on the turn of mind of those who have to decide.'[87]

3. Counter-restitution Impossible

The ability to rescind in equity is, as at common law, conditional on the claimant making counter-restitution to the defendant. As seen, the difference between the two is that, because rescission in equity is dependent on an order of the court, monetary adjustments are possible so that counter-restitution will not be impossible simply because restitution *in specie* cannot be made. As Lord Blackburn explained in *Erlanger v The New Sombrero Phosphate Co*:

> It is . . . clear on principles of general justice, that as a condition to a rescission there must be a restitutio in integrum. The parties must be put in statu quo . . . It is a doctrine which has often been acted upon both at law and in equity. But there is a considerable difference in the mode in which it is applied in Courts of Law and Equity, owing, as I think, to the difference of the machinery which the Courts have at command.[88]

[86] (1866) LR 1 Eq 483.
[87] *Erlanger v New Sombrero Phosphate Co* (1878) 3 App Cas 1218, 1279–80.
[88] ibid 1278.

An example of the operation of the different equitable machinery is *O'Sullivan v Management Agency and Music Ltd*,[89] where various contracts were entered into as a result of undue influence. The Court ordered the agreements to be set aside, an account of the profits made by the defendants, the reconveyance of copyrights, and the delivery up of certain master-tapes. The order for the account of profits was, however, reduced to make allowance for the defendant's skill and labour in promoting the innocent party. It is not, of course, possible to make restitution *in specie* of skill and labour, so there could have been no rescission at law, assuming, of course, that a legal ground, such as fraudulent misrepresentation or duress, was present.

This does not, however, mean that counter-restitution will always be possible. In *Gray v New Augarita Porcupine Mines Ltd*,[90] Gray, a director of a mining company, had abused his powers by arranging for the issuance of the company's shares to himself as fully paid up, at a discount of 80 per cent, and then selling them on at a substantial profit. New directors were appointed and he entered into a settlement agreement with the company, according to which he was to transfer to it certain assets in return for a waiver of all claims against him. The company later sought rescission of the agreement on the grounds of fraud or non-disclosure. The Privy Council, on appeal from Ontario, held that the agreement could not now be rescinded as Gray had handed over the assets as agreed and they had been sold. Lord Radcliffe said that the fact that that the transaction could not now be undone meant that *restitutio in integrum* was impossible.[91]

4. Intervention of Third-Party Rights

Just as with rescission at law, the intervention of third-party rights will bar the availability of rescission in equity. Thus, in *Oakes v Turquand*,[92] the House of Lords held that a shareholder who had been induced by fraudulent misrepresentations of the company to take shares could not obtain an order that his name be removed from the share register once the company had gone into insolvency because that would prejudice the rights of the company's creditors. As with the discussion above of the position at common law, the third-party rights bar once again cannot be an aspect of a bona fide purchase for value defence, for there was no such purchase in *Oakes v Turquand*.

C. Role of the Court

The question then is how the transferor effects rescission in equity. The orthodoxy, as seen, is that it is not possible for the innocent party to do so on their own: rescission is ineffective until there is an order of the court.

There is no shortage of dicta to this effect. We have already seen Lord Blackburn's description of the differences between law and equity and the ability of the latter to make

[89] [1985] QB 428.
[90] [1952] 3 DLR 1. Another example is *Murad v Al-Saraj* [2005] EWCA Civ 959, [2005] WTLR 1573.
[91] *Gray v New Augarita Porcupine Mines Ltd* [1952] 3 DLR 1, 11.
[92] (1867) LR 2 HL 325.

money orders to ensure *restitutio in integrum* in *Erlanger v New Sombrero Phosphate Co.*[93] In the same case, and after referring to the fact that the remedy of damages is only available at law, he said:

> But a court of equity could not give damages, and, unless it can rescind the contract, can give no relief. And on the other hand, it can take accounts of profits, and make allowance for deterioration. And I think the practice has always been for a court of equity to give this relief whenever, by the exercise of its powers, it can do what is practically just, though it cannot restore the parties precisely to the state they were in before the contract.[94]

These words would make no sense were we to see the claimant themselves as effecting rescission; his Lordship's talk throughout of 'the court' shows that what he is speaking of is an order of the court.

The decision of the High Court of Australia in *Alati v Kruger*[95] is often cited as authority for the view that rescission in equity is the act of the innocent party, not the court. However, it is a good illustration of the opposite proposition. Although the majority cite the decision of the House of Lords in *Reese River Silver Mining Co v Smith*[96] to say it is the 'act of the party', that case turned on a peculiarity of the statutory scheme in question. In any event, the point was not in issue in *Alati*. Furthermore, there were difficult questions concerning the plaintiff's ability to make *restitutio in integrum*. It was held that though this might have barred any claim to rescind at law, it was

> necessary here to apply the doctrines of equity, and equity has always regarded as valid the disaffirmance of a contract induced by fraud where the situation is such that, by the exercise of its powers, as for example the power to take accounts of profits and to direct inquiries as to allowances proper to be made for deterioration, it can do what is practically just and thereby replace the parties substantially, even though not precisely, in statu quo.[97]

Such a statement is, once again, inconsistent with rescission being the act of the innocent party themselves. Moreover, it is simply illogical to say, as the High Court asserts:

> The function of a court in which proceedings are taken is to adjudicate upon the validity of the purported disaffirmance as an act avoiding the transaction ab initio, and, if it is valid, to give effect to it and make appropriate consequential orders.[98]

[93] (1878) 3 App Cas 1218, 1278.
[94] ibid.
[95] (1955) 94 CLR 216.
[96] (1869) LR 4 HL 64, 73.
[97] ibid 223.
[98] *Alati v Kruger* (1955) 94 CLR 216, 224.

The possibility, indeed, necessity, of consequential orders gives the lie to the notion of equitable rescission as the act of the party.

Elliott, however, has recently argued that the point is 'determined by the authority of *Abram Steamship Co Ltd v Westville Shipping Co Ltd* in favour of the view that the power to rescind for innocent misrepresentation lies with the representee',[99] which, if correct, would logically extend to rescission in equity more generally. We must therefore examine *Abram Shipping*[100] in detail. As will be seen, it cannot bear the weight Elliott ascribes to it.

The facts are complex. A contracted with a shipbuilder for the construction and sale of a steamer. Before it was finished, A contracted to and did assign the shipbuilding contract to B. A, however, made false but innocent representations about the state of construction of the steamer, sufficient to allow B to rescind the contract of assignment. In ignorance of this, B contracted to and assigned the shipbuilding contract to C, innocently repeating the false representations. C then discovered the true position and gave notice to B that they 'repudiated' the contract of assignment on the ground of misrepresentation. B wrote to A telling them what C had done and informing A that C was applying to the court to rescind the assignment contract and gave notice to A that they likewise claimed rescission of their contract with A. C then commenced an action in the English courts[101] against B for rescission and return of the purchase price. Given that the misrepresentation was innocent, this would necessarily have been a suit for equitable rescission. Before the English proceedings were concluded, B issued proceedings against A in Scotland to reduce (rescind) the contract of assignment with A and likewise recover the purchase price. Just over a month later, the English proceedings formally came to an end, with judgment in the English action being entered by consent for C, B having been advised that they had no defence.

The dispute concerned the Scottish proceedings. A resisted the claim for rescission, among other things,[102] on the ground that, at the time when it was commenced, the shipbuilding contract was still vested in C, meaning that B was at that point unable to make counter-restitution. The argument was framed in terms of B having 'no title to sue', that their 'title' had to be tested by the circumstances existing at the date of issue of the summons. The argument failed at every stage. The Lord Ordinary, Lord Hunter, granted reduction of the contract and his decision was unanimously upheld by the First Division of the Inner House.[103] There, Lord President Clyde said:

> [T]he genuine and *bona fide* character of the English proceedings is not challenged; and, if the pursuers had no good answer to the sub-assignees' action, I cannot see that they were bound to postpone raising action in this Court until the rescinding order

[99] Elliott (n 2) 173.

[100] *Abram Steamship Co Ltd v Westville Shipping Co Ltd* [1923] AC 773.

[101] In fact, in the Cardiff District Registry.

[102] There was also an argument that C had 'homologated' (affirmed) the contract of assignment because of some negotiations with the shipbuilder. This too failed.

[103] *Westville Shipping Co v Abram Steamship Co* 1922 SC 571.

> was actually pronounced. All that actually stood between them and reinstatement in the benefits of the builders' contract was the pronouncement of this order which the sub-assignees were moving the English Court to make, and which, if the above stated hypothesis is correct, the pursuers had no means of resisting. I think in these circumstances the pursuers may properly be regarded as having a substantial title to sue, and as being substantially in a position to offer restitution to the defenders.[104]

Lord Mackenzie said that whilst it was true that B must 'offer restitution in order to make his averments relevant' and 'must be in a position at some point of time to make restitution', it was sufficient that they were in such a position at the date the record was closed.[105] Lord Skerrington described the issue as whether B had a good title after discovering their error although the resale had not 'actually' been rescinded. The answer was in the affirmative as B could prove that not only had C 'repudiated his contract, but that there were legal grounds which entitled him to do so'.[106] In such a case, he said, B had a 'substantial title' to sue, and that was enough.[107] Finally, Lord Cullen said that he could not see why B's action should fail 'merely because, at the inception of the action when they offered a *restitutio* which the defenders refused to accept, they could not there and then have made it had the defenders chosen to take it. No legitimate interest of the defenders has thereby suffered, so far as I am able to see.'[108]

Several points can be made about the decision of the First Division of the Inner House. First, at this stage at least, it had nothing to do with English law but was purely a decision on the Scots law as to the requirement of *restitutio in integrum*. In this respect, the decision was that, as a matter of Scots law, it was either sufficient for a claimant to be almost in a position to make counter-restitution at the time of commencement of proceedings or if they actually were in such a position by the time the case came on for hearing. Nothing whatever was said about whether English equity works on the basis of act of party rather than the order of the court. Second, it is implicit in what was said that they viewed the English position as being that the contract of assignment was not rescinded until the English proceedings were complete, for their reasoning would make no sense otherwise. Indeed, given, as we have seen, that decrees in equity are not self-executing and that there would have needed to be a reassignment of the shipbuilding contract from C to B, this is the only tenable position.

An appeal to the House of Lords failed.[109] Substantive speeches were given by Lord Dunedin, a Scottish judge, and Lord Atkinson. The Earl of Birkenhead agreed with both Lord Dunedin and Lord Atkinson, while Viscount Finlay agreed with Lord Dunedin alone. Lord Atkinson himself agreed with Lord Dunedin, while Lord Shaw,

[104] ibid 583.
[105] ibid 586.
[106] ibid 588.
[107] ibid.
[108] ibid 589.
[109] *Abram Steamship Co Ltd v Westville Shipping Co Ltd* [1923] AC 773.

another Scottish judge, simply expressed agreement with Lord President Clyde's judgment in the court below.

Lord Dunedin said that so long as the contract of assignment to C stood, B's action would be barred. Here, however, the contract no longer existed. It had, he said, 'been put out of the way by the decision in the English Courts.'[110] As to the question of 'date', he said:

> It is true that for the moment there seemed a good answer—namely: 'You have parted with the subject of the contract and therefore you have lost your interest,' but the moment that the instrument by which they had so parted was swept away the original title was then in all its force.[111]

Lord Atkinson, having, as noted, endorsed the reasoning of both Lord Dunedin and the Lord President below, said:

> Where one party to a contract expresses by word or act in an unequivocal manner that by reason of fraud or essential error of a material kind inducing him to enter into the contract he has resolved to rescind it, and refuses to be bound by it, the expression of his election, if justified by the facts, terminates the contract, puts the parties in statu quo ante and restores things, as between them, to the position in which they stood before the contract was entered into. It may be that the facts impose upon the party desiring to rescind the duty of making restitutio in integrum. If so, he must discharge that duty before the rescission is, in effect, accomplished; but if the other party to the contract questions the right of the first to rescind, thus obliging the latter to bring an action at law to enforce the right he has secured for himself by his election, and the latter gets a verdict, it is an entire mistake to suppose that it is this verdict which by itself terminates the contract and restores the antecedent status. The verdict is merely the judicial determination of the fact that the expression by the plaintiff of his election to rescind was justified, was effective, and put an end to the contract.[112]

He added:

> [I]t is not this judgment which puts an end to the voidable contract of March 13, 1920. That was done early in the month of July previous in the manner mentioned. This obviously brought it to an end, provided always that [C] was then entitled in law to take that course.[113]

Lord Atkinson, therefore, does seem to be endorsing a view of equitable rescission as the act of the party, not the court.

110 ibid 779.
111 ibid 780.
112 ibid 781.
113 ibid 785.

Standing back, there are a number of points to make about this decision. First and foremost, it is a decision on the position in Scots law on the impossibility of counter-restitution bar, not the English law of rescission in equity. The ratio is contained in the speech of Lord Dunedin, who held that it was sufficient that by the time the action was heard in the Scottish case, the English proceedings had come to a conclusion. This can only mean that he thought an order of the English equity court was needed. Second, Lord Atkinson agreed with both Lord Dunedin and the Lord President below. Third, Lord Atkinson's speech was a minority one, agreed with only by the Earl of Birkenhead. Fourth, even Lord Atkinson acknowledged, in the passage cited above, that B would need to make counter-restitution before the rescission was 'in effect, accomplished', the necessary implication being that it was ineffective until that happened. Fifth, he cited no authority for his statement that the expression of B was enough to effect rescission, which is obviously at odds with the point just noted. Sixth, his speech made no reference to the different approaches of law and equity. Indeed, the word 'equity' appears nowhere in his speech. Seventh, and finally, in the decision of *Boyd & Forest v The Glasgow Railway Co*,[114] decided a few years earlier, the same judge spoke unequivocally of the 'Court of Equity' setting aside contracts.[115] *Abram Steamship* cannot, therefore, be seen as having 'determined' the issue in favour of rescission in equity being the act of the party.

Elliott also relies on the endorsement of *Abram Steamship* by the Court of Appeal in *Brotherton v Aseguradora Colseguros SA*,[116] a claim for a declaration that a contract induced by fraudulent misrepresentation had been validly rescinded.[117] In upholding the grant by Moore-Bick J of the declaration sought,[118] Mance LJ said:

> It is clear that rescission in the general law of contract is by act of the innocent party operating independently of the court: see *Abram Steamship Co v Westville Shipping Co* [1923] AC 773 (rescission of a shipbuilding contract for misrepresentation) and *Horsler v Zorro* [1975] 1 Ch 302 (rescission of a contract for sale of land).[119]

Likewise, Buxton LJ said:

> [R]escission is an act of the party, effective as soon as made, and regarded by the courts as so effective provided that the appropriate circumstances for rescission existed at that time. That is established by . . . Lord Atkinson in *Abram Steamship* and Megarry J in *Horsler v Zorro*.[120]

[114] 1915 SC 20.
[115] ibid 30.
[116] [2003] EWCA Civ 705, [2003] 2 All ER (Comm) 298.
[117] Elliott (n 2) 176.
[118] See *Brotherton v Aseguradora Colseguros SA* [2003] EWHC 335 (Comm), [2003] 1 All ER (Comm) 774.
[119] *Brotherton v Aseguradora Colseguros SA* [2003] 2 All ER (Comm) 298 [27].
[120] ibid [45].

Elliott notes that the case would, before the Judicature Acts, have been brought in Chancery.

We should not make too much of this decision. First, since it was a case of fraudulent misrepresentation, rescission was possible at common law, which, as we know, is the act of the party. Indeed, the claimants only sought a declaration that this had in fact happened, that the position at common law was as the claimant said it was. It was not, therefore, a case of rescission in equity at all. Second, both Mance and Buxton LJJ rely on the decision of Megarry J in *Horsler v Zorro*. That, however, was concerned with termination for breach, decided shortly before the disentangling of the two concepts, rescission and termination, by the House of Lords five years later in *Johnson v Agnew*[121] and *Photo Production Ltd v Securicor Transport Ltd*.[122] Indeed, in light of these two decisions, it is a wonder that *Horsler v Zorro* was cited at all.

That rescission in equity is not the act of the party is confirmed by a wealth of other authorities. Thus, in *Pitt v Holt*,[123] where rescission was sought of the constitution of a trust, the Supreme Court described the equitable jurisdiction to set aside a voluntary disposition on the ground of mistake as exercisable whenever there was 'a causative mistake which was so grave that it would be unconscionable to refuse relief'.[124] This once again makes clear that the ultimate decision lies with the court, for it is only the court which can grant or refuse relief. Indeed, in relation to the related appeal in *Futter v Futter*, the Supreme Court indicated that relief on the ground of mistake, had it been claimed, would probably have been refused on the ground that it involved an artificial tax avoidance scheme,[125] a conclusion totally at odds with rescission being the act of the party.

That rescission in equity is not the act of the party but of the court is reinforced by the fact that there is a residual discretion in the court to refuse relief, even beyond the bars. Thus, in *Johnson v EBS Pensioner Trustees Ltd*,[126] the Court of Appeal had to consider whether a guarantee given by one of the defendants as security for a loan made by solicitors to his company should be rescinded because the solicitor acting for him had a conflict of interests and had been in breach of his fiduciary duty by failing to disclose that his firm received service charges on the loan. The Court upheld the judge's refusal to grant rescission, rejecting the submission that rescission was available as of right in such circumstances. Dyson LJ said:

> When exercising its equitable jurisdiction the court considers what fairness requires not only when addressing the question of the precise form of relief, but also when considering whether the remedy should be granted at all.[127]

[121] [1980] AC 367.
[122] [1980] AC 827.
[123] [2013] UKSC 26, [2013] 2 AC 108.
[124] ibid [128].
[125] ibid [135]. A recent example of relief being refused on these grounds is *Bhaur v Equity First Trustees (Nevis) Ltd* [2023] EWCA Civ 534, [2023] STC 1012.
[126] [2002] EWCA Civ 164, [2002] Lloyd's Rep PN 309.
[127] ibid [79].

Likewise, in *UBS AG (London Branch) v Kommunale Wasserwerke Leipzig GmbH*,[128] Briggs and Hamblen LJJ in their joint judgment in the Court of Appeal said:

> A claim . . . for rescission is a claim for an equitable remedy. Where a prima facie right to rescission is demonstrated, the court nonetheless retains what is traditionally called a discretion to refuse it where it would be unfair or disproportionate, or to afford some other more suitable remedy, such as equitable compensation or an account.[129]

Finally, the recent decision of the Supreme Court in *Hopcraft v Close Brothers Ltd* describes rescission as a discretionary remedy.[130]

A possible explanation for the confusion may be the compressed language often found in the cases. When it is said that the claimant can rescind, this is an unfortunate contraction of the phrase 'the claimant can petition the court of equity for an order of rescission'. The phenomenon is encountered elsewhere. One example is with the falsification and surcharge of accounts in equity. In *Libertarian Investments Ltd v Hall*,[131] for instance, Lord Millett NPJ said that if an account disclosed an unauthorised investment, 'the plaintiff may falsify it', and that if the account is shown to be defective, 'the plaintiff can surcharge' it.[132] However, both statements were immediately followed by words indicating that this would involve asking the court to do the things in question, precisely what should be the understanding here.

IV. Conclusion

Common law rescission is the act of the party whereas, despite the argument of Elliott, equitable rescission requires an order of the court. Indeed, it is difficult to see how it could be otherwise. Given that the claimant in equity often wants some form of consequential relief, there is clearly a need to obtain a court order, for they will require the invocation of the contempt jurisdiction of the court should the defendant refuse to comply. We would never think that a claimant can obtain orders for specific performance without going to court, and it is no different with orders for specific 'unperformance'.

There is one final point. If this account is right, then though it is correct to speak of rescission at law in terms of a power, not a right, the same language cannot be used for equitable rescission. Where a ground of rescission arises in favour of a person in equity, this is not a power, merely the ability to petition the court, no different from the ability of the victim of a breach of contract or a tort to seek an order for damages, or a contracting party to seek an order for specific performance. The cases speak of 'an equity' to rescind. Though this is not perhaps the most felicitous language, it is better than 'power'.

128 [2017] EWCA Civ 1567, [2017] 2 Lloyd's Rep 621.
129 ibid [157].
130 *Hopcraft v Close Brothers Ltd* [2025] UKSC 33, [2025] 3 WLR 423 [77], [238].
131 [2014] 1 HKC 368.
132 ibid [168], [170].

5

Corporate Rescission and Director Fraud

*Elise Bant**

I. Introduction

Debate has long raged over the implications of director fraud for corporate transacting.[1] The particular focus of this chapter is on whether transactions entered into by a corporation with an external counterparty, under the influence of the corporation's fraudulent director, are void or voidable (and, hence, liable to rescission) on the part of the corporation.[2] The answer to this seemingly simple and certainly recurrent question remains remarkably unclear and complex.

In unjust enrichment and restitution scholarship, the issue is variously approached through the lens of three different forms of 'unjust factor': mistake; 'ignorance' (or, more expansively, 'no intention to benefit the defendant');[3] and 'want of authority'.[4] A fourth potential source of claim arises from what might be called improper use of the director's power or authority.[5] Summarising grossly, contracts characterised as resulting from corporate mistake due to director fraud, or abuse of director authority, are

* Professor of Private Law and Commercial Regulation, The University of Western Australia, Perth, Australia, and Professorial Fellow, University of Melbourne, Melbourne, Australia (Orcid ID: 0000-0003-2188-0521). This article forms part of my Australian Research Council Future Fellowship project FT190100475: see <www.uwa.edu.au/schools/research/unravelling-corporate-fraud-re-purposing-ancient-doctrines-for-modern-times>. I thank most sincerely Professor Dame Sarah Worthington, Professor Lionel Smith, Mohammud Jaamae Hafeez-Baig, my colleague Rebecca Faugno, the editors of this collection, Jonas Atmaz Al-Sibaie and Jordan English, and the participants at the collection symposium for their generous and helpful feedback on this chapter. Responsibility for all remaining errors and infelicities rests with me.

[1] The inspiration for this chapter comes from Professor Dame Sarah Worthington's seminal article, Sarah Worthington, 'Corporate Attribution and Agency: Back to Basics' (2017) 133 LQR 118, the analysis and conclusions in which I largely echo, albeit through a holistic organisational analysis, and with a focus on director fraud rather than her broader examination of misbehaving agents.

[2] I see rescission as inherently restitutionary in nature: see E Bant, 'Rescission, Restitution and Compensation' in S Degeling and J Varuhas (eds), *Equitable Compensation and Disgorgement* (Hart 2017) 277; E Bant, 'Rights and Value in Rescission' in D Nolan and A Robertson (eds), *Rights and Private Law* (Hart 2012) 609. Rescission also applies to other forms of transacting, such as gifts and settlement, however the main focus for current purposes is contracting with parties external to the corporation.

[3] First posited in P Birks, *An Introduction to the Law of Restitution* (rev edn, OUP 1989) 141; see further M Bryan, 'No Intention to Benefit' in E Bant, K Barker, and S Degeling (eds), *Research Handbook on Unjust Enrichment and Restitution* (Edward Elgar 2020) 363. Examples include *non est factum*: *Ford v Perpetual Trustees Victoria Ltd* [2009] NSWCA 186, (2009) 75 NSWLR 42 [36]–[90] (mistake) and *Veall v Veall* [2015] VSCA 60, (2015) 46 VR 123 (undue influence).

[4] R Chambers and J Penner, 'Ignorance' in S Degeling and J Edelman (eds), *Unjust Enrichment in Commercial Law* (Lawbook Co 2008) 253.

[5] Worthington (n 1); L Smith, *The Law of Loyalty* (OUP 2023) 173–76; Bryan (n 3); and some observations below at Section III.B. See further Chapter 6 of this book (L Smith, 'Rescission in the Context of Fiduciary Relationships'). Whether this is an example of 'restitution for wrongs' or restitution for another reason is a further question, but one which cannot be addressed here.

generally regarded as binding on the company, but may be open to rescission subject to (amongst other elements) the counterparty being implicated in or sufficiently aware of the vitiating factor.[6] Where, by contrast, the analysis suggests that there is no corporate intention at all to enter the transaction, or no actual or ostensible director authority to do so, the putative transaction is more likely to be void from the outset.[7]

The different analyses therefore provide quite divergent answers to our core question.[8] But which is right, when, and why?

This chapter argues that the answer lies in understanding how corporations as organisational entities 'think' and act, including through directors. This enables us to demarcate the fundamental boundary between void and voidable corporate transacting, the latter constituting the territory of rescission. Mapping this terrain must, I think, presage enquiries into the more granular (and generally applicable) requirements of the other conditions of corporate rescission, such as what kinds of mistake support rescission of contracts, what kinds of knowledge a counterparty must have of the mistake, the role of election, and the nature and consequences of rescission.[9] If a transaction is void, rather than voidable, those enquiries fall away.

The analytical vehicle for this enquiry is a novel, holistic model of corporate responsibility, entitled 'Systems Intentionality'.[10] Recently adopted in the High Court of Australia,[11] this posits that corporations manifest (in the dual senses of reveal and instantiate) their states of mind through their adopted or deployed systems of conduct, policies, and practices. Section II of this chapter introduces this model to explain how and why, through a systemic lens, corporations will generally have acted intentionally in circumstances of director fraud. On this account, therefore, such cases should not be

[6] *Taylor v Johnson* (1983) 151 CLR 422 [5], [12], [13], [14], discussed in J Edelman and E Bant, *Unjust Enrichment* (Hart 2016) 141–48; *Great Investments v Warner* [2016] FCAFC 85, (2016) 243 FCR 516 [56]–[57].

[7] This means that the putative contract will form no 'juristic reason to retain' the benefit, and so it will be unnecessary for it to be set aside as a condition to restitution of any benefits that have been conferred. Whether there are other juristic reasons that justify retention (such as statute, or a process of registration) must also be considered: Edelman and Bant (n 6) 130–67; *Great Investments v Warner* [2016] FCAFC 85, (2016) 243 FCR 516 [70]–[76].

[8] The complexity may explain why these boundaries are, seemingly, sometimes simply ignored: see eg *Fistar v Riverwood Legion and Community Club Ltd* [2016] NSWCA 81, (2016) 91 NSWLR 732. A corporation was tricked by its fraudulent CEO into making payments through its designated payment system to an external fraudster, who in turn transferred the value of that sum to an innocent recipient. The transactions were described variously in terms of 'theft' and 'fraud'. Contrast *Great Investments Ltd v Warner* [2016] FCAFC 85, (2016) 243 FCR 516 [52]. The cases are discussed in E Bant and M Bryan, 'Outflanking *Barnes v Addy*? The Persistence of Strict Recipient Liability (2017) 11 J Eq 271, 279.

[9] For my views on these topics, see: Edelman and Bant (n 6) 142–49, 229–50; JM Paterson and E Bant, 'Automated Mistakes: Vitiated Consent and State of Mind Culpability in Algorithmic Contracting' in E Bant (ed), *The Culpable Corporate Mind* (Hart 2023) 255 (what kinds of mistake support rescission and the role of defendant knowledge and inducement); E Bant, 'Reconsidering the Role of Election in Rescission' (2012) 32 OJLS 467 (the conditions of rescission); Bant, 'Rights and Value in Rescission' (n 2) 609; Bant, 'Rescission, Restitution and Compensation' (n 2) 277 (the nature and consequences of rescission).

[10] The core of the model is set out in E Bant, 'Systems Intentionality: Theory and Practice' in Bant, *The Culpable Corporate Mind* (n 9) 183; E Bant, 'Modelling Corporate States of Mind through Systems Intentionality' in Bant, *The Culpable Corporate Mind* (n 9) 231; Paterson and Bant, 'Automated Mistakes' (n 9). See also E Bant, 'Culpable Corporate Minds' (2021) 48 UWAL Rev 352; E Bant and JM Paterson, 'Systems of Misconduct: Corporate Culpability and Statutory Unconscionability' (2021) 15 J Eq 63; E Bant, 'Corporate Mistake' in J Gardner and others (eds), *Politics, Policy and Private Law*, vol 2: *Contract, Commercial and Company Law* (Hart 2025) 123. Project publications and findings are found at <https://unravellingcorporatefraud.com/>.

[11] *Productivity Partners Pty Ltd v Australian Competition and Consumer Commission* [2024] HCA 27, (2024) 419 ALR 30 [108]–[111], [134], [143], [199]–[200], [236]–[241], [282], [307], [340].

characterised in terms of corporate 'ignorance'. Rather, director fraud may have operated to *subvert* or undermine the usual corporate decision-making process in which the director was a key component. Systems Intentionality suggests this subversion means that the corporation's decision-making system may have been vitiated, manifesting a form of corporate mistake. Consistently with the position for natural persons, and in accordance with the objective approach to consent in contract formation, such a corporate mistake will generally render a contractual transaction entered into with a third party pursuant to the mistake voidable, not void.[12] The transaction will only therefore be liable to rescission as against an external counterparty where the counterparty assisted in or was sufficiently aware of the director's fraud. Section III expands on this analysis to explain how a fraudulent director will generally have been authorised to act in the impugned transaction, although they may well have abused that authority. Such cases will not, therefore, be ones of 'want of authority'. Rather, and consistently with the analysis of corporate mistake, the adopted or deployed system resulting in the impugned transaction will generally have been the corporation's designated system for that purpose, albeit some component of it misfired (here, because of director fraud). In addition to the possibility of corporate mistake, there may also be a separate ground for rescission arising from abuse of authority, which is the subject of some brief, additional, observations. Section IV concludes by acknowledging the reduced role left to the concept of ostensible authority on this analysis.

Before turning to this task, some final observations and caveats are necessary. First, the analysis draws on the facts and reasoning of key cases to illustrate the operation of the model of Systems Intentionality, and its implications for our key question. However, it does not claim to be an interpretive account. Leading authorities reflect the individualistic focus of traditional attribution rules. On the other hand, the analysis aims to be more than a thought experiment, divorced from doctrinal realities. It argues that thinking in organisational terms helps to avoid a range of critical, diagnostic, slippages that have prevented courts from addressing the consequences of director fraud in a consistent and principled way.[13] Third, in this, it is also implicitly normative: it suggests that thinking in organisational terms better grounds existing attribution approaches and, hence, the availability of corporate rescission. Finally, and relatedly, while not an interpretive account, the analysis proceeds on the basis that the model of Systems Intentionality exemplifies and makes transparent nascent conceptions of organisational responsibility that emerge (albeit in a sporadic and incomplete way) throughout the law. This is most apparent in Australia, where recurrent legislative patterns express similar ideas,[14] and where recent Royal Commissions have adopted and

[12] Likewise, payments made pursuant to such a mistake will generally be effective to transfer value, although the corporate plaintiff may be entitled to restitution, subject to defences and other factors.

[13] A prime example is *Stone & Rolls Ltd (in liq) v Moore Stephens* [2009] UKHL 39, [2009] 1 AC 1391, discussed below in Section II.D. See further Worthington (n 1) 119.

[14] In particular, the Australian Consumer Law (ACL) ss 21 and 22, in sch 2 of the Competition and Consumer Act 2010 (Cth). The equivalent prohibition for financial services is the Australian Securities and Investments Commission Act 2001 (Cth), ss 12CB, 12CC. cf the 'Corporate Culture' provisions of the Criminal Code Act 1995 (Cth), s 12.3(2); Criminal Law Officers Committee of the Standing Committee of Attorneys-General, *Model*

applied Systems Intentionality as a principled supplement to the more traditional attribution approaches.[15] Further, as foreshadowed, the model has recently been cited with approval, and reasoning consistent with it applied,[16] in the High Court of Australia decision in *Productivity Partners Pty Ltd v Australian Competition and Consumer Commission*.[17] Justice Gordon (Steward J and Beech-Jones J separately agreeing)[18] and Edelman J adopted systemic analyses to find that the corporate wrongdoer in that case had engaged knowingly and intentionally in conduct that should, therefore, be characterised as 'unconscionable' and, so, contrary to the applicable statutory prohibition.[19] While the decision concerned a statutory prohibition, their Honours' key reasoning was expressed in general terms, as part of discussions about foundational questions of how corporations 'think' and act.[20] While accepting, therefore, that the analysis is a novel one, it is arguably deeply connected with existing and evolving principles of private and corporate law, all of which are relevant for corporate rescission.

It is to this systemic model of corporate responsibility, and the role of directors as (part of) key decision-making systems, that we now turn.

II. Systems Intentionality

A. The Model Outlined

In a nutshell, Systems Intentionality posits that corporations manifest (in the dual senses of reveal and instantiate) their states of mind through their adopted or deployed systems of conduct, policies, and practices. Lacking natural minds, corporations necessarily work through systems of conduct, policies, and practices to engage purposively in and with the world. As Gordon J put it in *Productivity Partners*:

> A 'system of conduct' connotes 'an internal method of working' or a plan of procedure. Such a system may develop organically as a practice, operate at a level of policy or be a combination of practice and policy. Corporations 'think' and act through systems.[21]

Criminal Code Chapters 1 and 2: General Principles of Criminal Responsibility (Report, 1 December 1992); Australian Law Reform Commission, *Corporate Criminal Responsibility* (ALRC Final Report, April 2020) ch 2 [4.73]-[4.79], and the recommendations in ch 6.

15 *Royal Commission into the Casino Operator and Licence* (Report, October 2021) (RCCOL Report) vol I, 174-78 and vol III, 58-59; *Perth Casino Royal Commission* (Final Report, 4 March 2022) (PCRC Report) vol I, 50.

16 This analysis accepts that the endorsement in the High Court was necessarily partial and constrained, not least because it was limited to the issues arising in the case.

17 (2024) 419 ALR 30.

18 ibid [282], [307], [340].

19 ibid [143], [242], [246], applying ACL, ss 21 and 22.

20 See eg E Bant and R Faugno, 'Corporate Culture and Systems Intentionality: An Essential Part of the Regulatory Toolkit' [2023] JCLS 345; E Bant, 'Rethinking Corporate Groups: Insights from Systems Intentionality' (2025) 47 Syd LR 1; Bant, 'Corporate Mistake' (n 10).

21 *Productivity Partners Pty Ltd v Australian Competition and Consumer Commission* (2024) 419 ALR 30 [108] (citations omitted).

Systems Intentionality proposes that, by engaging in an objective process of interpretation or (better) construction of these corporate systems, it is possible to ascertain corporate mindsets, relevant to corporate responsibility.[22] Each case will depend on its particular facts, and the particular state-of-mind element or definition in issue. However, some broad rules of thumb assist in identifying the relationship between corporate systems and states of mind. Again, citing Gordon J:

> Systems are inherently purposive. Systems are objectively designed to achieve certain ends; they coordinate and connect steps and processes to an end. Knowledge of certain matters is often implicit in a system—for example, that a predatory business model will only be profitable if a certain class of vulnerable customer exists and is successfully exploited.[23]

Thus, the starting point for analysis is that all forms of corporate systems nudge, direct, and coordinate behaviours on the ground to achieve corporate purposes. The 'general' intentionality manifested through systems of conduct arises from the very fact of them being systems: systems, schemes, plans, strategies, processes, and equivalents all exist for a purpose—at the least to produce the coordinated conduct the subject of the scheme. In some cases, additionally, the systems will be geared, as a matter of objective interpretation or construction, to achieve certain outcomes from that coordinated conduct (a 'specific' intention).[24] Further, Systems Intentionality posits that corporations may be taken to know the critical features of their systems, required for them to deploy successfully (that is, according to their terms).[25] Otherwise, the successful deployment of a system depends upon accidental or coincidental application of its steps or elements in the correct, synchronised, way. While not impossible, this is sufficiently unlikely to warrant placing the onus of demonstrating (for example) accident or mistake onto the corporation that has deployed the system, according to its terms. Knowledge of other matters may also be implicit in a system, as Gordon J's observations make clear.

From these basic propositions, Systems Intentionality can be used to identify a wide range of doctrinal mental elements and associated normative standards relevant to responsibility.[26] Thus, suppose a mistake is made when 'a person's decision is based on incorrect data'.[27] On this definition, a mistake signifies that one of the person's reasons for action is vitiated or impaired because it does not accord with the true or correct

[22] cf *Meridian Global Funds Management Asia Ltd v Securities Commission* [1995] UKPC 26, [1995] 2 AC 500, 506–11: attribution is always 'a matter of interpretation' (at 507) or 'construction' (at 511).

[23] *Productivity Partners Pty Ltd v Australian Competition and Consumer Commission* (2024) 419 ALR 30 [108].

[24] Bant, 'Modelling' (n 10) 233–35, 246–48.

[25] ibid 239–40, 249–50.

[26] The model is neutral as to state-of-mind definitions, which may vary over jurisdictions, matters, and time. The model works as an analytical tool, to whichever definition applies.

[27] Edelman and Bant (n 6) 172. See also *Great Peace Shipping Ltd v Tsavliris Salvage (International) Ltd* [2002] EWCA Civ 1407, [2003] QB 679 [28]; *Roles v Pascall & Sons* [1911] 1 KB 982, 987; *Westpac Banking Corp v Hilliard* [2006] VSC 470 [211], approved on appeal in *Hilliard v Westpac Banking Corp* [2009] VSCA 211, (2009) 25 VR 139 [68].

state of affairs.[28] Systems Intentionality suggests that a genuine corporate mistake of this kind may arise where its system of conduct is not deployed or is not implemented correctly, including in the sense that one of the component steps is omitted or fails. The omitted or failed step vitiates the corporate reasons for action, as manifested in the 'true' or correct system of conduct. The mistake is generally disclosed by comparing the combination of steps adopted on the occasion in question with the true or correct system of conduct, as adopted or routinely deployed by the corporation.

In identifying the 'true', instantiated system,[29] against which claims of a corporate mistake must be assessed, care must be taken to adopt an appropriate level of generality, relevant to the legal issue at play.[30] Here, the model of Systems Intentionality posits an expansive approach to identifying, and then characterising, the instant system. Thus, systems of conduct commonly comprise both positive and negative (omitted) steps.[31] Omitted steps, including through 'default settings' that determine the way in which a system deploys at critical junctures or pressure points, are often very expressive of corporate choices, preferences, and overall intentions.[32] Elements are also commonly proactive and reactive (such as audit and remedial mechanisms). How a corporation responds to the impacts of its behaviour in the world itself reflects and sheds light on its capacities and choices as a normatively responsible juristic person.[33] It is the integrated system of positive and omitted, proactive and reactive, elements, viewed holistically and over time that most clearly manifests the corporate intention(s). Adopting an expansive temporal as well as structural lens to the task of interpreting or construing corporate states of mind with which a specific action was taken is appropriate, given that systems of conduct generally deploy repeatedly over time.[34] Thus, returning to corporate mistake, the longer that a system is deployed without adjustment, the less likely it becomes that an alleged 'mistake in the system' is indeed a 'mistake', rather than a step that, over time, has become an accepted (and intended) part of the system or, indeed, was an intended element from the outset. Adopting that broader lens, a better characterisation of the claimed 'systems error' may be that the conduct as instantiated was intended: the nature of the system is simply different from how it was formally represented.

[28] cf PA French, *Collective and Corporate Responsibility* (Columbia University Press 1984) 40, discussed in Bant, 'Modelling' (n 10) 233–34. An example is given in Section II.B below.

[29] On the evidence, both internal and external to the corporation, relevant to proving a 'system of conduct', see *Productivity Partners Pty Ltd v Australian Competition and Consumer Commission* (2024) 419 ALR 30 [110] (Gordon J) and Bant, 'Systems Intentionality: Theory and Practice' (n 10) 197.

[30] Bant, 'Systems Intentionality: Theory and Practice' (n 10) 197.

[31] E Bant, 'Corporate Evil: A Story of Systems and Silences' in P Crofts (ed), *Evil Corporations: Law, Culpability and Regulation* (Routledge 2024) 223.

[32] Strikingly apparent in the context of automated systems: see E Bant, 'Where's WALL-E: Corporate Fraud in the Digital Age' in PS Davies and H Tjio (eds), *Fraud and Risk in Commercial Law* (Hart 2024) 55, 69-73, and JM Paterson, E Bant, and H Cooney, '*Australian Competition and Consumer Commission v Google*: Deterring Misleading Conduct in Digital Privacy Policies' (2021) 26(3) Comms L 136. An example is given in Section II.B below.

[33] Adopting and adapting B Fisse, 'Reactive Corporate Fault' in E Bant (ed), *The Culpable Corporate Mind* (n 9) 139; PA French, 'The Principle of Responsive Adjustment in Corporate Moral Responsibility: The Crash on Mount Erebus' [1984] J Bus Ethics 101.

[34] See further Bant, 'Corporate Evil' (n 31) 223.

B. The Model Illustrated

This section illustrates the potential application of the model. Given that mistake is a recognised ground of rescission, it focuses on scenarios that illustrate the practical value of the model as a means to establish, but also to challenge, the presence of corporate mistake.

As I have explained elsewhere,[35] *Barclays Bank Ltd v WJ Simms Son & Cooke (Southern) Ltd*[36] provides a useful factual template to which Systems Intentionality reasoning may readily apply.[37] Put shortly, a bank clerk paid out on a countermanded cheque. The fact of a mistake on the part of the bank, in 'overlooking' the stop order, was not contested before Robert Goff J. However, clearly, the clerk was not a director or senior officer and so was not part of the bank's 'directing mind and will' on traditional attribution approaches.[38] A clerk might nonetheless constitute its 'responsible agent' for payments made at the service counter on a broader attribution approach, which looks to the actions and mindsets of the individual that has been allocated the company's decision-making powers.[39] However, Robert Goff J's judgment discloses no enquiry at all into the employee's identity or their subjective reasons for making the payment. This may be because they were acting in a purely clerical or executive capacity,[40] exercising no active judgment or discretion. Indeed, on a Systems Intentionality approach, whether they paid out by mistake, deliberately to impress a colleague, or maliciously, is neither here nor there. The only salient facts, considered by Robert Goff J in considerable detail, were that there was a system in place to deal with countermanded cheques and that this system was not followed. It is precisely these facts that support a finding of organisational mistake, as viewed through the lens of Systems Intentionality.

Another illustration, to countervailing effect, arises from the Australian 'fees for no services' cases.[41] A number of these involved banks charging dead customers fees for life insurance through automated fee deduction processes. Banks commonly claimed that this form of misconduct was an 'administrative error' or 'mistake'. In some cases, banks claimed that as directors and senior officers were wholly unaware of the problem,

[35] See further Bant, 'Corporate Mistake' (n 10).

[36] [1980] QB 677.

[37] ibid 684. See also *Chambers v Miller* (1862) 13 CBNS 125, 143 ER 50; *Chase Manhattan Bank NA v Israel-British Bank (London) Ltd* [1981] Ch 105, 115.

[38] *Lennard's Carrying Co v Asiatic Petroleum Co Ltd* [1915] AC 705, 713; *HL Boulton (Engineering) Co Ltd v TJ Graham and Sons Ltd* [1957] 1 QB 159, 172; *Tesco Supermarkets Ltd v Nattrass* [1972] AC 153, 170.

[39] *Meridian Global Funds Management Asia Ltd v Securities Commission* [1995] 2 AC 500, 506–11. See further R Leow, '*Meridian*, Allocated Powers, and Systems Intentionality Compared' in E Bant (ed), *The Culpable Corporate Mind* (Hart 2023) 119, 123-26; S Watterson, 'Agents and Organisation: Attribution Rules in Unjust Enrichment Claims' [2017] RLR 254, 264; C Mitchell, P Mitchell, and S Watterson (eds), *Goff & Jones on Unjust Enrichment* (10th edn, Sweet & Maxwell 2022) [9-67]–[9-76].

[40] Watterson (n 39) 264.

[41] Commonwealth of Australia, *Royal Commission into Misconduct in the Banking, Superannuation and Financial Services Industry* (FSRC Final Report, 1 February 2019) 136–64, the subject of repeated analysis in eg Bant, *The Culpable Corporate Mind* (n 10); E Bant, 'Catching the Corporate Conscience' [2022] LMCLQ 467; Bant, 'Corporate Evil' (n 31); Bant, 'Where's WALL-E' (n 32); E Bant, 'Rethinking Public Responsibility: Insights from Systems Intentionality' (2024) 52 UWAL Rev 121.

so too was the corporation. On this account, individual ignorance meant that there could be no corporate intention at all to engage in the impugned conduct.

Through the lens of Systems Intentionality, another interpretation is possible. Here, it is striking that the automated processes typically contained no audit or adjustment mechanism to respond to the inevitability that some customers (paying, after all, for life insurance) would die. Rather, the default setting of these 'set and forget' automated systems was to keep 'taking',[42] presumably until some manual intervention occurred. Yet no manual intervention process existed, leaving correction to ad hoc and isolated remediation. Tellingly, when the families of deceased customers complained, banks generally continued their automated takings while 'investigating' the problem.

On the model of Systems Intentionality, these basic features of the fee deduction systems manifested a range of corporate knowledge: (i) all fee deductions for life insurance from customers' accounts must be authorised; (ii) some customers for life insurance would evidently die, affecting existing authorisations; and (iii) unless there was a responsive mechanism in place, the bank would inevitably engage in unauthorised takings from those customers. Against that background, the decision to deploy the automated system *without* such a mechanism expresses an organisational choice to prefer profit over legality. To adapt and paraphrase Edelman J in *Productivity Partners*, while it can be accepted that the banks did not 'desire' effectively to steal from particular customers, as ends 'good' in themselves, their automated systems manifested a corporate choice to adopt unauthorised takings from customer accounts as a means to maximise profits.[43] From this perspective, the inevitable carrying out of unauthorised takings cannot be readily construed as arising from a mistake, 'systems error', or an unwitting accident. The systems were operating perfectly as designed, in the sense of 'according to their terms'. Rather, a characterisation of the banks' conduct as knowing and deliberate, and consequently, likely reckless and dishonest, is fortified by the banks' repeated responses to the inevitable consequences of their automated conduct, over time: a strong example of 'reactive corporate fault'.[44]

C. Systems, Directors, and Agents

We have seen that Systems Intentionality posits an organisational rather than individualistic approach to corporate responsibility. However, this does not necessitate some radical rejection of traditional corporate attribution rules. To the contrary, Systems Intentionality conceptualises the board of directors as the most fundamental of corporate decision-making systems that enable and guide corporate conduct. From this perspective, it makes sense that early attribution rules focused on the board as the

[42] Royal Commissioner Hayne's descriptor, FSRC Final Report (n 41).
[43] *Productivity Partners Pty Ltd v Australian Competition and Consumer Commission* (2024) 419 ALR 30 [242], [246]; see also [143].
[44] Fisse (n 33).

corporation's indubitable directing mind and will.[45] But beyond very small and hierarchical entities, these decision-making systems are hardly sufficient to enable most modern corporations to operate successfully. So, more diffused systems of conduct are deployed, such as through devolved lines of authority.[46] As expressed by Lord Hoffmann in *Meridian Global Funds Management Asia Ltd v Securities Commission*,[47] in all cases the question of attribution becomes 'whose act (or knowledge or state of mind) was *for this purpose* intended to count as the act etc of the company?'[48] This question of attribution is fundamentally one of interpretation or construction.[49] Beyond applicable statutory requirements, it generally requires interpreting or construing the *corporate structure*, and the *roles* of individuals acting 'as' the corporation for the purposes of the disputed transaction or transactions in issue.[50]

Systems Intentionality endorses this implicitly systemic approach to this inquiry. But it also makes transparent that systems of conduct through which a corporation 'thinks' and acts go beyond corporate hierarchies centred around apex individuals, to encompass coordinated teams of employees and agents, such as commonly occurs when employees act in accordance with 'standard operating procedures' and more granular and organic practices.[51] In adopting this more expansive approach, the model recognises proxy or 'vicarious conduct' (to be distinguished from vicarious liability) as integral to corporate existence.[52] Lacking hands and feet, corporations must always 'conduct' their business in the world through some independent means.[53] This may certainly be through individual natural or corporate agents, being separate legal entities, and having independent agency. But corporations frequently also act purposefully through teams of natural and corporate agents, across jurisdictions, space, and over time.[54]

[45] The relationship is most fully explored in E Bant, 'Rethinking Corporate Groups' (n 20). On this account, the model supplements traditional attribution rules, placing them on a more principled, organisational basis: cf *Productivity Partners Pty Ltd v Australian Competition and Consumer Commission* (2024) 419 ALR 30 [199] ('also') and [237] ('alternative'); *Automotive Invest Pty Ltd v Commissioner of Taxation* [2024] HCA 36, (2024) 419 ALR 342 [114]-[115], [135].

[46] R Leow, *Corporate Attribution in Private Law* (Hart 2022) 40–41. See also C Witting, 'The Place of Managers in the Corporate Governance Architecture' [2024] JCLS 267.

[47] [1995] 2 AC 500.

[48] ibid 506–11.

[49] ibid 507, 511.

[50] Worthington (n 1) 124–25. A systemic approach arguably avoids the difficulties associated with adopting a one-size, right-sided approach to discerning the 'purpose' for this inquiry, identified in Leow, *Corporate Attribution in Private Law* (n 46) 20–22.

[51] *Productivity Partners Pty Ltd v Australian Competition and Consumer Commission* [2024] HCA 27, (2024) 419 ALR 30 [108]. Leow also endorses the salience of corporate practices to reveal to whom the corporation's powers to act have been allocated, or delegated: Leow, *Corporate Attribution in Private Law* (n 46) 41. However, Leow may take a more restrictive, formal approach to construction of scope: 41–44.

[52] cf *CCIG Investments Pty Ltd v Schokman* [2023] HCA 21, (2023) 278 CLR 165 [48]-[81], helpfully distinguishing cases where a defendant's liability is primary, but founded on another party's acts (proxy or 'vicarious conduct'), which are attributed to the defendant, from true 'vicarious liability' where it is the other's *liability* that is ascribed to the defendant. Their Honours described 'vicarious conduct' as referring, 'loosely', to agency, in which the relevant acts formed part of a joint enterprise (and so, were agreed), or were procured, authorised, or ratified by the defendant. The possible tension between my broad conception of vicarious conduct and the traditional agency rules, and indeed Edelman J's expression of their application to systems of conduct in *Productivity Partners*, is explored at length in Bant, 'Rethinking Corporate Groups' (n 20).

[53] cf *Productivity Partners Pty Ltd v Australian Competition and Consumer Commission* (2024) 419 ALR 30 [236] on the corporation as 'heuristic'.

[54] Powerfully illustrated by the generational and iterative processes of developing even basic automated and algorithmic tools: see AS McConnell, *Code Complete* (2nd edn, Microsoft Press 2004) 502.

Further, systems of conduct may comprise automated and algorithmic tools that cannot strictly or sensibly be described as 'agents' (at least, not in the sense of having independent agency and capacity for responsibility).[55] The 'fees for no services' scenarios are examples. As Edelman J observed in *Productivity Partners*, a 'systems liability' approach (his Honour's preferred terminology) enables proof of state-of-mind elements relevant to corporate liability rules without requiring evidence to be brought of responsible individuals within the corporation, whose mental states can be attributed to the corporation.[56] By assessing the default settings, guiding parameters, and overall 'choice architecture' of an automated and algorithmic system, it becomes entirely possible to identify the corporate choices, values, intentions, and preferences sought to be achieved even through complex amalgams of agentic and non-agentic tools.[57]

While such an approach may seem novel, on closer reflection it seems clear that there is no sharp boundary between agentic and non-agentic systems of conduct, or 'mixed' elements of systems of conduct. Many systems of conduct seek actively to constrain the discretion or independent judgement of natural agents within the system: again, 'standard operating procedures' are a well-known example. And relevantly for current purposes, in many cases, individual employees within a corporate system of conduct will act in a purely executive capacity, applying no independent judgement at all to the task at hand. As we saw in *Barclays Bank v Simms*, an employee's state of mind will often be irrelevant to ascertaining the corporate intention with which some conduct occurred. Whether the employee was daydreaming, motivated by malicious or mischievous inclinations, trying to do their best or worst, the primary issue will generally be whether they performed their role correctly, that is, according to the terms of the system of conduct in which they were embedded. Where they have, an unimpaired corporate intention is manifested. Conversely, where the system has not deployed according to its terms (eg through some step failing or being omitted), corporate mistake may be present. Depending on the nature of the system, the private and subjective mindset of the employee may be irrelevant to that assessment.[58]

It follows that, even in cases of directors embedded within relevant corporate systems, where we commonly equate their subjective mental states with the corporation's 'mind and will', it may be neither necessary nor appropriate to determine the corporate purposes etc manifested by those systems through a subjective inquiry.[59] Recall that when corporations deploy a system of conduct, that system manifests a corporate 'general' intention to act. Suppose some step within a system goes awry. A system may stipulate, for example, that a director's authorisation of some transaction be conditional on

[55] Paterson and Bant, 'Automated Mistakes' (n 9) 265; Bant, 'Where's WALL-E' (n 32) 57-58.

[56] *Productivity Partners Pty Ltd v Australian Competition and Consumer Commission* (2024) 419 ALR 30 [198]-[200], [247]. For the common law's gradual recognition of corporate capacity to hold mental states, see S Walpole, 'Criminal Responsibility as a Distinctive Form of Corporate Regulation' (2020) 35 Aust J Corp Law 235; Bant, 'Corporate Mistake' (n 10) 125–28.

[57] Paterson and Bant, 'Automated Mistakes' (n 9); Bant, 'Where's WALL-E' (n 32).

[58] Bant, 'Corporate Mistake' (n 10) 134–41.

[59] ibid.

certain matters (the transaction being for less than a certain price, or for certain purposes). Where that consent is given in circumstances that do not meet the condition, the reasons why the director performed her role within the system incorrectly may not matter for the purposes of discerning the corporate state of mind. Consistently with the position of the clerical staff in *Barclays Bank v Simms*, the director may have been mistaken herself, or unthinking, or malicious. The critical point, for analytical purposes, is that the usual system of conduct (here, a transaction protocol) was not followed, or did not deploy, correctly, potentially manifesting a corporate mistake.[60] We return to this analysis when considering the role and nature of 'actual' authority, in the next section.

Finally, we have seen that, through an organisational lens, directors may be conceived as part of core corporate decision-making systems, required to transform unthinking 'shell' companies into purposive corporate persons. Reflecting this critical role, directors will have individual, positional[61] responsibilities owed to the corporation, which no doubt will be breached in cases of director fraud. In such a case, the corporation is, vis-à-vis the director, a victim of their fraud and may bring an action accordingly. Directors may also be independently liable to third parties, or through regulator action, as alternate or additional, principal wrongdoers arising from the facts of corporate wrongdoing.[62] Or they may constitute accessories to the corporate wrongdoing, through being knowingly concerned or involved in the wrong.[63] But these forms of liability must be kept strictly separate from the role of director 'as' the corporation, when acting as part of the corporate decision-making process vis-à-vis external parties. Generally, the very fact that the director's act or mind counted as the corporation's act or mind for the purposes of the impugned transaction explains why the fraud will have been effective. Through a de-personalised, systemic lens, the critical distinction is maintained between the director's positional liability and the corporation's responsibility for its systems of conduct, of which the director formed part.

[60] See also the discussion of *Tesco Supermarkets Ltd v Nattrass* [1972] AC 153 in Bant, 'Corporate Mistake' (n 10) 142.

[61] They will also owe personal responsibilities to a range of persons, potentially also including the corporation, which are independent of their position as director. A director who trashes his office in a rage commits a range of common law wrongs quite independently of his position within the company. These personal, and so too 'private', duties, such as pursuant to child maintenance legislation, can be put to one side here. cf Dr Tim Peters' conception of corporate office: T Peters, 'Corporate Office, Corporate Irresponsibility and the Constitutive Vicariousness of Corporate Power' in Crofts (ed), *Evil Corporations* (n 31) 141. Peters makes the point powerfully that performance of one's office becomes detached from full personal or private responsibility. Organisational conceptions of the corporation can serve to reconnect vicarious acts of office with direct corporate responsibility. As this chapter seeks to show, however, this does not absolve agents of their spectrum of responsibilities: these exist in parallel to and in support of the corporation's liabilities.

[62] *Standard Chartered Bank v Pakistan National Shipping Corp (Nos 2 and 4)* [2002] UKHL 43, [2003] 1 AC 959 [21]-[24], addressing the liability of a director in deceit for false statements made to a bank in order to obtain payment under a letter of credit in favour of the company; cited in *Lifestyle Equities CV v Ahmed* [2024] UKSC 17, [2025] AC 1 [44]. See also *4VVV Ltd v Spence* [2024] EWHC 2434 (Comm).

[63] As occurred in *Productivity Partners Pty Ltd v Australian Competition and Consumer Commission* (2024) 419 ALR 30: see eg [193], [194], [275], [279], [280]. See further *Lifestyle Equities CV v Ahmed* [2025] AC 1 [24]-[40], [52], on the analogous accessory liability of directors for wrongs committed by their company. See also *Australian Competition and Consumer Commission v Get Qualified Australia Pty Ltd (in liq) (No 2)* [2017] FCA 709, (2017) ATPR ¶42-548 [7].

D. Conclusions for Director Fraud: Illustrated

This section has outlined the model of Systems Intentionality, and its key implications for traditional conceptions of corporate attribution and responsibility that underpin corporate rescission. Thus, where the director acts as part of the identified corporate system of conduct for engaging in the impugned transaction, the analytical starting point is that the corporation will have acted intentionally vis-à-vis the external counterparty. The corporation will therefore be bound by the transaction. However, where director fraud has the consequence of subverting or vitiating the corporate reasons for action, expressed in the corporate system of conduct, director fraud may manifest a corporate mistake. This may support the possibility of corporate rescission of the impugned transaction. It is a separate question whether the corporation may bring a claim against its director for breach of a duty owed to the corporation arising from the director's misconduct.

Amongst other benefits, this systemic lens avoids the temptation of treating 'one-man companies' as warranting some special status, whereby the separate legal personhood of corporation and controller are collapsed.[64] It also explains when and why dishonest corporations should be both bound by and responsible for transactions involving external counterparties, and yet be permitted to recant and seek redress against directors who have led them astray, or third parties that have contributed to the corporate misconduct.

Consider the basic facts of *Stone & Rolls Ltd (in liq) v Moore Stephens*.[65] A one-man company (Stone & Rolls) was set up and used by its sole director and shareholder to perpetrate a series of frauds on third-party banks. By the time the frauds came to light, both the proceeds of those frauds and the director had disappeared. Under the new stewardship of its liquidator, the corporation sued its auditors in negligence for their seemingly abject failure to uncover the fraud over several years. The auditors successfully defended the case on the basis that the corporation could not be permitted to profit from its own wrongdoing.

As Professor Dame Sarah Worthington has demonstrated, this decision wrongly confounded the corporate form and the positional obligations owed by director and auditors alike.[66] The better view is that throughout the corporate misconduct, and from a traditional attribution perspective, the director was clearly the person whose acts and intentions counted for those of the company. Systems Intentionality endorses that conclusion but underscores the distinction between the positional obligations of the director and the corporation acting purposefully through a system of conduct of which the director formed part (or even, the whole). So far as the corporation's own responsibility is concerned, the focus must be on the corporate systems through which a

[64] Worthington (n 1) 124. See now (postdating Worthington's analysis) the careful discussion of the 'dis-attribution fallacy' of directors who have procured or assisted their company to breach some duty: *Lifestyle Equities CV v Ahmed* [2025] AC 1 [35], [37]–[40], [52], [81]–[85]. cf *Keller v LED Technologies Pty Ltd* [2010] FCAFC 55, (2010) 268 ALR 613, criticised in S Lo, 'Dis-Attribution Fallacy and Directors' Tort Liabilities' (2016) 30 Aust J Corp Law 215.

[65] [2009] UKHL 39, [2009] 1 AC 1391.

[66] Worthington (n 1) 121–22.

corporation 'thinks' and acts. As explained earlier, directors commonly form part of the core decision-making processes of the corporation. Where they act as part of those processes or systems, they act 'as' the company. Or to put it the other way around, the corporation manifests its decision-making through the system of conduct resulting in the transaction, of which the director formed part. That process of analysis and characterisation cannot be affected by whether the corporation is a one-person company or not. Thus, had Stone & Rolls been a huge, multinational corporation and the director was the person, within the corporate structure, tasked with dealing with the banks, the conclusion would be the same. Similarly, where a director is the chief or only component or element in the corporate system of conduct, the nature of the task of interpretation or construction remains the same: identify the corporate system of conduct implicated in the transaction and then engage in a process of characterisation to discern the corporate purposes and knowledge manifested through the system. Through this systemic lens, the analysis does not and cannot equate or confound the individual and corporation.

This analysis further underscores that the subversion of a prudent corporate system of conduct (eg a payment process, or protocol for approving a deal) by a rogue director may result in the corporation's intention to enter the contract with an external third party being vitiated. This may support corporate rescission for mistake but will not render the dealing void. Conversely, in some cases, of which *Stone & Rolls* was one, the corporate system of conduct may be inherently corrupt.[67] In such cases, the corporation will be knowingly engaged in the misconduct and must be held to account for it vis-à-vis third parties. There will be no corporate mistake, given that the (corrupt) system of conduct deployed as it was designed to (ie in accordance with its terms), and so no grounds for denying or reducing corporate responsibility for that misconduct, or ground for rescission founded in mistake.[68]

Finally, on this systemic account, it is worthwhile re-emphasising that a fraudulent director within a one-man company certainly may be understood as abusing the corporation's inherent structural vulnerability to and reliance on the director. The corporation can and should be permitted both to seek relief on its own account from and against the director, as well as third parties who fail to assist it in those efforts, such as incompetent auditors. There is nothing inherently improper about this and it may indeed be critical for rehabilitation of the corporate person under the influence of more benign and prudent leadership, for example in the form of a liquidator or new board. Here, it is no answer for the fraudulent director to say that the corporation necessarily 'knew' of their fraud and so waived, or shared, or conspired in the director's misconduct.[69] These internally facing accountability mechanisms, however, must not

[67] Bribery practices are another example: see Section III.A.

[68] The possibility of rescission for abuse of authority provides an additional and hence potentially valuable route to rescission: see Section III.B.

[69] The province of the 'Hampshire Land principle', named after *Re Hampshire Land Co (No 2)* [1896] 2 Ch 743, and explained by Worthington (n 1) 126–28. See also *Bilta (UK) Ltd (in liq) v Nazir* [2015] UKSC 23, [2016] AC 1 [7], [37]–[44], in particular; see also *Crown Prosecution Service v Aquila Advisory Ltd* [2021] UKSC 49, [2021] 1 WLR 5666 [59]-[60]. cf *Grimaldi v Chameleon Mining NL (No 2)* [2012] FCAFC 6, (2012) 200 FCR 296 [282]-[286].

be conflated with the issue of whether the corporation is bound by and responsible for transactions entered into with external parties, pursuant to the director's wrongful influence or abuse of authority. And as explained, such contracts entered as a result of the director's fraud will generally be voidable, not void.

III. 'Actual' Authority and Director Fraud

A. Construing the Scope of Actual Authority

A related complicating factor in determining the boundary between void and voidable contracting behaviour concerns the scope of a director's authority to act for the company. There is authority for the view that an agent can have no *actual* authority to act contrary to the corporation's interests.[70] If this approach is adopted, corporate transactions entered into through the conduct of a fraudulent director will not bind the company. After all, there can be no corporate interest in being induced to act to defraud innocent third parties, nor for a corporation to be, itself, a victim of director fraud. Either option brings serious financial, reputational, and even existential risks.[71]

However, the previous section suggests that this approach may unduly protect the corporation from the consequences of what may well have been corporate-intentional behaviour. The better approach is to acknowledge that, where the corporation acted with intention through some system of conduct in which the director played a part, it is prima facie responsible for that conduct. The corporation can, of course, sue the director separately for breach of their positional obligations to the corporation arising from their misconduct, but that is a quite separate matter from whether the corporation is bound by its acts vis-à-vis the external counterparty. This means that relief from transactions entered into with outsiders to the corporation will depend on the corporation satisfying the conditions of rescission, such as proving the existence of a relevant corporate mistake arising from the director's fraud, and that the counterparty sufficiently knew of or participated in the director's fraud. The outsider is otherwise entitled to assume that the corporation's internal processes resulting in the transaction were operating according to their terms.[72]

If, then, director fraud does not automatically take director conduct outside the scope of the director's authority, how do we know when the line between authorised

[70] The line of modern authorities commencing with *Hopkins v TL Dallas Group Ltd* [2004] EWHC 1379 (Ch), [2005] 1 BCLC 543 [88], [87] is carefully unpacked and criticised in Worthington (n 1) 132–39. See further *Philipp v Barclays Bank UK plc* [2023] UKSC 25, [2024] AC 346 [70]–[74]; but cf [101]–[105], which aligns with the analysis of corporate mistake offered here.

[71] *Australian Securities and Investments Commission v Cassimatis (No 8)* [2016] FCA 1023, (2016) 336 ALR 209 [483]–[484].

[72] The relationship between ostensible authority, the 'rule in *Turquand's* case', also known as the 'indoor management rule' and statutory provisions such as Corporations Act 2001 (Cth), ss 128 and 129, expanding indoor management assumptions on the part of persons external to the corporation must await another day, but they appear largely aligned in outcome to this analysis: see further Section IV.

and unauthorised conduct is crossed, such that the director's conduct is not attributed to the corporation? To put this in systemic terms, when is a system of conduct in which a director plays some role *the corporation's* system of conduct? Individualistic attribution approaches tend to frame this question as one of the scope of a director's actual authority, express or 'implied'.[73] This is a matter of objective interpretation or construction, looking at the facts and context as a whole.[74] Thus, while explicit authorisation will generally arise through formal mechanisms (such as resolutions of the board of directors), actual authorisation may also be construed from the corporation's course of dealing.[75]

Systems Intentionality similarly directs attention to whether the system of conduct was objectively 'adopted or deployed' by a corporation (including, to adapt Edelman and Steward JJ's recent phrase, where it is procured, authorised, or ratified, or adopted as part of a joint enterprise).[76] Certainly, senior officers of a corporation may have known of, or expressly authorised, the impugned system of conduct.[77] However, Systems Intentionality posits that even in the absence of such express authorisation, the terms of the overall corporate arrangement may be express, or inferred[78] from the conduct of the corporate principal and agent and the circumstances of the case, including the course of business between agent and principal.[79] The very recognition of 'practices' within the model of Systems Intentionality as constituting corporate systems reflects this reality.[80]

This approach reinforces, therefore, the proposition that the fact that directors behave badly, even in breach of express (formal) contractual terms, does not mean their contributions do not form part of the corporate principal's business model, or system of conduct, for which harmful, external consequences the principal is responsible.[81]

[73] *Freeman & Lockyer v Buckhurst Park Properties (Mangal) Ltd* [1964] 2 QB 480, 502.

[74] cf *Meridian Global Funds Management Asia Ltd v Securities Commission* [1995] 2 AC 500: the question is always 'a matter of interpretation' (at 507) or 'construction' (at 511).

[75] cf *Hely-Hutchinson v Brayhead Ltd* [1968] 1 QB 549, 560–61 discussing the 'set-up' of the company decision-making processes. This reflects what would be understood in Systems Intentionality terms as the adopted practices of the company. Roskill J's factual analysis was approved on appeal by Lord Denning MR (at 583, 584), Lord Wilberforce (at 587), and Lord Pearson (at 592) in terms of actual authority 'implied' from the course of conduct.

[76] *CCIG Investments Pty Ltd v Schokman* [2023] HCA 21, (2023) 278 CLR 165 [50]; see also at [55], [62], [66]. cf the more limited formulation expressed in *Productivity Partners Pty Ltd v Australian Competition and Consumer Commission* (2024) 419 ALR 30 [237], discussed in Bant, 'Rethinking Corporate Groups' (n 20).

[77] *Productivity Partners Pty Ltd v Australian Competition and Consumer Commission* (2024) 419 ALR 30 [237] (Edelman J); *Australian Competition and Consumer Commission v Get Qualified Australia Pty Ltd (in liq) (No 2)* (2017) ATPR ¶42–548 [179], [190].

[78] cf 'implied': inference necessarily being a matter of objective construction, rather than (potentially) subjective intention. Again, this underscores that we are here concerned with construing the corporation's acts vis-à-vis an external counterparty, not with the corporation's possible claims internally as against a delinquent director.

[79] See eg *Australian Competition and Consumer Commission v Cornerstone Investment Aust Pty Ltd* [2016] FCA 445 [221]-[222], [225]-[227]; *Cargill Australia Ltd v Viterra Malt Pty Ltd (No 28)* [2022] VSC 13 [3088]; cf [3091] and [3092]. This is consistent with the idea of implied actual authority: *Hely-Hutchinson v Brayhead Ltd* [1968] 1 QB 549; *Brick and Pipe Industries Ltd v Occidental Life Nominees Pty Ltd* [1992] 2 VR 279. This expansive approach means, in turn, a limited role for 'ostensibly authorised' systems of conduct, discussed below in Section IV.

[80] *Productivity Partners Pty Ltd v Australian Competition and Consumer Commission* (2024) 419 ALR 30 [108]: 'a system may develop organically as a practice, operate at a level of policy or be a combination of practice and policy.'

[81] *Australian Competition and Consumer Commission v Australian Institute of Professional Education Pty Ltd (in liq) (No 3)* [2019] FCA 1982 [33].

Consistently with this analysis, rather than focusing on the formal terms of individual agency arrangements, Australian courts applying its statutory prohibitions on unconscionable systems of conduct have been willing and able to construe the impugned system of conduct, and the corporate state of mind it manifests, as a whole. While encouraged by the statutory context, this broad approach to the objective process of interpretation or construction is, arguably, a generally applicable one:[82] 'identification, assessment and characterisation of the system of conduct is, by reference to the totality of the circumstances, both internal and external to the corporation.'[83]

Rebecca Faugno and I have argued elsewhere that this approach is apt to reveal the true intentionality and culpability of corporations that have, for example, adopted corrupt practices in their business models.[84] Thus, in one such case, Rolls-Royce engaged in widespread and long-standing bribery practices over many years, and across many jurisdictions. Sometimes, directors were caught with their hands in the till. In other cases, only lower-level individuals could be identified. In deferred prosecution agreement approval proceedings following exposure of the problems, the liability consequences for Rolls-Royce sharply diverged on traditional attribution approaches.[85] Where directors were clearly implicated, the corporation was directly responsible for the corrupt conduct. Where middle management or more junior employees were caught, the corporation was liable for the much less culpable offence of 'failure to prevent bribery'. This divergence is problematic: the malpractices were 'endemic' to the corporation: they were how Rolls-Royce did business. Through the lens of Systems Intentionality, and whether or not specific directors were found with their hands in the till, from time to time, and jurisdiction to jurisdiction, this was corporate-deliberate malpractice. And no formal, glossy website policy, or contractual undertaking or exclusion, to the contrary could make a difference to that conclusion.

When discovered, and given the ubiquity of the problem, the very existence of Rolls-Royce was imperilled.[86] Again, it could hardly be in a corporation's interests to engage in such criminal malpractices.[87] And in all cases, no doubt, the conduct was in breach of a wide range of directors' and employees' contractual and other positional obligations.

[82] *Freeman & Lockyer v Buckhurst Park Properties (Mangal) Ltd* [1964] 2 QB 480; *Hely-Hutchinson v Brayhead Ltd* [1968] 1 QB 549.

[83] *Productivity Partners Pty Ltd v Australian Competition and Consumer Commission* (2024) 419 ALR 30 [110]. See also *Freeman & Lockyer v Buckhurst Park Properties (Mangal) Ltd* [1964] 2 QB 480; *Hely-Hutchinson v Brayhead Ltd* [1968] 1 QB 549.

[84] Bant and Faugno (n 20).

[85] *Serious Fraud Office v Rolls-Royce plc* [2017] Lloyd's Rep FC 249. As the Australian Law Reform Commission has explained, the same attribution enquiries affect civil and criminal corporate responsibility: ALRC Final Report (n 14) para 3.71; A uniform approach is also appropriate if, as we are told, the state of a corporation's mind is (like that of a natural person) a matter of fact: *Edgington v Fitzmaurice* (1885) 29 Ch D 459, 483; *Warner-Lambert Company LLC v Generics (UK) Ltd* [2018] UKSC 56, [2019] 3 All ER 95 [171].

[86] It was only because the corporation had wholly transformed, so that it was no longer the criminogenic person of former times, that a deferred prosecution agreement was approved: *Serious Fraud Office v Rolls-Royce plc* [2017] Lloyd's Rep FC 249 [62]. A similar approach was taken to the problematic corporate culture that infected the Crown Casino group of companies, in the Victorian and Perth Royal Commissions. As Commissioner Finkelstein put it: 'systemic and sustained change is needed for a culpable corporation to reform its character, as revealed through its systems, policies and processes': RCCOL Report (n 15) 178, para 6.101.

[87] *Australian Securities and Investments Commission v Cassimatis (No 8)* (2016) 336 ALR 209.

But to say that, accordingly, conduct performed by its agents in implementing Rolls-Royce's bribery practices did not belong (could not be attributed) to the corporation, including as against external counterparties, is arguably nonsensical. Yet we have seen that this should be the conclusion reached from the view, criticised earlier, that a corporate agent has no 'actual' authority to act against the corporation's interests, with the consequence that all such dealings are void. So far as director misconduct was concerned, that position contradicts basic attribution rules. It also requires that the question of authority must be interpreted or construed restrictively, in formalistic terms and contrary to the reality of corporate practices. A better approach is that questions of actual authority must be assessed as a matter of substance, by reference to the system of conduct as actually adopted or deployed. To repeat the point made earlier, this recognises that a director operating as part of a corporate process, who subverts its usual operation, may have committed a range of wrongs vis-à-vis the corporation. Indeed, even where a corporation has become criminogenic, this does not and should not stop the corporation (under the later influence of more ethical parties) suing its directors for breaches of duty. That course will often be quite right and proper, supporting or enabling rehabilitation of the corporate citizen, as ultimately occurred in Rolls-Royce's case.[88] But this possibility is quite a separate matter from whether the corrupt conduct was, at the time it took place, corporate conduct, so exposing the corporation to obligation and liability alike to third parties and to enforcement or penalty proceedings by public authorities. Importantly, on this analysis, there is no whiff of corporate mistake that could support rescission as against good faith counterparties (or any relevant defences or mitigating considerations for remedy or penalty).

Adopting another scenario, suppose a director is the designated person within the corporate structure for signing publishing deals.[89] Viewed in the expansive way encouraged by Systems Intentionality, this process will presumably have other, key elements preceding the point of signature: a nominated person or team who identifies and negotiates with the author early in the process; perhaps required integrity checks comprising both manual and automated, or algorithmic, elements; quality assurance steps, including independent review; and so on. Consistently with the analysis of the facts in *Barclays Bank v Simms* offered earlier, one of these broader steps could founder or misdeploy, yielding (on the Systems Intentionality analysis) a potential corporate error. None of these would be expected to render the transaction void rather than voidable. Rescission of the publication deal on the ground of corporate mistake would depend on (amongst other matters) whether the contracting party, the author, induced or knew of the failure.[90] For example, the author may have misrepresented some matter that resulted in the deal clearing a hurdle stage at an earlier phase in the process, contrary to the usual requirements. In those circumstances, it may be possible for the corporation

[88] Bant and Faugno (n 20).
[89] Worthington (n 1) 132. cf Leow, *Corporate Attribution in Private Law* (n 46) 42.
[90] *Taylor v Johnson* (1983) 151 CLR 422.

to rescind the transaction, notwithstanding that the director has 'signed off' on that transaction.

Suppose, then, that the director signs a publishing contract in circumstances that are contrary to the corporation's interests, dishonestly and in breach of their fiduciary obligations to the company. On an individualistic attribution approach, and taking a substantive approach to the question of characterising the relevant corporate structure, it is clear that 'the nominated [director] is the person whose acts count as the acts of the company for the purposes of entering into such deals. This is regardless of whether the contract turns out to be against the company's interests, motivated by improper purposes, negligent or disloyal.'[91] Pursuant to traditional (individualistic) attribution rules, the focus 'is simply on *which person*, within that internal structure, is the appropriate person to act for the company in the given contractual deal. This is a question about the *scope* of the individual's role in the company.'[92] The conduct here is within scope, notwithstanding that it is against the corporation's interests, or to further the director's personal interest.

Through the organisational lens of Systems Intentionality, this focus on the relevant corporate structure, and within it the role of discrete officers and agents, is innate and central in every case. One asks: was the corporate process (procedure, system, method) for signing up the author on the instance in question the usual corporate system for this transactional purpose (albeit one of its constituent steps misfired)? If so, then the conduct was the corporation's and manifested its general purpose, whatever the motivations of the individuals who contributed to that systemic conduct. Far from the transaction being void as beyond authority, the corporation will be bound to the dealing. The corporation will then need to establish the conditions for rescinding the contract as against the counterparty, including that they sufficiently knew of or induced the grounds for rescission.

Meridian itself may provide another illustration of the same point. As is well known, in that case, Koo was the chief investment officer of the corporate appellant, Meridian. Ng was its senior portfolio manager. Koo and Ng misused their corporate authority to buy and sell shares, as part of a secret scheme to gain control of another company. Lord Hoffmann explained that a statutory obligation on the company arose in the circumstances of the case to make immediate disclosure of the purchase of the shares. In this case, the directors of Meridian were wholly ignorant of Koo and Ng's secret agenda and misconduct. Nonetheless, Koo and Ng were the relevant persons within the corporate hierarchy with authority to engage in this sort of share trading, and therefore the relevant persons who acted 'as' the company for the statutory purpose. As Lord Hoffmann observed: '[t]he fact that Koo did the deal for a corrupt purpose and did not give such notice because he did not want his employers to find out cannot . . . affect the attribution of [corporate] knowledge and the consequent duty to notify.'[93]

[91] Worthington (n 1) 136.
[92] ibid 137–38.
[93] *Meridian Global Funds Management Asia Ltd v Securities Commission* [1995] 2 AC 500, 511.

B. The Role of 'Abuse of Authority'

Worthington advocates in these circumstances for an 'abuse of actual authority' analysis, whereby the fact of abuse is relevant to the company's rights against its defaulting agent (for our purposes, a director). By contrast, the 'scope'/'whose acts' attribution question is relevant between the principal and the third party. It follows that abuse of authority generally will result in voidable, not void, transactions. It may be that 'abuse of authority' is a related wrong to breach of the no-conflict fiduciary duties vis-à-vis the external counterparty, which also support rescission on the part of the wronged principal.[94] In this volume, Professor Lionel Smith argues that rescission arising from misuse of fiduciary power does not arise in response to a breach of duty in the Hohfeldian sense.[95] Rather, it is a condition for the fully valid exercise of that power. Resolution of these views lies outside the scope of this chapter. Both provide arguably additional grounds for rescission that do not require proof of corporate mistake. This may be helpful where rescission for mistake is not possible: for example where the corporate systems of conduct reflected genuinely corrupt corporate purposes, as in the *Stone & Rolls* and bribery scenarios.

For current purposes, it must suffice to note that fiduciaries can be understood to serve to extend their principal's autonomy in decision-making.[96] Returning to observations made earlier, there is little doubt that directors serve as a key decision-making structure for corporations. They necessarily wield enormous influence over the corporate person's autonomy in decision-making. Indeed, without them or equivalent core decision-making organs (such as shareholders voting in general meeting), corporations are mere zombies. In that light, Equity's fiduciary prohibitions on directors acting in circumstances of conflict serve to focus and police the directors' necessarily excessive or undue influence over the corporation's decision-making. These rules arguably have the consequence that, where a corporation acts under the influence of a director in conflict, the corporation's decision-making has necessarily been subverted.[97] Through the lens of Systems Intentionality, abuse of authority therefore likely provides a related, additional reason for rescission as between corporation and external counterparty, as well as (potentially) a form of positional wrongdoing which may support the director's independent liability, as between director and corporation. This seems largely consistent with Worthington's and Smith's analyses, albeit reached through an organisational (as opposed to more individualistic) lens.

[94] cf *Great Investments Ltd v Warner* [2016] FCAFC 85, (2016) 243 FCR 516 [55].

[95] Chapter 6 of this book (L Smith, 'Rescission in the Context of Fiduciary Relationships'). See further Smith, *The Law of Loyalty* (n 5) 57–60, 172–82.

[96] JM Paterson and E Bant, 'Mortgage Brokers, Regulatory Failure and Statutory Design' (2020) 31 JBFLP 7, 11–13; Leow, *Corporate Attribution in Private Law* (n 46) 43; L Smith, 'Fiduciary Relationships: Ensuring the Loyal Exercise of Judgement on Behalf of Another' (2014) 130 LQR 608, 613.

[97] M Davis, 'Introduction' in M Davis and A Stark (eds), *Conflict of Interest in the Professions* (OUP 2001) 3, 12, 16.

C. Conclusion

This section has sought to demonstrate how the holistic perspective of Systems Intentionality addresses the bounds and nature of 'actual' agent authority, in cases where directors misuse their authority to act for their corporate principal. Here, a key takeaway is that care must be taken not to collapse the distinctions between the positions as between principal and wrongdoing agent, and the principal and contracting third parties. Thus, acts done in abuse of authority may provide good grounds for bringing a claim of breach of contract against the director, or a tort of abuse of authority, or equitable breach of duty, amongst others. But these acts may still bind the corporation vis-à-vis the contracting party. From a systems perspective, the question is whether the transaction resulted from the corporation's (adopted or deployed) system concerned with, or geared towards, that form of transaction, so constituting corporate-intentional behaviour. In some cases, as in the bribery and Stone & Rolls scenarios, the misconduct will be corporate-intentional and manifest no corporate mistake, notwithstanding director fraud. In others, corporate mistake arising from director fraud may be present, opening up the possibility of corporate rescission. We have seen that another ground of rescission, namely of misuse or abuse of authority, may be possible. Importantly, on both mistake and misuse of authority approaches, whether the instant system operated properly or not is a question of internal governance for the corporation to assess and remediate, as against the director. In the absence of some knowledge or involvement, third parties cannot be expected to know of or take responsibility for, for example, some mis-deployment or error within a corporation's internal system.[98] Transactions entered into by the corporation through director fraud will therefore be voidable, not void.

IV. W(h)ither Ostensible Authority?

The final point to make, which must now be made very briefly, is the role for general law and statutory conceptions of ostensible authority on this analysis.[99] 'Ostensible' or 'apparent' authority arises where a principal represents that the agent has actual authority to act on the principal's behalf. Its basis in corporate contexts is debated, with support for it falling within the principles of estoppel,[100] or as promoting various grounds of

[98] See further Section IV.

[99] For discussion of the interplay between ostensible authority, the 'indoor management rule', or the rule in *Turquand's* case, and the expansive and supplementary statutory provisions of the Corporations Act 2001 (Cth), ss 128 and 129, addressing statutory indoor management assumptions arising from 'dealings' between a fraudulent agent and external counterparty, see *Caratti v Mammoth Investments Pty Ltd* [2016] WASCA 84, (2016) 50 WAR 84 [337], [380], [466]-[511], [529].

[100] cf *Freeman & Lockyer v Buckhurst Park Properties (Mangal) Ltd* [1964] 2 QB 480, 503 adopted in *Philipp v Barclays Bank UK plc* [2024] AC 346 [76], and *Caratti v Mammoth Investments Pty Ltd* (2016) 50 WAR 84 [275], [320], [326]-[334] (discussing the different juridical bases for the rule advanced in *Northside Developments Pty Ltd v Registrar-General* (1990) 170 CLR 146).

policy.[101] A key practical consideration supporting the doctrine is the difficulty, sometimes impossibility, of external counterparties ascertaining that a corporation's internal processes have been followed.[102]

As Sections II and III have explained, Systems Intentionality posits that corporations manifest their states of mind through their adopted or deployed systems of conduct, policies, and practices. The existence and nature of a corporate system of conduct is a matter of objective interpretation or construction. A corporation acting through its systems of conduct will therefore innately represent, and also instantiate or realise, its corporate intention. Where directors act as part of the corporation's relevant system of conduct for entering an impugned transaction, the corporation will have acted purposefully, even if it transpires that the particular system misfired for some reason. The mis-deployment of a corporate system may manifest a corporate mistake, but does not necessarily mean that the corporation did not act with intention. Rectifying the future deployment of the system of conduct, to avoid future corporate mistakes, is an internal matter for the corporation to address.

Even more pointedly, as Section III explains, a director may well be performing their role within a corporate system of conduct, notwithstanding that (for example) it is entirely contrary to formal corporate policy, and indeed the law. Corporations that engage in bribery practices often involve this sort of director misconduct: the directors may be both assisting and performing the corporation's purposive act, and all in defiance of existing compliance obligations and undertakings.[103] Indeed, even where a director subverts the applicable corporate process, if it *is* the applicable corporate process, then it may still be a corporate-intentional act and therefore 'authorised' as a matter of organisational (structural, procedural) reality.

This strongly objective and contextual approach to construction of corporate-intentional acts likely reduces the need and role for ostensible authority. Where, by contrast, the director is operating wholly outside the bounds of any true (de facto) corporate system, any representation as to their authority to do so would need to be made by the corporation. In so doing, the corporation may be adopting the director's conduct as its own.[104] In such circumstances, ostensible authority will again not be necessary.

For current purposes, it is only possible to acknowledge this overlap and alignment between operation of general law and statutory conceptions of ostensible authority, and the objective approach to interpretation or construction posited by Systems Intentionality, in assessing how corporations 'think' and act through their systems of conduct.[105]

[101] *Freeman & Lockyer v Buckhurst Park Properties (Mangal) Ltd* [1964] 2 QB 480, 505; *Northside Developments Pty Ltd v Registrar-General* (1990) 170 CLR 146, 198, 207.

[102] *Caratti v Mammoth Investments Pty Ltd* (2016) 50 WAR 84 [335]; *Northside Developments Pty Ltd v Registrar-General* (1990) 170 CLR 146 164–65, 175-77, 189; *Philipp v Barclays Bank UK plc* [2024] AC 346 [78].

[103] See eg *Serious Fraud Office v Rolls-Royce plc* [2017] Lloyd's Rep FC 249, examined in Bant and Faugno (n 20).

[104] Discussed in Section III.A.

[105] The analysis seems largely aligned, or consistent, with the courts' approach to Corporations Act 2001 (Cth), ss 128 and 129, which govern the circumstances in which statutory 'indoor management' assumptions apply: see eg *Caratti v Mammoth Investments Pty Ltd* (2016) 50 WAR 84 [148], [380] and the discussion of objective approaches to characterising parties' dealings. Where they apply, the corporation is bound by the transaction: *Caratti v Mammoth Investments Pty Ltd* (2016) 50 WAR 84 [158]-[159], [169], [465]-[511], [593]. cf Worthington (n 1)

V. Conclusion

The purpose of this chapter was to chart the boundaries of void and voidable transacting by corporations in cases of director fraud and in doing so to illuminate the province of corporate rescission. Its simple premise is that, to navigate that landscape, it is helpful to understand how corporations 'think' and act through their systems of conduct. These systems must be assessed through an objective process of interpretation or construction by reference to the real-life, actual, or instantiated systems of conduct, policies, and practices. Through this lens, corporations may engage in purposive conduct even where a director has acted fraudulently. It is precisely because the director is the relevant 'cog in the machine'[106] for the purposes of the corporate system at hand that they will generally be well situated to commit fraud on behalf of, or upon, the corporation, for their personal benefit. In such cases, the corporation can and should be able to sue the director for breaches of their positional duties. These breaches may be contractual, equitable, tortious (as in an 'abuse of authority' claim), statutory, or some combination of these. However, in such cases, because the director is the relevant cog in the machine, it will be very difficult on this systemic analysis to find that their conduct, as part of the corporate system, cannot relevantly be attributed to the corporation. The fact that a corporation's organisational intention (manifested through the deployed system of conduct) was undermined, subverted, or vitiated through director fraud does not necessarily stop it from being the corporation's generally intended conduct. The corporate intention may, rather, simply have been vitiated. On this analysis, the transaction resulting from its intended conduct will be voidable, not void, and belongs in the territory of rescission.

Does this mean that a corporation can never deny a director acted 'as' the corporation, so as to bind the corporation? To put it another way, when might a director act in such a way that the corporation can be said to give 'no consent' to the transaction, being ignorant of or powerless to prevent the director misconduct, so as to support a conclusion that the resultant transaction is void? Here, as previously discussed, we might think that a corporation, as an inherently inert entity, is particularly susceptible to the influence of its directors. Directors help transform shell corporations into purposive entities. No doubt this is why they are subject to stringent fiduciary duties, which require that inherently undue (excessive) influence be exercised in the corporation's interests. Equity's conflict rules here are, arguably, particularly powerful expressions of the law's concerns to protect the corporation's decision-making processes. Abuse of influence (or abuse of authority) may operate in a supportive and related way. Does

142 on the position at general law. Also echoing the position for rescission, s 128(4) disentitles a person to make an assumption in s 129 when the person, at the time of the relevant dealings, knew or suspected that the assumption was incorrect. cf *Philipp v Barclays Bank UK plc* [2024] AC 346 [70]–[74], favouring an apparent authority analysis, but then adopting a mistake analysis at [101]–[105] that reflects the actual authority/corporate mistake approach adopted here.

[106] *Tesco Supermarkets Ltd v Nattrass* [1972] AC 153, discussed in Bant, 'Corporate Mistake' (n 10) 142.

this pervasive influence, and corresponding corporate helplessness, mean that a corporation will sometimes be 'powerless' to prevent rogue directors from misbehaving, or will be 'ignorant' of the very fact of transacting by rogue directors, at least in some cases? As explained at the outset of this chapter, if a corporation had no intention at all to enter a transaction, it may be more likely to be void at the outset.

I think the category of cases in which a director may act *as a director*, and yet the corporation will simultaneously be ignorant or powerless to prevent the act, so as to deny any corporate consent (however severely vitiated) to the transaction, must be limited. Again, this requires a systemic analysis. A director is inherently part of a corporation's baseline decision-making systems. The director would have to be operating outside any extant corporate system in order for them to be acting in a wholly unauthorised way. And in those cases, the director may be conceptualised as acting privately, on their own account. The fact that such a person is a director may provide the context in which the misconduct occurred, but they were not acting, or misbehaving, 'as' a director. A director who raids the corporate bar for drinks for their child's twenty-first birthday party may be most simply characterised as a thief.

6

Rescission in the Context of Fiduciary Relationships

*Lionel Smith**

I. Introduction

In 1989, Mr Justice William Gummow said:

> Breach of fiduciary duty brings into play a range of remedies. They include: injunction, prohibitory and mandatory; rescission of transactions between principal and fiduciary; declaration and enforcement of constructive trust in respect of assets acquired in breach of duty; account of profits wrongly made, that is, a pecuniary rather than an *in specie* remedy; and compensation for loss inflicted by breach of duty.[1]

This is a long list. It could be longer still; as we will see, rescission of other transactions is also possible. But it would be a mistake to think that 'breach of fiduciary duty' is a single wrong, whose commission activates all these potential consequences. There are multiple fiduciary duties, since a 'fiduciary duty' is nothing but a duty that arises from a fiduciary relationship, just as a 'contractual duty' is a duty that arises from a contractual relationship.[2] There are many ways to breach these diverse fiduciary duties, and each of the remedies on that long list is logically related to the duty that the remedy exists to protect. Indeed, if we are to be particularly careful, we would say that many of the rules of fiduciary law are not 'duties' in the strictest sense of that word. They are rules of law and non-compliance with them has legal consequences, but they are not duties whose violation may lead, for example, to an order for compensation. If this seems like a strange claim, we need only remember that a contract may be rescinded for innocent misrepresentation or for undue influence. Neither of those involves the breach of a duty in the strict sense, but both of them allow rescission.

In the same way, many rules of fiduciary law have important legal consequences that do not depend on the breach of a duty. The Supreme Court of the United Kingdom has

* Professor of Comparative Law, University of Oxford, and Professorial Fellow of Brasenose College, Oxford, United Kingdom. I intended to present a draft of this paper at the symposium in Oxford on 14 March 2025, but I was unable to attend. On short notice, my generous friend and colleague, Robert Stevens, presented on my behalf, and by all accounts did a better job than I would have. I thank him, and I thank also the editors for their helpful suggestions.

[1] W Gummow, 'Compensation for Breach of Fiduciary Duty' in T Youdan (ed), *Equity, Fiduciaries and Trusts* (Carswell 1989) 57, 61.

[2] For a full argument, see L Smith, 'Prescriptive Fiduciary Duties' (2018) 37 UQLJ 261.

recently affirmed the holding in *Regal (Hastings) Ltd v Gulliver*[3] that when a fiduciary acquires an unauthorised profit, the fiduciary's obligation to hold that profit for the benefit of the beneficiary does not actually depend on any breach of duty, fiduciary or otherwise.[4] That obligation is nothing but an aspect of the accountability that applies to all fiduciaries in relation to the fiduciary relationship, from the moment the relationship is constituted. It is fiduciary accountability, but not, if we speak carefully, accountability for breach of fiduciary duty.

Of course, it is not possible to explore all of the rules and duties of fiduciary law in a chapter on rescission in the fiduciary context. But the points just made are important. First, in the fiduciary context there are two distinct patterns of rescission and, in each of them, the justification for rescission is quite different. Second, in only one of these patterns is a breach of duty required; moreover, even in that case, rescission is not founded directly on the breach of a duty.

Before introducing these two patterns, it is valuable to notice that rescission generally is not founded directly on breach of duty. When we discuss rescission, we are usually discussing the rescission of contracts; but we can also rescind unilateral legal acts like gifts or settlements.[5] In all of its manifestations, the rescission of a legal act is possible because the legal act is in some way defective when measured against the rules for the performance of the act. A fraudulent misrepresentation is, of course, a breach of duty and a legal wrong; it may permit rescission; but this rescission is available because the rescinding victim's consent to the legal act was impaired by some mistake that *they* made. We may well insist on a misrepresentation, rather than a one-sided mistake, because where a contract is made the law must take account of the interests of both parties, not merely those of the mistaken one. But the ultimate justification for allowing rescission is that the rescinding party contracted mistakenly; the insistence on misrepresentation is an insistence that the misrepresenting party be responsible for the mistake that the rescinding party made, so that the misrepresenting party's interest in the maintenance of the contract is less worthy of protection than it would be otherwise. My claim here, that wrongdoing is not the direct foundation of rescission, is shown more clearly by the case of rescission for innocent misrepresentation, which does not involve any wrongful act. A mistake on the part of the rescinding party is required; and in the case of a contract, a misrepresentation is usually needed to show that the other party is *responsible* in law for that mistake; but the misrepresentation need not be legally wrongful. Of course, if the victim of a fraudulent misrepresentation claims compensation for loss caused by the misrepresentation, *this* is a claim that is founded directly on the wrongful breach of a duty by the misrepresenting party.

[3] [1967] 2 AC 134.

[4] *Recovery Partners GP Ltd v Rukhadze* [2025] UKSC 10, [2025] 2 WLR 529; confirmed in *Stevens v Hotel Portfolio II (UK) Ltd* [2025] UKSC 28, [2025] 3 WLR 293.

[5] It may be correct that rescission is always of unilateral legal acts; on this view, when we speak of rescission 'of a contract', we mean rescission by one party of its offer or acceptance, as the case may be. The rescission of that legal act necessarily rescinds the contract. This is the understanding in German law: BS Markesinis, W Lorenz, and G Dannemann, *The Law of Contracts and Restitution: A Comparative Introduction* (Clarendon Press 1997) 205.

Rescission in the fiduciary context can be of both of the kinds mentioned above in the non-fiduciary context: that is, rescission of contracts or of unilateral legal acts. But these are not the two different patterns in fiduciary rescission to which I referred earlier.

The first pattern of fiduciary rescission is the rescission of the exercise by a fiduciary of a fiduciary power. If the exercise of the fiduciary power created a contract, the rescission of that exercise will lead to rescission of the contract; in such a case, the interests of any innocent counterparty to that contract must be considered and may preclude rescission. On the other hand, if the exercise of the fiduciary power was merely a unilateral act, such as under a dispositive discretion, then it is this unilateral act that will be rescinded (although again the intervention of other interests might stand in the way). As in the general law of rescission, rescission of the exercise of a fiduciary power is available because the legal act was in some way defective when measured against the rules for the performance of the act. There are, however, at least two important differences between rescission of the exercise of a fiduciary power and the rescission of non-fiduciary legal acts. The first difference is that the *grounds* of rescission are more numerous. This is simply because there are more legal requirements for the unimpeachable exercise of a fiduciary power than there are for the unimpeachable exercise of a non-fiduciary power (such as the power to make an ordinary contract or a gift). The second difference is that impeachably exercised fiduciary powers can be challenged by a wider range of persons. In rescission outside of the fiduciary context, the person rescinding is almost certainly the person who carried out the legal act that they are now, themselves, rescinding. But in fiduciary law it is very different. To take a simple example: assume that a trustee exercises a fiduciary dispositive power, but in a way that is defective in some respect and makes the exercise voidable. At least the following people can demand rescission: the trustee who exercised the power, a co-trustee or successor trustee, and any beneficiary of the trust. It is quite possible that objects of that dispositive power (or of other powers) who are not beneficiaries of the trust could also demand rescission.[6] If the trust were a charitable trust, which does not have beneficiaries in the 'trust law' sense of that word, rescission could be demanded by the Attorney-General, by the Charity Commission,[7] and by interested members of the public.[8]

How do we explain these differences? Fiduciary law is different from the rest of private law inasmuch as in fiduciary law, people do not act for themselves; rather, they act for and on behalf of others. This is why there are more grounds of rescission. Fiduciary powers are voidable for the same reasons as non-fiduciary powers, such as mistake or undue influence, because legal powers should be exercised with an unimpaired volition and understanding. But they are also voidable for further grounds, precisely because they are powers that the fiduciary holds in order to accomplish some other-regarding

[6] L Smith, *The Law of Loyalty* (OUP 2023) 290–93.

[7] Charities Act 2011, s 114.

[8] Charities Act 2011, s 115. For the limits of this section's requirement that leave of the Charity Commission be obtained, see *Bhamani v Sattar* [2021] EWCA Civ 243. Before the current legislation, the Court of Chancery sometimes allowed members of the public to take proceedings without any legislative authority (eg *Re Beloved Wilkes's Charity* (1851) 3 Mac & G 440, 42 ER 330).

assignment. This is why fiduciary powers (but not non-fiduciary powers) can be voidable, as we will see, for such grounds as having been exercised for an improper purpose.

What about the second difference, that is, the wider range of persons who have standing to demand rescission? This also follows from the other-regarding nature of fiduciary relationships. In non-fiduciary powers, the rules that allow rescission for mistake (for example) protect the integrity of the decision-making of the person who exercises the power. This also needs to be protected in the case of fiduciary powers. But in fiduciary powers, which by definition are held to allow the fiduciary to better accomplish some mission that extends beyond the fiduciary's own self-interest, the additional grounds of rescission exist in order to try to ensure that the power is properly used in the pursuit of that mission and for no other reason. These extra grounds, which will be discussed below, include such rules as that a fiduciary power can only be exercised for a proper purpose. But these extra grounds are rightly provided by the law in order to protect not only the interests of the fiduciary but the interests of those *on whose behalf the fiduciary is required to act.* This is why, where there is some infringement of those other grounds—for example, where the power has been exercised for an improper purpose—the law grants standing to demand rescission to those on whose behalf the fiduciary is required to act. These rules aim to protect them and their interests, so an infringement of one of these rules is something that they need to be able to act upon in law.[9]

The second pattern of fiduciary rescission only involves the rescission of contracts, not of unilateral acts. This is in the context of the 'fair-dealing' rules, which govern where a fiduciary contracts with their own beneficiary. In this setting, no fiduciary power is involved. Where the rules are not complied with, the beneficiary can rescind the contract that they made with the fiduciary. As we will see, the basis of rescission is that the *beneficiary's* consent to the contract was impaired due to non-disclosure by the fiduciary.

The goal of this chapter is to elucidate the different justifications for rescission of legal acts done by and with fiduciaries in these different settings.

II. Rescission of the Exercise of Fiduciary Powers

In *Pitt v Holt*,[10] a settlement was set aside on the ground of mistake. Although the settlement was made by someone acting in a fiduciary role, rescission for mistake can just as well be invoked by someone exercising a non-fiduciary prerogative, and for this reason I leave discussion of it to others. The decision also addressed rescission of the exercise of fiduciary powers for grounds that are particular to such powers. Since that case, it has become commonplace to classify improper exercises of fiduciary powers into

[9] For other principles that apply in fiduciary relationships but not when people are acting for themselves, see Smith, *The Law of Loyalty* (n 6) 431–32 and generally.

[10] [2013] UKSC 26, [2013] 2 AC 108 [60]–[61]; see L Smith, '*Pitt v Holt*: The Ambiguity of "Breach of Fiduciary Duty"' in J Russell and L Graham (eds), *Private Law and the UK Supreme Court: Key Cases and Decisions* (Routledge 2026) 190.

three groups.[11] 'Excessive execution' is the impropriety that arises from an attempt to do something with the power that is not authorised by it; for example, the objects of a dispositive power are A and B, and the power-holder purports to dispose relevant assets to C. This, I also leave aside; like mistake, it is not confined to fiduciary law or fiduciary powers; moreover, it leads not to potential rescission (which is the result of a voidable exercise) but to a total failure to exercise the power (voidness). 'Inadequate deliberation' is the impropriety that arises from exercising the power within its scope, but while 'failing to give proper consideration to relevant matters in making a decision which is within the scope of the relevant power'.[12] 'Improper purpose' is the impropriety that arises from exercising the power within its scope, but not in the pursuit of at least one of the purposes for which the power was conferred.[13]

Earlier decisions articulated other restrictions on fiduciaries.[14] In *Re Hay's Settlement Trusts*,[15] it was said that a trustee (and by extension any other fiduciary):

> must, first, consider periodically whether or not he should exercise the power; second, consider the range of objects of the power; and third, consider the appropriateness of individual appointments.[16]

The first of those could not easily be a reason for setting aside the exercise of a power, although it might be a reason for other intervention, such as removal of a trustee. The other two could also be grounds for such intervention, but they could reveal examples of inadequate deliberation. *Re Hay's* also articulates a rule against delegation, but holds that a delegation is (unless expressly authorised) void as an excessive execution.[17] Another case is *Turner v Turner*,[18] in which trustees slavishly and without exercising their own judgement simply followed the instructions of the settlor. Lord Walker suggested in *Pitt* that this situation needed a separate label, namely 'equitable *non est factum*'.[19]

There is a simpler view of all this, which is that inadequate deliberation, improper purpose, and indeed '*equitable non est factum*' are all examples of a single defect: using a fiduciary power within its scope but in a manner that is improper as judged against the reason or reasons for which it was granted. Those reasons entail that the fiduciary, if acting properly, will exercise their judgement in relation to all legally relevant matters

[11] See eg *Grand View Private Trust Co v Wong (No 2)* [2022] UKPC 47, [2023] WTLR 149 [52], stating that counsel's summary of this passage from *Pitt* provided 'a helpful and accurate summary of three major duties and restrictions applicable to the exercise of fiduciary powers'.

[12] *Pitt v Holt* [2013] 2 AC 108 [60].

[13] *Grand View Private Trust Co Ltd v Wong (No 2)* [2023] WTLR 149 [52], noting that a power may have more than one proper purpose.

[14] Note that in *Grand View Private Trust Co Ltd v Wong (No 2)* [2023] WTLR 149 it was said that counsel's summary was of 'three major duties and restrictions', implying not only that there are restrictions that are not duties, but that there are more than those three. The phrase 'duties and restrictions' also appears at [51].

[15] [1982] 1 WLR 202.

[16] ibid 210.

[17] ibid 212–13. We might also classify as excessive execution the effect of another rule, that a fiduciary power-holder may not fetter their discretion in advance.

[18] *Turner v Turner* [1984] Ch 100.

[19] *Pitt v Holt* [2013] 2 AC 108 [43].

(will deliberate adequately) and will not take account of legally irrelevant matters (improper purposes). Since all of these cases address the improper exercise of a fiduciary power but one that is within its scope, it makes sense that the exercise is voidable and not void in all of these cases.[20]

This assertion could be challenged on at least two grounds. First, the label 'equitable *non est factum*' implies, as some think is the case, that the exercises in *Turner* were void. It is true that in that case, Mervyn Davies J said at one point that one appointment was 'wholly void';[21] but on the same page he said three times that all three appointments were 'set aside' retroactively by his order (and he used 'set aside' and 'put aside' in discussing the law); this is the language of voidability, since in the case of a wholly void act there is nothing to set aside.

Second, *Cloutte v Storey*[22] stands for the proposition that an exercise made in 'fraud on the power' is void. Recent decisions reveal an assumption that 'fraud on a power' is nothing but an outdated name for 'improper purposes'.[23] Thus it might be thought to follow that the implication of the holding in *Cloutte* is that the exercise of a fiduciary power for an improper purpose is void, not voidable.[24] But this may be a misunderstanding. *Non*-fiduciary power-holders can generally use the powers for such purposes as they wish; the fiduciary rules on proper purposes simply do not apply. And yet there are important decisions addressing 'fraud on a power' by the holders of such non-fiduciary powers.[25] This implies that they must be addressing something other than what we now call (fiduciary) proper purposes. I would suggest that what these cases were addressing under the label of 'fraud on a power' was actually the problem of concealed excessive execution. In *Vatcher v Paull*,[26] Lord Parker said that for fraud on a power, '[i]t is enough that the appointor's purpose and intention is to secure a benefit for himself, or some other person not an object of the power'.[27] That is concealed excessive execution, and it is exactly what had happened in *Cloutte v Storey*.[28] If fraud on a power is hidden excessive execution, then voidness would make perfect sense.[29]

[20] There is a line of reasoning that doubts this distinction between *absence* of power and *misuse* of power, and argues that since a misuse is not authorised, it amounts to an absence of power: P Matthews and others, *Underhill and Hayton: Law Relating to Trusts and Trustees* (20th edn, LexisNexis 2022) [60.33]–[60.36], [60.57]; cf P Sales, 'Use of Powers for Proper Purposes in Private Law' (2020) 136 LQR 384, 399–400. But this elides an important conceptual distinction; in the words of Richard Nolan, it is 'entirely artificial . . . simply a sleight of hand' (R Nolan, 'Controlling Fiduciary Power' (2009) 68 CLJ 293, 300). It is also inconsistent with an enormous body of fiduciary law holding that misuse of fiduciary power within its limits leads to voidability, not voidness.

[21] *Turner v Turner* [1984] Ch 100, 111.

[22] [1911] 1 Ch 18.

[23] See *Pitt v Holt* [2013] 2 AC 108 [61]–[62], [93]; *Eclairs Group Ltd v JKX Oil & Gas plc* [2015] UKSC 71, [2016] 3 All ER 641 [15]; *Grand View Private Trust Co Ltd v Wong (No 2)* [2023] WTLR 149 [56].

[24] It was so held, on exactly this reasoning, in *FS Capital Ltd v Adams* [2025] EWCA Civ 53; but see *Tianrui (International) Holding Co Ltd v China Shanshui Cement Group Ltd* [2024] UKPC 36, [2025] AC 709 [74].

[25] *Cloutte v Storey* [1911] 1 Ch 18; *Re Cohen* [1911] 1 Ch 37; *Vatcher v Paull* [1915] AC 372.

[26] [1915] AC 372.

[27] ibid 378.

[28] See also *Re Cohen* [1911] 1 Ch 37.

[29] Moreover, if concealed excessive execution leads to voidness this should be true also in the case of a fiduciary power, which seems to have been held in *Wong v Burt* [2004] NZCA 174, [2005] 1 NZLR 91 [30] ('[I]f the power is exercised with the intention of benefiting some non-object of the discretionary power, whether that person is the person exercising it, or anybody else for that matter, the exercise is void.'). The difference between void and voidable, however, was not material in that case.

This, however, is a much narrower doctrine than setting aside the exercise of a fiduciary power for improper purposes.[30]

My own view is that whether or not it is necessary to differentiate between inadequate deliberation and improper purposes (and, indeed, 'equitable *non est factum*'), any of them will make the exercise of a fiduciary power voidable; and if it is avoided, this is an example of rescission.[31] It is, moreover, rescission for a peculiarly fiduciary ground. If the exercise of the power was part of the creation of a contract (ie either the offer or the acceptance was by exercise of a fiduciary power), then rescission of the exercise will entail rescission of the contract (subject to the protection of third parties, particularly the other party to the contract).

There is still more to say about the grounds of rescission of the exercise of fiduciary powers. The exercise of fiduciary powers (but not non-fiduciary powers) can also be set aside if such a power was exercised while the fiduciary was in a situation in which their personal interests were in conflict with the requirement that they use the power according to the purposes for which it was granted (in abbreviated form, 'a conflict of (self-)interest and (fiduciary) duty'). The same recourse is available if the fiduciary exercised the power in a situation in which their fiduciary duty to one beneficiary was in conflict with their fiduciary duty to another beneficiary. We will discuss the justification for these rules in more detail in the next section,[32] because the 'self-dealing' rule discussed there exists to regulate conflicts of self-interest and fiduciary duty. Summarising that discussion, a conflict of either kind makes it impossible to know whether the power has been exercised for a proper purpose. For this reason, in the presence of a conflict, it is not necessary to prove that there was an actual improper purpose; the exercise is automatically voidable, as it would be if an improper purpose were proven.[33] But while every case of self-dealing involves a conflict of self-interest and fiduciary duty, not every disqualifying conflict is necessarily a case of self-dealing.[34] For this reason it

[30] And this would support the suggestion in *Pitt v Holt* [2013] 2 AC 108 [62] that an exercise for an improper purpose is voidable, not void.

[31] It has been said by the Privy Council in the context of inadequate deliberation that the correct reading of *Pitt v Holt* [2013] 2 AC 108 is that the court has a discretion whether to allow rescission: *Gany Holdings (PTC) SA v Khan* [2018] UKPC 21 [54]; *Dawson-Damer v Grampian Trust Co Ltd* [2025] UKPC 32, [2025] 1 WLR 353 [59]. On my argument, this should also apply to improper purposes.

[32] Section III.A.

[33] The problem of bribery is topical thanks to *Hopcraft v Close Brothers Ltd* [2025] UKSC 33, [2025] 3 WLR 423. Among the multiple remedies generated by bribery (see P Perell, 'Remedies for the Victims of a Bribe' (1999) 22 Advocates' Q 198; D Rendleman, 'Commercial Bribery: Choice and Measurement Within a Remedies Smorgasbord' (2017) 74 Wash & Lee L Rev 369), it allows a principal to avoid any contract made by their bribed agent, without inquiry into the contract's fairness (eg *Logicrose Ltd v Southend United Football Club Ltd* [1988] 1 WLR 1256, 1260–61; *Otkritie International Investment Management Ltd v Urumov* [2014] EWHC 191 (Comm) [67]–[73]). An unauthorised profit, as such, is not the same thing as a conflict (see *Rowland v Chapman* (1901) 17 TLR 669, an unusual case in which there was no conflict despite the taking of an unauthorised profit (explained below at n 69); and see the judgment of Lord Leggatt in *Recovery Partners GP Ltd v Rukhadze* [2025] 2 WLR 529 [112]–[118], concurring in the result and not dissenting on this point). Almost always, however, a bribed agent is in a conflict when exercising their fiduciary agency power to bind their principal to a contract (for discussion, see Smith, *The Law of Loyalty* (n 6) 170–71). Thus rescission is available according to the principle that any exercise of a fiduciary power while in a conflict is automatically voidable.

[34] Bribery illustrates this. Speaking generally, such a case would not be described as within the self-dealing rule, as there is no need for the bribed fiduciary to be, in any sense, a party to the contract that was procured in connection with the bribe. Other examples could be given; self-dealing involves a bilateral transaction, which is not present in every case of the conflicted exercise of a fiduciary power.

is necessary to notice here, at the outset, that these rules on conflicts are another general ground for making the exercise of a fiduciary power voidable.

In my view, rescission based on any of these peculiarly fiduciary grounds does not depend on any breach of duty in the strict sense. Just as with rescission for mistake or undue influence (whether of the exercise of a fiduciary power or outside of the fiduciary context), rescission of the exercise of a fiduciary power for improper purposes or for inadequate deliberation arises because there is a defect in the proper exercise of the power.[35] As for rescission in the presence of a conflict, again it is available because it is impossible to know whether there is a defect in the proper exercise of the power.

As was mentioned above, in the case of the exercise of a fiduciary power, the voidability of the exercise of a fiduciary power can be invoked by persons other than the one (the fiduciary) who exercised the power. In the context of trusts, at least, we might say that anyone who has standing to enforce the trust has standing to ask that the exercise of a fiduciary power be set aside. This is because the idea of enforcement of the trust is much wider than ensuring that those who are entitled to trust property receive it; in a broader sense, it extends also to all aspects of the proper administration of the trust.[36] But this does not *exclude* rescission by the one who exercised the power: in *Turner*, and in *Pitt* and many of the cases cited therein, proceedings were taken by the trustees themselves.

III. Self-dealing and Fair-dealing

Tito v Waddell[37] is well-known as containing a restatement of the rules on 'self-dealing' and 'fair-dealing':

> (1) *The self-dealing rule*: if a trustee purchases trust property from himself, any beneficiary may have the sale set aside ex debito justitiae,[38] however fair the transaction.
>
> (2) *The fair-dealing rule*: if a trustee purchases his beneficiary's beneficial interest, the beneficiary may have the sale set aside unless the trustee can establish the propriety of the transaction, showing that he had taken no advantage of his position and that the beneficiary was fully informed and received full value.[39]

Although they are often lumped together, Megarry V-C was right to separate them, because they deal with two situations that are very different juridically.

[35] This seems to be why the Privy Council used the word 'restrictions' when discussing rescission of the exercise of fiduciary powers in *Grand View Private Trust Co v Wong (No 2)* [2023] WTLR 149 (see the discussion in n 14).
[36] Smith, *The Law of Loyalty* (n 6) 290–93.
[37] *Tito v Waddell (No 2)* [1977] Ch 106.
[38] This Latin phrase means 'as a matter of right', 'automatically', and implies that the court has no discretion (see DM Walker, *The Oxford Companion to Law* (Clarendon Press 1980) sv 'ex debito justitiae').
[39] *Tito v Waddell (No 2)* [1977] Ch 106, 225 (italics in original); see also 240–41 and generally.

A. Self-dealing

'Self-dealing' concerns the use by a fiduciary (including a trustee) of a fiduciary power to enter into a transaction of some kind in which the fiduciary is, in some sense, on the opposite side of the transaction. Every case of self-dealing involves a conflict between the trustee's self-interest and the duties that they owe in relation to that fiduciary power *or* a conflict between the duties that they owe in relation to that fiduciary power and the demands of a fiduciary duty owed to someone else.[40] For example, a trustee may have the power to sell property held in trust. That is an administrative fiduciary power and must be exercised in what the trustee thinks is in the best interests of the beneficiaries; otherwise it would be exercised for an improper purpose.[41] If the sale is to (for example) a company in which the trustee has a financial interest, then the trustee's self-interest (their financial self-interest that the company does well) conflicts with their fiduciary duty to exercise the power in what they perceive to be the best interests of the beneficiary.[42] The legal response to this conflict of self-interest and fiduciary duty is that the exercise of the fiduciary power is automatically voidable by any beneficiary, without any inquiry into whether the sale was at a fair price. In this case, this means that the sale is voidable, because the fiduciary power was used to constitute the contract of sale. The only way to insulate the transaction is to secure in advance the fully informed consent of all the beneficiaries, all being fully capacitated; or, the approval of the court.[43]

The logic of this is that there is a natural human tendency to favour one's own interests, even unconsciously. The law grants the remedy of voidability since it is impossible to know whether the fiduciary, even if they were trying to act in good faith, actually favoured their own interests above those of the beneficiary.[44] As AL Smith LJ said in *Re Lamb*:

[40] Thus every case of self-dealing involves a conflict; but not every conflicted exercise of a fiduciary power is a case of self-dealing (see n 34).

[41] This would not be the correct formulation in the case of a charitable trust; in such a trust, the trustees must exercise their administrative powers in what they believe is the best way to advance the trust's charitable purpose(s). In recent debates about knowing receipt it has become popular to invoke the example of charitable trusts as a way of showing that we must be wary of overgeneralisation about trusts: L Smith, 'The Continuing Interest of Knowing Receipt' (2024) 83 CLJ 238, 239. Charitable trusts are structures in which privately conferred powers are required to be used in the public interest, and it is not surprising that not all things that are true of private trusts are true of such public trusts.

[42] I use the typical formulation here, although I have suggested above that this 'fiduciary duty' is in the nature of a restriction or a requirement for unimpeachable exercise of the power.

[43] If we are dealing with a private fiduciary relationship, the fiduciary's powers are held (and only held) for the benefit of the beneficiaries (including perhaps, in the case of a trust, objects of dispositive powers who are not true beneficiaries). The rules about conflicts, like all of the other restrictions on the exercise of fiduciary powers, exist only to protect those persons. If, therefore, they are content with what is proposed, the exercise will be effective because there is no one else who has a legally protected interest in objecting. The court may have a role to play if any beneficiary or potential beneficiary lacks capacity to consent, or in the case of a public fiduciary relationship such as a charity.

[44] See Smith, *The Law of Loyalty* (n 6) 154–59. It is sometimes said that the conflicted fiduciary is 'irrebuttably presumed' to have acted for an improper purpose, especially in the context of bribery (see *Otkritie International Investment Management Ltd v Urumov* [2014] EWHC 191 (Comm) [68]), but this is unhelpful because an 'irrebuttable presumption' of some fact is always a way of saying that it is immaterial whether the fact is true or not. A better formulation is that of Millett J (as the then was) in *Logicrose Ltd v Southend United Football Club Ltd* [1988] 1 WLR 1256, 1261: 'The principal, having been deprived by the other party to the transaction of the disinterested advice

> It is obvious—everybody knows it who has any knowledge of life—that when a man has a pecuniary interest, his mind is naturally warped in favour of his own interest. It is human nature, and no one can doubt it.[45]

Thus the self-dealing rule is just an example of the principle we have already noticed: if a fiduciary exercises a fiduciary power while in a conflict, that exercise will be voidable, due to the possibility—incapable of being disproved—that the exercise was improper in the sense that it was affected by the fiduciary's own self-interest, or by their fiduciary duty owed to some other beneficiary:

> There is no need to show—and it would often be impossible to determine—that the conflicting interest affected the fiduciary's conduct or judgment. The inherent danger that the fiduciary may have acted disloyally is reason enough to allow the principal to require the transaction to be undone.[46]

This, in turn, is nothing but the particular implementation, in the context of conflicts, of the more general rules already discussed on the rescission of exercises of fiduciary powers where the powers have been positively shown to have been used improperly.[47]

In a typical self-dealing situation in trust law, the beneficiary is not a party to the impugned transaction, although they are potentially affected by it, because the transaction involves trust property. This also shows the connection with the general rules on the rescission of fiduciary powers: the voidability of such powers can be invoked by any beneficiary, not as a party to the legal act but as one for whose benefit the power exists. Conversely, if all of those for whose benefit the power exists are content (with full knowledge of the conflict) that the self-dealing transaction should go ahead, there will be no infirmity in the exercise of the power. Thus, in a case of informed consent to

of his agent, is entitled to a further opportunity to consider whether it is in his interests to affirm it.' But even this is not wide enough to cover all conflicts, because not all are like bribes in having been generated by a counterparty to the transaction. For example, a conflicted unilateral legal act by a fiduciary is voidable, even though the fiduciary (for example a trustee) was not in an advisory relationship with the beneficiary.

[45] *Re Lamb* [1894] 2 QB 805, 820, cited by Lord Leggatt in *Recovery Partners GP Ltd v Rukhadze* [2025] 2 WLR 529 [115]. Note that AL Smith LJ was *not* saying that everyone is corrupt; the effect he describes can operate subconsciously upon those in good faith. For psychological research showing that the law is correct in responding to this subconscious effect, see Smith, *The Law of Loyalty* (n 6) 155–59.

[46] Lord Leggatt in *Recovery Partners GP Ltd v Rukhadze* [2025] 2 WLR 529 [116]. The same response is attracted if the trustee is in a 'conflict of duty and duty' (Smith, *The Law of Loyalty* (n 6) 159–63). Here their own self-interest is not implicated; but if, for example, a trustee sold trust property to a company of which the trustee was a director (and to which company, therefore, the director owed a conflicting fiduciary duty in that role), there would be a conflict of duty and duty and the sale would be voidable. A similar problem arises: it is impossible (in many cases, even for the trustee) to say whether the trustee favoured the interests of the company over those of the trust beneficiaries.

[47] The formulation of Megarry V-C (*Tito v Waddell (No 2)* [1977] Ch 106, 225) that the self-dealing rule generates an automatic power to rescind does, however, seem inconsistent with the idea that proven misuses of fiduciary power give the court a discretion in relation to rescission (see n 31). Even in the case of a contract secured by the bribery of an agent, however, Millett J suggested that the principal does not have an automatic right to rescind (*Logicrose Ltd v Southend United Football Club Ltd* [1988] 1 WLR 1256, 1260). The formulation of Megarry V-C may only have meant to indicate that the fairness of the self-dealing transaction is irrelevant; on his formulation, this was in contrast to the fair-dealing rule.

self-dealing, what the beneficiaries (or the court) are consenting to is the exercise of the fiduciary power in a situation in which its exercise might otherwise be thought to have been affected by the fiduciary's self-interest or some conflicting fiduciary duty.

B. Fair-dealing

The 'fair-dealing' rule, by contrast, does not usually involve the exercise of a fiduciary's *fiduciary* powers. In the case of a trust, it applies where the trustee transacts, in their personal capacity, with a beneficiary of the trust; in the trust context this has usually meant the acquisition by the trustee (for himself) of the beneficiary's equitable interest under the trust. Here, differently from self-dealing, the trustee is not exercising any of the powers that they hold as a trustee; the trustee is acting for their own account as the buyer, in dealing with the beneficiary as a seller. Also differently from self-dealing in trust law, here the beneficiary *is* a party to the contract in question. The beneficiary is the seller of their own rights; the trustee is not buying or selling trust property as a trustee. Indeed, none of the trust property (which is held in trust by the trustees) is being sold when the beneficiary sells their own equitable interest in the trust; the beneficiary's equitable interest *in* the trust property is not, itself, the property held in trust. Moreover, the trustee is not on both sides of the transaction in two different roles, as they are in the case of self-dealing. The beneficiary is acting personally, in selling their interest; moreover, they do not need the trustee to do that; the beneficiary could sell their interest to anyone. The trustee is also acting personally, in acquiring that interest. The trustee is not acting 'as trustee' or exercising any power that they hold as trustee.

Having said all that about trusts, it is important to note that today, and historically, the fair-dealing rule has more often been applied to non-trustee fiduciaries, especially advisory fiduciaries.[48] For example, if a fiduciary advisor, like a lawyer, contracts with their own client (buying from or selling to the client, or lending money to or borrowing from the client), the fair-dealing rule is activated.

In some fiduciary relationships there will be a presumption of undue influence. Undue influence, which may lead to rescission according to its own logic, is left aside here. Although in earlier cases, from the seventeenth century well into the twentieth century, undue influence was not clearly distinguished from the rules governing fiduciary relationships, it is now the case that the rules governing fiduciary relationships, including the fair-dealing rules, are different from the principles of undue influence, which can operate in non-fiduciary relationships.[49]

[48] This label is used to refer to a fiduciary who does not have *legal* fiduciary powers, as does a director, trustee, personal representative, agent, or business partner, but only the factual power involved in giving advice (see *Hopcraft v Close Brothers Ltd* [2025] 3 WLR 423 [164]). The clearest example of an advisory fiduciary is a solicitor. See AB Laby, 'Advisors as Fiduciaries' (2020) 72 Florida L Rev 953; S Degeling and L Smith, 'Exporting Fiduciary Obligations: The Case of Advisors' in S Agnew and M Smith (eds), *Law at the Cutting Edge: Essays in Honour of Sarah Worthington* (Hart 2024) 171.

[49] Thus in the current law, there can be undue influence without any invocation of a fiduciary relationship (eg *Waller-Edwards v One Savings Bank plc* [2025] UKSC 22, [2025] 2 WLR 1263); conversely, the fiduciary

Fair-dealing situations generate duties of disclosure that would not apply if there were not a fiduciary relationship.[50] We saw above that when a transaction is set aside because a trustee exercised their fiduciary powers while in a conflict (self-dealing), it is because of a concern that the trustee did not properly use their fiduciary powers. By contrast, when a transaction is set aside under the fair-dealing rule, it is because of a concern that the *beneficiary* did not properly agree to the transaction: their personal consent to it is vitiated because they did not have all the relevant information to make a fully informed decision. I will expand on this important difference in the next section.[51]

The consequence of attracting the fair-dealing rule, as it applies in trusts, is this: 'if a trustee purchases his beneficiary's beneficial interest, the beneficiary may have the sale set aside unless the trustee can establish the propriety of the transaction, showing that the trustee had taken no advantage of their position and that the beneficiary was fully informed and received full value.'[52] Thus such transactions are not forbidden, and may not even be voidable if the trustee can prove full disclosure and fairness (while a self-dealing transaction is automatically voidable, without inquiry into fairness, unless authorised in advance). Professor Matthew Conaglen has argued that in fair-dealing, it is only necessary to show that full disclosure was made by the trustee; it is not separately necessary to show that the transaction was fair. He argues that the role of unfairness is as evidence of inadequate disclosure.[53] On that view, which seems plausible, *if* the trustee makes full disclosure to the beneficiary of everything material to the transaction before the transaction, then it will not be liable to be set aside. If there is, however, a separate inquiry into fairness, then that inquiry must also be satisfied, or the beneficiary can set the transaction aside.

One category of case has caused difficulties for a long time: the company director who wishes to contract with the company of which they are a director.[54] The company is a legal person and the proposed transaction is therefore between the beneficiary and the fiduciary (or, perhaps, another company in which the fiduciary is interested). This makes it look like a fair-dealing case. On the other hand, the director is a member of the company's board, and it is the board that holds fiduciary powers in relation to the company. If those powers need to be exercised to approve the transaction, this looks like a self-dealing case. As is often the case when multiple norms apply in fiduciary law, all

fair-dealing rules can apply without any suggestion of undue influence (eg *Swindle v Harrison* [1997] 4 All ER 705, discussed below). For more discussion of the relationship between fiduciary duties and undue influence, see Degeling and Smith (n 48) 183–87.

[50] For discussion, see Smith, *The Law of Loyalty* (n 6) ch 5, s VIII.D. Some people deny that these are duties properly so called; I return to this below.

[51] Section IV.

[52] *Tito v Waddell (No 2)* [1977] Ch 106, 225.

[53] M Conaglen, 'A Re-Appraisal of the Fiduciary Self-Dealing and Fair-Dealing Rules' (2006) 65 CLJ 366, 374–90.

[54] Some cases of this kind are frequently cited and quoted; eg *Aberdeen Ry Co v Blaikie Brothers* (1854) 1 Macq 461, 1 Paterson 394; *North-West Transportation Co v Beatty* (1887) 12 App Cas 589.

of the relevant norms must be complied with. The standard technique to manage this situation, sometimes mandated by the corporate constitution or by legislation, is full disclosure and recusal from the decision. Recusal tends towards taking the case out of the self-dealing category (although recusal is not resignation), because the conflicted fiduciary is not participating (at least formally) in the decision relating to the fiduciary power. Even if this is correct, though, the fair-dealing aspect remains.[55] This may be why, in at least some jurisdictions, the transaction may be impeachable in relation to substantive fairness, even if all of the rules governing full disclosure and recusal have been followed.[56]

IV. Understanding the Foundations

In *Tito v Waddell*,[57] it was debated before Megarry V-C whether self-dealing and fair-dealing were two separate rules, or rather two aspects of a single rule. The judge treated the rules as separate. Like Mowbray QC in that litigation, however, Conaglen argues that they are aspects of a single principle: 'both the self-dealing rule and the fair-dealing rule are most appropriately understood as applications of the general fiduciary conflict principle.'[58]

In my view, this is true in a very general sense, but it is likely to confuse rather than clarify our understanding of the law. It would be as if we said that the rules on communication of contractual acceptance, and the rules on remoteness of contractual damages, are both applications of the general principle that seriously made promises are legally enforceable. It is broadly true, but it does not help us to understand, analyse, and evaluate the detailed legal rules in question. To do that, we must pay more detailed attention to the particular and differing concerns that underlie those rules.

Once we have a clear and sound definition of what is a fiduciary conflict, we see that the self-dealing rule does not respond directly to fiduciary conflicts but rather to other aspects of the fiduciary relationship.

[55] In Canadian federal corporate law, the relevant provisions (Canada Business Corporations Act, RSC c C-44, s 120) apply not only to directors but also to 'officers', who are fiduciaries but who are not on the board; such persons are (depending on their other fiduciary powers) less clearly within the self-dealing norms, but they are clearly within the fair-dealing ones.

[56] This is true under the Canadian federal statute (s 120(7)(c)), even if there has been shareholder ratification (s 120(7.1)(c)). Similarly, in Delaware corporate law, such transactions attract what is called the 'entire fairness' standard. An example can be seen in the detailed holding allowing rescission of a shareholder-approved compensation award worth US$55.8 billion in *Tornetta v Musk*, 326 A3d 1203 (Del Ch, 2024). Note however that the emigration of the corporation to Texas has apparently allowed the package's approval, albeit in reduced amount: J Ewing, 'Tesla Grants Musk $29 Billion in Stock to Keep "Elon's Energies Focused"' *New York Times* (4 August 2025).

[57] *Tito v Waddell (No 2)* [1977] Ch 106, 224–25, 240–41.

[58] Conaglen (n 53) 395.

A. Defining 'Conflict of Interest'

Conaglen's definition is that there is a disabling conflict if the fiduciary's self-interest conflicts with any duty that the fiduciary owes to the beneficiary.[59] The trouble with this definition is that it is too broad; on this view, the fiduciary will be in a conflict of this kind whenever they are acting in their fiduciary role. For example, a fiduciary's self-interest is to do the least amount of work for what they are being paid for their fiduciary role (even if, or especially if, the amount is zero). Since the fiduciary owes a duty to the beneficiary to do at least some work in their fiduciary role, it follows that the fiduciary's self-interest always conflicts with the duties owed to the beneficiary. Conversely, the self-interest of a fiduciary who is paid by time spent is to do as much work as possible, even if it does not usefully assist the beneficiary; again, the fiduciary's self-interest always conflicts with the duties owed to the beneficiary.

Note that these points do not turn on the fiduciary ever doing anything remotely wrongful. These examples do not posit that the fiduciary inappropriately favours their own interests, or in any way breaches their duties. The point is simply to observe that the fiduciary's self-interest (whether or not they pursue it) systematically conflicts with the duties they owe to the beneficiary. This, therefore, is not a fiduciary *conflict of interest*, which is something that must be avoided or at least be managed; this is simply a conflict of *interests*, the interest of one party conflicting with the interest of the other.[60] This conflict of *interests* is routine and unavoidable. It is regulated by a range of objective legal rules, such as the duty to comply with the terms of the trust or other fiduciary role, and the duty of care, skill, and diligence that gives an objective answer to how much work a fiduciary must devote to their fiduciary duties when the fiduciary would rather be playing tennis.[61]

This observation does not mean that I believe that fiduciary obligations are somehow all-encompassing. They are not, or at least they need not be. A person might be the trustee of a small charitable trust whose trustees meet four times a year. I do not argue that this person is always in a situation where their personal interests conflict with their fiduciary duties. My point is that whenever they are acting in their fiduciary role, their personal interests conflict with their duties towards the beneficiary (again, this is the case even if the trustee complies scrupulously with their duties). This is why we must seek a better definition of 'conflict of interest' in fiduciary law.

[59] M Conaglen, *Fiduciary Loyalty: Protecting the Due Performance of Non-Fiduciary Duties* (Hart 2010) 63 ('A fiduciary is prohibited from acting in a situation in which there is a conflict between [any non-fiduciary] duty that he owes to his principal and his own personal interest').

[60] For more on this distinction, see Smith, *The Law of Loyalty* (n 6) 144–49.

[61] In *Recovery Partners GP Ltd v Rukhadze* [2025] 2 WLR 529, Lord Burrows disagreed with the majority holding that fiduciary accountability for unauthorised profits grows directly out of the fiduciary relationship of accountability; he opined that this accountability depends on a wrong. Such a view demands a careful analysis of what exactly are the elements of the relevant wrong, and exactly when it is committed. As to this, Lord Burrows used more than one formulation. Some of them (eg at [264]) are, like Conaglen's formulation, too wide because they refer to the conflict of *interests* that is present at all moments of the fiduciary relationship and so cannot sensibly amount to a legal wrong.

The phrase 'conflict of interest' is potentially misleading if we forget that it is a contraction. It actually means 'conflict of self-interest and (or with) *fiduciary* duty'.[62] This is captured in a sentence of Lord Goff:

> [F]iduciaries . . . must not put themselves in a position where there is a conflict between their personal interests and their duties as fiduciaries.[63]

Note that on this formulation, differently from Conaglen's, 'their duties as fiduciaries' are not the duty (or rule) that they must avoid conflicts. 'Their duties as fiduciaries' refers to their duties *in the exercise of their fiduciary powers*: that is, the duties and restrictions which aim to ensure that those powers are used properly. This means that a conflict of this kind—a fiduciary conflict of interest (or of duty and duty)—can only arise where the fiduciary is exercising fiduciary powers. The reason this particular situation is so strictly regulated by fiduciary law is that discretionary fiduciary powers involve the exercise of judgement, and whether the fiduciary has used their powers properly involves a subjective element relating to the fiduciary's decision-making process.[64] As we have seen, conflicts (of self-interest, or of duty and duty) raise the spectre that the fiduciary's judgement might have been influenced in an unknowable way by self-interest, or by a conflicting fiduciary duty to another. Where a fiduciary owes an *objective* duty (like the duty of care, skill, and diligence, or the duty to comply with the trust instrument), the fiduciary's judgement is not implicated in measuring whether the duty has been fulfilled; it is the law that tells us whether the duty has been breached. Here, rules on conflicts have no place.

Thus the rules about conflicts (conflicts of self-interest and fiduciary duty, and conflicts of fiduciary duty with fiduciary duty) exist entirely to protect the proper exercise of fiduciary powers.[65] This focused understanding of the norms relating to conflicts of interest helps us to see that it is entirely unnecessary, and indeed it is analytically counterproductive, to have any reference to these norms in the context of unauthorised profits. If a fiduciary takes a bribe, or makes a less morally questionable but still unauthorised profit from their fiduciary role, they are accountable for it, simply because they are acting in a role in which they act for and on behalf of another.[66] There is no need to rely on wrongdoing, and in particular there is no need to rely on conflict of interest as playing the role of some ill-defined breach of duty. The mistaken and confusing view that fiduciary accountability for unauthorised profits depends in some way

[62] Or, in the case of a conflict of duty and duty, conflict of one fiduciary duty with another.

[63] *Guinness plc v Saunders* [1990] 2 AC 663, 700. The High Court of Australia has also stated that the concern is with a conflict between the fiduciary's self-interest and their *fiduciary* duty: *Chan v Zacharia* (1984) 154 CLR 178, 199; *Warman International Ltd v Dwyer* (1995) 182 CLR 544, 557; both cited in *Howard v Federal Commissioner of Taxation* [2014] HCA 21, (2014) 253 CLR 83 [33], [108].

[64] *Eclairs Group Ltd v JKX Oil & Gas plc* [2016] 3 All ER 641 [15]; *Grand View Private Trust Co Ltd v Wong (No 2)* [2023] WTLR 149 [72].

[65] In *Recovery Partners GP Ltd v Rukhadze* [2025] 2 WLR 529, Lord Leggatt adopted this view of the nature of a fiduciary conflict of interest ([115]–[116]).

[66] *Regal (Hastings) Ltd v Gulliver* [1967] 2 AC 134; *Recovery Partners GP Ltd v Rukhadze* [2025] 2 WLR 529; *Stevens v Hotel Portfolio II (UK) Ltd* [2025] 3 WLR 293.

on wrongful conduct has now been rejected twice by the House of Lords[67] and twice also by the Supreme Court of the United Kingdom.[68] Rather than being a free-standing wrong, the presence of a conflict of interest makes the exercise of a fiduciary power voidable, as illustrated by (among other illustrations) the self-dealing rule. In this, it functions like other non-wrongs that make legal acts voidable (including mistake and undue influence). The independence of the conflict rules from the rule on unauthorised profits solves a number of otherwise intractable puzzles.[69]

B. Implications for Understanding Self-dealing and Fair-dealing

What are the implications for the present study? Self-dealing is a straightforward example of the conflicted exercise of a fiduciary power. As we have seen, such an exercise is automatically voidable because the conflict of interest makes it impossible to know whether the fiduciary power was exercised properly.

In the fair-dealing context, as we have seen, there is no exercise of a fiduciary power that could or might be rescinded. It is true that in the case of an advisory fiduciary, it is the giving of advice that stands in the place of the exercise of a fiduciary power, and an advisory fiduciary could certainly be said to be in a conflict of self-interest and fiduciary duty when advising the beneficiary in a self-dealing setting. The fiduciary's self-interest could taint that advice just as it can taint the exercise of a fiduciary power of sale over trust property. But as we have seen, the way the rules about conflicts protect the exercise of fiduciary powers is by making conflicted exercises subject to rescission. It is not possible to rescind the giving of advice. Anyway, the beneficiary does not want to somehow rescind the advice; the beneficiary wants to rescind the *contract* made with the fiduciary, or sometimes (as we will see) to claim compensation from them. Fair-dealing cases, therefore, play out differently, without any need to rely on the rules about conflicts of interest and their effects on the exercise of fiduciary powers.

[67] *Regal (Hastings) Ltd v Gulliver* [1967] 2 AC 134; *Boardman v Phipps* [1967] 2 AC 46.

[68] *Recovery Partners GP Ltd v Rukhadze* [2025] 2 WLR 529; *Stevens v Hotel Portfolio II (UK) Ltd* [2025] 3 WLR 293. This principle is also arguably implicit in *FHR European Ventures LLP v Mankarious* [2014] UKSC 45, [2015] AC 250 and *Crown Prosecution Service v Aquila Advisory Ltd* [2021] UKSC 49, [2021] WLR 5666.

[69] See the judgment of Lord Leggatt in *Recovery Partners GP Ltd v Rukhadze* [2025] 2 WLR 529 [112]–[136]. It is clear that there can be conflicts without profits, since a conflicted legal act is voidable without any need to show an unauthorised profit. There can also be unauthorised profits without any conflict, when 'conflict' is understood carefully. See Smith, *The Law of Loyalty* (n 6) 200–07, and also *Rowland v Chapman* (1901) 17 TLR 669. In that case, the six plaintiffs had contracted to buy an interest in land and were seeking rescission of the contract, which had been made by their agent who had allegedly taken a secret commission from the vendor. The unusual feature of the case is that the agent was *also* a purchaser; they were all seven buying the land together. The commission was 1.5 per cent of the price, but the agent was a 1/7 contributor to the price. Thus for any increase in the price of £100, he would gain (converting to decimal currency) £1.50 of commission, but his required contribution to the price to be paid would go up by £14.29. Buckley J held that whether or not this was an unauthorised profit, for which the agent would have been accountable to the principals (the factual question whether the commission had been authorised did not have to be decided), rescission was not available because the agent did not have an interest conflicting with his fiduciary duty to his principals. Just as in *Regal (Hastings) Ltd v Gulliver* [1967] 2 AC 134 and *Boardman v Phipps* [1967] 2 AC 46 (see Smith, *The Law of Loyalty* (n 6) 205–06; *Recovery Partners GP Ltd v Rukhadze* [2025] 2 WLR 529 [118]), the agent's interest was *aligned* with the interests of his principals, not in conflict.

Let us consider a decision from the formative period of this body of law: the judgment of Lord Eldon in *Gibson v Jeyes*.[70] An attorney had sold a life annuity to his elderly client, now deceased, and the client's administrator sought to set aside the transaction and recover the price paid. This claim was successful. Lord Eldon did not refer to the relationship as fiduciary, since this terminology arose later; moreover, the grounds of the claim included what would now be called incapacity, as well as undue influence and the fiduciary fair-dealing rule. But the judgment is informative as to the logic of the fair-dealing rule. Lord Eldon made it clear that it was lawful for an attorney to contract with his own client (or for a trustee to contract with his own beneficiary); but the attorney must give the client the same advice as he would properly give if the client was contracting with some third party:

> Therefore I say, [the attorney] might contract [with his client]: but then he should have said, if he was to deal with her for this, she must get another attorney to advise her as to the value: or, if she would not, then out of that state of circumstances this clear duty results from the rule of this Court, and throws upon him the whole *onus* of the case; that, if he will mix with the character of attorney that of vendor, he shall, if the propriety of the contract comes in question, manifest, that he has given her all that reasonable advice against himself, that he would have given her against a third person. It is asked, where is that rule to be found. I answer, in that great rule of the Court, that he, who bargains in matter of advantage with a person placing confidence in him is bound to shew, that a reasonable use has been made of that confidence; a rule applying to trustees, attorneys, or any one else.[71]

The attorney's duty of disclosure, he went on to say, extended to 'all the information, that would have given her any advantage'.[72] For example, the attorney being ten years older than the client, he should have pointed out to her that if the attorney should predecease the client, she would have to prove as a creditor against his estate for the payment of the annuity. Thus this duty of disclosure goes far beyond disclosing the *fact* that the fiduciary's interest is opposed to that of the client, which in any event is usually obvious.

In squaring this state of the law with his view that the fair-dealing rule is all about conflicts, Conaglen argues:

> In a transaction falling within the *fair-dealing* rule, the principal will ordinarily, although not always, know that she is dealing with her fiduciary and will therefore ordinarily have consented to the fiduciary having some personal interest in the transaction. However, fiduciary doctrine requires that consent to be of a high quality—there must be full disclosure on the part of the fiduciary of all material facts within

[70] (1801) 6 Ves Jun 266, 31 ER 1044.
[71] *Gibson v Jeyes* (1801) 6 Ves Jun 266, 278; 31 ER 1044, 1050.
[72] ibid 279 and 1050.

his control—before the fiduciary's conflicting personal interest in the transaction is effectively neutralised and the transaction immunised against the fiduciary conflict principle.[73]

We have already seen that conflicts are not obviously relevant to these cases, since the contract being challenged was not created by the exercise of a fiduciary power.

The simpler explanation is to take seriously the language of 'duty of disclosure', which is ubiquitous in these fair-dealing cases. In fair-dealing, the fiduciary has a duty to disclose all information of which they are aware that is relevant to the beneficiary's decision-making process. This is because, as a fiduciary, they are by definition acting for and on behalf of the beneficiary. We have already seen that the law, in such a relationship, attributes to the beneficiary any profit that the fiduciary extracts, not as a remedy for a wrong, but for the bare reason that the fiduciary is acting for and on behalf of the beneficiary.[74] Information cannot be attributed in exactly the same way as financial profit, through being held in trust for the beneficiary; but it can be attributed through the imposition of a duty of disclosure. Requiring the fiduciary to disclose the information is the law's means of attribution of information. It makes sure that the information is acquired by the person for whose benefit the fiduciary is acting: the beneficiary. The duty of disclosure ensures that the law does not allow the fiduciary unilaterally to step out of the fiduciary relationship for the purposes of a particular contract.[75]

Full disclosure in fair-dealing, then, is not required to secure the beneficiary's consent to the fiduciary's acting in a conflict; it is required in order for the fiduciary to comply with a fiduciary duty of disclosure that is generated by the contractual negotiation between a fiduciary and their own beneficiary. If the fiduciary fails to comply with this exacting duty of disclosure, the beneficiary may well enter into the contract under a mistake; a mistake, that is, in relation to whatever material information the fiduciary failed to disclose. The beneficiary may indeed be entirely ignorant of some relevant fact which ought to have been disclosed. A mistake is a ground for rescission of a contract if the other party is responsible in law for the mistake. Usually this requires a misrepresentation, but where there is a duty of disclosure, then a breach of that duty has a comparable effect.[76] Thus in the fair-dealing scenario, where there has been non-disclosure by the fiduciary, the beneficiary is empowered to rescind *their own* consent to the contract. This is not rescission of the exercise of a fiduciary power.

Until the late nineteenth or early twentieth century, it might have been said that this 'duty' of disclosure was not a duty in the strictest sense. It was in the nature of

[73] Conaglen (n 53) 391 (emphasis in original; footnotes omitted).

[74] *Recovery Partners GP Ltd v Rukhadze* [2025] 2 WLR 529.

[75] For a fuller discussion of why the fiduciary must disclose (as Lord Eldon said in *Gibson*) anything that is relevant to the beneficiary's decision-making process, see Smith, *The Law of Loyalty* (n 6) 228–37, esp (in relation to fair-dealing) 233–36. As discussed there, the same principle explains, among other things, why fiduciaries must disclose their own wrongdoing.

[76] E Peel, *The Law of Contract* (15th edn, Sweet & Maxwell 2020) [9-157], [9-177]; J Cartwright, *Misrepresentation, Mistake and Non-Disclosure* (6th edn, Sweet & Maxwell 2022) [17-39]–[17-40]. Outside of fiduciary law, the same logic is also familiar in contracts of indemnity insurance, where there is also a duty to disclose and non-disclosure also permits rescission.

a requirement for the creation of an unimpeachable contract. Breach of the 'duty' allowed the beneficiary to rescind; this might include a money award in a case of what is often called 'pecuniary rescission'. Thus a breach had significant legal consequences. If, however, it only allowed rescission, and not compensation for consequential loss caused by the breach, then it was not a wrong in the strictest sense; rather, it was like innocent misrepresentation, as it was before any statutory intervention: a non-wrong that allowed rescission. Turning that around, we might say that compliance with the fiduciary 'duty' of disclosure in fair-dealing was *only* a requirement for the creation of an unimpeachable contract. This changed definitively in *Nocton's case*,[77] and we moved into a world in which the 'duty' of disclosure became a genuine duty of disclosure, such that breach gave rise to claims for compensation for loss caused.[78] And since this duty arises from the fiduciary relationship, it is a prescriptive fiduciary duty of disclosure.[79]

Since the 1990s, some have accepted a view that fiduciary duties are only proscriptive: they forbid certain conduct but never require conduct. The present chapter, although focused on other issues, shows that this is an ahistorical view.[80] The idea seems to have originated in a paper by Professor Paul Finn,[81] although this view is inconsistent with what he said both earlier[82] and later.[83] Although the proscriptive-only view remains popular (but not universally held) in Australia,[84] it is not tenable as an understanding of the positive law of England and Wales.[85] The proscriptive-only view seems to require that the fiduciary duty of disclosure become once again only a 'duty' of disclosure as it was until *Nocton's case*,[86] but for a different reason. Before that case, we might have said it was not a real duty because the only recourse generated by violation was rescission (including pecuniary rescission), and compensation for consequential losses was not available. On the prophylactic-only view of fiduciary duties, it cannot be a fiduciary duty because it requires positive action; it is prescriptive. Holders of this view therefore say that this 'duty' of disclosure is not a duty but only a way of *not* breaching the duty 'not to be in a conflict' or perhaps 'not to act while in a conflict'.[87]

[77] *Nocton v Lord Ashburton* [1914] AC 932.

[78] The story is told in detail in J Grower, 'From Disability to Duty: From Constructive Fraud to Equitable Wrongs' (PhD thesis, University College London 2021).

[79] See Gummow (n 1) 64–66.

[80] See further Smith, 'Prescriptive Fiduciary Duties' (n 2).

[81] PD Finn, 'The Fiduciary Principle' in Youdan (n 1) 1.

[82] PD Finn, *Fiduciary Obligations* (Law Book Co 1977).

[83] PD Finn, 'Fiduciary Reflections' (2014) 88 ALJ 127, 131 fn 41.

[84] See Smith, 'Prescriptive Fiduciary Duties' (n 2) and R Derrington, 'Commentary on Professor Lionel D Smith's Paper, "Prescriptive Fiduciary Duties"' (2018) 37 UQLJ 289.

[85] *Pitt v Holt* [2013] 2 AC 108 [70]–[73]; *Eclairs Group Ltd v JKX Oil & Gas plc* [2016] 3 All ER 641 [37], [39] (speaking here for the whole Court); *Lehtimäki v Cooper* [2020] UKSC 33, [2022] AC 155; *Grand View Private Trust Co Ltd v Wong (No 2)* [2023] WTLR 149 [56]. The holding that a fiduciary holds an unauthorised profit in trust for their beneficiary, not as a remedy for wrongdoing but as a matter of primary right (so held in *Recovery Partners GP Ltd v Rukhadze* [2025] 2 WLR 529 and *Stevens v Hotel Portfolio II (UK) Ltd* [2025] 3 WLR 293, and arguably implicit in *FHR European Ventures LLP v Mankarious* [2015] AC 250 and *Crown Prosecution Service v Aquila Advisory Ltd* [2021] WLR 5666) is also a holding that fiduciary accountability (including for unauthorised profits) is a prescriptive fiduciary duty.

[86] *Nocton v Lord Ashburton* [1914] AC 932. Grower (n 78) ch 6 argues that the change was foreshadowed by the House of Lords in *Cavendish Bentinck v Fenn* (1887) 12 App Cas 652.

[87] eg *Maguire v Makaronis* (1997) 188 CLR 449, 466–67; *Blackmagic Design Pty Ltd v Overliese* [2011] FCAFC 24, (2011) 191 FCR 1 [105]. This understanding is also embraced by Derrington (n 84) 294–96.

But this tortured and unintuitive approach cannot, it seems, succeed as a way of understanding the law.[88] We have already seen that the understanding of 'conflict' upon which it depends is unworkable as the definition of a legal wrong.[89]

Nor does this 'non-duty' approach fit the positive law. *Swindle v Harrison*[90] is a leading English fair-dealing case in which compensation was sought. Mrs Harrison was trying to purchase a hotel and some of the financing she expected to get fell through. She would have forfeited a deposit of £44,000 and been in breach of contract if she failed to complete; she would also lose the many thousands of pounds that she had spent, with the vendor's consent, on improvements to the building. One day before completion, she was therefore in desperate need of £75,000 of financing to close the deal. Her solicitors, including Mr Swindle, arranged a loan that allowed Mrs Harrison to complete. She knew very well that she was contracting with her solicitors. The terms of the loan were fair in the circumstances. The loan was made through the use by the solicitors of their borrowing facility with a bank. The solicitors did not disclose to her, however, the extent of their profit on the loan, because they had a share in the 'arrangement fee' that was payable to the bank, and they were also to receive some of the interest payable.

Mrs Harrison's business failed; not, however, due to anything that the solicitors had done, but simply because the business did not prosper. Her home was repossessed and she lost a great deal of money. Her solicitors now sought possession of the hotel, on which their loan was secured, which is why Mr Swindle was the claimant. Mrs Harrison counterclaimed against the solicitors, seeking to recover her losses. She was not seeking rescission, pecuniary or otherwise, of the contract with the solicitors; she was seeking to recover all the losses she had suffered as a result of the failed venture. What was the basis of the relevant part of her claim against them? We read in the three judgments of the Court of Appeal:

> [The fiduciaries'] *breach of duty consisted in failing to disclose material facts* to [Mrs Harrison], as the judge held, and it can be assumed that she would be entitled to claim rescission of the loan agreement, if recission was possible, and that she is now entitled to recover damages, or compensation, for the consequences of that breach.[91]
>
> [The fiduciary Mr Swindle] was dealing with his principal. He, therefore, was under *an additional fiduciary duty to prove affirmatively* that the transaction was fair and *that, prior to the making of the contract, he made 'full disclosure of all facts material to the transaction'.* This *fiduciary duty* is additional to his contractual duty... The judge held that... in breach of *his fiduciary obligation to make full disclosure,* [Swindle] did not disclose that his firm were making a 'hidden profit'... He also found that Mr Swindle was *in breach of his fiduciary duty in not disclosing* [other relevant information].[92]

[88] For further reasons why, see Smith, 'Prescriptive Fiduciary Duties' (n 2) 281–83.
[89] Section IV.A. For more detail, see Smith, *The Law of Loyalty* (n 6) ch 4, esp section II.
[90] *Swindle v Harrison* [1997] 4 All ER 705.
[91] ibid 718 (Evans LJ) (emphasis added).
[92] ibid 720 (Hobhouse LJ) (emphasis added). The other information referred to by Hobhouse LJ is omitted from my summary of the facts above.

> [The fiduciaries'] *duty was to make full disclosure of material facts relevant to the bridging loan* to enable [Mrs Harrison] to make a fully informed decision about it. They were in breach of that *duty*[.][93]

I am not sure how anyone can read that case and say that English law does not know of prescriptive fiduciary duties of disclosure.[94] Moreover, this and other cases on compensation cannot be understood as based on any supposed duty not to be, or act, in a conflict. The reason is that the fiduciary's being or acting in the conflict is not usually plausibly a but-for cause of the claimant's loss. In *Swindle*, the beneficiary's loss was through the failure of her business. She could not say that if the fiduciary had not been conflicted, she would not have suffered a loss; indeed in that counterfactual, she would have suffered the same loss. What she could and did say was simpler: that if she had been told all of the facts, which it was his duty to tell her, she would not have gone ahead at all, and so would not have suffered the loss. That is the logic of non-disclosure, although on the evidence, she failed to prove the causal link that was essential to her claim. This is because it was found as a fact by the trial judge that she was so committed to the transaction that even if full disclosure had been made, she nonetheless would have gone ahead and she would have suffered the same losses.[95]

In a case involving fiduciary accountability for unauthorised profits, there is no need to prove any causal link between any wrongful act and the profit. This is because the claim is not based on any wrongful act, but on the primary duty of accountability to which every fiduciary is subject.[96] But in *Swindle*, it was essential for Mrs Harrison to prove a causal link between the breach of the fiduciary duty of disclosure that had occurred and the losses that she had suffered. This is because her claim *was* based on that

[93] ibid 735 (Mummery LJ) (emphasis added). Mummery LJ also said (at 732) of *Nocton v Lord Ashburton* [1914] AC 932 that it stood for the proposition that '[a] solicitor who enters into a financial transaction with his client is under a fiduciary duty, when advising his client, to make full disclosure of all relevant facts known to him'. Note that as in Lord Eldon's judgment in *Gibson v Jeyes* (1801) 6 Ves Jun 266, 31 ER 1044, this positive fiduciary duty is not described as disclosure of the *conflict*; its ambit is much wider, limited only by relevance.

[94] For an equally unambiguous example from the High Court of Australia, see *Daly v Sydney Stock Exchange Ltd* (1986) 160 CLR 371, in which Gibbs CJ, for the majority, referred to a fiduciary duty to disclose arising from self-dealing (377, 379); see also Brennan J, concurring (385–88, citing *Gibson v Jeyes* (1801) 6 Ves Jun 266, 31 ER 1044). In the Privy Council, see *London Loan & Savings Co v Brickenden* [1934] 3 DLR 465 and *Clark Boyce v Mouat* [1994] 1 AC 428, 437. In the Supreme Court of Canada, see eg *Canson Enterprises Ltd v Boughton & Co* [1991] 3 SCR 534, 542, 558, 560, 572–73. The decision of Millett LJ (as he then was) in *Bristol & West Building Society v Mothew* [1998] Ch 1 that a fiduciary's duty of care, skill, and diligence is not a fiduciary duty is not universally shared (see R Walker, 'The Changing Face of Trust Law' (2017) 31 TLI 19, 24–26; *Silven Properties Ltd v Royal Bank of Scotland plc* [2003] EWCA Civ 1409, [2004] 1 WLR 997 [29]). The relevant part of the judgment in *Bristol & West Building Society v Mothew* [1998] Ch 1, 17–19, is idiosyncratic and difficult to follow; but in any event, it includes an *obiter dictum* to the effect that in fair-dealing, there is a fiduciary duty of disclosure (at 18).

[95] *London Loan & Savings Co v Brickenden* [1934] 3 DLR 465 can be read as suggesting that once non-disclosure is established, there is a kind of irrebuttable presumption of causation. In *Swindle v Harrison* [1997] 4 All ER 705, the court did not read *Brickenden* as establishing any such principle. Very thorough discussions of the treatment of *Brickenden* all over the common law world are found in C Mitchell, 'Equitable Compensation for Breach of Fiduciary Duty' [2013] CLP 307, 328–30 and in *Sim Poh Ping v Winsta Holding Pte Ltd* [2020] SGCA 35. In that case it was held (at [240]), in line with most of the decisions cited by Mitchell, that upon proof of non-disclosure the burden of proof should be reversed, but the fiduciary can escape liability by showing that the same loss would have been suffered even if disclosure had been made.

[96] *Regal (Hastings) Ltd v Gulliver* [1967] 2 AC 134; *Boardman v Phipps* [1967] 2 AC 46; *Recovery Partners GP Ltd v Rukhadze* [2025] 2 WLR 529; *Stevens v Hotel Portfolio II (UK) Ltd* [2025] 3 WLR 293.

wrongful act. It is obviously not helpful to think that we should say things like 'in claims for breach of fiduciary duty, it is not necessary to prove causation'. This is an illustration of the point made at the start of this chapter: it is a mistake to think that 'breach of fiduciary duty' is a single thing.

V. Conclusion

The rules governing conflicts and the rules governing unauthorised profits grow out of the fiduciary relationship, as a relationship in which one person acts for and on behalf of others. But they are distinct bodies of rules governing different aspects of that relationship in different ways and with different remedies.[97] We could say the same thing about the rules on self-dealing and the rules on fair-dealing. They are both part of fiduciary law, but they govern different aspects of the fiduciary relationship in different ways and with different remedies.[98]

Conflicts have a particular role in impugning the unimpeachable exercise of fiduciary powers. Like inadequate deliberation and improper purpose, they give a ground upon which beneficiaries can ask that the exercise of fiduciary powers be set aside. Self-dealing is merely an example of that.

Fair-dealing is a situation in which the beneficiary is empowered to rescind their own consent to a contract and thereby rescind the contract. That power arises upon the breach of the wide duty of disclosure that falls on any fiduciary who seeks to contract with their own beneficiary. A breach of that duty used only to give a power of rescission (and consequential relief, sometimes in the form of pecuniary rescission). Some have expressed regret that since *Nocton's case*,[99] if not before, it now gives rise also to compensation for loss caused by non-disclosure;[100] but the law evolves, and this die seems to have been cast.

The most important point for understanding rescission in these contexts is that the legal act that is impugned in the two situations is entirely different. In self-dealing or

[97] Section IV.A.

[98] Professor Dame Sarah Worthington also argues that the two sets of rules should not be rolled together: S Worthington, 'Fiduciaries: Following Finn' in T Bonyhady (ed), *Finn's Law: An Australian Justice* (Federation Press 2014) 33, 51–53. Confusingly to me, however, she argues that fair-dealing applies to non-fiduciaries who are in 'service engagements'; but the cases treat it as a rule of fiduciary law, and treat the duty of disclosure that arises in this situation as a fiduciary duty. The Court of Appeal recently suggested that fiduciary duties could apply to non-fiduciaries (*Wood v Commercial First Business Ltd* [2021] EWCA Civ 471, [2022] Ch 123), but the Supreme Court has rejected this (see *Hopcraft v Close Brothers Ltd* [2025] 3 WLR 423 [201]). Worthington also suggests that the justification for the fair-dealing rule is that the fiduciary's role has given them 'superior knowledge of the sale property' (at 52, here citing Finn). Often this is true, but this is not enough to explain the wide scope of the duty. The discussion above of *Gibson v Jeyes* (1801) 6 Ves Jun 266, 31 ER 1044 shows that the duty of disclosure goes well beyond things that the fiduciary knows about the sale property. Leading cases like *Swindle v Harrison* [1997] 4 All ER 705 (where no property was being sold) and *Daly v Sydney Stock Exchange Ltd* (1986) 160 CLR 371 (where the fiduciary was required to disclose its own precarious solvency) also illustrate this.

[99] *Nocton v Lord Ashburton* [1914] AC 932.

[100] eg LS Sealy, 'Fiduciary Obligations, Forty Years On' (1995) 1 J of Contract L 37; J McCamus, 'Prometheus Unbound: Fiduciary Obligation in the Supreme Court of Canada' (1997) 28 CBLJ 107; see the balanced and detailed survey in Mitchell (n 95) (compromised, in my respectful view, by taking a version of the mistaken proscriptive-only view of fiduciary duties).

other conflicted exercises of fiduciary powers, just as in direct attacks based on inadequate deliberation or improper purpose, the attack is on the exercise of a fiduciary power. In fair-dealing, the beneficiary invokes their own mistake, induced by the breach of a fiduciary duty of disclosure, to set aside their own consent to the contract made with the fiduciary.

7

Rescission of Unconscionable Gifts

*Man Yip**

I. Introduction

The law has to tackle the difficulty in 'defining and preventing those gifts that a legal system considers dangerous while at the same time allowing gift-giving to continue'.[1] The trouble is that private law is chiefly formulated for market-related activities and struggles to comprehend 'the fundamentally different social dynamic that governs gift-giving'.[2] Market-related activities are for-profit activities, and pursuit of self-interest is the accepted norm. The motivations for making a gift, on the other hand, are various, and most gift situations involve mixed motives. But pure altruism is also rare, as significant gifts are frequently made to one's family, close friends, or charity, with the expectation of non-financial returns.[3] In the context of making a gift to family and friends,[4] communications are generally informal and may take place over a long period of time; transfers are not conducted under the same degree of scrutiny and caution as commercial transfers;[5] some degree of persuasion and influence are commonplace;[6] family dynamics and affection could change; and the donors are more vulnerable for a multitude of reasons when they are past their prime,[7] but these circumstances do not necessarily amount to *non est factum* or mental incapacity.[8]

Placed in the social context of an ageing population (with the attendant issues of waning physical health and mental capacity) and the increasing awareness of the various forms of mental impairment, the issue of rescission of gifts made by vulnerable individuals is a strikingly important one. Yet, defining when social or familial behaviour

* Professor of Law, V3 Group Professor in Family Entrepreneurship, Singapore Management University, Singapore. I would like to thank Jonas Atmaz Al-Sibaie, Jordan English, Nuncio D'Angelo, Joshua Getzler, Goh Yihan, Lusina Ho, Robyn Honey, John Mee, Ben McFarlane, Charles Mitchell, Helen Scott, Alvin See, and CH Tham for their helpful comments. All views and errors are my own.

[1] R Hyland, *Gifts: A Study in Comparative Law* (OUP 2009) 12.

[2] ibid 9–10.

[3] A Farnsworth, 'Promises to Make Gifts' (1995) 43 Am J Comp L 359, 359–60. For example, the gift may be made to promote loyalty or allegiance.

[4] Charitable gifts fall outside of the scope of this chapter.

[5] Legal advice is not generally sought or expected in gift transactions, unlike commercial/contractual transactions.

[6] As Professor Pauline Ridge has noted, '[a] strong theme in the case law on probate undue influence is the social acceptability of lobbying testators for bounty': P Ridge, 'Equitable Undue Influence and Wills' (2004) 120 LQR 617, 628.

[7] eg they are easily tired, more forgetful, sick, and under long-term medication.

[8] Capacity is concerned with an individual's capability to understand the information, instead of demonstrating an actual understanding. See *Re Bearney* [1978] 1 WLR 770, 773 (test for *inter vivos* gifts).

concerning gratuitous transfers is unacceptable and impacts upon the donor's free will is a complex task for the law. The scope of application of the different doctrines and the precise rules for the successful invocation of each doctrine inform society as to the proper behaviour the law expects between individuals in non-commercial contexts.

This chapter focuses on the doctrine of 'unconscionable transactions' as a ground for rescission of *inter vivos* gifts, a subject that is given scant treatment or simply dismissed as unhelpful in practice.[9] The English doctrine, in particular, is neither frequently invoked nor highly developed.[10] Some English cases even suggest that the doctrine, also commonly referred to as 'unconscionable bargains', does not apply to gifts.[11] And even accepting that the doctrine is in principle applicable to both contracts and gifts,[12] difficulties and confusion remain. First, whilst the doctrine is recognised to be distinct from undue influence,[13] there is a clear overlap between them in terms of broad rationale. This has not escaped judicial and academic scrutiny. In cases where 'unconscionable transactions' is argued, undue influence is almost always invoked and may even be prioritised as the primary argument in non-commercial relationships. This raises the further inquiry as to the conceptual distinctiveness of 'unconscionable transactions' and its practical utility as a tool to protect vulnerable individuals. Second, and more importantly, there is little investigation as to the criteria of the doctrine of 'unconscionable transactions' that should be applied to gifts. It is assumed that the criteria that apply to contracts would apply without any modification. There is a need to reflect on the values that underpin relationships where gifts are made and how to construct a sensible legal understanding of acceptable conduct in the social practice of gift-giving which has immense social value.[14] The discussion will therefore deal with the second question first, to establish a proper understanding of the doctrine in the context of gifts before turning to the first question.

II. Historical Origins and Requirements: Current Law

A. Historical Origins

The doctrine of 'unconscionable transactions' is said to have developed in the later seventeenth century to 'police transactions which offended against the spirit of the usury legislation', although its genesis might be even earlier.[15] There were two limbs

[9] C Stanley, 'Vulnerable Gifts Made by Vulnerable People' (2017) 23 T&T 542, 553. Stanley explained that its practical utility was constrained by the requirement of showing moral culpability on the part of the counterparty.

[10] D O'Sullivan, S Elliott, and R Zakrzewski, *The Law of Rescission* (3rd edn, OUP 2023) [7.72].

[11] See *Langton v Langton* [1995] 2 FLR 890, 908–09 (Mr AWH Charles QC, sitting as deputy High Court judge, set aside the case on the basis of indue influence and his comments in relation to unconscionable transaction were therefore *obiter*); *Randall v Randall* [2004] EWHC 2258 (Ch), [2005] WTLR 119 [94] (approved *Langton* by way of *obiter* without fully engaging with the underlying issues).

[12] *Wilton v Farnworth* (1948) 76 CLR 646. See also B McFarlane, 'Fraud, Undue Influence and Unconscionable Transactions' in S Elliott (ed), *Snell's Equity* (35th edn, Sweet & Maxwell 2025) [8-039] (it is briefly stated, whilst noting conflicting authorities, that the doctrine of unconscionable transactions should also apply to gifts).

[13] See eg *Lawrence v Poorah* [2008] UKPC 21 [20].

[14] Tang HW, 'Restitution for Mistaken Gifts' (2004) 20 JCL 1.

[15] KL Fletcher, 'Review of Unconscionable Transactions' (1972) 8 UQLJ 45, 48.

to the doctrine: general relief from unconscionable bargains and an equity for heirs and expectants to relieve them from 'catching bargains'.[16] Relief was said to be more readily available to expectants and heirs than other claimants due to the policy concern of 'maintenance of family estates', and expectants were thus denied the right of free alienation of property.[17] The favoured expectant-heir plaintiffs enjoyed a rebuttable presumption of sharp practice which the defendant could rebut by demonstrating the fairness of the transaction and that the plaintiff had confirmed the transaction voluntarily and freely.[18] In practice, it was often the case that moneylenders had taken advantage of the expectant heirs in some way.[19]

In respect of the general limb concerning relief from unconscionable transactions for other types of claimants, historically,[20] equity intervened in four instances of sharp practice: (i) transactions at undervalue; (ii) lack of independent advice; (iii) misrepresentation; and (iv) where one party's weaknesses (eg illiteracy, lack of education, or impecuniosity) made the other party's sharp practice of taking advantage of their disparate positions more egregious.[21] The plaintiffs in this category did not enjoy a presumption of sharp practice.

As the general limb could not be extended to all instances of sharp practice, it did not provide adequate protection against unregulated moneylending.[22] Eventually, the Moneylenders Act 1900 was introduced to regulate moneylenders, which included various grounds to reopen harsh and unconscionable moneylending transactions, including one that represented the equitable doctrine of unconscionable transactions. The general limb was then relied on primarily to relieve the ignorant or aged applicants from unconscionable transactions relating to the disposition of their property.[23] The equity relating to heirs and expectants also progressively lost its vitality and, by the twentieth century, it was only invoked twice and unsuccessfully on both occasions.[24] In the case of *Fry v Lane*,[25] Kay J, identifying both limbs as common examples where the doctrine had been invoked,[26] extracted the following general principle from the then case law:

[16] ibid. A 'catching bargain' is a transaction entered into with an heir or expectant for the purchase of their expectancy for inadequate consideration.

[17] ibid 48–50. Fletcher further observed that there are conflicting viewpoints as to which limb developed first and endorsed Fonblanque's view that the second limb, which was originally vested in the Court of Star Chamber, was assimilated to the Chancery Court's developing jurisprudence on relief against oppressions when the Court of Star Chamber was abolished in 1641, resulting in the creation of a doctrine to relieve against unconscionable transactions. See J Fonblanque, *A Treatise on Equity* (5th edn, J & WT Clarke 1820) 134–39. Modern literature tends to trace the development of the doctrine to the expectant heirs cases: see D Capper, 'The Unconscionable Bargain in the Common Law World' (2010) 126 LQR 403; O'Sullivan, Elliott, and Zakrzewski (n 10) [7.76].

[18] Fletcher (n 15) 49–50.

[19] See eg *Tylor v Yates* (1870–71) LR 6 Ch App 665.

[20] This limb became 'the sole bulwark against unconscionable bargains' for most plaintiffs after the repeal of the usury legislation. See Fletcher (n 15) 52–53.

[21] ibid 56. See *Strachan v Brander* (1759) 1 Eden 303, 28 ER 701 (the court found 'misrepresentation, imposition, and undue advantage taken of the necessitous situation' of the destitute claimant who was ignorant of his rights as an heir and the value of his inheritance).

[22] Fletcher (n 15) 57.

[23] ibid 58.

[24] ibid.

[25] (1888) 40 Ch D 312.

[26] ibid 321.

> The result of the decisions is that where a purchase is made from a poor and ignorant man at a considerable undervalue, the vendor having no independent advice, a Court of Equity will set aside the transaction . . . The circumstances of poverty and ignorance of the vendor, and absence of independent advice, throw upon the purchaser, when the transaction is impeached, the onus of proving, in Lord Selborne's words, that the purchase was 'fair, just, and reasonable.'[27]

The reference to Lord Selborne LC's words was a reference to his judgment in *Earl of Aylesford v Morris*,[28] a case concerning equity relieving expectant heirs from unconscionable bargains. Kay J's statement of the principle amalgamated requirements under both limbs of the doctrine. The doctrine thereafter went into 'hibernation in England until *Cresswell v Potter* in 1968' and took on a reincarnated form.[29] Although the precise reasons as to why the doctrine became dormant in that period were unclear, there were suggestions that this might be a result of English law being much more focused on certainty in contract law from the nineteenth century onwards.[30] Indeed, the Sales of Reversions Act 1867 was passed primarily to curb what was perceived to be excessive judicial intervention in contracts—the preamble stated that 'it is expedient to amend the law, as administered in Courts of Equity with respect to Sales of Reversions'.[31] It reduced the need to rely on the equitable doctrine in the context of a sale of reversionary interests at undervalue.[32] Tracing the historical developments of the equitable doctrine reveals that the doctrine was primarily developed as a legal tool to regulate contracts, with the focus being on protecting vulnerable individuals from unfair contracts and unconscionable contracting behaviour.[33]

In *Cresswell v Potter*,[34] the doctrine began to morph. Megarry J clarified that even though the principle remained the same, the words 'poor' and 'ignorant' used by Kay J in *Fry v Lane* would need to be reinterpreted to suit the modern societal conditions which were very different from the ones prevailing at the time *Fry v Lane* was decided.[35] Megarry J also said that the requirements laid down in *Fry v Lane* would not be the only circumstances in which equity would intervene to set aside the transaction, thereby suggesting that Kay J's statement of principle was not truly a test.[36]

[27] ibid 322. In the case, two poor and ignorant brothers entered into sales of their shares in the estate at clear undervalue, having received no independent advice. The solicitor acted for both sides, and was observed by the court to be inexperienced and 'must have been considering the purchaser's interest too much properly to guard that of the vendors' (at 323).

[28] (1873) LR 8 Ch App 484, 490–91.

[29] Capper, 'The Unconscionable Bargain' (n 17) 404.

[30] RW Clark, 'The Unconscionability Doctrine Viewed from an Irish Perspective' (1980) 31 NILQ 114, 125–34; SR Enman, 'Doctrines of Unconscionability in Canadian, English and Commonwealth Contract Law' (1983) 16 Anglo-Am LR 191.

[31] See Clark (n 30) 125.

[32] The statute did not permit the setting aside of sales solely on the ground that the transaction was at undervalue, if it was entered into in good faith, without fraud or unfair dealing. It had been re-enacted in the Law of Property Act 1925, s 174.

[33] *Langton v Langton* [1995] 2 FLR 890, 908.

[34] [1978] 1 WLR 255.

[35] ibid 257.

[36] ibid.

B. The Modern Doctrine and Its Requirements

Peter Millett QC's judgment in *Alec Lobb (Garages) Ltd v Total Oil (Great Britain) Ltd*[37] is generally taken to be an authoritative statement[38] of the modern doctrine of unconscionable transactions, which has three criteria:[39]

> First, one party has been at a serious disadvantage to the other, whether through poverty, or ignorance, or lack of advice, or otherwise, so that circumstances existed of which unfair advantage could be taken . . . secondly, this weakness of the one party has been exploited by the other in some morally culpable manner . . . and thirdly, the resulting transaction has been, not merely hard or improvident, but overreaching and oppressive.

The three criteria of special disadvantage, unconscionable conduct, and oppressive terms set out in *Alec Lobb* do not operate independently from each other and must be considered in the round. The proof of one requirement 'may have a strong effect on the court's finding of another'.[40] I unpack the three criteria below, to establish a proper understanding of how these criteria operate in the contractual context before turning to critique their operation in the gift context.

1. Serious Disadvantage

A serious disadvantage is one that 'seriously affects the ability of the innocent party to make a judgment as to his/her own best interests'.[41] As alluded to, the harsh terms of 'poverty' and 'ignorance' have been given a contemporary reinterpretation. 'Poverty' refers to a range of financially inferior circumstances, including being 'a member of the lower income group',[42] 'not wealthy',[43] or someone who has 'barely enough . . . to live on'.[44] 'Ignorance' is taken to mean being 'less highly educated'.[45] In *Cresswell v Potter*, the transferor was a telephonist and had conveyed her half share in the matrimonial home (to which purchase she had made a substantial contribution) to her former husband in exchange for a release from existing mortgage liabilities. She had signed the release thinking it was a document that would enable the property to be sold without affecting her interest in it. It was held that a telephonist may be considered as 'poor' and 'ignorant' in the context of property transactions and conveyancing documents.[46] More importantly, there are many kinds of 'serious disadvantage' other than poverty

[37] [1983] 1 WLR 87.

[38] See eg *Jones v Morgan* [2001] EWCA Civ 995, [2001] Lloyd's Rep Bank 323 [35]; *Pakistan International Airline Corp v Times Travel (UK) Ltd* [2021] UKSC 40, [2023] AC 101 [24].

[39] *Alec Lobb (Garages) Ltd v Total Oil (Great Britain) Ltd* [1983] 1 WLR 87, 94–95.

[40] Y Liew and D Yu, 'The Unconscionable Bargains Doctrine in England and Australia: Cousins or Siblings?' (2021) 45 MULR 206, 210.

[41] *Commercial Bank of Australia Ltd v Amadio* (1983) 151 CLR 447 [38].

[42] *Cresswell v Potter* [1978] 1 WLR 255, 257.

[43] *Backhouse v Backhouse* [1979] 1 WLR 243, 251.

[44] *Dickinson v Lowery* (KBD, 23 March 1990) (the weaker party only had 'a small private income' and old-age pension).

[45] *Cresswell v Potter* [1978] 1 WLR 255, 257.

[46] ibid 257–58.

and ignorance, including sickness, age, infirmity of body or mind, drunkenness, illiteracy, lack of education, lack of assistance or explanation where such would be necessary,[47] and unfamiliarity with the language used for the transaction document.[48]

The different kinds of serious disadvantages do not operate in the same way in establishing the weaker party's inability to judge their own best interests. Poverty, in the bargain context, may demonstrate the weaker party's immediate need of money and therefore makes them an easy victim to manipulation/exploitation.[49] Sickness, age, infirmity, drunkenness, and illiteracy, on the other hand, go towards showing the weaker party's capacity to understand the nature and consequences of the transaction and/or whether they did in fact understand those matters. Sickness and age may help to establish that the weaker party is dependent on and/or susceptible to the exploitation of the stronger party.[50] The proof of special advantage brings the party seeking rescission a step closer to proving that there was unconscionable conduct because they are in a position to be taken advantage of, manipulated, or exploited. It also underlines the need for independent advice and the lack of such professional aid casts doubt on the gift having been an expression of the donor's free will.

2. Oppressive Terms and Unconscionable Conduct

Although the modern restatement is not framed in contractual language, *Alec Lobb* involved a claim to set aside the contract for being an unconscionable bargain. The Court of Appeal clarified that the

> whole emphasis is on extortion, or undue advantage taken of weakness, unconscientious use of the power arising out of the inequality of the parties' circumstances and on unconscientious use of power which the court might in certain circumstances be entitled to infer from a particular—and in these days notorious—relationship unless the contract is proved to have been in fact fair, just and reasonable.[51]

Unequal bargaining power, one party's weakness (eg poverty or mental incapacity) or objectively unreasonable terms, without impropriety on the part of the counterparty, would not establish unconscionable conduct.[52] Nor would knowledge or belief that the transferor is foolish by itself suffice.[53] These points have been emphatically

[47] *Blomley v Ryan* (1956) 99 CLR 325, 405. cf *Kakavas v Crown Melbourne Ltd* [2013] HCA 25; (2013) 250 CLR 392 [126]–[135] (pathological gambling condition was not considered a special disadvantage so as to make the weaker party (the gambler) susceptible to exploitation).

[48] *Commercial Bank of Australia Ltd v Amadio* (1983) 151 CLR 447.

[49] *Langton v Langton* [1995] 2 FLR 890, 908.

[50] *Radley v Bruno* [2006] EWHC 2888 (Ch).

[51] *Alec Lobb (Garages) Ltd v Total Oil (Great Britain) Ltd* [1985] 1 WLR 173, 182.

[52] ibid 183; *Hart v O'Connor* [1985] AC 1000 (a sale between a mentally incapable individual who was independently advised by his own solicitor and his neighbour which contained unfavourable terms to the former (as proposed by his own solicitor) but the neighbour was not aware of the former's mental incapacity).

[53] *Wu v Ling* [2016] NSWCA 322 [11]. The Court noted (at [2] and [15]) that the plaintiff, Ms Wu, was 'an experienced and astute businesswoman of considerable wealth' and had received independent legal advice in relation to the loans. It also observed (at [16]) that she was willing to pay high interest rates to the defendant because she believed in taking 'large risks to achieve large rewards'.

made by Lord Templeman in *Boustany v Pigott*,[54] also a case concerning the setting aside of a contract (a lease). Unconscionable conduct includes pressuring the plaintiff into executing the transfer with undue haste.[55]

Unconscionable conduct can be inferred from the circumstances—for example, if the transaction was based on clearly disadvantageous terms. A transaction at a substantial undervalue coupled with the weaker party having not received any independent advice would make it 'impossible' for the stronger party to prove that the transaction is fair, just, and reasonable.[56] In *Alec Lobb*, Peter Millett QC observed:

> Where there has been a sale at undervalue, the under-value has almost always been substantial, so that it calls for an explanation, and is in itself indicative of the presence of fraud, undue influence or other such feature.[57]

Millett QC found that there was no advantage taken of the weaker contracting party in the case because it 'was advised throughout by its own solicitors and accountants, who were completely independent of the defendants'. The defendant did not press for a hasty decision,[58] and the transaction was not at undervalue.

Another case to illustrate that unconscionable conduct can be inferred from the disadvantageous terms of the transaction is *Boustany v Pigott*.[59] In that case, Miss Pigott, who had entrusted her business affairs to her cousin (George Pigott), granted a new lease to her existing tenant, Mrs Boustany, when George was temporarily away. Miss Pigott's solicitor, who had prepared the first lease, considered the terms of the new lease to be disadvantageous[60] to Miss Pigott. There was no personal attachment between the two women that might account for Miss Pigott's generosity. The solicitor summoned Miss Pigott, Mrs Boustany, and her husband to his chambers so he could explain the unfair terms to Miss Pigott before everyone. The parties went ahead to sign the new lease nonetheless. The lease was ultimately set aside as the Privy Council agreed with the trial judge's inference from the circumstances that Mrs Boustany and her husband 'had prevailed upon Miss Pigott to agree to grant a lease on terms which they knew they could not extract from Mr George Pigott or anyone else'.[61] Similarly, in *Radley v Bruno*,[62] the elderly Mrs Radley[63] sought to set aside a lease granted to her nephew

[54] (1995) 69 P & CR 298.
[55] *Bridgewater v Leahy* (1998) 194 CLR 457 [15].
[56] *Dickinson v Lowery* (KBD, 23 March 1990).
[57] *Alec Lobb (Garages) Ltd v Total Oil (Great Britain) Ltd* [1985] 1 WLR 87, 95.
[58] ibid.
[59] (1995) 69 P & CR 298.
[60] It was a lease for ten years, with an option to renew for a further ten years, and the rent, which was below market price, was fixed for the entire duration (including for the further ten years if the option to renew was exercised).
[61] *Boustany v Pigott* (1993) 42 WIR 175, 181. cf N Bamforth, 'Unconscionability as a Vitiating Factor' [1995] LMCLQ 538, 544. Bamforth considered the Privy Council's treatment of the facts to be problematic. He pointed out that inferences were necessary in the case because Miss Pigott was incapable of giving evidence at the original trial and Mrs Boustany refused to do so.
[62] [2006] EWHC 2888 (Ch).
[63] She was 92 years old when she executed the lease and was suffering from various ailments that weakened her: ibid [32].

(Mr Bruno), his wife (Mrs Bruno), and herself. The lease was over her property bought with her late husband, which was worth a lot of money. The lease was to last for 99 years or until the death of the last surviving lessee, whichever was earlier. The rental was a peppercorn until the death of Mrs Radley and thereafter at a rate far below the market rental price, to be paid by Mr and Mrs Bruno. It contained no forfeiture clause. Collins J held that the terms of the lease were 'so clearly disadvantageous' that the Court could infer that Mr and Mrs Bruno had behaved unconscionably.[64]

In contractual transactions, the inequality or unreasonableness of terms, a matter of substantive fairness, is adjudged based on market norms. The underlying assumption is that people look for a broadly fair exchange of value or equality of terms in contractual dealings, reflecting the contractual norm that contracting parties are expected to pursue their respective commercial self-interests, which is usually taken to mean financial interests.[65] It is thus possible and reasonable to infer unconscionable conduct constituted by victimisation or exploitation from disadvantageous terms.

More generally, the possibility of inferring unconscionable conduct brings into view an uncertain but important aspect of this requirement: whether the strong party must subjectively know of the weaker party's serious disadvantage and actively take advantage of it in entering into the transaction (subjective approach); or is it sufficient that the strong party, on an objective assessment, ought to have been aware of the serious disadvantage and passively accepted the benefit of the transaction (objective approach)?[66] A subjective approach would be consistent with a 'defendant-sided' account of the doctrine which pins liability on the moral reprehensibility of the defendant's conduct.[67] An objective approach, on the other hand, falls somewhere between a 'defendant-sided' account and a 'plaintiff-sided' account (where the focus is on the weaker party's impaired consent).[68] The resort to inferences from circumstantial evidence, which is a necessary judicial technique, has the potential to blur the distinction between the two approaches in practice.[69]

Judicial articulation of the law is also not necessarily sensitive to the distinction between the two approaches. In *Hart v O'Connor*,[70] it was stressed that the doctrine requires proof of 'victimisation, which can consist of either of the active extortion of a benefit or the passive acceptance of a benefit in unconscionable circumstances'.[71] In *Jones v Morgan*,[72] Chadwick LJ said that '[t]he enquiry is not whether the conscience

[64] ibid [34].
[65] *Pakistan International Airline Corp v Time Travel (UK) Ltd* [2023] AC 101 [1], [97]–[99].
[66] Bamforth (n 61) 548–50.
[67] ibid 550, referencing the discussion of the 'plaintiff-sided' and 'defendant-sided' approaches in P Birks and N-Y Chin, 'On the Nature of Undue Influence' in J Beatson and D Friedmann (eds), *Good Faith and Fault in Contract Law* (Clarendon Press 1995) 57.
[68] Bamforth (n 61) 550, citing the discussion of the two approaches in Birks and Chin (n 67).
[69] In *Jones v Morgan* [2001] EWCA Civ 955 [38], the Court of Appeal reversed the lower court's finding of fact that one of the contracting parties (the appellant) 'undoubtedly appreciated' that the other contracting parties (the respondents) had made a mistake by deleting certain contractual provisions. The Court of Appeal was of the view that as the contract was prepared by the respondents' experienced solicitor, it was not open to the court to infer, in the absence of evidence, that the appellant came to a different conclusion.
[70] [1985] AC 1000.
[71] ibid 1024. This was endorsed in Australian law: see *Bridgewater v Leahy* (1998) 194 CLR 457 [34].
[72] [2001] EWCA Civ 995.

of the party who has obtained the benefit of the transaction is affected in fact; the enquiry is whether, in the view of the court, it ought to be'.[73] If the stronger party has actual knowledge of the weaker party's serious disadvantage and passively accepts the benefit of the transaction in the circumstances, can the former not be said to exploiting the latter? Surely the stronger party's actual knowledge would make their acceptance, even in the absence of any persuasion or extortion, not strictly passive. Should it make any difference if the disadvantage is so manifest that it would be obvious to anyone who deals with the weaker party in the same circumstances but the stronger party nevertheless denies that it was obvious to them? I would suggest not.

Undoubtedly, an objective approach would allow more transactions to be unwound than a subjective approach.[74] Considering bargains to be different from gifts, some tentatively suggest that it may be easier to set aside gifts.[75] Unfortunately, the courts have not fully explored this issue.[76] Presumably, the justification lies in the policy of protecting the security of bargain transactions. I will return to this issue below in Section III.B, arguing that the issue cannot be approached from a strictly policy perspective.

3. Reversal of Onus?

It has been noted that English cases do not speak with one voice as to whether there is a reversal of onus on the defendant to prove that the transaction is 'fair, just, and reasonable' upon the claimant proving some elements of the doctrine.[77] Reversal of the onus of proof makes it easier for the weaker party to invoke the doctrine of unconscionable transactions. On the analysis of Professor Ying Khai Liew and Ms Debbie Yu, there is no reversal of onus based on the current state of English law.[78] Australian law, on the other hand, puts the burden on the defendant to show that the transaction is 'fair, just and reasonable' upon the claimant showing that their 'special disability' was 'sufficiently evident to the stronger party to make it prima facie unfair or 'unconscientious' that he procure, or accept, the weaker party's assent to the impugned transaction in the circumstances in which he procured or accepted it'.[79] From the perspective of norm-setting, reversal of the onus of proof affords the law an opportunity to directly define what is proper conduct on the part of the donee.[80]

[73] ibid [35].

[74] Bamforth (n 61) 550.

[75] McFarlane (n 12) [8-039] (by comparing the criteria for setting aside a contract with the criteria for setting aside a voluntary disposition in equity for mistake); *Nitopi v Nitopi* [2022] NSWCA 162, (2022) 109 NSWLR 390 [31]–[32] (discussed below at text to and around nn 127–29).

[76] Bamforth tentatively observed that a subjective approach was adopted in *Louth v Diprose* (1992) 175 CLR 621, a case concerning a gift; whereas the courts had applied both approaches in contract cases: Bamforth (n 61) 549. cf O'Sullivan, Elliott, and Zakrzewski (n 10) 613–14 (it is observed that '[g]ifts inter vivos are more vulnerable than contracts to rescission' in various aspects because the policy of protecting bargains is not engaged where gifts are concerned); McFarlane (n 12) [8-039] (fn 294).

[77] Liew and Yu (n 40) 25.

[78] ibid 26.

[79] *Commercial Bank of Australia Ltd v Amadio* (1983) 151 CLR 447, 474.

[80] The onus of proof is sometimes reversed on the defendant because they are in the best position to lead evidence on the matter.

4. Lack of Independent Advice

If the donor has received independent advice from a qualified person, it demonstrates that the nature and effect of the transaction was explained to them. Having received independent legal advice is considered to be the 'most obvious way' to establish that the transfer was the result of an exercise of free will.[81] If it is usual to have a solicitor assisting in a particular type of transaction (eg conveyancing), then 'the more striking will be his absence, and the more closely will the courts scrutinise what was done'.[82] This requirement might have developed by reason that a great number of authorities concerned conveyancing transactions where having the aid of a solicitor was standard practice.[83] Hence, lack of independent advice is 'not so much an essential freestanding requirement, but rather a powerful factor confirming the suspicion of nefarious dealing which the presence of advice would serve to dispel'.[84]

Conversely, the fact that one of the parties to the transaction has not received independent legal advice does not, by itself, establish unconscionability, if the other elements of the doctrine are not satisfied. For example, if the allegedly weaker party does not in fact suffer from any special disadvantage that calls for the aid of a professional advisor, its absence would not by itself cast doubt on the free will of this party in entering into the transaction.[85] On the other hand, the fact that the weaker party has received independent legal advice against entering into the transaction because the agreement contains grossly unreasonable terms but still goes ahead to sign the agreement could contribute to an inference of unconscionable conduct on the part of the stronger party.[86]

III. Gifts—Transfers for No Value

A. Scope of Application of the Doctrine

As a matter of principle, the doctrine of unconscionable transactions should apply to gifts. This is the position taken under Australian law, Irish law, and Singapore law. It is therefore surprising that under English law, this point has not been definitively settled. In *Langton v Langton*,[87] the Court observed, by way of obiter, that the doctrine does not apply to gifts for three reasons.[88] First, the doctrine was historically developed

[81] *Inche Noriah v Shaik Allie Bin Omar* [1929] AC 127, 135–36. Although the case concerned undue influence, the same rationale would apply in respect of this requirement in the context of unconscionable transactions.

[82] *Cresswell v Potter* [1978] 1 WLR 255, 258.

[83] ibid.

[84] *Portman Building Society v Dusangh* [2000] 2 All ER (Comm) 221, 232.

[85] In *Yedina v Yedin* [2017] EWHC 3319 (Ch) [284], the Court described the allegedly weaker party as 'a seasoned businessman and politician who had acquired considerable wealth in the Ukraine in the post-communist era'.

[86] See *Thorne v Kennedy* [2017] HCA 49, (2017) 263 CLR 85. In this case, the stronger party (the fiancé) created a sense of urgency for the weaker party (the fiancée) to sign the prenuptial agreement.

[87] [1995] 2 FLR 890.

[88] ibid 908–09. The transaction in the case was regarded by parties as a gift, although the court took the view that it could be treated as a bargain.

to protect vulnerable parties from unfair or unconscionable bargains. Further, gifts are frequently scrutinised under the doctrine of undue influence. Finally, the description 'fair, just, and reasonable' applies to bargains and not gifts. However, in *Evans v Lloyd*,[89] Judge Keyser QC (sitting as a deputy high court judge) held to the contrary for several reasons.[90] First, there was no authority where the proposition that the doctrine is inapplicable to gifts formed part of the ratio.[91] Second, the doctrine's origin in bargains ought not to constrain its contemporary scope of operation. Third, in equity, substance must prevail over form. To exclude gifts from the doctrine's scope of application would be to do the contrary. In fact, *Cresswell v Potter* was characterised as a case concerning a gift 'in substance', even though the transfer was not for nothing.[92] Fourth, it is possible to provide a principled statement of the law supported by a defensible rationale that does not draw unmeritorious distinction between bargains and gifts. Fifth, there were no downsides to allowing equity to set aside gifts for being unconscionable transactions; for this latter proposition, Judge Keyser QC drew support from Australian and Irish law, which conventionally recognised the application of the doctrine to gifts.

Whilst affirming the doctrine's application to both bargains and gifts, Judge Keyser QC did briefly note that '[m]ost gifts would be unaffected by the doctrine'.[93] This brief remark merits a couple of preliminary responses. It may be that *most* gifts would be unaffected by the doctrine for two main reasons. First, at least under English law, it would be easier to invoke undue influence, which does not require proof of unconscionable conduct, to set aside a gift.[94] I will return to the relationship between undue influence and unconscionable transactions in Section IV. This first reason is, however, not an adequate justification for confining the doctrine of unconscionable transactions to bargains. Second, proving that a gift is an unconscionable transaction is not quite so straightforward. This is the point made in *Langton*. We are not able to evaluate fairness and reasonableness of the gift through the bargain lenses of exchange of monetary value and pursuit of self-interest. Put another way, a gift is made with no expectation of returns and, on that basis, how could the terms of a gift ever be overreaching and oppressive? It is inherently economically imbalanced. In fact, a gift is frequently made to affirm or advance a relational bond or out of moral and other personal convictions that cannot be explained in monetary terms and is therefore 'foolish' from the bargain perspective. That the donor would often be unable to testify at trial only intensifies the challenge of discerning their motivations. Conversely, short of direct physical/emotional abuse and fraudulent misrepresentation, what amounts to a 'taking of advantage'

[89] [2013] EWHC 1725 (Ch), [2013] WTLR 1137.

[90] ibid [52].

[91] See eg *Langton v Langton* [1995] 2 FLR 890. See further D Capper, 'Unconscionable Bargains and Unconscionable Gifts' [1996] Conv 308.

[92] Mr Keyser QC referred to both Megarry J's own comments in *Cresswell v Potter* [1978] 1 WLR 255, 259, as well as the views on the case set out in *Snell's Equity* (n 12).

[93] *Evans v Lloyd* [2013] EWHC 1725 (Ch) [52].

[94] See eg *Humphreys v Humphreys* [2004] EWHC 2201 (Ch), [2004] WTLR 1425.

in close, personal, relationships is harder to identify or define where relationships are not characterised by pursuit of self-interest as a starting point. Social and family relationships can be considered as collaborative pursuits that prioritise collective benefit and mutual assistance, values that require some degree of self-sacrifice and tolerance. Parties therefore make requests of each other or expect and readily accept gifts. Intergenerational wealth transfers are a family norm and a topic that is often discussed between the family members, especially when the senior family member is progressively weakened by old age and health issues. This second reason simply underscores the need to clarify the criteria and how they are applied to set aside gifts. It is not a reason for restricting the doctrine to bargains.

The doctrine of unconscionable transactions is broadly speaking concerned with predatory behaviour in both contractual and gift contexts. Where gifts are concerned, we are specifically concerned with *relational* predatory behaviour. Therefore, the same general criteria ought to apply for both contracts and gifts. However, the criteria must be understood in their respective contexts. Unfortunately, there is little reflection on the contextual differences in case law and existing scholarship. My analysis below seeks to plug the gap. Through a review of case law, I identify the distinctive features of gift-giving in personal relationships and propose how the criteria are to be understood or modified in the gift context. Given that much of English case law is on unconscionable contracts, I will also draw upon the case law from Australia,[95] Ireland,[96] and Singapore[97] to examine the diverse fact patterns in which unconscionable gifts may be made. Whilst acknowledging that there may be differences between the different versions of the doctrine in each jurisdiction, there are sufficient similarities between them to justify studying them together to gain insights into the relational dynamics in the gift-giving context.

Before diving into an analysis of the case law, it should be highlighted that the fact patterns usually involve transfers of property where title to the property has been conveyed to the donee. It is conceivable that an individual may make a gift of services, that is to say, one may render services to another gratuitously. My chapter does not deal with 'gifts' of services because services, once performed, cannot be rescinded. They should

[95] For an excellent analysis of the differences between the Australian doctrine and the English doctrine, see Liew and Yu (n 40). The authors observe that English law requires actual knowledge of the claimant's serious disadvantages and exploitation of the same in a morally culpable manner, whereas under Australian law, categories (i)–(iv) of Baden degrees of knowledge would be sufficient to bring the doctrine into play, even in the absence of overt exploitation. Further, the authors point out that English law requires the claimant to prove that the transaction is 'overreaching and oppressive', whereas Australian law reverses the burden on the defendant to show that the transaction was 'fair, just and reasonable'.

[96] See *Secured Property Loans Ltd v Floyd* [2011] IEHC 189; *Allied Irish Bank plc v DX* [2020] IECA 308. Contrary to the earlier decision of *Prendergast v Joyce* [2009] IEHC 199, and aligning with the modern approach under English law, Irish law now requires 'impropriety or moral culpability' on the part of the stronger party. In *Allied Irish Bank*, the Irish Court of Appeal also stated that it is sufficient that the stronger party 'ought' to have known of the weaker party's serious disadvantage.

[97] See *BOM v BOK* [2018] SGCA 83, [2019] 1 SLR 349. A two-stage test applies under Singapore law: under the first stage, the claimant bears the burden to show that they suffer from an infirmity of sufficient gravity and evident to the counterparty which the counterparty exploited in procuring the transaction; on satisfying the first-stage requirement, the burden then shifts to the defendant at the second stage to show that the transaction was fair, just, and reasonable. In other words, Singapore applies the reversal of onus approach.

be analysed as claims for restitution.[98] My discussion below is thus exclusively focused on gifts involving transfer of property.

B. Context and Criteria

1. Pre-existing Relationship and Gift-Giving

In *Irvani v Irvani*,[99] Buxton LJ observed:

> Undue influence is concerned with the prior relationship between the contracting parties, and whether that was the motivation or reason for which the bargain was entered into. Unconscionable bargain is, as its title suggests, concerned with the nature and circumstances of the bargain itself, and can arise without there being any relationship, outside of that immediate contract, between the parties.[100]

The distinction between undue influence and unconscionable transactions is much more apparent in the contractual context than in the context of gifts. This is because bargains can be entered into between the weaker party and the stronger party as a one-off transaction, without there being a prior relationship. Where gifts are concerned, most gifts are made to family members or friends—that is to say, there is usually a pre-existing *personal* relationship.[101] That relationship provides the motivation and occasion for making the substantial gift, as well as supplying the occasion for exploitation or manipulation. In the cases examined above, the parties were family members[102] (or formerly family members),[103] akin to family members,[104] or in a courtship.[105] This is not to say that the doctrine of unconscionable transactions can never be applied in respect of gifts made outside of a prior relationship. But such cases are likely to be rare. Outside of charitable gifts, the making of a substantial gift to a stranger by itself looks suspicious and could be challenged on various possible grounds, including mistake.

Small gifts are commonplace in non-commercial relationships because they serve to affirm the affection and bond or are given as a reward for loyalty or return of affection. Conversely, it is harder to prove or infer unconscionable conduct because it may not take a lot of persuasion or pressure for the stronger party to extract gifts of small

[98] On the distinction between a test for rescission and a test for restitution, see the brief discussion in J English, 'Deeds, Rescission and Restitution' (2023) 139 LQR 363.

[99] [2000] 1 Lloyd's Rep 412.

[100] ibid 424.

[101] *Langton v Langton* [1995] 2 FLR 890, 909.

[102] *Bosschieter v Howitt* [2024] NSWSC 1676 (grandmother and granddaughter); *Prendergast v Joyce* [2009] IEHC 199 (aunt and nephew (by marriage)); *BOM v BOK* [2019] 1 SLR 349 (father and infant son).

[103] *Backhouse v Backhouse* [1978] 1 WLR 243 (married couple who separated after the wife committed adultery with another man).

[104] *Evans v Lloyd* [2013] WTLR 1137. In this case, a farmer made a gift of his entire estate to the proprietors of the farm where he had spent his entire working life and they were observed by the court (at [11]) to have enjoyed the 'closest and warmest of relationships'.

[105] *Louth v Diprose* (1992) 175 CLR 621.

value from the weaker party with whom they are in a pre-existing personal relationship. Practically, donors are unlikely to pursue legal proceedings to set aside gifts of small value, given the prohibitive costs of litigation.

It is the substantial gifts, which often constitute a substantial part/the entirety of the donor's wealth, that look suspicious. In *BOM v BOK*,[106] the husband was misled by the wife into settling all his assets on an *inter vivos* trust for their infant son. In *Wilton v Farnworth*,[107] the husband transferred his entire interest in his wife's estate to the defendant, his wife's son from a previous marriage. Substantial gifts look especially suspicious in cases where the donor had closer relations to whom they would be expected, in the normal course of things, to give the assets,[108] or if the donor, who is not in the last years of their life, would be left with close to nothing for themselves after making the gifts.[109] The substantial gift would also raise eyebrows if parties were not as close and affectionate as to account for the donor's generosity.[110] The court has to grapple with this question: could the gift be accounted for by normal human motivation in the context of the pre-existing relationship? What is normal human motivation must surely be drawn from general societal experience and the circumstances, personality, and experience of the particular donor. In *Evans v Lloyd*, for instance, Wynne Evans (a farmer) made a gift of his entire estate, comprising two agricultural holdings he inherited from his brother, to the proprietors of the farm (David and Elizabeth) on which he had been working on since he was fourteen years old, first under the employ of David's grandparents and later under David and Elizabeth. The Court found that the gift was not unconscionable. On David's evidence, Wynne gave them the two agricultural holdings because one of them required substantial renovations which Wynne was not willing to pay for, given that he was 70 years old at the time and had no intention to set up his own home.[111] Further, the Court took into account the fact that Wynne's consideration as to who should receive his agricultural holdings was similar to that which his grandfather took on board in deciding to leave the agricultural holdings to the farmers in the family.[112]

Finally, the existence of a pre-existing relationship in the context of gifts helps to explain how the various criteria of the doctrine of unconscionable transactions operate in such cases. It is to those criteria we now turn.

2. Special Disadvantage

As the cases demonstrate, any physical, mental, or emotional condition that would prevent the transferor from independently judging their best interests could constitute a

[106] [2019] 1 SLR 349.
[107] (1948) 76 CLR 646.
[108] *Evans v Lloyd* [2013] WTLR 1137. Wynne had brothers related by blood.
[109] *BOM v BOK* [2019] 1 SLR 349; *Wilton v Farnworth* (1948) 76 CLR 646; *Louth v Diprose* (1992) 175 CLR 621.
[110] *Backhouse v Backhouse* [1978] 1 WLR 243 (the transfer was made when the couple, though remaining legally married, had separated); *Wilton v Farnworth* (1948) 76 CLR 646 (the gift was made to the donor's deceased wife's son from a previous marriage).
[111] *Evans v Lloyd* [2013] WTLR 1137 [28].
[112] ibid [64].

serious disadvantage. The relevant serious disadvantage may prevent the transferor from fully appreciating the nature and consequences of the transaction. Emotional condition, in particular, may make the weaker party susceptible to the influence of, and manipulation by, the stronger party. In *Louth v Diprose*,[113] a man was utterly infatuated with a woman to the degree that constituted 'an enormous weakness' because he lavished her with gifts even though she did not reciprocate his affection. He even used a large part of his assets to buy her sister's house for her when she informed him that it would have to be sold and further told him that she would attempt to kill herself if she lost the house. The house was the subject matter of the claim for rescission. The man's unusual degree of emotional attachment and susceptibility to her influence rendered the relationship between them 'to be different in kind from the ordinary relationship between a man courting a woman'.[114] The High Court of Australia set aside the unconscionable gift, ruling that the woman had acted dishonestly to induce the man to buy the house for her as a gift.[115]

Another example would be *BOM v BOK*. In that case, the husband had been induced by his wife to sign a trust deed settling all his assets on trust for his son. He signed the deed a week after his mother's tragic death, at a time when he was undergoing acute grief. The wife had drafted the deed by hand on the day when the mother's will (comprising SGD 54m assets) was read. When she broached the matter to him that evening, the husband initially refused to sign the deed. He relented after the couple had an argument. The husband alleged that the wife had misrepresented to him that the trust of all of his assets in favour of his infant son was to take effect on his death when in fact it took effect immediately, a matter he belatedly learned after signing the deed. He also alleged that she threatened to kick him out of the house if he did not sign the deed. The husband was neither poor nor ignorant. To the contrary, he was very rich and well-educated, having earned an LLM from University College London by long-distance learning. His special disadvantage was his acute grief at the material time which impaired his ability to make decisions, rendering him susceptible to his wife's influence,[116] of which the wife was aware and took advantage The Singapore Court of Appeal upheld the lower court's decision that the deed could be set aside on the grounds of unconscionability, mistake, undue influence, and duress.

Conversely, one party's ability to manipulate and influence the other party, which usually occurs in relationships of a certain degree of closeness, may enable the stronger party to create the special disadvantage to which the victim is subject. This was what happened in *Thorne v Kennedy*.[117] Although the facts concerned setting aside financial agreements made under Part VIIIA of the Family Law Act 1975 (Cth), the relational dynamics and special disadvantage could equally arise in a gift transaction. In that case,

[113] (1992) 175 CLR 621.
[114] ibid 7.
[115] The trial judge, King CJ observed that the defendant was aware of the man's infatuation with her and her influence on him. He described her as having manufactured 'an atmosphere of crisis where no crisis existed' and that the conduct 'smacked of fraud': *Louth v Diprose* (1990) 54 SASR 438, 448.
[116] *BOM v BOK* [2019] 1 SLR 349 [154].
[117] (2017) 263 CLR 85.

Ms Thorne applied to the Court to set aside two financial arrangements, one of which was a prenuptial agreement entered into with her then fiancé, Mr Kennedy, the terms of which solely protected Mr Kennedy's interests. Ms Thorne was 36 years of age and living in the Middle East when she met Mr Kennedy, who was 67 years old, through an online dating website. While she had no substantial assets and spoke limited English, he was very wealthy. A year later, Ms Thorne moved to live with him in Australia and planned for a wedding in September that year, as her Australian visa was soon to expire and she could not remain in Australia unless she married Mr Kennedy. Less than two weeks before the wedding, Mr Kennedy told her that she must sign an agreement or the wedding would be cancelled, with no promise on his part to assist Ms Thorne and her family to return home in that event. The next day, the first time she became acquainted with the terms of the agreement, she was given independent advice by a family law solicitor that the terms of the agreement were entirely disadvantageous to her. At that stage, Ms Thorne's family had flown to Australia to attend the wedding, her wedding dress had been made, wedding guests had been invited, and the wedding reception was booked. Four days before her wedding, she signed the agreement (which incorporated minor amendments to the terms) against her solicitor's strong advice not to do so. After the wedding, again against her solicitor's advice, she signed a second agreement—the postnuptial agreement—on substantially identical terms as the prenuptial agreement and revoked the prenuptial agreement. She also applied to set aside this second agreement.

The High Court of Australia ruled that the agreements were vitiated by unconscionable conduct. The plurality (Kiefel CJ, Bell, Gageler, Keane, and Edelman JJ) held that Ms Thorne had found herself in a situation where 'she saw no choice but to enter the agreements' because Mr Kennedy 'created the urgency with which the pre-nuptial agreement was required to be signed and the haste surrounding the post-nuptial agreement and the advice upon it'.[118] In the circumstances, Ms Thorne was not able to 'make a judgment as to her best interests'.[119]

However, emotional conditions are not clear-cut matters like sickness, physical impairment, advanced age, or mental impairment, which can be established more readily by objective medical evidence. In some cases, such as *BOM v BOK*, the weaker party's emotional condition was not created or related to the stronger party. In other cases, such as *Louth v Diprose*, the weaker party's emotional condition related to and could be said to be made worse by the stronger party's deliberate manipulation. However, emotional attachment to the transferee—for example, infatuation and consequent clouded judgement—ought not by itself to be considered a serious disadvantage.[120] Otherwise,

[118] ibid [63]–[64].

[119] ibid [65].

[120] *Mackintosh v Johnson* [2013] VSCA 10, (2013) 37 VR 301 [77]. In this case, a 73-year-old man had a five-month intimate relationship with a 45-year-old woman and, whilst they were together, he had paid her about $175,000 to support her business and spent $480,000 to buy a house registered in her sole name. The court rejected his pleaded serious disadvantage based on his advanced age, loneliness, vulnerability, and the fact that he was retired and wanted a companion.

many gifts made in the context of a romantic relationship would be liable to be set aside after the relationship has come to an end.

Oddly, emotional strain arising from marital disloyalty was considered a serious disadvantage in *Backhouse v Backhouse*.[121] The wife in that case had committed adultery and left the matrimonial home registered in the married couple's joint names to live with the other man. After an unsuccessful reconciliation attempt, the wife executed a transfer form, prepared by the husband's solicitors, to transfer the matrimonial home, which was her only substantial capital asset, into the husband's sole name for no monetary consideration. She was released from the mortgage liability.[122] The Court found that the real reason the wife had signed the transfer form was because 'she felt a sense of guilt at what she had done'.[123] It rejected any suggestion that the husband had used threats to secure the wife's execution of the transfer form.[124] One would have thought that the guilt and emotional strain were but a normal emotional response to the state of affairs brought about by the claimant herself. The better explanation for the outcome in *Backhouse v Backhouse* is that the marriage had broken down and the parties were expected to conduct themselves in the transaction as if it were a bargain.

Finally, poverty may be a less relevant special disadvantage in cases involving gifts because the donor is necessarily not too poor if they are able to make a substantial gift to the donee, even though they may not be objectively rich.[125] More pertinently, poverty is usually not the reason they are unable to appreciate the nature and consequences of the voluntary transaction, unlike in contracts where the weaker party may be overly eager to sell for a profit by reason of their own impecuniosity.

3. Knew or Ought to Have Known?

In *Nitopi v Nitopi*,[126] Bell JA observed that the Australian authorities are inconsistent as to whether the stronger party must have actual knowledge of the weaker party's serious disadvantage or whether it is sufficient that the stronger party ought to have known of the same.[127] He accepted that constructive knowledge of the weaker party's serious disadvantage would suffice, by interpreting *Kakavas v Crown Melbourne Ltd*[128] (one of

[121] [1979] 1 WLR 243.

[122] It may be questioned whether *Backhouse v Backhouse* [1979] 1 WLR 243 is properly a case of gift, and not bargain as the transfer of her interest in the property was *not* for nothing. Its factual pattern is similar to that in *Cresswell v Potter* [1978] 1 WLR 255, 258, where Megarry J scrutinised whether the ex-wife's transfer of her interest in the matrimonial home to the husband was at undervalue by reference to the value of the discharge of mortgage liability in comparison with what her interest would have been worth. The headnotes of *Backhouse*, however, had labelled it as involving a 'voluntary transfer'. The court also kept emphasising that the transfer was for no monetary value.

[123] *Backhouse v Backhouse* [1979] 1 WLR 243, 249.

[124] ibid 249–50.

[125] What constitutes a substantial gift must be considered in relation to the overall financial position of the transferor (ie the weaker party). In principle, even a gift of £50 could be a substantial gift if it is nearly everything that the transferor owns. Such a gift is liable to be rescinded for being an unconscionable transaction if the criteria are satisfied. Of course, in real life, we only have case law dealing with objectively substantial gifts because claims to rescind gifts of small value are not worthwhile to pursue. Nor would a poor donor be able to afford litigation.

[126] (2022) 109 NSWLR 390.

[127] ibid [4]–[8].

[128] (2013) 250 CLR 392.

the relevant authorities) to have decided that constructive notice, and not constructive knowledge, would be insufficient.[129]

This inconsistency harks back to the wider controversy on whether the doctrine adopts an objective or subjective approach. As mentioned above, gifts usually take place within an existing personal relationship. The line between whether the donee knew or ought to have known of the donor's conditions/arrangements is blurry. I suggest that the court's recourse to an objective approach is not strictly a policy decision as to how interventionist equity ought to be. In a great number of the cases, the objective approach is applied as a matter of practicality and forms part of the court's toolbox to determine what actually happened.

In many of these cases, the donor might be deceased[130] or too infirm to give testimony in trial, making it difficult to directly challenge the veracity of the donee's subjective (and rather implausible) account of what happened in respect of the transfer. The court might infer from the circumstances that there was actual knowledge, a factual finding that can be supported based on the often long-term personal relationship between the parties. In other cases, the court might apply the objective test of 'ought to have known' as a device to test the veracity of the donee's testimony. *Bosschieter v Howitt*[131] illustrates the later judicial technique. In that case, the elderly donor grandmother was physically and emotionally dependent on her donee granddaughter for daily care and arrangements of any sort. On whether her grandmother (deceased at the time of trial) received independent legal advice in respect of the gift, the granddaughter's testimony was that she thought that she had already spoken to her legal advisor. The Court did not accept the testimony.[132] The Court stressed that the improvidence of the gift (constituting the grandmother's life savings) 'would have been obvious to any reasonable person in [the granddaughter's] position and must have been obvious to [the granddaughter]' and that the grandmother's 'weakness and dependence' upon the granddaughter 'must also have been obvious to [her] as must have been [the grandmother's] lack of independent legal advice'.[133]

4. Unconscionable Conduct in Personal Relationships

What the law considers to be unconscionable conduct in the context of gifts is significant: it dictates the norms of gift-giving in close, personal relationships. When does exerting influence, excessive persuasion, or proposing a certain gift be made cross the line? Conduct in contractual settings may be evaluated by objective standards, such as: (i) measuring contractual consideration against market value; (ii) determining the fairness and reasonableness of the contractual terms by benchmarking against industry norms; (iii) that parties are free to pursue their self-interests; and (iv) independent

129 *Nitopi v Nitopi* (2022) 109 NSWLR 390 [9].
130 See eg *Prendergast v Joyce* [2009] IEHC 199.
131 [2024] NSWSC 1676.
132 ibid [171].
133 ibid [173]–[174].

legal advice may be necessary, or even conventional, for certain types of commercial transactions.

In the context of gifts, where the stronger party clearly took advantage of the weaker party through active misrepresentation or deceit, the court would not hesitate to find that the stronger party had acted unconscionably.[134] Unconscionable conduct is also readily established in circumstances where the donor was rushed into executing the gift with unseemly haste and the donee made no attempt to explain the transaction to them.[135] If the gifts were made in circumstances where the donor was clearly unable to judge their best interests and the donee was aware of the donor's vulnerability, the gifts were clearly obtained by the donee through unconscionable exploitation. In *Bosschieter v Howitt*, Covid-19 restrictions applied around the time of the transfer and the grandmother (the donor), who was 92 years of age, had been isolated from the rest of her family. She was very weak, began to show periods of confusion, and was fully dependent on her granddaughter (the donee), with whom she lived in the same house, for daily care and arrangements (including arrangements to consult her legal advisor). In *Prendergast v Joyce*,[136] a wife (the donor) had, after the death of her husband, transferred a series of payments from bank accounts in the couple's joint names into new joint accounts in the names of the husband's nephew (the donee) and herself. These payments were made when the wife was 70 years old and had Alzheimer's disease[137] and just a week after her husband's death, which left her in a state of shock. After the wife's death, her niece, the administrator of her estate, successfully set aside these transactions under the Irish equivalent of the doctrine of unconscionable transactions.

Nitopi is more unusual. It concerned a claim to set aside payments made by a father to his adult daughter. The father, a successful businessman, had made the transfers when he was nearly 70 years old, had short-term memory deficit, and was diagnosed with alcoholic dementia. The trial judge held that the daughter had unconscientiously taken advantage of her father by exerting 'moral pressure' on the latter.[138] Bell CJ astutely commented:

> There is a question as to whether an adult child's making known a need to a parent for money for one purpose or another, absent any trickery or pretence in the making of the request (and none was found by the judge), could amount to the kind of moral pressure sufficient to attract equitable intervention?[139]

[134] *BOM v BOK* [2019] 1 SLR 349; *Louth v Diprose* (1992) 175 CLR 621.
[135] *Wilton v Farnworth* (1948) 76 CLR 646.
[136] [2009] IEHC 199.
[137] She started to become forgetful five years before her husband passed away and became unable to care for herself even before his death. Two years before his death, she was described to be 'very frail, depressed, and severely anxious, and suffered from poor concentration and memory'. Shortly after her husband's death, she required 24-hour care: ibid 264–65.
[138] *Re Estate of Nitopi (No 2)* [2021] NSWSC 748 [247].
[139] *Nitopi v Nitopi* (2022) 109 NSWLR 390 [18].

In view of the father's vulnerable mental state at the point of transfer, the outcome was undoubtedly correct.

Relevantly, Bell CJ accepted that even passive retention coupled with knowledge of the claimant's serious disadvantage (which may be acquired post-receipt) would be sufficient to bring the Australian doctrine into play in the context of gifts, although setting aside contracts under the doctrine might require active procurement by unconscionable conduct.[140] In other words, Bell CJ is in favour of making it easier to set aside gifts. However, the endorsement of knowing retention as being sufficient to engage the doctrine means that even 'an unsolicited gift to a child' could be set aside.[141] This merits serious reconsideration as it is inconsistent with the established rationale underlining the doctrine of unconscionable transactions as being based on unconscionable *exploitation* of the weaker party's vulnerability. The normative basis for allowing gifts to be unwound in the absence of unconscionable conduct of the donee will require full investigation and is likely to be focused on impairment of autonomy. It will drive a schism between setting aside contracts and setting aside gifts on the basis of unconscionability. Further, the law will need to review the current list of recognised special disadvantages, which includes matters (eg emotional attachment) that do not by themselves cause the weaker party to be *unable* to judge their own best interests. If the law decides to travel in this direction of development, it will also need to develop defences (eg change of position) to protect the gift recipient who might have dissipated the gift (or part of it) between receipt and acquiring knowledge of the donor's special disadvantage.

5. Transaction at Undervalue and Oppressive Terms

We have discussed above how unconscionable conduct may be inferred from disadvantageous or oppressive terms of transfers.[142] Where bargains are concerned, the fact of a transaction at undervalue goes to demonstrate that the terms of the bargain are unreasonable/improvident and, coupled with the transferor's weakness/vulnerability, contributes to the inference that the transferee has taken advantage of the transferor. If a serious disadvantage on the part of the transferor and unconscionable conduct on the part of the transferee could be shown, the contract should be set aside even where the transfer was at a market value.[143] Transaction at undervalue is therefore an evidentiary factor.

On the other hand, gifts, as was pointed out in *BOM v BOK*,[144] are always transactions at undervalue. This factor therefore does not perform the same function in the context of gifts as it does in the context of bargains. To speak in terms of a transaction at undervalue in the context of gifts is to misdirect our attention to the inquiry as to why the transferor gave away a substantial asset for no monetary consideration, seemingly

[140] ibid [31]–[32].

[141] M Leeming, 'Unconscionable Transactions—the Roles of Knowledge and "Predatory State of Mind"' (2023) 97 ALJ 13.

[142] See Section II.B.2.

[143] It may be that the plaintiff would never have wanted to sell the relevant asset to the transferee, if not for the latter's manipulation or oppression.

[144] *BOM v BOK* [2019] 1 SLR 349 [155].

suggesting that a sensible transferor would have asked for value in return. This line of inquiry may make sense for transactions which one would have expected to be bargains (or involve substantial monetary consideration even if not at full market value) in the ordinary course of things. *Backhouse v Backhouse* is a good example—it concerned a transfer of property between a couple at the point of their separation to effect a clean break. Such kinds of transfers, which are not uncommon, should be subject to a bargain-esque line of inquiry.

However, there are many other transactions where the proper question to ask is whether the gift would have been made at all, not whether the transfer should have been made for (full) value. The proper inquiry to undertake is whether the transaction can be accounted for by normal human motivation based on the circumstances of the donor and their relationship with the donee. This inquiry emerges clearly in the Court's reasoning in *Evans v Lloyd* where the Court was satisfied that the donor, a farmer, had very good reasons to make the generous gift to the proprietors of the farm on which he had worked for his entire working life.

Returning to Mr Charles QC's comment in *Langton* that 'fair, just and reasonable' is not a description that can be used for gifts, the above cases demonstrate that the court has evaluated the fairness and reasonableness of the gift by reference to two factors: (i) whether they constitute a substantial part of the donor's assets, and (ii) whether the donor might require the subject matter of the gift for their own maintenance/purposes. The unarticulated value underlining these two factors is that an individual would and ought to prioritise self-care and pursuits before caring for others. In the context of family and friendship, this value is firmly rooted in the belief in intergenerational independence and an orientation towards individual development. This is not to say that an individual cannot, in complete disregard of their own care, maintenance, and pursuits, give away their entire estate. However, the law will only let such a gift stand, out of respect of that individual's autonomy, if the individual did it out of their free will, in the absence of pressure or manipulation from the donee. Thus, the value of the gift and self-interest, factors that are relevant to bargains, are also relevant to the assessment of the fairness and reasonableness of gifts. The difference is that in the context of gifts, self-interest is not equiparated with commercial or financial interests. The understanding of oppressive terms from which unconscionable conduct could be inferred should therefore be reoriented accordingly.

6. Norm-setting: Independent Legal Advice and Reversal of Onus

My final point is on the norm-setting function of equity. Two matters are relevant to this function within the doctrine of unconscionable transactions: (i) independent legal advice, and (ii) the reversal of the onus onto the defendant to show that the gift is fair, just, and reasonable. We turn first to independent legal advice.

Ensuring that the donor received independent legal advice in respect of the gift does more than ensuring that the donor has proper assistance in understanding the terms of the transaction and the consequences on the donor's financial position. In practice, as many of the donors are elderly and weak and because loss of mental capacity is a gradual process requiring expert determination, ensuring the donor has consulted a legal advisor will also ensure mental incapacity or impairment can be detected. However, independent legal advice does not ensure that the donor has made the gift in their own best interests, a matter that is hard to assess outside of bargains. The weaker party may do so in circumstances involving some form of compromise. Independent legal advice can however ensure that the donor has had the nature, terms, and consequences of the gift explained to them and increases the chance that the donor makes the gift out of their free will. An adequate legal advisor may also be able to point out signs of oppressive or manipulative conduct emanating from the stronger party. There are therefore many benefits in requiring that a would-be donor of a substantial gift be independently advised by a lawyer.

In *BOM v BOK*, the Singapore Court of Appeal considered the lack of independent advice to be an evidential factor in determining whether the transaction is fair, just, and reasonable. In the context of gifts, we are even less concerned with substantive fairness (ie fairness of terms of the transaction) as we are with procedural fairness—that is to say, the donor, where they have a serious disadvantage, should not be making the gift until they have, at the very minimum, been independently advised by a solicitor. This establishes a protocol for protecting vulnerable donors when they make substantial gifts.[145] The reversal of the onus onto the defendant (ie the stronger party) to show that the transaction is fair, just, and reasonable can further strengthen the protection. As has been pointed out, the Australian approach, which clearly adopts the reversal of the burden of proof, 'sends the message that, if D is aware of C's special disadvantage, equity will intervene *unless* D discharges their positive duty to ensure that the overall transaction is fair, just and reasonable'.[146] The Australian version is focused on *prevention* of unconscionable conduct. This may be a more effective way of protecting vulnerable donors,[147] instead of simply providing a legal recourse to the donor to set aside gifts on proving that these gifts have been obtained by unconscionable conduct.

IV. Conceptual Distinctiveness and Practical Utility

The doctrine of unconscionable transactions is often, though not exclusively,[148] compared with the doctrine of undue influence.[149] The latter has been described as being

[145] Whether the quality of the independent legal advice ought to be taken into account is a separate question.

[146] Liew and Yu (n 40) 30.

[147] The protection is especially needed in cases of what I would describe as early 'inheritance' cases, a proliferating social problem. Essentially, younger family members may pressure their ageing and physically frail family members into giving away their substantial assets by way of *inter vivos* gifts, instead of waiting for their inheritance through testamentary bequests after their relatives have passed away. I thank Dr Nuncio D'Angelo for highlighting this point.

[148] A neighbour doctrine is impaired capacity based on mental infirmity and intoxication. Unlike the doctrine of unconscionable transactions, rescission on the grounds of mental infirmity and intoxication does not require demonstrating exploitation or that the transaction was at undervalue. See O'Sullivan, Elliott, and Zakrzewski (n 10) [7.42]. We will return to this doctrine shortly.

[149] See generally R Honey, 'Deconstructing the Equitable Concept of Undue Influence: Insights from a Genealogy' (2020) 14 J Eq 58.

concerned with victimisation,[150] although some varieties of undue influence do not involve wrongdoing at all.[151] No doubt, there are differences between the two doctrines—most notably, the requirements of serious disadvantage and unconscionable conduct under the doctrine of unconscionable transactions are not requirements under the doctrine of undue influence. The requirements under the two doctrines may, however, be stretched to form significant overlap. The overlap between the two doctrines is particularly well noted in the contractual context,[152] and has prompted much discussion as to whether the two doctrines should be merged (with one being subsumed by the other)[153] or kept separate.[154] I am interested in the narrower and more practical question as to whether the doctrine of unconscionable transactions has any major role to play in the context of gifts.

Under Australian law, the High Court has recently affirmed the conceptual demarcation between undue influence (plaintiff-sided) and unconscionable transactions (defendant-sided) in *Thorne v Kennedy*. Interestingly, in that case, whilst the plurality found that the financial agreements were vitiated by both unconscionable conduct and undue influence, Gordon J took the contrary view that Ms Thorne did not sign the agreements pursuant to undue influence because her 'will was not overborne'.[155] Gordon J found that she was 'able to comprehend what she was doing, she knew and recognised the effect and importance of the advice she was given and wanted the marriage to Mr Kennedy to proceed and prosper'.[156] Gordon J's judgment shows that in some cases of non-bargain transactions where parties are in a pre-existing relationship, it may be that undue influence is not available. However, whether someone's will was overborne when subjected to unconscionable manipulation so as to amount to undue influence is really a matter of evaluative judgment for the court.[157]

Crucially, the reversal of the burden of proof onto the defendant to show that the transaction is fair, just, and reasonable under Australian law makes the doctrine of unconscionable transactions comparatively more generous and therefore more frequently invoked.[158] Indeed, in *Bosschieter v Howitt*, a case in which both doctrines were argued, Slattery J set aside the transfer on the basis of unconscionable bargains but commented, by way of *obiter*, that 'there probably was a relationship of actual undue influence' on the facts.[159]

Under English law, on the other hand, the claimant is required to prove exploitation or some kind of morally culpable conduct on the part of the defendant, a 'steep hurdle'

[150] *National Westminster Bank v Morgan* [1985] AC 686, 705. cf *Macklin v Dowsett* [2004] EWCA Civ 904, [2004] 2 EGLR 75 [10] (Auld LJ said that the rationale of the doctrine is 'the protection of the vulnerable in dealings with their property').

[151] McFarlane (n 12) [8-015], citing *Allcard v Skinner* (1887) 36 Ch D 145.

[152] Clark (n 30) 114.

[153] D Capper, 'Undue Influence and Unconscionability: A Rationalisation' (1998) 114 LQR 479.

[154] Birks and Chin (n 67).

[155] *Thorne v Kennedy* (2017) 263 CLR 85 [108].

[156] ibid [80]–[81].

[157] ibid [43].

[158] Leeming (n 141). See also Liew and Yu (n 40). For other common law jurisdictions, the introduction of reversal of onus may change the interplay between undue influence and unconscionable transactions.

[159] *Bosschieter v Howitt* [2024] NSWSC 1676 [177].

that makes it less attractive to invoke unconscionable bargains in the context of gifts.[160] Where there is a pre-existing relationship, presumed undue influence (based on an established relationship of influence or actual proof of a relationship of influence) can be more easily established, without proving wrongdoing. Further, the types of serious disadvantage recognised under the doctrine of unconscionable transactions constitute facts that help to establish that the relationship is one of influence. The role of unconscionable transactions is therefore residual, to fill the gaps left by undue influence—typically in cases where there may be no relationship of influence (presumed or actual) and where there is no coercion, threats, or misrepresentation that may give rise to actual undue influence. There are at least two gaps.

First, consider the following example.[161] A claimant gratuitously transfers his home into the joint names of himself and an acquaintance (the defendant), to be held on trust for themselves as tenants in common (50:50). The claimant is illiterate and has the functional age of six years where mathematical ability is concerned. The parties are not close at all, but the claimant's impaired mental acuity is evident to the defendant. The claimant, who has no relatives or friends, proposes the transaction to enable the defendant to live with him and care for him and his property, although the object could be and is often, in the ordinary course of things, achieved via other means. The claimant is advised by a solicitor but the solicitor does not repeatedly explain the provisions of the deed to him over a sufficient period of time for the claimant to understand the nature and consequences of the transaction. The defendant passively accepts the gift nonetheless.

On the facts of the hypothetical scenario, which may be unusual but not impossible, the doctrine of undue influence would not apply. If the claimant's impaired mental acuity prevented him from forming any views or making any assessments about the transaction, it may not be straightforward to establish an operative mistake, although inferences from circumstances could help to establish one. Perhaps this is a case where the doctrine of unconscionable transactions could provide redress.

Second, there may be cases of relational predatory conduct which is not solely or even substantially dependent on the pre-existing relationship between the donor and donee, although that relationship provides the occasion for the predatory conduct to arise. To put it simply, the direct relationship between the donor and donee would not enable the donee to exert any influence upon the donor but the donee would be able, through that relationship, to manipulate the donor. The facts of *Wilton v Farnworth*,[162] with some modification, would illustrate this. In that case, a husband (the plaintiff) gave away his share in his wife's estate to the wife's son from a previous marriage (the defendant). It was clear from the facts that he was still sentimentally attached to his wife even though they had parted ways before her demise, as he requested her wedding ring as a keepsake. He also expressed regret for not making it in time for her funeral.

[160] Stanley (n 9) 553.

[161] The example is largely based on the hypothetical scenario discussed in Stanley (n 9) 556, where the author considers that the law presently does not have a doctrine to address the situation.

[162] (1948) 76 CLR 646.

Described by the Court as a person of 'dull intellect',[163] and without understanding that he had a substantial share in her estate by the operation of intestacy laws, the plaintiff gave away that interest by signing a document prepared by the defendant, having been bustled into the transaction with 'unseemly haste'.[164] The Court did not explicitly identify the plaintiff's emotional attachment to his wife as a possible special disadvantage and it may be that, on the facts of the case, that emotional attachment was not overwhelmingly strong. But where the emotional attachment is sufficiently strong, it would be strongly arguable that the stepson could have exploited the husband's emotional state to bustle the husband into signing away his interest in his wife's estate to the stepson, manipulating the husband to think that would be the best way to honour his wife's wishes.

Even finding possible gaps does not negate the observation that the doctrine of undue influence is likely to do much more of the work in the context of gifts. But as Professor Peter Birks and Dr Nyuk Yin Chin highlighted: '[i]f there are two doctrines, there are two doctrines, and the fact that one might do perhaps 95% of the work is no reason for pretending that the other does not exist.'[165] Moreover, common law jurisdictions do allow concurrent claims.

V. Conclusion

In this chapter, through unpacking the criteria of the doctrine of unconscionable transactions, I have made a positive case that the doctrine should also apply to gifts and on the same general criteria. However, the criteria must be understood differently in the gift context, in view of the characteristic relational dynamics inherent in gift-giving and the fact that gifts are by definition transactions at undervalue. I have highlighted that unconscionable gifts are concerned with relational predatory conduct as gifts are generally made in the context of a pre-existing personal relationship between the donor and the donee. That pre-existing personal relationship requires some reorientation of our understanding of special disadvantage and unconscionable conduct. That gifts are transactions at undervalue also means that we need to understand oppressive terms, an evidentiary factor from which to infer unconscionable conduct, differently. In the second part of the chapter, I investigated the relationship between unconscionable transactions and undue influence in the context of setting aside gifts. I made the point that where a claimant is required to prove a positive case of unconscionable conduct as under English law, the role of unconscionable transactions is residuary, to plug the gaps left by undue influence. The Australian doctrine, which reverses the burden onto the defendant to show that the transaction was fair, just, and reasonable once the claimant has proved that they laboured under a special disadvantage which the

163 ibid 650.
164 ibid 654.
165 Birks and Chin (n 67) 95.

defendant was aware of, is far more vigorous and has overtaken undue influence under Australian law to regulate gift-giving. This comparison is not a mere intellectual exercise. It should prompt greater reflection on how the law can protect vulnerable donors from their family members' predatory conduct, a social issue that is becoming increasingly important.

8

The Scope of Rescission for Duress

*Robert Stevens**

I. Introduction

The central claim of this chapter is that rescission is justified by a number of different reasons. Rescission for duress where justifiable always concerns unlawful pressure, but in one of three distinct senses.

'Rescission' describes the exercise of a form of legal power: the power to set aside a juridical act, such as entering into a contract, making a will, declaring a trust, accepting a gift, or, in principle, an earlier act of rescission.[1] Just as with other forms of right, such as subrogation, it should not be surprising that such a power arises for more than one reason. One example, differing from all those discussed in this chapter, is where a contract by its terms provides for one or both parties to be able to avoid the contract where certain conditions are satisfied.

This chapter is confined to the law of contract (the 'rescission' of wills, in particular, raises different considerations).[2] Duress is taken to mean a form of illegitimate pressure applied by another. After considering the kinds of reasons that could in principle justify rescission, the chapter concludes that duress may impact upon a contract in the following ways.

First, starting with the most extreme case, duress may be so acute that the promisor is not responsible for the impression of agreement created, and no contract is validly entered into, unless they subsequently choose to ratify what was done.

Second, a wrong committed by the promisee that enables them to obtain agreement from the counterparty, through the subsequent application of pressure or otherwise, may be rescinded. Contractual rights acquired wrongfully may be set aside.

Third, the pressure applied by the promisee may constitute the threatened commission of a wrong, and thereby suffice for rescission.

Fourth, where the pressure constitutes a threat to do something lawful that would worsen the counterparty's position (eg prosecute the promisor or disclose humiliating information) and it is applied for an improper purpose (eg obtaining a contract) it thereby becomes wrongful, and rescission is available.

* Professor of English Private Law, University of Oxford, and Professorial Fellow of Lady Margaret Hall, Oxford, United Kingdom.

[1] Chapter 6 of this book (L Smith, 'Rescission in the Context of Fiduciary Relationships'); Chapter 2 of this book (B Häcker, 'Explaining the Right to Rescind').

[2] On the impact of undue influence on a will, see P Ridge, 'Equitable Undue Influence and Wills' (2004) 120 LQR 617.

Fifth, the category of 'lawful pressure' may be dispensed with in the context of rescission, although it may possibly have a role in establishing that there was no justification for a payment made. Threats to withhold benefits should never, without more, constitute duress.

II. A Little Light Theory

If I have a right against you, you owe a duty to me. The form of the relationship restricts the range of reasons that may legitimately justify it. If we are to justify why you should have an entitlement against me, we must appeal to reasons that relate me to you. 'You deliberately punched me on the nose' appeals to such a reason. It describes the parties as the 'doer and the sufferer of the same wrong'.[3] It could potentially justify why the puncher now owes a duty to the punchee to compensate them.

If we appeal to reasons unrelated to the putative duty bearer as a necessary part of its justification, they are entitled to respond 'what has that got to do with me?' If we argue that the law ought to require you to clean my windows because my time is very valuable and you will do a better job than I would, you may legitimately respond that you have no responsibility for this state of affairs.

Conversely, if we appeal to reasons unrelated to the putative right holder, the putative duty bearer is entitled to respond 'what has that got to do with you?' If I argue that you ought to pay me money if you fail to drive your car with due care, in order to deter you and others from behaving in such a way in the future, you may legitimately respond that how you drive is not, without more, my affair.

Reasons that relate to one party or the other in isolation, or which are unrelated to either of them ('policy' reasons) cannot, alone, legitimately justify our rights one against another.

In contract law, this restriction on the justification for rights most prominently manifests itself in the requirement of agreement. If one party subjectively consents to do something, that does not suffice; there must be an offer from one party that is accepted by the other. This offer and acceptance is not a matter of the parties' subjective intentions. Those intentions may, fortuitously, exactly coincide, but, absent the external actions of offer and acceptance, we have no agreement.[4] Those actions in the world have an existence independent of the parties themselves. They are objectively interpreted because that is how, inside and outside the law, we interpret the words and actions of persons. Meaning is not determined by anyone's state of mind. Contractual obligations are made by the actions of the parties together, for which they are jointly responsible.[5]

The banal truism of the kinds of reasons that may justify the rights we have one against another should not be pushed too far. Different kinds of reasons may be relevant

[3] E Weinrib, *The Idea of Private Law* (OUP 1995).
[4] cf *Tinn v Hoffman* [1873] 29 LT 271 (cross offers).
[5] R Stevens, 'What is an Agreement?' (2020) 136 LQR 599.

to the enforceability (as opposed to the existence) of a right. Once the issue of the exercise of state power and the deployment of its resources comes into play—as it does at the stage of the court making an order—that creates a new kind of public duty on those subject to it; further reasons may become important in refusing an order.

Sometimes a right may be either wholly unenforceable or the availability of some orders restricted, in order to protect one party alone. Focusing on contract law, a contract may be unenforceable because of the lack of capacity of one party (eg a child) in order to protect them and other similarly situated people. A contract for the provision of services is not, generally, specifically enforceable because we do not wish to destroy the promisor's future freedom of action (ie we do not facilitate a system akin to slavery even where voluntarily entered into). The rule against restraint of trade seems based upon the same idea of protecting autonomy, but here goes further so as to rule out a claim for damages for breach too.

Sometimes a contract may be unenforceable (again, either wholly or in part) because of reasons that are not necessarily related to the parties to the contract at all. If an agreement is illegal for one or both parties to either enter into or perform, this may render it wholly or partially unenforceable. Limitation statutes generally have the goal of allowing all of us to close the books on the past, so that we are free from claims that arose a considerable time ago. Where required, the justification for formality requirements should also render the agreement unenforceable and not void,[6] but alas this is no longer the position in England because of legislative error.[7]

By contrast, if we wish to either invalidate, or give one party the power to set aside, a right based upon some kind of countervailing reason, that reason too must relate the duty bearer to the right holder. Just as the reasons justifying rights must relate the parties to one another, the countervailing reasons that may justify there either being no rights or why such rights may be set aside must also do so. And this is, again, the pattern we find in the law. Rescission for misrepresentation, undue influence,[8] and unconscionable bargains all follow this pattern of being based upon reasons relating one party to the other. It is a mistake to think, when it comes to rescission, that the grounds for doing so could legitimately be 'claimant-sided', 'defendant-sided', or unrelated to either party based upon some kind of public reason.[9]

The distinction above between unenforceability and invalidity is not merely of theoretical importance in explaining the different forms of countervailing reason, but of practical legal significance. If a contract is rescinded, once it is avoided there is no justification for the performance rendered by either party, and so they must be unwound, insofar as that is now possible. By contrast, where a contract is merely unenforceable, a payment or other performance rendered cannot be recovered (unless having been

[6] Statute of Frauds 1677, s 4, partially repealed by the Law of Property Act 1925 but requiring that contracts for the sale of land must be evidenced in writing (s 40).

[7] Oral contracts for the sale of land under the Law of Property (Miscellaneous Provisions) Act 1989, s 2(1).

[8] cf M Chen-Wishart, 'Undue Influence: Vindicating Relationships of Influence' (2006) 59 CLP 231.

[9] But see P Birks, *Restitution: The Future* (Federation Press 1992).

agreed to be conditional, and that condition having failed).[10] If a third party procures the breach of an unenforceable contractual duty, they may themselves be liable for damages under the rule in *Lumley v Gye*,[11] whereas this cannot be so if the obligation is a nullity or is set aside. An unenforceable agreement may be the vehicle for the passing of title to goods ('property passing when intended to pass')[12] but this cannot be so if it is a nullity,[13] and title will revest in the seller if the contract is avoided.[14] A party who deliberately breaches an unenforceable obligation in order to cause harm to a third party may be liable for causing loss by unlawful means, which cannot be so if there is no obligation at all.

If we are to justify rescission for duress specifically, the reasons appealed to must relate the parties to the contract together. Where a contract is signed at gunpoint, we might say that it may be set aside either because of the promisor's wrongdoing, or because of the promisee's vitiation of consent.[15] However, these formulations are deficient. More accurately, rescission may be justifiable because of the wrong committed by the promisee and suffered by the promisor or because of the promisee's vitiated consent for which the promisor is responsible.

III. Negativing and Nullifying

The vitally important distinction between negativing and nullifying,[16] the latter being the province of rescission, is most familiar from, and most easily explained in, the context of mistake. This distinction is also relevant to duress, and means that care must be taken before analogising across from cases where duress establishes that there is no reason why a payment has been made, and those where it is used as a reason to rescind a contract. This is best demonstrated through examples where the source of the mistake or the pressure is a third party.

For example:

X represents to C that C owes D £100. C believes X and pays D. C owed D nothing.

Here the induced mistake, that explains why C paid D, establishes that there is no good reason for the payment having been made and that C did not consent to D having the payment in any event. It must be established that the mistake as to the obligation

[10] *Moses v Macferlan* (1760) 2 Burr 1005, 1012; 97 ER 676, 680–81. At one time gaming contracts were by legislation void (Gaming Act 1845, s 18). This appears to have been done in order to enable the losing party, who had not placed a stake (which were expressly irrecoverable) but who had paid out on a losing bet, to recover the payment. Bookmakers did not, of course, in practice ever seek restitution as, if they did so, their business would be destroyed. The Gaming Act 1845, s 18 was repealed by s 334(1)(c) of the Gambling Act 2005.

[11] (1853) 2 El & Bl 216, 118 ER 749.

[12] *Singh v Ali* [1960] AC 167.

[13] *Cundy v Lindsay* (1878) 3 App Cas 459.

[14] *Car & Universal Finance v Caldwell* [1965] 1 QB 525.

[15] S Smith, 'Contracting Under Pressure: A Theory of Duress' (1997) 56 CLJ 343.

[16] But see A Burrows, 'Professor Guenter Treitel' in J Goudkamp and D Nolan (eds), *Scholars of Contract Law* (Hart 2022): 'an impossible distinction', criticising Treitel's insistence on the same divide.

to pay caused the payment because it is in this way that C establishes that it was for this (bad) reason that they paid, and not for one of the many justifiable reasons that there are (eg they intended to make D a gift of the money). The mistake does not however have to be the responsibility in any sense of D, nor does D need to know of the mistake or be on notice at the time of payment, as there is no entitlement, whether contractual or otherwise, that it is necessary to set aside.

By contrast:

> X (innocently?)[17] represents to C that the oats D is selling are old. C buys the oats from D. The oats are in fact new oats, for which D has no use.

If X is not D's agent, and D is unaware of the misrepresentation that X has committed, the contract between C and D ought in principle to be perfectly valid. The unilateral error of one party cannot be enough to invalidate the deal.

It may be that, in some cases, such a unilateral error is sufficiently serious so as to render the agreement (partially) unenforceable. In *Malins v Freeman*,[18] a bidder at an auction muddled up the lots he was bidding on, and purchased entirely the wrong property from that which he had intended. The seller sought specific performance to compel the buyer to accept the conveyance, that would then satisfy the condition of being entitled to the price. The unilateral mistake was sufficiently serious as to justify the refusal of specific performance, although damages would still be available to the seller, but not to justify setting aside the contractual right altogether.[19]

Orthodox contract law tells us that if C wishes to negative the apparent contract that they have entered into based upon the mistake they have made, they must show that the mistake was both one as to the terms of the deal (ie they had mistakenly thought that D warranted that the oats were old) and that D knew of the mistake they were making.[20] Ordinarily we are bound by the objective impression of agreement that we create. Where, however, C is mistaken as to what they are agreeing (ie the mistake is as to the terms of the deal) and D knows of C's mistake, D cannot rely upon the impression that they knew to be false. Mistakes of the promisor that are not induced by the counterparty do not suffice to set aside a contract, although, as we shall see, in very limited circumstances they may negative the existence of a contract altogether.

Of course, it may be that the deal turns out to be a good one for C, the market for oats may dramatically rise. In which case C should have the option of ratifying what they have earlier mistakenly done, validating the contract. The parties' agreement should not therefore be void for all purposes.

There are some cases concerning guarantees that seem to contradict this analysis, saying that a guarantee from a connected party to a transaction is vulnerable to be set

[17] It may be that where the misrepresentation by the third party is fraudulent, a more generous approach to rescission should and does apply.
[18] (1847) 2 Keen 25, 48 ER 537.
[19] *Malins v Freeman* (1838) 4 Bing New 394, 132 ER 839.
[20] *Smith v Hughes* (1871) LR 6 QB 597, 607, 610–11.

aside for misrepresentation unless the bank takes steps to ensure the guarantor takes legal advice, regardless of the bank's ignorance of the mistake the guarantor is making.[21] Just as with the requirement that guarantees are in writing, this is best understood as a special rule in relation to contracts of guarantee. Unlike the position under most bargains, a guarantor personally receives no (direct) benefit from the counterparty. They are peculiarly suspicious transactions. This special treatment of guarantees has now been extended to 'any non-commercial hybrid transaction where, on the face of the transaction, there is a more than de minimis element of borrowing which serve to discharge the debts of one of the borrowers and so might not be to the financial advantage of the other'.[22]

We find the same pattern in the area of duress as we do in relation to misrepresentation. For example:

> X threatens to seize C's goods unless C pays D £100. C pays D.

It should not matter whether D knows of the duress or what the relation, if any, is between X and D. The threats establish that the payment was unjustified, in the circumstance C did not consent to D having the payment in any event, and so D is obliged to repay.

Where duress is used to establish that a payment was without justification, it should again be necessary to show that it caused the payment. In *Maskell v Horner*,[23] the plaintiff was a trader outside Spitalfields market who had for a dozen years paid tolls demanded by the owner of the market. The plaintiff objected on the grounds that he was not in the market, whereupon the defendant threatened to seize his goods. He paid up and continued to do so but always under protest. Subsequent litigation established that there was no right to the tolls. Rowlatt J refused recovery on the basis that the plaintiff had acquiesced;[24] this was overturned on appeal. Lord Reading CJ stated:

> If a person with knowledge of the facts pays money, which he is not in law bound to pay, and in circumstances implying that he is paying it voluntarily to close the transaction, he cannot recover it . . . [but it can be recovered if] the payment is made for the purpose of averting a threatened evil and is made not with the intention of giving up a right but under immediate necessity and with the intention of preserving the right to dispute the legality of the demand.[25]

[21] The earlier cases required knowledge: *Stone v Compton* (1838) 5 Bing NC 142, 156–57; 132 ER 1059, 1065; *Spencer v Handley* (1842) 4 Man & G 414, 418; 134 ER 169, 171; *Cobbett v Brock* (1855) 20 Beav 524, 528, 531; 52 ER 706, 707, 708; *Kempson v Ashbee* (1874) 10 Ch App 15, 21; *Barclays Bank v O'Brien* [1994] 1 AC 180; *Credit Lyonnais Bank Nederland NV v Burch* [1997] 1 All ER 144; *Royal Bank of Scotland v Etridge (No 2)* [2001] UKHL 44, [2002] 2 AC 773.

[22] *Waller-Edwards v One Savings Bank plc* [2025] UKSC 22, [2025] 2 WLR 1263 [57]. Whether this judicial legislation makes policy sense is impossible to tell.

[23] [1915] 3 KB 106.

[24] ibid 111.

[25] ibid 118.

Again, and by contrast, the same approach to knowledge should not apply when it comes to setting aside a contract:

> X threatens to seize C's goods unless C agrees to buy oats from D. C does so but has no use for oats.

In such a case the contract should not be capable of being set aside unless D knew of the duress or X was D's agent.[26]

Further, as with mistakes, it is arguable that the kinds of pressure that negative the consent to a payment should be and are wider than those that suffice to nullify or rescind a contract.[27] This certainly was the law at some point in the past. In *Morgan v Palmer*,[28] the claimant was a publican who had paid a fee to a local justice of the peace for the renewal of his pub licence. The defendant had no authority to demand such a fee. The defendant argued that the payment was a voluntary one, being made with full consent. Notice that it was not understood that it was for the plaintiff to establish his state of mind[29] in bringing the claim; the claim arose because there was no justification for the payment, to which the plea of voluntariness was a defence. It was held that the payment was recoverable because not voluntary, as the parties were not on equal terms and the defendant could not impose conditions on the publican. The kind of pressure sufficient to establish that a contract could be set aside was absent, at least in the era before the law became more generous in its approach.

Whether, today, the scope of duress differs in the two contexts is doubtful following the decision of the Court of Appeal in *CTN Cash and Carry v Gallaher*.[30] A buyer ran a cash and carry business, and paid a sum of money to their regular supplier of cigarettes. This sum was not owed. The buyer paid because of threats by the seller to discontinue further supplies to which the buyer had no contractual entitlement. The suppliers made the threats in the honest belief that the sum was owed. The buyers had acceded to the demand because the sellers were the sole UK distributor of the brands of cigarettes supplied, and the buyers threatened to no longer extend the sellers credit if they did not pay.

Recovery was denied because the claimants had paid the money knowing full well that it was not due.[31] If the buyers had stipulated that they paid reserving their rights to recover back the payment at a later date ('without prejudice'), then recovery should have been allowed because this would have shown that they did not consent to the position that they now found themselves in. But they did not.

[26] *Kesarmal v Valliappa Chettiar* [1954] 1 WLR 380; *Witham v Commercial Union Capital Ltd* [2002] EWCA Civ 1776 [11]; *Halpern v Halpern* [2006] EWHC 603 (Comm), [2006] 2 All ER (Comm) 251 [96]; *Smith v William Charlick* (1924) 34 CLR 38, 56.

[27] To the contrary, see J Beatson, 'Duress as a Vitiating Factor in Contract' (1974) 33 CLJ 97, 108.

[28] (1824) 2 B&C 73, 108 ER 652. See also *Parker v Great Railway Company* (1844) 7 M&G 253, 135 ER 107; *Steele v Williams* (1853) 8 Exch 625, 155 ER 1502; *Fraser v Pendlebury* (1861) 34 LJCP 1.

[29] See also R Stevens, *The Laws of Restitution* (OUP 2023) 71–72, discussing *Kelly v Solari* (1841) 9 M&W 54, 152 ER 24.

[30] [1994] 4 All ER 714.

[31] See also *Smith v William Charlick Ltd* (1924) 34 CLR 38, 51–52.

A threat to discontinue the conferral of a benefit, where not wrongful as a threatened breach of contract, as opposed to a threat to cause harm, cannot possibly constitute duress sufficient to set aside a contract.[32] However, it might be argued that the case ought to be different where the payment is unjustified, and the claimant seeks to show that they were involuntary. However, this distinction may now be lost to English law.

Again, as with mistake, if it were true that contract depended upon the actual consent of the parties, the matching of their wills, rather than upon their actions in entering into their agreement as objectively construed, then the case for concluding that the application of anything constituting duress always renders a contract void, regardless of whether the pressure came from the promisee or a third party, would be strong. As, however, the 'will theory' (if it deserves the name of a theory) does not reflect the positive law and has no normative appeal, it is not.[33]

IV. No Contract Cases?

It is basic contract law that we are bound by the objective impression of agreement that we are responsible for creating. That we did not subjectively intend to enter into a contract on particular terms, or any contract at all, does not prevent us from being bound by such an impression.

However, it must be that we are responsible for the apparent agreement objectively made. If through forgery or fraud, a rogue, for whom I am not responsible, creates the impression that I am offering to sell my home, I am not bound by any apparent agreement created, however reasonable the counterparty's belief that I am the one making the offer.[34]

We find this principle most prominently in the doctrine of *non est factum* in relation to purported contractual documents that have been signed. If a celebrity, scribbling her name outside of a movie premiere, signs what they reasonably believe is an autograph book but which is in fact a document guaranteeing a loan with a third party, it will not be binding. If the document is fundamentally different from that which it was believed to be, and the signature was not careless, it will not bind.[35]

It is possible that there may be extreme cases of duress where the same applies.[36] The modern authorities concerning duress of the person are thin, but the Privy Council's decision in *Barton v Armstrong*[37] might be thought to approach such a case. The

[32] *Times Travel (UK) Ltd v Pakistan International Airlines Corp* [2021] UKSC 40, [2023] AC 101; *Smith v William Charlick* (1924) 34 CLR 38.
[33] *Crescendo Management Pty Ltd v Westpac Banking Corp* (1988) 19 NSWLR 40, 45–46; *Dimskal Shipping Co SA v International Transport Workers Federation (The Evia Luck)* [1992] 2 AC 152, 166.
[34] *Henkel v Pape* (1870) LR 6 Ex 7.
[35] *Gallie v Lee* [1971] AC 1004.
[36] 'Luca Brasi held a gun to his head, and my father assured him that either his brains or his signature would be on the contract' (Michael Corleone, *The Godfather* (Paramount Pictures and Alfran Productions 1972)).
[37] [1976] AC 104.

claimant entered into an agreement in the form of a deed to transfer a shareholding in a company. The defendant had made threats to kill if the agreement was not signed, which had left the claimant in a state of 'very real mental torment'.[38] The majority's conclusion that the executed deed was 'void'[39] is often criticised as wrong, as duress usually operates so as to render a contract voidable. Ordinarily it establishes that although the elements of a valid contract had been satisfied, a countervailing reason arises as to why it may be set aside. Here, however, it may be that the threats were so extreme that we may legitimately conclude that the promisor was not responsible for the apparent promise at all (although they should have the option of ratifying the bargain once free from the pressure if they so choose).

The apparent oddity of the case was that it was not established that the deed would not have been entered into anyway regardless of the pressure. The bargain was, in fact, a good one so far as the seller was concerned. If, however, this is a case where no contract was ever validly made this should make no difference, as it would also not matter in an example of *non est factum*. If no contract has been made, this is unaltered by the fact that it would have been made if circumstances had been different.

The majority concluded that it sufficed that although the claimant 'would have executed the documents even if [the defendant] had made no threats and exerted no unlawful pressure to induce him to do so the threats and unlawful pressure in fact contributed to his decision to sign'.[40] The difference between causing, which requires making a difference, and contributing may be illustrated by considering voting in an election. One vote amongst thousands does not (save exceptionally) cause a successful candidate to be elected, because it makes no difference. It merely contributes to the result. Although no one vote causes the result, each voter for the successful candidate is (partially) responsible for it. So, in this context, the majority of the Privy Council concluded that in cases of high degrees of fault it suffices that the serious threats merely contributed to, but did not cause, the contract to be concluded.

If it is correct that there are some cases where the threats are so serious that there is no responsibility at all for promises apparently made, it may be that the same result would follow if the threats of death had come from a third party, of which the counterparty was unaware and for which they were not responsible.

The same might also be true in a limited category of duress of circumstances cases. Although not a case of pressure applied by anyone, *The Medina*[41] illustrates that, in some extreme cases, a contract may not bind because of pressure from another source, at least where this is known to and exploited by the counterparty. In that case, 550 pilgrims being carried from Sumatra to Jedda on board the *Medina* were shipwrecked on a rock in the Red Sea. In answer to distress signals, the steamship the *Timor* arrived. The master of the ship agreed to rescue the pilgrims and carry them to Jedda for the

[38] ibid 120.
[39] ibid.
[40] ibid. See also *The Law Debenture Trust Corp plc v Ukraine* [2023] UKSC 11, [2024] AC 411 [143].
[41] (1876) 2 PD 5. cf *The Port Caledonia and The Anna* [1903] P 184. But see the careful discussion in C Kennefick, 'The Just Price in Salvage Contracts' (2025) 141 LQR 203, which casts doubt on any such general principle.

sum of £4,000. This was exorbitant for a few days of work, and the Court of Appeal refused to enforce the promise to pay.

However, the Court did award a reasonable sum for the work done, £1,800. This may indicate that the agreement was merely unenforceable and not void, the sum awarded being a claim for restitution of the value of the work rendered on the agreed condition of payment, a condition that had failed. Such a claim is dependent upon there being an agreement between the parties.[42] This may indicate that duress of circumstances, however extreme, renders the extracted agreement unenforceable, rather than wholly void.

V. Rescission for Wrongs

The (only) explanation for some cases of rescission is that a right against another has been acquired through wrongdoing, a breach of a duty owed to the promisor. One response to such a wrong is that the right acquired is vulnerable to being set aside. In the world where the wrong had not been committed there would be no such right. Placing the parties as near as possible in the position they would have been in had the contract not been wrongfully procured may therefore mandate rescission, just as much as wrongdoing commonly requires compensation for consequential loss suffered.

As we have seen, it may not necessarily be required that the wrongdoing caused the promisee to enter into the contract. Especially in cases of high degrees of fault it may suffice that the wrongdoing merely contributed to the decision. In the context of deceit, it suffices that a misrepresentation contributed to the promisor's decision-making process, but it is not required that it caused the deal to be entered into.[43] However, the world we are seeking to replicate, by treating the contract as void *ab initio*, once the promisee elects to do so, is the counterfactual one where the contract had never been entered into.

An alternative explanation for rescission in some cases is that the promisee's conduct induced a defect in the promisor's consent. As we shall see, just as not all misrepresentations are actionable wrongs, not all examples of illegitimate pressure may constitute actionable wrongs. It is understandable that the induced vitiation of consent may sometimes justify rescission despite the absence of wrongdoing.

A nice illustration of when rescission may only be available for wrongdoing, because there is no vitiation of the promisor's consent, is *Zurich Insurance Co plc v Hayward*.[44] A liability insurer entered into a settlement agreement with a claimant, based upon fraudulent misrepresentations made as to the scope of his injuries. However, the insurance company never believed those representations; they had

[42] Stevens, *The Laws of Restitution* (n 29) ch 7.

[43] *Edgington v Fitzmaurice* (1885) 29 Ch D 459, 483; *BV Nederlandse Industrie van Eiprodukten v Rembrandt Enterprises Inc* [2019] EWCA Civ 596, [2020] QB 551 [32]. cf *Barton v Armstrong* [1976] AC 104.

[44] [2016] UKSC 48, [2017] AC 142.

entered into the settlement because of doubts as to whether they could establish their falsity in litigation. Once they had obtained proof of his fraud, because of the testimony of his neighbours, they sought to have the settlement set aside. The deceit was a 'material cause' of the decision to enter into the settlement (in the sense that it contributed to it, even if it made no difference), despite the fact that the insurers had never believed the statements made. There was, however, no 'vitiation of consent' in the sense of any error induced by the counterparty: they had always thought he was lying.[45] It might be said that they were making a mistake as to whether they would subsequently be able to establish that he was lying, but that error was never induced by the counterparty. Rather, the deceit, the wrong, had induced the settlement, and so it could be set aside.

Zurich Insurance therefore illustrates that there are two possible reasons for rescission for a misrepresentation, governed by different rules, not one. If the misrepresentation is innocent, it must induce a belief in its truth, which influences the decision to contract. It 'vitiates' the promisor's consent, regardless of whether it is wrongful or not. By contrast, if the misrepresentation constitutes deceit, it suffices that it contributed to the entering into of the contract, regardless of whether it is believed or not. Rescission is then justified by the wrong committed in acquiring the right, rather than by any defect in the promisee's consent.

Similar to *Zurich Insurance* in the context of illegitimate pressure is the decision in *Borrelli v Ting*.[46] Mr Ting was the CEO of a company that went into insolvent liquidation. The liquidator wanted to enter into a scheme of arrangement so as to fund the liquidation, which would also fund claims against Mr Ting. Mr Ting controlled companies with a blocking minority shareholding and so demanded a settlement of any claims against him before he removed that block and consented to the scheme. The liquidator agreed and then sought to set aside the settlement. The Privy Council accepted that this could be done on the basis of duress.

Here, the only reason why Mr Ting was in a position to obtain such a settlement was because of earlier wrongs that he had committed. He had forged board resolutions of the companies he controlled, authorising votes to block the scheme. He had failed to cooperate with the liquidator in providing necessary information, as former office holders are required to do. These acts had sufficiently delayed the scheme of arrangement such that the liquidators subsequently had no option but to agree to the settlement, unless all was to be lost. The earlier wrongdoing sufficed to justify rescission, regardless of whether the pressure subsequently applied by Mr Ting would have been, in isolation, legitimate or not. The last-minute pressure was simply the mechanism by which the earlier wrongdoing became effective. Focusing on the promisor's 'vitiation

[45] Which has led some commentators to claim the result was wrong: P Davies and W Day, 'A Mistaken Turn in the Law of Misrepresentation' [2019] LMCLQ 390; C Mitchell, P Mitchell, and S Watterson, *Goff & Jones on Unjust Enrichment* (10th edn, Sweet & Maxwell 2023) [9-63]; J Cartwright, *Misrepresentation, Mistake and Non-Disclosure* (6th edn, Sweet & Maxwell 2022) [3-53].

[46] [2010] UKPC 21, [2010] Bus LR 1718. cf K Loi, 'Pre-contractual Misrepresentation: Mistaken Belief Induced by Mis-statements' [2017] JBL 598.

of consent' at the time of entering into the settlement is to fail to appreciate the significance of the earlier (wrongful) conduct of the promisee.

Speaking of 'rescission for breach of contract' is usually misleading, made worse by saying that the requisite breach is a 'breach of a condition'.[47] This is for four reasons. First, as is now generally accepted, where one party does not perform his contractual obligations, thereby entitling the counterparty not to perform theirs, the effect is not to avoid their contract. Rather the obligations to perform cease. Second, this is not a remedy for, or justified by, the wrong of breach of contract. Unlike in *Zurich Insurance* or *Borrelli* the contract has not been obtained by the breach of a duty, the breach of duty occurs because there is a contract. Third, a counterparty is entitled to refuse to perform because the condition of his obligation to do so is not satisfied. This is so regardless of whether the non-fulfilment of the condition is also a breach of contract. Fourth, it is a misuse of the English language to talk of 'breach of condition', although English unlike American lawyers often fall into this mistake.[48] Something, such as an obligation, may be conditional upon something else occurring, and there may be an obligation to bring about the fulfilment of that condition, but if there is a breach it is of the obligation, not the condition.

An exceptional, genuine, case of rescission for breach of contract is *The Cenk K*.[49] The claimant charterers had entered into an agreement with the owners of the *Cenk K* for the carriage of scrap metal to China. The charterers' contract with their Chinese buyers stipulated for a fixed shipment date. In repudiatory breach of contract, the owners chartered the vessel to another party. The owners acknowledged that they had made a mistake but stated that they would find an alternative and compensate for loss caused by the delay. The owners then offered another vessel, but at a rate that did not compensate the charterers for the loss that they suffered as a result of having to renegotiate with their buyers. The sale contract was then renegotiated at a lower price, and the owners made a 'take it or leave it' offer, at a slightly discounted freight rate but requiring a waiver of all claims for damages. This the charterer was commercially compelled to accept.

The 'take it or leave it' offer was not the threat of a wrong. The repudiatory breach of contract was already in the past. Rather, it was an offer to contract that the charterers had no alternative but to accept because of the breach of the original charter. Their breach of contract was what enabled the owners to extract the agreement to the new terms. Again, here the operative fact is not the threat, which in isolation was legitimate. Rather, the threat was the mechanism by which the earlier wrong of breach of contract caused the new contract to be entered into. Because the new contract had been obtained by a breach of contract, it was vulnerable to being set aside, or rescinded.

[47] The best discussion is now J English, *Discharge of Contractual Obligations* (OUP 2025) esp [2.38]–[2.39].
[48] ibid.
[49] *Progress Bulk Carriers Ltd v Tube City IMS LLC* [2012] EWHC 272 (Comm), [2012] 2 All ER (Comm) 855.

VI. Rescission for Threats of Wrongs

It is helpful to draw a parallel between the law of duress and the so-called 'tort' of intimidation. The intentional infliction of loss is not, without more, actionable in the English common law.[50] If, however, unlawful means are used, the position changes. If, for example, I open a barbershop next door to your hairdresser in direct competition, you have no claim against me for your lost income, but if I beat up your customers to deter them from having their hair cut by you, you do have a claim. This presents us with something requiring explanation. The persons whose rights have been violated, the victims of a tort, are your injured potential customers. Why can you claim for the loss I have intentionally caused you, when no specific right of yours has been infringed?

It might be said that the central purpose of law is to give each of us the ability to live our lives independently of the choices of others. If rights afford us the space within which we may pursue our own ends, equally with others, abusing the freedom that the law accords us with the intention of harming others (and thereby inhibiting their freedom) may be thought to be contrary to a system of rights.[51] Although making such intentional infliction of harm actionable may be justifiable, it could not be because such behaviour constitutes a tort, in the sense of the violation of a specific claim-right. English law limits the actionability of such intentionally inflicted loss to cases where unlawful means are used because in such cases there can be no countervailing reason for permitting the conduct in question (as there may be in other cases of intentionally causing loss such as competition or an industrial dispute). 'Causing loss by unlawful means' is an 'abuse of rights' (or, more accurately, abuse of liberties) rule. It is not accurately described as a tort.

Intimidation is a justifiable extension, or species, of the rule against intentionally causing loss by unlawful means. If I deliberately cause you loss by threatening a wrong, either to you or another whilst falling short of actually committing that wrong, the means I have used also cannot be justifiable. Threats to seize goods or imprison your daughter or breach a contract, or to commit a crime with the intention of causing the claimant loss, should suffice for intimidation where such loss is suffered. Again, it is inaccurate to describe this rule as a tort. Unlike all torts properly so called, the intention of the defendant is central to its justification.

We find the same pattern in the law of duress, where the threat to commit a wrong may constitute duress even though not itself a wrong. Threats to seize goods may suffice,[52] as may threats of violence against either the counterparty or someone else. Such pressure is illegitimate because the act threatened is a wrong, even if the threat alone

[50] *Allen v Flood* [1898] AC 1; *Mogul Steamship Co v McGregor Gow & Co* [1892] AC 25; *Bradford v Pickles* [1895] AC 587.

[51] See E Weinrib, 'Private Law and Public Right' (2011) 61 UTLJ 191, discussed in JW Neyers, 'Explaining the Inexplicable? Four Manifestations of Abuse of Rights in English Law' in D Nolan and A Robertson (eds), *Rights and Private Law* (Hart 2011).

[52] *Astley v Reynolds* (1731) 2 Str 915, 93 ER 939.

does not constitute a wrong to the counterparty. This rule appears justifiable in the same way as the actionability of causing loss by intimidation. The application of some kinds of pressure in order to acquire rights is justifiable, but not where the pressure constitutes the threat to commit a wrong. We therefore give the party subject to such pressure the option of setting aside the rights the counterparty has thereby acquired. It is 'unlawful' even if not a specific tort, because of the intention with which the threats are made.

In principle, threats of all wrongs, whether to defame, to convert goods, to reveal private information, or to continue to unlawfully confine to a lunatic asylum,[53] should all constitute duress.

Most problematic, however, and the source of much litigation, are threats to breach a contract. Other wrongs threaten to worsen the counterparty's position. Threats to break another's legs, or ruin their reputation, or bespoil their land are all of this kind. Ordinarily, however, a threat to break a contract is a threat to withhold a benefit from the counterparty that they do not yet have. A threat not to pay what is owed, or not to deliver goods, or not to perform a service are all of this kind. It is perhaps for this reason that the courts have required something more to be shown before treating a threatened breach as constituting duress.

The counterparty is faced with two unpalatable options when demand is made to enter into or vary a contract in the face of threats of breach, if they are to seek to avoid the adverse consequences. Either they treat the threatened breach of contract as a repudiation, accept it, and sue for damages, or they concede to the demand, perform, and seek to rescind subsequently. On either side of the ledger of choice, the necessity of legal proceedings appears. English law appears to restrict duress to cases where the choice to accept the repudiation and claim damages is not viable.[54]

One reason why suing for damages may be an inadequate alternative is that the loss may be irrecoverable as too remote. In *North Ocean Shipping v Hyundai*,[55] a shipbuilder agreed to build a tanker for a price fixed in dollars. The dollar then devalued by 10 per cent, and the shipbuilder insisted upon an increase in the price to reflect this. However, this demand was made in the honest belief that they were entitled to the higher price under the terms of the agreement. The buyers agreed to pay the higher price. The reason for the buyers doing so was that they had agreed to charter the vessel to Shell for a very good rate and subsequently made a substantial profit out of the fixture. There was a substantial risk that if they had treated the shipbuilder's demand for a higher price as a repudiation, and sued for damages, their loss would not have been recoverable as too remote.[56] If the buyers had not affirmed, the Court would have permitted rescission.

[53] *Cummings v Ince* (1847) 11 QB 117.
[54] *Times Travel (UK) Ltd v Pakistan International Airlines Corp* [2023] AC 101 [79]; *DSND Subsea Ltd v Petroleum Geo-Services ASA* [2000] BLR 530, 545–46.
[55] [1979] QB 705.
[56] cf *Victoria Laundry v Newman Industries* [1949] 2 KB 528.

Similar is *D&C Builders Ltd v Rees*.[57] Builders carried out work for the defendants who refused to pay the £482 still owed. The employer offered to pay £300 in settlement, implying that if they refused they would get nothing. The builders accepted the lower sum because of their financial difficulties: they were in danger of being put into winding up because of their cashflow problems. Refusing the lower sum and suing for damages was not an option as they would be, commercially, dead.

That what is threatened must be a wrong recognised by English (domestic) law was determined by the Supreme Court in *The Law Debenture Trust Corp plc v Ukraine*.[58] The Russian Federation sought to enforce Eurobond notes issued by Ukraine. Ukraine alleged that these notes had been obtained through a variety of threats, most seriously of violence through invasion. The Supreme Court had no difficulty in concluding that threats of violence could constitute duress, but concluded that threats of economic sanctions, in breach of a number of Russia's treaty obligations, could not do so. Those treaties, as unincorporated into UK domestic law, created no rights under that law. Threats to discontinue trade could not, therefore, amount to threats of wrongs under English law, which governed the bond issue.

Where legislative policy has provided for an immunity from actionability for a wrong, that policy may also justify the conclusion that the threat to commit the wrong is legitimate. In *Universe Tankships Inc of Monrovia v International Transport Workers Federation (The Universe Sentinel)*,[59] an international union of seamen sought to improve conditions of employment by 'blacking' ships sailing under flags of convenience. The claimant's tanker, the *Universe Sentinel*, sailing under such a flag was detained at Milford Haven because it was deprived of the services of tugs operated by union workers.

Although sometimes described as a case of 'lawful pressure',[60] it was not.[61] The union's procuring of a breach of contract by its members was wrongful and was used as a means for causing the claimant loss and compelling the employer to meet its demand. But unions have long had statutory immunities from suit for the various economic torts, at the time contained in the Trade Union and Labour Relations Act 1974 covering acts in furtherance of a trade dispute. However, an immunity is not a privilege rendering an action lawful.[62]

The shipowners, in order to secure the release of the ship, paid money to the union's welfare fund. They subsequently sought restitution. The claim succeeded because a majority concluded that the action was not 'in furtherance of a trade dispute' within the terms of the immunity. Here, the statutory immunity was being used in an indirect way, as by its terms it only applied to an action based upon a tort. The legislation indicated where the line between legitimate and illegitimate conduct lay.[63]

[57] [1966] 2 QB 617.
[58] [2024] AC 411.
[59] [1983] 1 AC 366.
[60] Most recently by the Supreme Court in *The Law Debenture Trust Corp plc v Ukraine* [2024] AC 411 [140].
[61] P Birks, *An Introduction to the Law of Restitution* (rev paperback edn, Clarendon Press 1989) 350.
[62] WN Hohfeld, 'Some Fundamental Legal Conceptions as Applied in Judicial Reasoning' (1913) 23 Yale LJ 16.
[63] cf *The Evia Luck* [1992] 2 AC 152.

VII. Rescission for Wrongful Threats

Causing other people harm, in the sense of worsening their position from that which currently obtains, is often not wrongful. Prosecuting people, bringing civil proceedings against them, disclosing embarrassing truths about them, or ending long-standing relationships of affection, may all leave another worse off than they were. Without more, however, these acts are not wrongful.

Threats to prosecute for an offence committed or threats to institute proceedings against another are not threats to do an action that, if carried out, would be a wrong to the counterparty. Today, the disclosure of information about another that is true potentially amounts to a wrong of invasion of privacy, but even where this is not so, the threat to disclose such information, such as threats to tell one partner of the other's adultery, may potentially constitute duress.[64] In all these cases, the threat is to worsen the counterparty's position compared to the present, but the action itself, if carried out, would not be wrongful. However, they are not mere threats to withhold a benefit. If I threaten that I will not continue to supply you with free widgets, as I have done in the past, I am not threatening to worsen your current position.

An action may be lawful in itself, but if threatened for an improper purpose, such as the obtaining of a gain for oneself or causing harm to another, may then constitute an independent wrong. Such threats of harm made for an improper purpose constitute the gist of the crime of blackmail.[65] Although there is no tort of blackmail, we find the same idea operative in the wrong of malicious prosecution.[66]

An example of a threat for a proper purpose is *R v Attorney-General for England and Wales*.[67] The claimant, a member of the SAS, was threatened with being returned to the regiment from which he had joined, unless he signed a confidentiality agreement. Even if we assume that this was a threat of harm, it was done for a proper purpose and so did not amount to duress.

On the other side is the decision of the House of Lords in *Williams v Bayley*.[68] A father agreed to pay on various promissory notes that had been forged, secured by a charge over his property, in order to avert the bank's implied threat to prosecute his son for forging his signature. The agreement was found to be invalid on the basis that it was procured by undue influence.

It is common today to suggest that cases of this kind, although decided in equity on the basis of undue influence, are simply cases of illegitimate pressure, or duress, under a different label.[69] It might be objected that the crux of cases such as this is the relationship between the father and the son, which is exploited by the third party,[70] in which

[64] cf *Norreys v Zeffert* [1939] 2 All ER 187.
[65] *Thorne v Motor Trade Association* [1937] AC 797, 822; Theft Act 1968, s 21.
[66] *Willers v Joyce* [2016] UKSC 43, [2018] AC 779.
[67] [2003] UKPC 22, [2003] EMLR 24.
[68] (1866) LR 1 HL 200. See also *Kaufman v Gerson* [1904] 1 KB 591; *Mutual Finance Ltd v John Wetton and Sons Ltd* [1937] 2 KB 389.
[69] *Times Travel (UK) Ltd v Pakistan International Airline Corp* [2023] AC 101 [8].
[70] M Chen-Wishart, 'Undue Influence: Vindicating Relationships of Influence' (2006) 59 CLP 231.

case it should remain aligned with other cases in equity of 'undue influence'. However, it is perfectly possible to imagine cases where the threat is to prosecute the promisor unless he enters into a contract, removing any relationship of dependence from the story.[71] Such a case would have to be analysed as an instance of 'illegitimate pressure' or duress. The better view, therefore, is that the availability of rescission in *Williams v Bayley* can be explained in two different independent ways.

An unusually difficult example of this category might be *Cooper v Crane*.[72] Here the claimant had entered into a marriage ceremony because she was induced by the threats of her husband that if she did not appear at the church door, he would immediately 'blow his brains out'. Collins J refused the declaration of nullity on the basis that the claimant had known what she was doing. Although suicide is no longer criminal, presumably where a contract is procured through a threat of suicide, it may potentially be vulnerable to be set aside.

VIII. Lawful Pressure

The leading case on lawful pressure, falling outside of each of the three categories of unlawful pressure drawn above, is *Times Travel (UK) Ltd v Pakistan International Airline Corp*.[73] Pakistan International Airlines Corporation (PIAC) was the only provider of direct international flights between the United Kingdom and Pakistan. Times Travel (TT) was a travel agent, almost all of whose business was selling flights operated by PIAC. PIAC failed to pay £1.2m in commission owed to TT. PIAC then gave notice that the agency contract between them would be terminated, as they were entitled to do, and that TT's ticket allocation would be cut from 300 to 60. Under the pressure of this threat, which would put them out of business, TT agreed to a new contract under which it waived all claims to the £1.2m in unpaid commission. TT subsequently sought rescission of this new agreement and recovery of the outstanding commission of £1.2m.

In a decision given by Lord Hodge (with whom Lords Reed, Lloyd-Jones, and Kitchin agreed), a majority of the Supreme Court[74] accepted that a category of 'lawful act duress' existed but confined it to two kinds of case: first, the exploitation of knowledge of criminal activity (exemplified by *Williams v Bayley*) and second, using illegitimate means to manoeuvre the claimant into a position of weakness (exemplified by *Borrelli v Ting*). They refused to extend the category of 'lawful act duress' beyond these cases.

However, the majority's reasons for confining 'lawful act duress' to these two categories are not convincing ('difficult to anchor the extension in any recognised legal

[71] *Smith v Monteith* (1844) 13 M&W 427, 153 ER 178; *Mutual Finance v John Wetton & Sons Ltd* [1937] 2 KB 389, 395.
[72] [1891] P 369.
[73] [2023] AC 101.
[74] The approach of the majority was endorsed in *The Law Debenture Trust Corp plc v Ukraine* [2024] AC 411.

principle',[75] 'unwanted uncertainty',[76] 'of limited utility'[77]) and some strongly worded academic commentary has criticised the decision as wrong.[78]

In the light of the above discussion, a better basis for distinguishing the two categories identified is that they are not examples of 'lawful act duress' at all.

The first category is not best understood as one concerned with the exploitation of criminal activity but of threats of harm for an improper purpose (as is blackmail more generally). However, in *Times Travel* PIAC were not threatening harm in the relevant sense. They were threatening to withhold further tickets in the future from TT. They were merely threatening to withhold the conferral of a benefit, not to worsen TT's position. It is easy to lose sight of this because PIAC were threatening to make TT worse off than they would be in the future if the supply of tickets continued as before. They were also threatening to do an action (terminate the agreement) but this is not the relevant test.

The correct baseline is whether the threats are to worsen your current position, not whether the threats would worsen your position compared to a world where the counterparty continued to confer the benefit upon you as they had in the past.

Lord Burrows, in a concurring judgment with which the other members of the Court did not join, proposed that if the threat by PIAC had been made in 'bad faith' it would have sufficed for the purpose of duress. Here he concluded there was no 'bad faith' because PIAC had genuinely, but wrongly, believed that it was not liable for the unpaid commissions.

If what had been threatened was harm in the relevant sense, then the fact that this had been done for an improper motive would indeed have sufficed for a finding of duress. However, a threat to withhold a benefit, such as continued supplies of flight tickets, should be legitimate for the purposes of rescission regardless of the motive of the party making the threat.

As we have seen, the second category, exemplified by *Borrelli v Ting*, is best understood as rescission for a wrong anterior to the application of pressure. In *Times Travel* itself, of course, PIAC were in breach of contract in failing to pay the commission. Why then could the new contract not be rescinded on the same basis as that in *The Cenk K*?[79] The answer is that it was not the breach of contract, nor the threat not to pay the commission, that caused TT to agree to the new contract. The non-payment of the commission was not what caused the agreement to waive the commission. It was not the earlier breach that gave PIAC the ability to extract the concessions from TT, but the fact that TT's business would be destroyed if future tickets were not forthcoming. The force of the threat did not derive from any anterior wrong.

[75] *Times Travel (UK) Ltd v Pakistan International Airline Corp* [2023] AC 101 [49].
[76] ibid [50].
[77] ibid [51].
[78] I Branford and J Gardner, 'Reconceiving Wrongdoing in Lawful Act Duress' (2023) 139 LQR 629; M Chen-Wishart and J Gardner, 'Schrödinger's Lawful Act Duress: Dead or Alive?' in E Peel and R Probert (eds), *Shaping the Law of Obligations: Essays in Honour of Professor Ewan McKendrick KC* (OUP 2023) 75.
[79] '[O]n all fours': Chen-Wishart and Gardner (n 78) 75, 88.

The 'gist' of duress is wrongfulness (or unlawfulness) in one of the three senses identified above. The behaviour of PIAC was, no doubt, wanting in virtue. However, just as the law does not impose duties upon us to confer benefits upon others,[80] we do not act contrary to any justifiable legal norm in threatening not to do so, whatever our state of mind. The language of 'good faith' is best avoided, appearing to import as it does the idea that our rights against others should be capable of being lost if we fail to behave as the virtuous person should.[81]

IX. Conclusion

There are, of course, forms of rescission in equity that are unrelated to wrongdoing in any sense.[82] Although, as we have seen, it is possible to characterise the conduct in *Williams v Bayley* as an example of illegitimate (= undue) pressure (= influence), that is not true of the behaviour of the lady superior of the 'Sisters of the Poor' in *Allcard v Skinner*.[83] That transaction was vulnerable to being set aside because of the relationship of too much (= undue) dependence (= influence). The further and other reasons for rescission are not reducible into the genus of the same kind of reasons that apply in cases of duress. Why do we allow rescission outside of the categories of wrongdoing in one of our three senses at all?

If we are to permit rescission outside of a courtroom, as we do at common law, it is justifiable to restrict such cases to the clearest cases, instances of unlawfulness or wrongdoing. All of the grounds for rescission at common law other than duress (most obviously fraud, bribery, breach of duty by an agent) also involve wrongdoing. Beyond such relatively easy cases, it may be necessary for a judge to determine the potentially incommensurable considerations in play, and so restrict rescission to being required to be done by a court order.[84] Put more formally, equity when exercising its exclusive jurisdiction could and does go further than the common law in allowing rescission because necessarily taking effect by court order.

Even in cases of duress (or fraud, or bribery etc), however, if we are to allow rescission outside of a courtroom, this power may be easily lost. If the party seeking to rescind cannot readily return the counterparty to the position they were in before the contract was entered into, then if rescission is to be permitted it ought to be done by court order so as to settle the terms of doing so (eg a monetary adjustment where what has been received cannot be exactly returned).

80 *Sutradhar v Natural Environment Research Council* [2006] UKHL 33, [2006] 4 All ER 490; *Robinson v Chief Constable of West Yorkshire Police* [2018] UKSC 4, [2018] AC 736; *Tindall v Chief Constable of Thames Valley* [2024] UKSC 33, [2025] AC 1046 [1]. See R Stevens, *Torts and Rights* (OUP 2007) 9; S Steel, *Omissions in Tort Law* (OUP 2024) 30.
81 But see *Al Nehayan v Kent* [2018] EWHC 333 (Comm), [2018] 1 CLC 216 [187].
82 Chapter 6 of this book (L Smith, 'Rescission in the Context of Fiduciary Relationships').
83 (1887) 36 Ch D 145.
84 Chapter 4 of this book (W Swadling 'Rescission—The Role of the Court').

Again, put more formally, in exercising its concurrent jurisdiction, equity could, and still can, allow rescission for duress (or fraud or bribery etc) when to do so would no longer be possible at common law. The court can take into account a number of potentially incommensurable factors (eg How serious was the duress? How long has now passed? How unbalanced was the bargain? Was the promisor also at fault? What value should the performance rendered in the past now have? Have the parties' positions changed since the contract was entered into?) that allow it to set aside the contract on terms, which it is impossible to achieve without a court order.

It is not mere antiquarianism to think that a system that has restrictive rules permitting rescission outside of a court, and a more liberal regime, with fewer restrictions, of court-ordered rescission, is justifiable.

9

The Power to Prevent Disproportionate Relief

*Steven Elliott KC**

I. Introduction

Section 2(2) of the Misrepresentation Act 1967 empowers an adjudicator to withhold or override rescission for non-fraudulent misrepresentation on the basis that damages are to be awarded instead. How are we to understand it? The legislation presents three questions.[1] First, is the power available where rescission is barred? Second, on what principles should the power be exercised? And third, most questionable of all, what is the nature and measure of the damages that may be awarded in lieu of rescission? These issues have provoked a diversity of views and, while the first question now seems to have been settled in favour of a negative answer,[2] nearly sixty years after the enactment of the legislation the second and third questions continue to vex the courts.[3]

Section 2(2) of the 1967 Act provides:

> Where a person has entered into a contract after a misrepresentation has been made to him otherwise than fraudulently, and he would be entitled, by reason of the misrepresentation, to rescind the contract, then, if it is claimed, in any proceedings arising out of the contract, that the contract ought to be or has been rescinded, the court or arbitrator may declare the contract subsisting and award damages in lieu of rescission, if of opinion that it would be equitable to do so, having regard to the nature of the misrepresentation and the loss that would be caused by it if the contract were upheld, as well as to the loss that rescission would cause to the other party.

The three questions are often treated as being independent each of the other, but this chapter argues that the questions are connected in that the answer to each is shaped

* Professor, National University of Singapore, Singapore; Barrister, One Essex Court, London, United Kingdom. I am grateful to the participants in the symposium held on 14 March 2025 at the University of Oxford, out of which this volume came, for their comments on earlier versions of this chapter and especially to the editors and to Matthew Frey.

[1] There is a controversial question in the wider law as to whether rescission for innocent misrepresentation occurs by the election of the aggrieved party or by court order. Section 2(2) accommodates both possibilities ('if it is claimed ... that the contract ought to be or has been rescinded'), and the argument advanced in this chapter is similarly agnostic. Accordingly, where I refer to disproportionate relief I mean either relief already obtained on a self-help basis or relief sought from the court. As to the controversial question, see S Elliott, 'The Basic Structure of Rescission' in B McFarlane and S Elliott (eds), *Equity Today: 150 Years after the Judicature Reforms* (Hart 2023) 167, 172–73.

[2] *Salt v Stratstone Specialist Ltd* [2015] EWCA Civ 745, [2016] RTR 17.

[3] Most recently in *Electric Mania Ltd v Avon Trading Ltd* [2025] EWHC 159 (Comm).

by the same legislative purpose. That purpose is to prevent disproportionate relief, which the legislation achieves by empowering adjudicators to refuse rescission where it would be disproportionate compared with the loss caused by the misrepresentation. The interests of the aggrieved party are protected by requiring an award of damages in respect of this loss. Section 2(2) is best understood as creating a power to prevent disproportionate relief which operates as a bar to rescission.

This legislative purpose explains why the power is unavailable where rescission is barred. In those circumstances the adjudicator cannot be compelled to grant or uphold disproportionate relief so that the power is not required. The purpose also helps us to understand in what circumstances the power should be exercised. It is where the loss rescission would cause to the misrepresenting party would be disproportionate to the loss the misrepresentation causes to the aggrieved party that the adjudicator should consider declaring the contract subsisting and awarding damages instead. Because exercise of the power deprives the aggrieved party of a remedy to which they are entitled, this should only be done where their losses are comparatively modest and will be adequately compensated.

The legislative purpose also indicates that damages awarded in lieu of rescission are compensatory in nature. The chapter accordingly disagrees with the popular and persistent opinion that s 2(2) provides for a kind of pecuniary rescission, replicating in money the specific relief the court is empowered to refuse. It will be argued that relief of that kind would perpetuate the disproportionality s 2(2) is intended to prevent. The statutory expression 'damages in lieu of rescission' does not identify a *sui generis* type or measure of damages. It just means damages instead of rescission.

The argument will be developed by first considering the origin of s 2(2) to identify its mischief and purpose. Once this is understood, the chapter will proceed to consider the three questions in turn.

II. Origin of the Power

The 1967 Act substantially enacted the recommendations of the Law Reform Committee's 1962 report on innocent misrepresentation.[4] One of the Committee's recommendations was that rescission for innocent misrepresentation should no longer be barred by the performance of the contract, except in cases of contracts for the sale or disposition of certain interests in land, in which case finality was the predominant consideration.[5] Outside that excepted category, the Committee considered there to be cases where the inability to rescind a contract after it had been performed could work serious injustice.[6] The Committee emphasised cases where a buyer's first real opportunity to

[4] Law Reform Committee, *Innocent Misrepresentation* (Tenth Report) (Cmnd 1782, 1962) (LRC Tenth Report). Where statutory language is not clear and unambiguous, reports of bodies such as the Law Reform Committee are admissible 'to assist the court to identify not only the mischief which [a statute] addresses but also the purpose of the legislation, thereby assisting a purposive interpretation of a particular statutory provision': *R (O) v Secretary of State for the Home Department* [2022] UKSC 3, [2023] AC 255 [30]. Hoffmann LJ relied on passages from the LRC Tenth Report to explain aspects of s 2(2) in *William Sindall plc v Cambridgeshire CC* [1994] 1 WLR 1016, 1036.

[5] LRC Tenth Report (n 4) [6].

[6] ibid [3].

identify defects occurred after the sale had completed, by which time the right to rescind had been lost.[7] The Committee's recommendation that rescission should not be barred by the performance of the contract was implemented by s 1 of the 1967 Act.

The Committee was concerned that by correcting one injustice, its recommendation might cause another. This was because of the 'drastic character' of rescission.[8] The Committee explained its concern in these terms:

> Unless the Court's power to grant rescission is made more elastic than it is at present, the court will not be able to take account of the relative importance or unimportance of the facts which have been misrepresented. A car might be returned to the vendor because of a misrepresentation about the mileage done since the engine was last overhauled, or a transfer of shares rescinded on account of an incorrect statement about the right to receive the current dividend. In some cases the result could be as harsh on the representor as the absence of a right to rescind under the present law can be on the representee.[9]

To meet this concern, the Committee recommended:

> that wherever the court has power to order rescission it should, as an alternative, have a discretionary power to award damages if it is satisfied that these would afford adequate compensation to the plaintiff, having regard to the nature of the representation and the fact that the injury suffered by the plaintiff is small compared with what rescission would involve.[10]

The Committee considered that where the contract had not been performed rescission was less likely to be unjust, because 'the parties can be relatively easily restored to their original positions'.[11] But while the Committee considered that it would only rarely be appropriate to exercise the power in respect of an unperformed contract, it recognised that such cases might occur. The Committee therefore recommended that the power should be made available, not only where the contract had been performed, but 'wherever the consequences of rescission would be out of all proportion to the injury suffered by the plaintiff'.[12] This disproportion lay at the heart of the Committee's thinking about what became s 2(2).

It is important to appreciate that s 2(2) did not spring from a view that the range of remedies available for purely innocent misrepresentation was inadequate and that a damages remedy should be made generally available in addition to rescission.[13]

[7] ibid [4].
[8] ibid [11].
[9] ibid.
[10] ibid [12].
[11] ibid [11].
[12] ibid [13].
[13] The Committee did consider that damages should be available where the representor had been careless, and that the burden in this regard should be placed on the representor. This recommendation resulted in s 2(1) of the 1967 Act.

An innocent misrepresentation is a misfortune rather than a wrong in any real sense, and the Committee did not depart from the basic position of our law that mere misfortunes do not warrant compensatory relief: 'In such a case the loss should lie where it falls.'[14]

Instead, having recommended expanding the availability of rescission in what became s 1 of the 1967 Act, the Committee's intention in what became s 2(2) was to prevent this expansion from leading to disproportionate relief. This was to be achieved by empowering the court to withhold or override rescission where it would have that consequence. But a complete denial of relief could cause its own injustice. Damages were therefore required to ameliorate the refusal of specific relief. The Committee's thinking was that where the court exercises its power to deny the aggrieved party the rescission to which they are otherwise entitled, instead of leaving the aggrieved party altogether empty-handed, the court should award a second-best remedy in the form of damages for whatever loss the misrepresentation may cause. Compensation for this loss would constitute sufficient justice for the aggrieved party.

With limited refinement, Parliament implemented the Committee's recommendations. Accordingly, the mischief to which s 2(2) responds is that rescission for innocent misrepresentation can be disproportionate and therefore drastic or harsh. This was thought to be especially likely where the contract has been performed. The purpose of the legislation is to prevent disproportionate relief of this kind, but to do so in a way that minimises the prejudice to the aggrieved party.[15] The mischief is ameliorated and the purpose achieved by empowering the adjudicator to declare the contract to be subsisting on the basis that damages are to be awarded instead, provided that these damages would adequately compensate the aggrieved party for the loss caused by the misrepresentation.

III. Availability of the Power

The conditions identified in s 2(2) for the exercise of the power include that the aggrieved party would be entitled, by reason of the misrepresentation, to rescind the contract. For some time there was a question whether this condition could be satisfied where rescission is barred for one reason or another. One judge thought yes, because 'rescission might or might not be available at the time of trial depending on a host of factors which have nothing to do with the behaviour of either party',[16] and that was also Professor Sir Guenter Treitel's view.[17] But several other judges thought no.[18]

[14] LRC Tenth Report (n 4) [17].

[15] '[I]ts object is to ameliorate for the innocent misrepresentor the harsh consequences of rescission . . . in a case where it is fairer to uphold the contract and award damages against him': *William Sindall plc v Cambridgeshire CC* [1994] 1 WLR 1016, 1044.

[16] *Thomas Witter Ltd v TBP Industries Ltd* [1996] 2 All ER 573, 590.

[17] GH Treitel, *The Law of Contract* (9th edn, Sweet & Maxwell 1995) 333.

[18] *Alton House Garages (Bromley) Ltd v Monk* (KB, 31 July 1981); *Floods of Queensferry v Shand Construction Ltd (No 3)* [2000] Building LR 81; *Government of Zanzibar v British Aerospace Ltd* [2000] 1 WLR 2333; *Pankhania v London Borough of Hackney* [2002] EWHC 2441 (Ch). Mustill J's obiter dictum in *Atlantic lines & Navigation Co Inc v Hallam Ltd (The Lucy)* [1983] 1 Lloyd's Rep 188, 202 seems also to have proceeded on this basis.

The Court of Appeal eventually settled the question in the negative in *Salt v Stratstone Specialist Ltd*.[19]

The Court of Appeal's decision was based on the wording of the provision—the words 'damages in lieu of rescission' are said to imply that rescission remains available. Earlier decisions to this effect were also based on textual considerations and these are compelling.[20] But, looking at the problem purposively, why must rescission remain available? If one assumed that the legislative purpose was to create a general damages remedy for innocent misrepresentation, then this limitation would appear capricious.[21] But that would misunderstand the legislative purpose. The requirement that rescission remain available makes perfect sense once it is understood that the purpose of s 2(2) is to prevent disproportionate relief. This is because the mischief to which the provision is directed does not arise where rescission is barred, for in such a case the adjudicator cannot be compelled to grant or uphold a disproportionate remedy.

IV. Exercise of the Power

Where the power is available, the adjudicator 'may' exercise it if 'of opinion that it would be equitable to do so'. If these words stood alone, the power would be exceptionally broad and shapeless. But, consistently with the mischief and purpose of the legislation, s 2(2) goes on to state that the adjudicator must form the opinion 'having regard' to 'the nature of the misrepresentation and the loss that would be caused by it if the contract were upheld, as well as to the loss that rescission would cause to the other party'.

This has been said to contemplate 'a balancing exercise between the situation if damages are awarded and that if rescission were granted'.[22] While the listed factors are not the only ones the adjudicator may consider, the adjudicator must have regard to them and they are the factors to which most weight should be given in all but an exceptional case.[23] The reason for this, it is submitted, is that these factors go to the key question of proportionality. This was clearly seen by the Court of Appeal of Singapore in *RBC Properties Pte Ltd v Defu Furniture Pte Ltd*:

> [T]he discretion is to be exercised only in accordance with established principles, the foremost of which is that, where the misrepresentation is slight or relatively unimportant in the circumstances of the case, so that rescission may be disproportionately harsh on the representor, damages may be awarded in lieu thereof.[24]

[19] [2016] RTR 17 [17].
[20] See esp *Government of Zanzibar v British Aerospace Ltd* [2000] 1 WLR 2333.
[21] eg E Peel, *Treitel on The Law of Contract* (16th edn, Sweet & Maxwell 2025) [9-070]: 'as a matter of policy it is hard to see why the factors which bar the right to rescind should limit the discretion to award damages.'
[22] *Government of Zanzibar v British Aerospace Ltd* [2000] 1 WLR 2333, 2342.
[23] *William Sindall plc v Cambridgeshire CC* [1994] 1 WLR 1016, 1042–43.
[24] [2014] SGCA 62, [2015] 1 SLR 997 [130].

A. The Proportionality Assessment

How does this operate? At its most basic, something is disproportionate if it is too large or too small when compared with something else. The comparison works most readily if the two things are commensurate and quantifiable. In principle there are two stages. First, the quantities must be established. Second, a normative judgment must be made. How much of a difference is too large or too small is influenced by the purpose for which the question is asked.

Proportionality was specified in s 2(2) by the legislative draftsperson in terms of loss caused. Losses are commensurate and so this specification permits a comparison of quantities and thus a proportionality assessment. That does not mean that, at the first stage of analysis, the adjudicator must fully or formally quantify the losses. Such an exercise might itself be disproportionate. Nonetheless, identification in the provision of the two losses indicates the comparison to which the adjudicator must have regard in their assessment.

On one side of the comparison lie the losses the misrepresenting party would suffer if the contract were rescinded. They will lose the benefit of a bargain, and one which may by now have been performed. It may be that upon rescission an asset a seller must now take back is worth less than the price they must repay, whether because it always was worth less or because the value has declined.[25] Or the misrepresenting party may have acted on the faith of the contract in ways that are not sufficient to make *restitutio in integrum* impossible or to require an adjustment, but which would nonetheless leave them suffering a loss if the contract were rescinded. For example, rescission might cause the waste of expenses incurred in connection with the contract but not pursuant to it.[26]

On the other side of the comparison are the losses the aggrieved party will suffer by reason of the misrepresentation if the adjudicator upholds the contract, meaning losses suffered in a world in which the contract stands. These are the losses for which damages would be given if the power were exercised.[27] They must be calculated in accordance with the principles intended by the legislation.[28] These principles are considered further below, where it is argued that the damages are compensatory in nature and compensate for the losses caused by the misrepresentation having been made.

Once these losses have been determined, at least in broad terms, it becomes necessary to ask whether the difference, if any, is disproportionate. This is a normative issue

[25] All else being equal, and absent culpable delay, the fact that the asset the aggrieved party received has declined in value as a result of the ordinary play of market forces will not prevent them from making sufficient *restitutio in integrum* by simply returning it. See *Cheese v Thomas* [1994] 1 WLR 129, 135 and the other authorities cited in D O'Sullivan, S Elliott, and R Zakrzewski, *The Law of Rescission* (3rd edn, OUP 2023) [18.93].

[26] O'Sullivan, Elliott, and Zakrzewski (n 25) [17.61]–[17.66].

[27] *William Sindall plc v Cambridgeshire CC* [1994] 1 WLR 1016, 1036, 1043.

[28] ibid 1037C; *SK Shipping Europe Ltd v Capital VLCC 3 Corp* [2022] EWCA Civ 231, [2022] 1 Lloyd's Rep 521 [82].

that is itself directed to the ultimate question whether the adjudicator should exercise the s 2(2) power. It is that ultimate question that guides the assessment of how large a difference is too large. The range of factors that may influence this normative assessment is in principle open-ended. As discussed further below, it includes the degree of fault involved.

Three points may usefully be made about the exercise of the power. First, it is necessary to start with the correct orientation. The question arises in circumstances where the aggrieved party has established an entitlement to rescission that is not subject to any bar. The adjudicator should normally grant that remedy unless the misrepresenting party can make a case for the exercise of the discretion.[29] Rescission is 'a strong starting point'.[30] To justify exercise of the power, the disproportion must displace this starting point.

This is essentially different from the power to order specific performance of a contract, which in principle should only be exercised where damages would not be adequate. The defendant car dealer in *Salt v Stratstone Specialist* invited the court to exercise the s 2(2) power on the ground that damages would be an adequate remedy. This invitation was roundly refused, Longmore LJ saying that rescission is the 'normal remedy for misrepresentation'[31] and that it 'should be awarded if possible'.[32] The legislation does not result in a general preference for financial relief; it only creates the possibility of a financial remedy where this will spare the adjudicator from granting specific relief that would be disproportionate.

A comparison may be drawn, however, with the principles that govern the award of damages under s 50 of the Senior Courts Act 1981 (known as Lord Cairns' Act) in substitution for the grant of an injunction to prevent an ongoing invasion of rights. Such relief is exceptional because it licenses a violation of rights. It may be granted, however, where the 'good working rule' AL Smith LJ articulated in *Shelfer v City of London Electric Lighting Co*[33] applies. That rule allows the court to refuse injunctive relief and award damages in substitution where the injury is small and can be estimated and adequately compensated in money, and an injunction would be oppressive to the defendant. This is similar to the class of cases to which s 2(2) applies. The Law Reform Committee had this comparison in mind, writing that since the decision in *Slack*[34] the power contained in Lord Cairns' Act had been 'exercised on principles similar

[29] *British & Commonwealth Holdings plc v Quadrex Holdings Inc* (1995) CLR 1169, 1200.

[30] *SK Shipping Europe Ltd v Capital VLCC 3 Corp* [2022] 1 Lloyd's Rep 521 [86].

[31] *Salt v Stratstone Specialist Ltd* [2016] RTR 17 [24].

[32] ibid [31].

[33] [1895] 1 Ch 287, 322–23. At least in cases of nuisance, the judgments in *Coventry v Lawrence* [2014] UKSC 13, [2014] AC 822 loosen the restrictive approach articulated in *Shelfer* to varying degrees, primarily where there are public interest considerations and where third parties are affected by the nuisance. After a full discussion, D Capper, *Injunctions in Private Law* (Edward Elgar 2024) concludes at [4.66]: 'It is far from clear at this stage that *Coventry v Lawrence* will bring about a revolution in the courts' approach to deciding between injunctions and damages.'

[34] *Leeds Industrial Co-operative Society Ltd v Slack* [1924] AC 851.

to those' they intended.[35] *Slack* was an ancient lights case within the 'good working rule'.[36]

Second, while a misrepresenting party cannot avoid rescission on the basis that damages would be adequate, the *inadequacy* of damages is likely to be an important factor in favour of an aggrieved party who wishes to rescind. This is not specified in the legislation, but it was emphasised by the Law Reform Committee,[37] and it was also mentioned by Hoffmann LJ in *William Sindall plc v Cambridgeshire County Council*.[38]

Take a case where the aggrieved party is suffering prejudice that could not be adequately compensated if the contract were upheld.[39] A consideration of this kind may have influenced Longmore LJ in *Salt v Stratstone Specialist*.[40] The purchaser of the Cadillac CTS in that case was a car enthusiast who believed he was buying a car described to him as 'brand new'. Compensation for depreciation may not adequately compensate an enthusiast for a car not being immaculate and authentically new. Another example where damages may not be adequate occurs where damages would be an empty remedy because of the defendant's impecuniosity.[41]

Third, the nature of the misrepresentation may be important to the normative assessment. This is a factor mentioned in the statute, and the courts have construed the expression broadly. It encompasses the comparative importance of the misrepresented fact to the overall transaction,[42] and an important question is whether the misrepresentation struck to the root of the bargain.[43] The courts also take into account the extent to which the misrepresenting party can be faulted.[44] While fraud takes a case out of s 2(2), absent fraud there may still be serious fault, and in such a case it may be that even a substantial discrepancy between the losses that may be suffered would not be considered disproportionate. In general, the less important the misrepresentation was, and the less fault is attributable to the misrepresenting party, the easier it will be to conclude that rescission would be disproportionate.

[35] LRC Tenth Report (n 4) [12].

[36] That the 'good working rule' applied had been established by the primary judge: *Slack v Leeds Industrial Co-Operative Society Ltd* [1923] 1 Ch 431, 432–33. The question for the House of Lords was whether there is jurisdiction under Lord Cairns' Act to award damages in substitution for an injunction on a *quia timet* basis; a majority concluding that there is. That, however, cannot be the point the Law Reform Committee had in mind when it made a comparison to *Slack*.

[37] LRC Tenth Report (n 4) [12], [27(3)].

[38] *William Sindall plc v Cambridgeshire CC* [1994] 1 WLR 1016, 1037.

[39] A similar principle was applied in *Tesco Stores Ltd v Union of Shop, Distributive and Allied Workers* [2024] UKSC 28, [2025] 2 All ER 565 [78] in the context of specific performance.

[40] *Salt v Stratstone Specialist Ltd* [2016] RTR 17.

[41] *TSB Bank plc v Camfield* [1995] 1 WLR 430, 439. The courts have arrived at much the same position in relation to the specific performance of contracts: *Gravelor Shipping Ltd v GTLK Asia M5 Ltd* [2023] EWHC 131 (Comm), [2023] 2 Lloyd's Rep 239 [99]–[101]; *Liberty Mercian Ltd v Cuddy Civil Engineering Ltd* [2013] EWHC 4110 (TCC) [18].

[42] *William Sindall plc v Cambridgeshire CC* [1994] 1 WLR 1016, 1036, 1043; *Huyton SA v Distribuidora Internacional de Productos Agricolas SA de CV* [1983] 1 Lloyd's Rep 780, 846.

[43] *Atlantic Lines & Navigation Inc v Hallam Ltd (The Lucy)* [1983] 1 Lloyd's Rep 188, 202; *SK Shipping Europe plc v Capital VLCC 3 Corp* [2021] 2 Lloyd's Rep 109 [234(i)].

[44] *William Sindall plc v Cambridgeshire CC* [1994] 1 WLR 1016, 1043; *SK Shipping Europe plc v Capital VLCC 3 Corp* [2021] 2 Lloyd's Rep 109 [234(ii)]. In principle, any fault on the part of the aggrieved party should also be relevant.

B. Illustration

An illustration inspired by a recent decision may help to explain how these principles operate.[45] Imagine that a trader bought tens of thousands of hand sanitiser units at the very peak of the market in April 2020 on the basis of a misrepresentation which turned out to be inconsequential. Unfortunately many other traders did the same thing and the market was flooded, so that the units became practically worthless. On these facts, rescission would be very hard on the seller, who would repay a price agreed at the top of an exceptional market and gain, in return, worthless units. On the other hand, the buyer suffered no loss in consequence of the misrepresentation. They paid what was then the market price for the hand sanitiser units. That the units then became practically worthless had nothing to do with the misrepresentation.

On assumed facts and findings resembling these, the judge in *Electric Mania Ltd v Avron Trading Ltd* considered that rescission should be refused and that no damages should be awarded in lieu of rescission. He asked himself whether the fact he would not award any damages indicated that it would be wrong to refuse rescission, but reached the opposite conclusion: 'The very reasons that the [buyer] has not suffered loss consequent upon the alleged misrepresentation is intimately bound up in my finding on this issue that rescission should not be permitted, since to allow rescission of the contract . . . would give the [buyer] an unjustified windfall.'[46] Put differently, that the seller would suffer a great loss if the contract were rescinded, while the buyer suffered no loss in consequence of the misrepresentation, indicated that rescission would be disproportionate and should be refused.

C. Summary

In summary, the Law Reform Committee's report and the text of s 2(2) itself tell us that the power created by that provision is to be exercised where rescission would be disproportionate to the loss the aggrieved party would suffer by reason of the misrepresentation if the contract were upheld, having regard to the significance of the misrepresentation and to fault, and provided that damages can provide adequate compensation. The jurisdiction is loosely modelled on the criteria articulated by AL Smith LJ in *Shelfer's case* for selecting between damages and injunctive relief.

V. The Nature and Measure of the Damages

Just as the statutory purpose shapes the grounds on which the s 2(2) power may be exercised, so it also shapes the damages that may be awarded where the power is exercised.

[45] *Electric Mania Ltd v Avron Trading Ltd* [2025] EWHC 159 (Comm). The actual decision is confused and so I have modified the facts to describe the scenario the judge seems to have thought he was addressing.
[46] ibid [105].

The statutory purpose points to the answer to an issue on which there has been much disagreement. For reasons that will be explained, what it points towards is damages of the usual compensatory sort. What it points away from is a pecuniary rescission analysis. This is so notwithstanding the views of commentators to some of whom I am indebted, all of whom I admire, and with all of whom I would prefer to agree.[47]

The argument will be developed in two stages. The first stage is concerned with the nature of the damages. The argument will be that these are compensatory rather than substitutionary, and they compensate for the loss caused by the misrepresentation rather than the loss caused by the refusal of specific relief. How exactly the loss caused by the misrepresentation is to be measured is considered at the second stage further below.

A. The Nature of the Damages

1. Pecuniary Rescission

The alternative view disputed at this stage is that the 'damages' referred to in s 2(2) should be calculated as a monetary form of rescission. On this view, the award would put the aggrieved party in the financial position they would have occupied if the contract had been rescinded. Such an award would be calculated as the difference between the value of the performance and of the counter-performance. In principle these values should be taken at the date of the order, because that is the date on which rescission would otherwise be given effect, although a sensible argument can also be made for the date of the election to rescind.[48] Taking values at the original date of the transaction would not replicate rescission in financial terms unless values have remained constant.

The difference between the two approaches can be illustrated by reference to the example given above involving a sale of hand sanitiser units that later become practically worthless. Whereas the buyer's loss in that case was considered to be nil, because the units were bought at the prevailing market price, a pecuniary rescission analysis would have required the seller to repay the price with no deduction on account of the now worthless units. This is substantially the outcome the judge in *Electric Mania* thought would give the buyer an unjustified windfall. Another difference is that, while a compensatory analysis naturally permits recovery of consequential loss, pecuniary

[47] E Peel (n 21) [9-088]; J Edelman (ed), *McGregor on Damages* (22nd edn, Sweet & Maxwell 2024) [50-082]–[50-090]; J Cartwright, *Misrepresentation, Mistake and Non-disclosure* (7th edn, Sweet & Maxwell 2025) [4.76] (I agree with Cartwright that the tort measure rather than the contract measure applies, but I do not agree that the tort measure results in 'damages to put him in the financial position in which he would have been if the contract had been rescinded'); H Beale (ed), *Chitty on Contracts* (35th edn, Sweet & Maxwell 2024) [10-117]–[10-119] ('a special measure', which is intended to reflect the outcome of rescission); N Venkatesan, 'Damages for Misrepresentation' (DPhil thesis, University of Oxford 2015) ch 10.

[48] E Bant, 'Reconsidering the Role of Election in Rescission' (2012) 32 OJLS 467, discussing pecuniary rescission under the general law, not s 2(2).

rescission does not permit it because rescission itself does not give recovery of consequential loss.[49]

Pecuniary rescission can be described as compensation for the loss caused, not by the misrepresentation but instead by the refusal of rescission. However, this is confusing because the event for which compensation is given is something done by the adjudicator rather than the opposing litigant. It is better to describe the award as substitutionary, for it provides a monetary substitute for rescission. Money awards are sometimes given on a similar basis where the court refuses for practical reasons to order the specific performance of a contract, for example because a monetary award would be simpler to express, supervise, or enforce.[50] The amount is usually calculated as the cost of purchasing a replacement performance.

2. The Positive Argument

The reasons why a compensatory analysis should be favoured are textual and purposive. As to the textual reasons, the primary and etymologically correct meaning of the word 'damages' is a money award that compensates for loss or injury.[51] The term is also used in a secondary sense to refer to non-compensatory awards, for example nominal damages, punitive damages, liquidated damages, and, by some writers, restitutionary damages and disgorgement damages.[52] But these are exceptional and for this reason where they are discussed the term 'damages' is always qualified by an adjective. By contrast, the term 'compensatory damages' sounds redundant to most lawyers and is usually used for contrast. 'Damages' standing alone implies compensation.

It follows that, on the face of it, the reference to 'damages' in s 2(2) is likely to be a reference to damages calculated as compensation for a loss. This is put beyond question by the link made in the provision between 'damages' and 'loss', particularly the loss caused by the misrepresentation. Any theory that results in gain-based or restitutionary relief is unlikely to be correct. The reference in s 2(2) to the loss caused by the misrepresentation also rebuts the theory that the damages are those caused by the refusal of rescission.

[49] Authors who consider that consequential loss should not be available under s 2(2) for this reason include Peel (n 21) [9-088], Beale (ed), *Chitty on Contracts* (n 47) [10-118], Edelman (n 47) [50-084], and H Beale, 'Damages in Lieu of Rescission for Misrepresentation' (1995) 111 LQR 60, 63. Professor Andrew Tettenborn and David Wilby KC contend that consequential losses should only be recoverable to the extent the claimant would avoid those losses if the contract were rescinded: A Tettenborn and D Wilby (eds), *The Law of Damages* (2nd edn, LexisNexis Butterworths 2010) [17.60]–[17.61].

[50] See the discussion in S Smith, *Rights, Wrongs and Injustices: The Structure of Remedial Law* (OUP 2019) 172–76, whose terminology I have adopted.

[51] *Broome v Cassell & Co Ltd* [1972] AC 1026, 1070 (citing Harvey McGregor QC's definition as 'the pecuniary compensation obtainable by success in an action for a wrong which is either a tort or a breach of contract'); *Leeds Co-operative Society v Slack* [1924] AC 851, 868–69 ('money compensation for a wrong done'); W Blackstone, 2 Bl Com 438 ('a compensation or satisfaction for some injury sustained'); CT Onions, *The Oxford Dictionary of English Etymology* (OUP 1966) 242. The point made in the text is developed at greater length in S Elliott, 'Compensation Claims against Trustees' (DPhil thesis, University of Oxford 2001) 69–71.

[52] Breaking with views expressed by Harvey McGregor QC in previous editions, the current editor of *McGregor on Damages* (n 47), Justice James Edelman, contends that the fact of these alternative kinds of damages, and especially disgorgement damages, mean that the term is now used in a sense that does not imply compensation (at [1-009]–[1-010]). For reasons stated in the text, I disagree.

Turning from textual to purposive considerations, a measure that seeks to put the claimant into a financial position equivalent to their position if the contract were rescinded would be directly inconsistent with the purpose of the legislation. This is because such a measure would deliberately replicate in money the disproportionate consequences of rescission. For example, where an asset has declined sharply in value for reasons unrelated to the misrepresentation,[53] damages designed to put the aggrieved purchaser in the same position as if the contract were rescinded would be just as hard on the seller as rescission itself. As Hoffmann LJ put it in the *William Sindall* case, the Law Reform Committee 'could not possibly have intended the damages in lieu to be assessed on a principle which would invariably have the same effect'.[54] Foxton J more recently considered the question in *SK Shipping* and reached the same conclusion.[55]

The legislative purpose is to empower the adjudicator to require a claimant to accept a second-best remedy, damages, where they would prefer rescission. This is only appropriate where the losses rescission would cause to the misrepresenting party are disproportionately greater than the aggrieved party's comparatively modest losses. Depriving the aggrieved party of a remedy to which they are otherwise entitled is only defensible on the basis that they are to be adequately compensated for the losses they suffer in a world in which the contract is upheld. It would therefore be inappropriate to select an approach that artificially limits the damages to anything less than compensation for the losses caused by the misrepresentation, for example by excluding all consequential losses.[56] But it would be equally inappropriate to select an approach that artificially inflates the damages to an amount greater than the losses the aggrieved party has suffered, as pecuniary rescission does in the hand sanitiser example. The legislative purpose therefore points towards the damages being compensatory in the usual sense.

A parallel can be found in a number of cases in which the courts have refused specific relief of other kinds, not for practical reasons, but where it would be disproportionate.[57] In such cases the courts refuse to award substitutionary financial relief, which would be equally disproportionate, but instead award compensatory damages in respect of any loss suffered. For example, in *Tito v Waddell (No 2)*,[58] Megarry J refused to enforce the mining company's contractual replanting obligation either specifically or by an award of damages measured by the cost of purchasing substitute performance where, as a result of bombing during the Second World War, the island was thought to be uninhabitable. Megarry J was prepared to order compensatory damages but he concluded that no loss had been suffered.

[53] As in *William Sindall plc v Cambridgeshire CC* [1994] 1 WLR 1016.

[54] ibid 1038.

[55] *SK Shipping Europe plc v Capital VLCC 3 Corp* [2021] 2 Lloyd's Rep 109 [237].

[56] Consistently with this, the cases indicate that consequential loss is recoverable: *Davis & Co (Wines) Ltd v Alfa-Minerva (EMI) Ltd* [1974] 2 Lloyd's Rep 27; *William Sindall plc v Cambridgeshire CC* [1994] 1 WLR 1016, 1044 (wasted transaction expenses); *SK Shipping Europe plc v Capital VLCC 3 Corp* [2021] 2 Lloyd's Rep 109 [256] (costs incurred by reason of delay).

[57] See Smith (n 50) 261–63, who also cites *Dennis v Ministry of Defence* [2003] EWHC 793 (QB), [2003] 2 EGLR 12; *Boomer v Atlantic Cement Co*, 26 NY2d 219 (1970); and other nuisance cases.

[58] [1977] Ch 107.

3. The Counter-Arguments

Why, then, have authors favoured a pecuniary rescission analysis? First, because the language of s 2(2) is said to entail it; second, because compensatory damages are thought to be inappropriate since innocent misrepresentation is not a wrong; and third, because of views expressed when the legislation was considered in Standing Committee. These arguments will be addressed in turn. A fourth counter-argument rooted in s 2(3) will be addressed at a later stage, once the contest between the tort measure and the contract measure has been adjudicated.

As to the first of these arguments, it has been suggested that the expression 'damages in lieu of rescission' means that the damages are 'explicitly a substitute for rescission'.[59] If the suggestion is that the damages are substitutionary in nature, that reads too much into the expression. A simpler and more natural meaning of the expression, consistent with the legislative purpose, is that damages are to be given instead of rescission.

As to the second argument, as a general matter it is certainly true that purely innocent misrepresentation is a misfortune rather than a wrong in any real sense and that our law has never previously given damages on this basis.[60] Because of this, it has been argued that the term 'damages' is unlikely to have been used in s 2(2) in its usual sense. For example, the position taken through several editions of *Treitel on The Law of Contract* has been that because the misrepresentation is wholly innocent and lacks contractual force, the damages should not be regarded as tortious or contractual, but that a measure that prevents the representing party from profiting would be appropriate.[61] This measure is said to be 'sui generis' and 'the monetary equivalent to rescission'. Professor Peter Birks's view was at one time that we are driven to this by the improbability of Parliament having meant what it said: 'Since the legislature did not turn purely innocent misrepresentation into a wrong or breach of contract, it must be understood as having used the word "damages" in a broad sense and as having meant to allow the courts to put a money value on the restitution which would otherwise have been effected under the label of rescission.'[62]

In more mature work, Birks rowed back from his earlier view, accepting that s 2(2) cannot be treated as a statutory remedy for unjust enrichment.[63] Instead, he came to see it as a 'contorted jurisdiction to treat an unjust enrichment as though it were a tort'.[64] Birks was right that by s 2(2) Parliament requires adjudicators to treat an innocent misrepresentation as though it were a tort, with damages given for the loss thereby caused. But it is important to appreciate that Parliament did not create a general damages remedy for innocent misrepresentation and nor did the Law Reform Committee recommend that.[65] Damages are only available under s 2(2) in specific circumstances,

[59] Edelman (n 47) [50-082].

[60] *Redgrave v Hurd* (1881) 20 Ch D 1. Indeed, the term 'damages' is sometimes defined to require a wrong. See the examples in n 52 and also Edelman (n 47) [1-001] ('Damages are an award in money for a civil wrong').

[61] Peel (n 21) [9-088].

[62] Peter Birks, 'Unjust Factors and Wrongs: Pecuniary Rescission for Undue Influence' (1997) 5 RLR 72, 75.

[63] Peter Birks, *Unjust Enrichment* (2nd edn, OUP 2005) 176–77.

[64] ibid 177.

[65] LRC Tenth Report (n 4) [17].

being where the adjudicator would otherwise be obliged to permit or grant rescission and that remedy would be disproportionate. It is in those circumstances and only in those circumstances that the adjudicator is empowered to require the aggrieved party to accept second best: compensation for their losses. Damages are the price the misrepresenting party pays to avoid a harsh remedy to which the aggrieved party is otherwise entitled. It is the minimum justice the aggrieved party must receive.

Turning to the third argument advanced in favour of a pecuniary rescission analysis, in his doctoral thesis entitled 'Damages for Misrepresentation',[66] Dr Niranjan Venkatesan KC cites notes of deliberations on the legislation in Standing Committee which indicate that the author of the notes (at least) believed that damages under s 2(2) would compensate for loss suffered by reason of rescission being refused.[67] The author relied on a comparison with the measure of damages awarded under Lord Cairns' Act in substitution for an injunction. Citing *Slack*,[68] the author asserted that the measure in that context is the 'loss (including prospective loss) suffered by the plaintiff by reason of his not obtaining the injunction to which he would otherwise have been entitled'. The suggestion was that damages under s 2(2) should likewise compensate the claimant for the refusal of rescission.

The author went on to illustrate this with an example that makes clear that what was intended was a remedy that would put the aggrieved party in the financial position they would have occupied if the contract had been rescinded. This is worth setting out:

> [I]n a simple case, where A had induced B to buy a car for £500, by misrepresenting its year of manufacture, the measure of damages would be the difference between £500 and the actual value of the car, because, if rescission were ordered, A would get the car back and B would recover his £500.
>
> In the example given above, by the time B's claim for rescission is tried there may have been a drop in the second-hand car market, so that the actual value of the car at that date had fallen by a further £100. If B could rescind, he would still have got his £500 back and A would have taken in return the depreciated car. So what B has lost by being held to his contract is now the difference between the £500 he paid and the depreciated car, less the value, if any, of the use he has made of it in the meantime.[69]

In the terms adopted earlier, this would be substitutionary rather than compensatory relief. For reasons already given, there are textual and purposive reasons why this is not what Parliament intended. There are also two particular difficulties with an argument based on these archival materials.

[66] Venkatesan (n 47) 304–05.

[67] The National Archives, *Misrepresentation Act 1967: Notes on Clauses and Amendments*, BT 258/2382, 3 (in which the particular proposed amendment is identified), and The National Archives, 'Notes on Amendment Nos 26 and 29' in *Misrepresentation Bill 196-: Notes on Amendments [Commons] Committee Stage*, LCO 2/7378 (in which the reasons for rejecting the amendment are recorded). The latter notes contain the passages to which Venkatesan chiefly refers.

[68] *Leeds Industrial Co-operative Society Ltd v Slack* [1924] AC 851.

[69] The National Archives, 'Notes on Amendment Nos 26 and 29' (n 67).

The first is that the author of the notes misunderstood the decision in *Slack*.[70] It is true that Viscount Finlay said at one point in his speech that the damages should give an 'equivalent for what is lost by the refusal of an injunction', but he made clear elsewhere that the damages are given as compensation for the injury that had been or would in future be caused by the tort,[71] which is not the same thing.[72] Lord Dunedin also spoke of the injury to be caused by the tort.[73] More recently, Lord Bingham MR and Millett LJ spoke in similar terms in passages in *Jaggard v Sawyer*[74] that were subsequently endorsed by the Supreme Court.[75] Like damages under s 2(2), damages in substitution for an injunction under Lord Cairns' Act are ordinary compensatory damages for losses caused by the tort, and not damages for loss caused by the adjudicator's refusal to grant an injunction.

Venkatesan contends that the Law Reform Committee itself considered that the damages should be assessed by what he calls 'the *Slack* measure': 'what has the claimant lost by reason of the refusal of the remedy that he seeks and to which he would otherwise be entitled'.[76] Even putting aside the question whether *Slack* is authority for this measure, in the passage in the Law Reform Committee's report to which Venkatesan refers[77] the Committee cited *Slack* to draw a comparison with the principles on which the power is exercised, not a comparison with the approach to the assessment of damages.[78] The measure Venkatesan advocates is unlikely to have been favoured by the Law Reform Committee for it would replicate the disproportionate consequences of rescission and thus undermine the Committee's recommendation.

The second difficulty is that the key document Venkatesan unearthed in the National Archives is not admissible in aid of the interpretation of s 2(2). There are important constitutional reasons why the materials admissible in the interpretation of legislation

[70] As, with respect, I believe Foxton J did in *SK Shipping Europe plc v Capital VLCC 3 Corp* [2021] 2 Lloyd's Rep 109 [236], [237(v)].

[71] Compare *Leeds Industrial Co-operative Society Ltd v Slack* [1924] AC 851, 859 with 857: 'damages . . . must necessarily cover not only injury already sustained but also injury that would be inflicted in the future by the commission of the act threatened.'

[72] eg a right to an injunction might give negotiating leverage worth more than the financial value of the injury caused by the tort.

[73] See *Leeds Industrial Co-operative Society Ltd v Slack* [1924] AC 851, 865: 'a pecuniary payment equalling the loss to be occasioned by the act against which, but for the provision in question, an injunction would have been obtained.'

[74] [1995] 1 WLR 269, 276 ('to compensate the plaintiff for future unlawful conduct'), 286 ('to compensate for those future wrongs which an injunction would have prevented').

[75] *One Step (Support) Ltd v Morris-Garner* [2018] UKSC 20, [2019] AC 649 [44]. Lord Reed's remarks in *Morris-Garner* at [47] should not be taken to indicate a different view, as to which see S Elliott (ed), *Snell's Equity* (35th edn, Sweet & Maxwell 2025) [20-053] and A Burrows, *Remedies for Torts, Breach of Contract, and Equitable Wrongs* (4th edn, OUP 2019) 317.

[76] Venkatesan (n 47) 304.

[77] Venkatesan refers to LRC Tenth Report (n 4) [12], which states:

> To meet these objections we recommend that wherever the court has power to order rescission it should, as an alternative, have a discretionary power to award damages if it is satisfied that these would afford adequate compensation to the plaintiff, having regard to the nature of the representation and the fact the injury suffered by the plaintiff is small compared with what rescission would involve. The courts were given power to award damages in addition to or in substitution for an injunction or a decree for specific performance by s 2 of Lord Cairns' Act (the Chancery Procedure Act, 1858), and *since the decision of the House of Lords in [Slack], this power has been exercised on principles similar to those we have just mentioned.* (emphasis added)

[78] See text to nn 35 and 36.

should be limited to those readily available to citizens and their legal advisers. Usually citizens should be able to rely on what they read in an Act of Parliament and regulate their conduct accordingly.[79] Reports recommending legislation, such as that of the Law Reform Committee, which are easily available to lawyers, may be admissible to show the background to the legislation and to reveal the mischief to which it was directed and its purpose.[80] By contrast, a transcript of the proceedings of a committee which goes on to recommend legislation will not usually be admissible even if it could be uncovered by diligent research.[81] Arguably any material which can only be found in archives should be excluded from consideration. But there is a more specific reason here which is that, by law,[82] the key document Venkatesan found was not released to the public for 30 years, for which reason the copy in the National Archives is marked 'Closed until 1997'.[83]

4. Summary

In summary, for textual and purposive reasons, the damages that are to be awarded where an adjudicator exercises their power to withhold or override rescission are compensatory, and the loss for which they compensate is that caused by the misrepresentation. The damages are not compensation for the refusal of rescission and nor are they to be calculated in such a manner as to put the aggrieved party in the same financial position they would have occupied if the contract had been rescinded.

B. The Tort Measure or the Contract Measure?

That leaves the question whether the loss caused by the misrepresentation is the loss caused by the statement having been made (which results in the tort measure) or the loss caused by the statement having been false (which results in the contract measure). In a 'no transaction' case involving a sale, the tort measure is the difference between the price and the actual value of the asset, whereas the contract measure is the difference between the value as warranted and the actual value.[84]

To adopt the contractual measure would be illogical and unprincipled.[85] The aggrieved party would gain the benefit of a warranty where they did not bargain for one.

[79] *R v Secretary of State for the Environment, Transport and the Regions, ex p Spath Holme Ltd* [2001] 2 AC 349, 397.

[80] *R (O) v Secretary of State for the Home Department* [2023] AC 255 [29]–[30].

[81] *Bilta (UK) Ltd v Tradition Financial Services Ltd* [2025] UKSC 18, [2025] 2 WLR 1015 [33].

[82] Public Records Act 1958, s 5(1), as amended by the Public Records Act 1967, s 1.

[83] As to the less important *Notes on Clauses and Amendments*, in *In Re Scottish Independence Referendum Bill* [2022] UKSC 31, [2022] 1 WLR 5435, the Supreme Court considered the use of a similar document in interpreting the Scotland Act 1998. The Notes on Clauses in that case were said (at [20]) to have 'accompanied the Scotland Bill when it was considered by the United Kingdom Parliament' and to have been published online and in hard copy. Notwithstanding these matters, the Supreme Court said (at [26]) that it did not attach particular weight to the Notes on Clauses because it was drafted by government officials and had not been endorsed by Parliament.

[84] *Karim v Wemyss* [2016] EWCA Civ 27 [23]–[25].

[85] In this I agree with the general consensus of commentators, and my reasons repeat those of others: Beale, 'Damages in Lieu of Rescission for Misrepresentation' (n 49) 64; Peel (n 21) [9-088]; Edelman (n 47) [50-080]

This produces a serious anomaly where the aggrieved party made a good bargain. Take a case where the aggrieved party bought goods for £100 which, as represented, would have been worth £200, but which in their flawed condition were in fact worth the price paid. The contract measure would deliver damages of £100—the difference between the £200 value as represented and the actual value of £100—whereas the tort measure would deliver no damages because the price and the actual value were the same. In other words, if the contract measure were to be adopted, the aggrieved party would recover £100 damages for innocent misrepresentation where they would have recovered no damages if the statement had been made fraudulently. Parliament is unlikely to have intended this, and the language of s 2(2) certainly does not require it. To the extent the Lords Justices in *William Sindall* favoured the contract measure,[86] their views are objectionable for these reasons.

The tort measure, by contrast, is principled and produces satisfactory outcomes. It is helpful to consider three scenarios that differ according to the causative impact of the representation.

First, assume an innocent misrepresentation that has no causative impact in that the parties would have contracted on the same terms if the representation had not been made. In these circumstances there is no sufficient ground for rescission so that the s 2(2) power is not engaged.[87]

Second, assume that had the innocent misrepresentation not been made, the parties would still have contracted but on different terms. Foxton J considered this scenario in *SK Shipping* and concluded that the damages should be measured by the value of the difference between the terms actually agreed and those that would have been agreed.[88] As he observed, damages calculated on this basis do not protect the aggrieved party from the consequences of a bad bargain, if there was one, or from later changes in asset values. The measure seems unobjectionable and altogether appropriate.

Third, assume that had the innocent misrepresentation not been made, the negotiations would have fallen through—in other words, a 'no transaction' case. In such a case the basic tort measure is the difference between the price and the actual value of the asset or other performance at the date of the transaction.[89] That is the loss the aggrieved

and [50-087]; Cartwright (n 47) [4.76]; Beale (ed), *Chitty on Contracts* (n 47) [10-117]; Venkatesan (n 47) 310–11 (second and third reasons).

[86] *William Sindall plc v Cambridgeshire CC* [1994] 1 WLR 1016. The views in question were obiter dicta in circumstances where the court concluded that there had been no misrepresentation. While Evans LJ favoured the contract measure as a second strand in his reasoning (at 1045–46), Hoffmann LJ only said that the contract measure caps recovery, expressing no view as to the circumstances in which the damages may be less (at 1038), and Russell LJ agreed with both (at 1046), so that even obiter dicta there is no majority analysis.

[87] O'Sullivan, Elliott, and Zakrzewski (n 25) [4.105]–[4.109].

[88] *SK Shipping Europe plc v Capital VLCC 3 Corp* [2021] 2 Lloyd's Rep 109 [253]–[255].

[89] *Waddell v Blockey* (1879) 4 QBD 678; *Cemp Properties (UK) v Dentsply Research & Development Corp (No 2)* [1991] 2 EGLR 197; *Smith New Court Securities Ltd v Scrimgeour Vickers (Asset Management) Ltd* [1997] AC 254, 283. The 'date of transaction' rule was developed in fraud cases, but it also applies in negligence cases (Peel (n 21) [9-086]) and cases to which s 2(1) of the 1967 Act applies (eg *Cemp Properties*). The rule is usually understood to be an aspect of the principle barring recovery of avoidable loss: A Summers, *Mitigation in the Law of Damages* (OUP 2025) ch 10.

party suffered by relying on the representation. If the aggrieved party is to be denied the specific remedy to which they are otherwise entitled, it seems appropriate that they should be compensated for this loss. If the contract was at the time it was made a bad bargain for the aggrieved party for reasons unrelated to the misrepresentation, they will be rescued from that, but this is unobjectionable because the rescission to which they are otherwise entitled would have the same consequence.

What if after the contract was made the asset bought by the aggrieved party declined in value? Could that loss be recovered as consequential loss and would that be objectionable in the context of s 2(2)? Such losses will usually be irrecoverable because of the date of transaction rule. But there are well-known exceptions. For example, the misrepresentation may continue to operate to induce the aggrieved party to retain the asset, or they may for some reason be locked into holding the asset.[90] In a 'no transaction' case that is exceptional in this way, the loss caught by the tort measure will include that attributable to the market decline after the date of the transaction. That is as it should be, because this loss is caused by the misrepresentation having been made.

Where loss associated with a market decline is caused by a misrepresentation in this way, such that it would be caught by the tort measure of damages, what good reason is there to exclude it from recovery under s 2(2)? If the aggrieved party is to be denied a specific remedy to which they are otherwise entitled, they must be compensated for the losses they suffer by reason of the misrepresentation. In these exceptional cases it cannot be objected that the remedy protects the aggrieved party from what turns out to have been a bad bargain because it was the misrepresentation itself that exposed them to the market decline. Moreover, if the consequence of including losses such as these is that the damages in a particular case are substantial, that may simply show that rescission is unlikely to be disproportionate.[91] Those are not cases in which the power was intended to be exercised. The power is only to be exercised where the aggrieved party's losses are comparatively modest.

This discussion enables us to see the much-criticised judgments in *William Sindall* in their proper context.[92] The buyer had paid about £5 million for land now worth only £2 million following a market collapse. Having originally gone to 'great lengths' to acquire the land, the buyer now regretted the purchase. Discovering a nine-inch drain under part of the land, the buyer claimed to rescind, notwithstanding that the alleged misrepresentation concerned 'a matter of relatively minor importance' which 'would have cost £18,000 to put right'.[93] The Court of Appeal agreed that there had been no misrepresentation, but went on to discuss in obiter whether, had there been a misrepresentation, it would have been appropriate to exercise the s 2(2) power. This

[90] *Smith New Court Securities Ltd v Scrimgeour Vickers (Asset Management) Ltd* [1997] AC 254, 267.

[91] If in some case the consequences of rescission would be disproportionately greater than the substantial losses the aggrieved party would suffer if the contract were upheld, the misrepresenting party should be pleased to pay damages in respect of those substantial losses rather than face the consequences of rescission.

[92] *William Sindall plc v Cambridgeshire CC* [1994] 1 WLR 1016; *Electric Mania Ltd v Avon Trading Ltd* [2025] EWHC 159 (Comm) is similar.

[93] *William Sindall plc v Cambridgeshire CC* [1994] 1 WLR 1016, 1036.

in turn required the Lords Justices to consider, for the purposes of the proportionality assessment, whether the damages in lieu of rescission would include the £3 million loss caused by the market decline. This issue was considered on the assumption that *William Sindall* was a 'no transaction' case, although this was scarcely credible on the facts.[94]

To shift the loss caused by the market collapse onto the seller on the basis of a fortuitous misrepresentation would have been unattractive and the only argument that led to this conclusion was the pecuniary rescission analysis which the Court unanimously rejected. Both the contract measure they favoured to varying extents and the tort measure yield more limited relief. Although characterised differently, in circumstances where the contract price otherwise accorded with the prevailing market value, both measures would deliver damages effectively measured by the cost of putting right the errant drain. Neither measure would have compensated William Sindall for the £3 million loss caused by the market collapse, in the case of the tort measure because of the 'date of transaction' rule. Indeed, Evans LJ recognised that the tort damages would have been limited to loss suffered at the date of the transaction.[95]

It can therefore be seen that on the assumed facts of *William Sindall*, the contract measure yielded an appropriate quantum of relief, being substantially the same as the quantum yielded by the tort measure. That is because the bargain was a neutral one in that it accorded with the prevailing market price. This circumstance conceals the difficulties with the contract measure, which come into focus where the aggrieved party's bargain was instead a good one, as illustrated above. Tort damages, by contrast, represent an appropriate measure of relief in all scenarios.

C. Section 2(3)

Finally, it has been suggested that s 2(3) precludes the tort measure of damages.[96] The provision did not feature in the Law Reform Committee's thinking and recommendations. It is possible to read too much into a provision introduced, perhaps unnecessarily, only to prevent double-counting.

The legislation provides:

> Damages may be awarded against a person under subsection (2) of this section whether or not he is liable to damages under subsection (1) thereof, but where he is so liable any award under the said subsection (2) shall be taken into account in assessing his liability under the said subsection (1).

[94] ibid 1043. More realistically, the parties would have contracted on the same terms (so anxious was William Sindall at the time to acquire the land), so that s 2(2) would not have been engaged; or else there would have been a minor adjustment in the price, this being the full extent of the damages recoverable on the tort measure.

[95] ibid 1044.

[96] P Atiyah and G Treitel, 'Misrepresentation Act 1967' (1967) 30 MLR 369; Edelman (n 47) [50-080].

So, take a case where a contract is induced by a misrepresentation which was not made fraudulently. The first part tells us that the power to award damages under s 2(2) is independent of the power under s 2(1). Damages may be awarded under s 2(2) even though there is no liability under s 2(1), which would be because the misrepresenting party had reasonable grounds to believe and did believe the statement to be true. And damages may also be awarded under s 2(2) where there is also liability under s 2(1). The second part tells us that where there is liability under both provisions, the adjudicator should first make their award under s 2(2), and must then take that award into account when assessing damages under s 2(1). The implication is that, to the extent losses are compensated by the award made under s 2(2), the adjudicator should not make a duplicative award under s 2(1).

If damages under s 2(1) and s 2(2) were to be calculated such that the quantum of awards made under the two provisions would always be the same, then s 2(3) might instead have been worded such as to prevent liability from arising concurrently under both provisions. Arguably, s 2(3) therefore tells us that there must be a difference in the principles that underpin the calculations. However, it is not necessary that these should lead to differences of outcome in every case or even in the generality of cases.

Section 2(3) should not cause us to adopt a measure which defeats the evident purpose of the legislation, unless this is really necessary, which it is not. This is because recovery of consequential loss in tort comes in more and less expansive variants. Damages under s 2(1) are awarded on the same basis as damages for deceit,[97] the remoteness criteria of which are unusually comprehensive.[98] This would not be appropriate for damages under s 2(2) because those damages may be given in respect of wholly innocent misrepresentations, although the courts have not yet considered whether the applicable test is foreseeability or something even more limited. In any event, there may be differences between the damages awarded under ss 2(1) and 2(2) such that overlapping awards, the relationship between which needs to be regulated by s 2(3), are possible.

Section 2(3) can therefore accommodate a tort theory of the measure of damages under s 2(2) and does not drive us to pecuniary rescission or the contract measure.

D. Summary

In summary, the damages that may be awarded under s 2(2) are what it says on the tin: damages for the loss caused by the misrepresentation. These damages are compensatory rather than substitutionary in nature. The popular pecuniary rescission

[97] *Royscott Trust Ltd v Rogerson* [1991] 2 QB 297, 304–05. While this decision has been controversial, it stands undiminished and evidently reflects the intentions of the Law Reform Committee and the draftsman. In recommending what became s 2(1), the Law Reform Committee stated that '[t]he damages obtainable for misrepresentation will be no less extensive' than those obtainable for deceit: LRC Tenth Report (n 4) [22].

[98] *Doyle v Olby (Ironmongers) Ltd* [1969] 2 QB 158, 167; *Smith New Court Securities Ltd v Scrimgeour Vickers (Asset Management) Ltd* [1997] AC 254, 265, 267, 269.

theory is untenable, being inconsistent with the purpose of the legislation, and it has rightly been rejected by the courts. Nor are the damages to be measured on the contract basis, for that would give the aggrieved party the benefit of a bargain they did not make. Instead, the damages are to be measured on the usual tort basis. There is nothing wrong with awarding tort damages for an innocent misrepresentation where those damages are the price the misrepresenting party pays to avoid a specific remedy which is disproportionately harder.

VI. Conclusion

The chapter has argued that s 2(2) of the Misrepresentation Act 1967 should be understood as creating a bar to rescission for innocent misrepresentation where rescission would be disproportionate. The provision thus protects the misrepresenting party from an injustice, but the price of this protection is that the aggrieved party must be compensated for any loss caused by the misrepresentation.

In starting with a proper understanding of what s 2(2) is for, the disproportionality thesis offers a principled and purposive account of the provision which is sometimes lacking in other explanations found in the literature. Disproportionality helps to explain not only the circumstances in which the power is available but also the grounds on which the power should be exercised, as well as the nature of the damages that may be awarded. Disproportionality links these elements together in such a way that they form a cohesive whole.

10

Third-Party Rights and Insolvency as Bars to Rescission

*Magda Raczynska**

I. Introduction

Where rights passed under a contract, rescission of the contract revests those rights or may generate new ('replacement') rights. In principle, the rights may revest on rescission even if they have passed to a third party.[1] However, a familiar rule states that a contract cannot be rescinded when a third party has acquired rights in reliance on the contract and without notice of the power to rescind, where those rights would be defeated by its rescission.[2] This is referred to as the third-party rights bar. The aim of this chapter is to show that the rule applies more narrowly than is generally thought.

First, the third-party rights bar has already come under incisive criticism in cases where a third party acquired a property right.[3] One reason is that the bar protects the third party while leaving the fraudster with an unwarranted windfall; another is that the bar in equity has little support in the authorities. The critics are correct. The chapter develops the critique, favouring the view that the acquisition of property rights by a third party does not bar rescission in equity but only precludes rescission having restitutionary effects as against third parties. In such cases, rescission of the contract brings about replacement rights which the claimant may assert against the fraudster.

Second, the chapter explores the related but almost entirely unexamined[4] argument that rescission is barred on the insolvency of the fraudster since that would prejudice the rights of the fraudster's creditors. General creditors of the insolvent fraudster do not hold, by definition, any proprietary rights in the insolvent's assets, and they certainly do not acquire any such rights because a bankruptcy order was made or a winding-up petition presented. But they obtain a (statutory) conditional right to receive a distribution

* Associate Professor, University College London, London, United Kingdom.

[1] See eg *Bainbridge v Bainbridge* [2016] EWHC 898 (Ch), [2016] WTLR 943 [20].

[2] *Tennent v City of Glasgow Bank (in liq)* (1879) 4 App Cas 615.

[3] B Häcker, 'Rescission and Third Party Rights' (2006) 14 RLR 21; B Häcker, *Consequences of Impaired Consent Transfers: A Structural Comparison of English and German Law* (Hart 2013) 259–74; S Zogg, *Proprietary Consequences in Defective Transfers of Ownership* (Intersentia 2020) 191–201; D O'Sullivan, S Elliott, and R Zakrzewski, *The Law of Rescission* (3rd edn, OUP 2023) ch 20; J English, 'Deeds, Rescission and Restitution' (2023) 139 LQR 363.

[4] One notable exception is Zogg (n 3) 201–05.

from the insolvent's estate.[5] Rescission does not take away that right. If insolvency is a bar to rescission at all, it is not a third-party rights bar in the strict sense. However, it is plausible to consider it as a third-party rights bar in a broader sense because rescission on insolvency shrinks the size of the pool of assets available for distribution, and so affects the enjoyment (realisation) of the general creditors' rights to distribution. The chapter shows that the 'insolvency bar' to rescission rests on some misconceptions and weak authority. It suggests that the insolvency of the fraudster does not preclude rescission of the contract as a matter of authority, although there are some exceptions relating to particular types of contract entered with corporate fraudsters where rescission after winding up is not generally possible.

The chapter is divided in two parts which correspond to the two arguments just outlined. The conclusion reflects on the scope of the third-party rights bar. Before proceeding, let us acknowledge that the current law of rescission is difficult to understand without a reference to the differences between the rules of common law and equity. Briefly, at common law, only contracts can be rescinded, and only for fraud and duress, mental incapacity, and, in the case of insurance contracts, non-disclosure and non-fraudulent misrepresentation. In equity, rescission is available more widely. No attempt is made here to rationalise or criticise the difference between those rules. For the purposes of this analysis, it is simply assumed that the difference exists.

II. Third-Party Property Rights

The following scenario illustrates the problem. B induces A by fraudulent misrepresentation (not giving rise to a fundamental mistake) to sell him a platinum ring on credit. Before A realises that B is never going to pay, B sells the ring to C. C pays B and is unaware of the fraud. It is clear that C acquires an indefeasible title to the ring at law and in equity. Can A rescind the contract with B if C acquired property rights in the ring?

The orthodox view is that a bona fide purchase by C of rights acquired by B under a contract with A operates as a total bar to rescission against B.[6] This means that (i) A remains bound by the contract with B; (ii) A cannot claim restitution against B of benefits conferred under the contract; and (iii) A cannot claim traceable proceeds/substitutes that B received in return for conferring property rights on C. This is generally thought to be the position at common law and in equity,[7] despite arguments that the bar has never existed in equity.[8] The following discussion endorses the view that the bona fide

[5] This is conditional on creditors proving their debts. An administrator or liquidator must distribute the asset realisations (subject to deductions) to the creditors who have proved in accordance with the order of priority: Insolvency (England and Wales) Rules 2016, rr 14.27–14.35.

[6] The orthodox view is set out in H Beale (ed), *Chitty on Contracts* (35th edn, Sweet & Maxwell 2023) [10-150]; E Peel, *Treitel on the Law of Contract* (16th edn, Sweet & Maxwell 2025) [9-121]. See also Chapter 4 of this book (W Swadling, 'Rescission—The Role of the Court').

[7] See eg *Moses v Moses* [2022] UKPC 42, where the Privy Council seem to have proceeded on this basis. I am grateful to Jordan English for this point, and see English (n 3).

[8] O'Sullivan, Elliott, and Zakrzewski (n 3) [20.23]–[20.27].

acquisition of property rights by third parties does not bar rescission in equity and suggests that, while the orthodox view applies at common law, it is even more limited than generally thought.

A. The Bar at Common Law

Various cases are cited in the literature for the proposition that a third-party intervention bars a power to rescind. One is *White v Garden*,[9] in which Cresswell J said:

> [T]he [defrauded] seller [A] may elect to treat [the contract] as a contract, [or] ... do the contrary [ie elect to rescind it] before the buyer [B] has acted ..., and re-sold the goods to a third party [C] ... And I see no difficulty or hardship in so deciding. One of two innocent parties must suffer: and surely it is more just that the burthen should fall on the [defrauded party].[10]

The first sentence may be understood as saying that the transfer of rights by B to C extinguishes A's power to rescind. However, it is clear from what immediately follows that the loss of the power to rescind contemplated by the Court is not against B but merely against C. In fact, the issue in *White v Garden* was whether a bona fide purchaser (C) had a claim against A, a party defrauded by a fraudster (B). A had removed 29 tons of iron from C's wharf. The Court held in favour of C, and directed A to pay C the value of the iron removed from the wharf. The case was about barring rights of a defrauded party against an innocent third party, and not about barring rights of a defrauded party against the fraudster.[11] The issue of the rescission of the contract against B was raised in argument[12] but it was not how the Court decided the case. This shows that the case concerned protection of innocent third parties and was not about rescission of the contract.[13]

That the concern is the protection of innocent third parties can also be gleaned from the reasoning of the judges in *White v Garden*, as they focus on explaining why the innocent third party should be protected as against the rescinding party. For example, Cresswell J thought that the rescinding party was 'guilty of negligence in parting with their goods upon the faith of a piece of paper which a little inquiry would have shewn to be worthless' while the innocent third party should be protected because he 'trusted

[9] (1851) 10 CB 919, 138 ER 364.

[10] *White v Garden* (1851) 10 CB 919, 926–28; 138 ER 364, 367; *Stevenson v Newnham* (1853) 13 CB 285, 302–03; 138 ER 1208, 1215. See also *Kingsford v Merry* (1856) 11 Exch 577, 579; 156 ER 960, 961 (revd on other grounds: (1856) 1 H&N 503, 156 ER 1299), cited elsewhere in this book: See also Chapter 4 of this book (W Swadling, 'Rescission—The Role of the Court').

[11] *Cundy v Lindsay* (1878) 3 App Cas 459, which is sometimes cited as authority for the third-party rights bar, in fact contained dicta about the rights of a defrauded party against an innocent third party, not the fraudster: see at 464, referring to 'settled and well known rules of law' that 'the original owner [A] of the goods ... will not be allowed to interfere with a title for valuable consideration obtained by some third party [C] during the interval while the contract remained unreduced [not set aside]'.

[12] *White v Garden* (1851) 10 CB 919, 920; 138 ER 364, 365.

[13] O'Sullivan, Elliott, and Zakrzewski (n 3) [20.09]–[20.17].

to the possession of the goods themselves.'[14] These are the sort of arguments that are familiar from discussions about the defences to the operation of the *nemo dat* rule (priority conflicts) and do not ground or justify barring the power to rescind the contract with the fraudster. In other words, they are about why the innocent third party should be protected, not about why the rescinding party should lose the power to rescind.

Furthermore, it is possible to interpret some dicta as suggesting that rescission of the contract between A and B is possible, even if C acquired indefeasible title. In *White v Garden*, Cresswell J said that the fraudster 'could not have enforced the contract'.[15] It is possible that the fraudster was thought not to be able to enforce the contract because it had been rescinded, which would admit the possibility of rescission of the contract between A and B while the rescission had no effect against a bona fide third party. Similarly, in *Stevenson v Newnham*,[16] the Court appeared to recognise that protection of third parties is separate from rescission of the contract between the defrauded party and the fraudster: '[a]n innocent purchaser from the fraudulent possessor may acquire an indefeasible title to [the property], though it is voidable between the original parties.'[17]

Against this, and in support of the orthodox view that a third-party intervention defeats a power to rescind is *Clough v London & North Western Railway Co*,[18] in which Mellor J said:

> [For as] long as [the defrauded party, A] has made no election he retains the right to determine it either way, subject to this, that if . . . an innocent third party [C] has acquired an interest in the property . . . it will preclude him from exercising his right to rescind [a contract with B].[19]

But the case did not concern an innocent purchaser, and the action was not even between C and A, but C and another third party.[20] In this case, a seller was induced by B's fraud to sell him some pianos for delivery by train to C, who knew about the fraud. Therefore, the support for the third-party property-rights bar is merely *obiter*.

Next, rescission of a contract between A and B is said to be barred when B pledges the goods in favour of C.[21] But it is submitted that the support in pledge cases for this proposition is not clear. They provide that A cannot sue C for trover until A discharges the duty that is secured by the pledge.[22] This suggests, first, that the pledge cases do not

[14] *White v Garden* (1851) 10 CB 919, 926; 138 ER 364, 367 and see also 927 (Talfourd J), 927 (Williams J), 928 (Jervis CJ).
[15] *White v Garden* (1851) 10 CB 919, 926; 138 ER 364, 367.
[16] (1853) 13 CB 285, 138 ER 1208.
[17] *Stevenson v Newnham* (1853) 13 CB 285, 302; 138 ER 1208, 1215.
[18] (1871) LR 7 Ex 26.
[19] ibid 35. See also *Whittaker v Campbell* [1984] QB 318, 327.
[20] See O'Sullivan, Elliott, and Zakrzewski (n 3) [20.13].
[21] *Parker v Patrick* (1793) 5 Term Rep 175, 101 ER 99; *Babcock v Lawson* (1880) 5 QBD 284; O'Sullivan, Elliott, and Zakrzewski (n 3) [20.15].
[22] *Kingsford v Merry* (1856) 11 Exch 577, 577; 156 ER 960, 960; *Pease v Gloahec* (1866) LR 1 PC 219, 229. See also *Attenborough v London & St Katharine's Dock* (1878) 3 CPD 450, 465–66 (although this case concerned an equitable charge as the 'contract to pledge' was never perfected).

involve indefeasible third-party rights; the pledgee's rights to the asset are very much contingent on the non-payment of the debt. In other words, these cases involve a bar that can be lifted by paying the third party. When the third-party property rights are discharged, there is no scope for a third-party bar to apply. That the rights of a pledgee can be discharged is unsurprising. Pledgees' rights in the asset are by way of security only, meaning that pledgees can exercise powers of enforcement in relation to the asset only to the extent that the obligations secured by the pledge are outstanding, and when those obligations are discharged, so is the pledge.[23] Second, once A discharges the pledge and acquires rights to the goods, it is not obvious that this necessarily suggests that the contract between A and B is rescinded. A could also be acquiring those rights by way of subrogation into the rights of the pledgee to secure the debt now owing by B to A.[24] After all, A has paid B's secured debt. This suggests that the pledge cases do not unequivocally support the proposition that no bar arises where the purchaser pledges the asset.[25]

The third-party rights bar appears to have some support as a matter of principle, albeit one that has received trenchant criticism.[26] The principle, as Professor Birke Häcker has explained, is that certain sale contracts operate in a particular way, and the existence of the bar appears to be a function of that.[27] In such contracts, title to the goods passes by force of contract[28] under what could be described as a consensual model of property transfer. Rescission of such a contract by either party should re-convey the title.[29] If a third party already purchased the goods from the fraudster, rescission would deprive the third party of the title to the goods. The third-party property rights bar operates as a means of protecting third parties, who otherwise would not have a valid defence: mere bona fide purchase is not, of course, a defence to legal property rights.[30] But the consensual model of property transfer is not the only way to

[23] See *Donald v Suckling* (1866) LR 1 QB 585, 618 (Cockburn CJ).

[24] This is so even though pledges are possessory, and a subrogated party may not necessarily be in possession. Subrogation is to the rights of pledgee, the most important of which is the right to the realisation of the value of the asset if the secured duty is not performed. But it does not mean that those exact rights are acquired: subrogation is a fiction; the creditor's actual rights are extinguished (*Banque Financière de la Cité v Parc (Battersea) Ltd* [1999] 1 AC 221, 236) and new rights arising in equity are acquired (*Boscawen v Bajwa* [1996] 1 WLR 328, and see C Mitchell and S Watterson, *Subrogation. Law and Practice* (OUP 2007) [3.10]–[3.18], [8.07], [8.12]–[8.15]). Here, these rights amount to an equitable security right (a lien or a charge). The new rights arise in response to unjust enrichment (*Banque Financière de la Cité v Parc (Battersea) Ltd* [1999] 1 AC 221, 236; *Cheltenham and Gloucester plc v Appleyard* [2004] EWCA Civ 291; *Menelaou v Bank of Cyprus* [2015] UKSC 66, [2016] AC 176; *Swynson Ltd v Lowick Rose LLP (in liquidation)* [2017] UKSC 32, [2018] AC 313 [19], [31]) and are not dependent on the same conditions (such as possession) as determined the existence of the old rights. In addition, it does not matter that the subrogated party has an equitable interest while the creditor's interest was legal: *Halifax plc v Omar* [2002] EWCA Civ 121, [2002] 2 P & CR 26 [84].

[25] To be clear, a contract between A and B could probably be rescinded even though the pledge of goods continued.

[26] Häcker, 'Rescission and Third Party Rights' (n 3); O'Sullivan, Elliott, and Zakrzewski (n 3) [20.18]–[20.21]; Zogg (n 3) 192–94.

[27] Häcker, 'Rescission and Third Party Rights' (n 3) 3–4.

[28] Sale of Goods Act 1979, s 17(1) and s 18 r 1.

[29] S Worthington, 'The Proprietary Consequences of Rescission' [2002] RLR 28, 36–37; R Stevens, *The Laws of Restitution* (OUP 2023) 194. But see W Swadling, 'Rescission, Property, and the Common Law' (2005) 121 LQR 123.

[30] The position of the third party could fit some other defence, eg under ss 24 and 25 of the Sale of Goods Act 1979. See eg *Newtons of Wembley Ltd v Williams* [1965] 1 QB 560.

explain the English law of sale. Professor Häcker argues persuasively that a contract of sale performs two functions: (i) a contractual function, and (ii) a proprietary function by which title passes—there is no necessary conceptual link between the two.[31] On this model (which is the preferred one), there is no necessity for a third-party property rights bar.[32] One could rescind a contract against the contracting party but not against a third party. A slight refinement of the dual-function (dual power) analysis suggested here is to notice that the contractual function, which determines the creation and content of the contract, will also include an obligation to pass property. In contracts that are also conveyances, this obligation is always either immediately executed or is at least self-executing in that it is the contract which passes title (eg where the parties agree that the title is to pass at a later date).[33]

The dual power analysis has been met with a challenge that it is inconsistent with case law which states that legal title to goods revests automatically as a consequence of the act of rescission of a contract.[34] The criticism appears to overlook the nature of Häcker's argument which is that, as a matter of principle, automatic revesting is not a necessary consequence of the English law position that some contracts convey property.

The dual effect of a contract of sale of goods is generally discussed in relation to contracts of sale of specific goods[35] because it is in relation to such contracts that the default rule is that the conveyance occurs when the contract is made.[36] But the dual effect is easier to identify in contracts for the sale of unascertained goods because parties to such contracts cannot simply convey property at any time they might intend.[37] There needs to be ascertainment.[38] When there is a contract for the sale of unascertained goods, parties are presumed to intend for property to pass when goods have been unconditionally appropriated to the contract.[39] There is a temporal gap between the contract and the passing of property, and so the two separate functions—contractual and proprietary—are easier to identify. Specifically, it is easier to notice a separation between an obligation to pass property contained in the contract, and the passage of property. In relation to such contracts it is perhaps even clearer that one could rescind a contract against the contracting party but not against a third party.

[31] Häcker, 'Rescission and Third Party Rights' (n 3) 16–18.

[32] This analysis has generally been met with approval: O'Sullivan, Elliott, and Zakrzewski (n 3) [20.20]; Zogg (n 3) 192–93; N Andrews, A Tettenborn, and G Virgo, *Contractual Duties: Performance, Breach, Termination and Remedies* (4th edn, Sweet & Maxwell 2023) [3-041].

[33] I am grateful to Jonas Atmaz Al-Sibaie for this last point.

[34] A Reilly, 'Voidable Title in the Sale of Goods: One Power to Rescind, or Two?' (2024) 35 KLJ 170, 194 (arguing in favour of a single power to rescind a contract with a proprietary consequence of revesting arising as a matter of operation of law).

[35] See Sale of Goods Act 1979, s 61, defining specific goods as goods identified and agreed at the time of the contract.

[36] Sale of Goods Act 1979, s 18 r 1. The dual effect can also be seen in relation to a contract for the sale of unascertained goods in which the parties provide that property is to pass after the goods become ascertained, and stipulate the time when property is to pass. In such a case property passes when intended by the parties.

[37] Sale of Goods Act 1979, s 16.

[38] See *Re Stapylton Fletcher* [1994] 1 WLR 1181.

[39] Sale of Goods 1979, s 18 r 5.

Enabling the defrauded party to wipe out the contractual consequences of the fraud against the fraudster while protecting an innocent third party (by leaving the proprietary effects of the contract intact) produces a better policy outcome. The current law has the undesirable effect of incidentally shielding a wrongdoer when protecting the third party.[40] While A will often have a claim for damages against the wrongdoer, rescission may offer a better relief in some cases.[41]

The argument is sometimes made that the defrauded party brought about their own misfortune by being duped.[42] While this might explain why, as between the innocent third party and the defrauded party, the innocent party's claim to an asset has greater merit, it does not justify an absolute bar on rescission, that is, one that precludes both contractual and proprietary effects. A better explanation for protecting innocent third parties is to protect security of receipt, such that a bona fide purchaser can be sure that the property rights acquired are free from 'infirmities'. This rationale would help justify protection of innocent third parties also *after* the defrauded party rescinded the contract. This is not the law at present, of course, but it should be.[43]

One difficult area is whether the rescinding party can trace into the substitutes obtained by the fraudster and in so doing assert a proprietary claim to those substitutes. This would be particularly useful if the claim against a third party is indeed barred. An absolute third-party property rights bar clearly precludes such an exercise. But barring only third-party effects of rescission opens the possibility of tracing into substitutes. What follows suggests how tracing might operate in this context, as a matter of legal principle, recognising, however, that there is no authority on this point.

If rescission of a contract with the fraudster is possible, rescission will remove the rights and obligations undertaken in the contract, including the obligation to pass property. As between the defrauded party and the fraudster, it is as if the obligation to pass property was never executed and rights from the defrauded party to the fraudster never passed. In reality they did, of course, pass. The disposition of the rights by the fraudster to a third party will then, from the perspective of the defrauded party, not be authorised.[44]

Put another way, by exercising the power to rescind, the defrauded party is withdrawing authority to dispose of the property rights, which would otherwise be conferred on the fraudster. The assumption made here is that an owner[45] of an asset has a

[40] O'Sullivan, Elliott, and Zakrzewski (n 3) [20.21].

[41] Häcker, 'Rescission and Third Party Rights' (n 3) 30–33, 35–36.

[42] *White v Garden* (1851) 10 CB 919, 138 ER 364; and see text to nn 14–15 above. S Elliott, 'The Basic Structure of Rescission' in B McFarlane and S Elliott (eds), *Equity Today: 150 Years After the Judicature Reforms* (Hart 2023) 167, 184.

[43] J O'Sullivan, 'Rescission as a Self-Help Remedy: A Critical Analysis' (2000) 59 CLJ 509, 532; Swadling, 'Rescission, Property, and the Common Law' (n 29) 131.

[44] There is a parallel here with the language found in *Nelson v Larholt* [1948] 1 KB 339, 342–43 (referring to an asset being taken from the right owner without his authority) and *Lipkin Gorman v Karpnale Ltd* [1991] 2 AC 458.

[45] The asset could itself be a right. It can sometimes be awkward to refer to 'ownership' of rights, so an 'owner' of rights should be understood to mean the right holder. The power to dispose of rights (power to assign) can be limited on account of the nature of the right (say, to personal services), but nothing turns on this point here.

power to dispose of rights to the asset. As part of that power, the owner is free to decide how (on what terms) the power is to be exercised.[46] For example, an owner of an antique clock might ask an antique dealer to sell it, and determine the terms of sale, for example for no less than £100. If the dealer sells it for £90, this is a breach of contract between the owner and the dealer, but the third party may well acquire good title if they are able to set up a defence to the operation of the *nemo dat* rule. The exercise of the power of sale by the dealer as against the third party is valid, even though it is unauthorised as between the owner and the dealer. It is conceptually possible to separate powers to dispose of rights from the authority to dispose of them such that a property right can pass from one person to another, but the authority to deal with it need not exist.

Rescission removes authority to dispose completely, but this need not affect the rights acquired by a bona fide purchaser from a fraudster. The removal of the authority ('de-authorisation') is retrospective. This might seem unusual, but the law already recognises an analogous concept of conferral of authority retrospectively. When the principal ratifies an unauthorised act undertaken by an agent, they confer antecedent authority (*ab initio*).[47] Rescission does the reverse—it removes authority *ab initio.* Unauthorised dispositions of one's rights will enable the defrauded party to trace into the proceeds of such dispositions.[48] The fraudster holds the rights they acquired in an unauthorised way on trust for the defrauded party. This shows that common law rescission should be supported by equitable tracing.

B. The Bar in Equity

The support for the third-party property rights bar in equity is even weaker than at common law. As the authors of *The Law of Rescission* show,[49] there are many cases in which contracts have been rescinded in equity even though the asset has been sold on to an innocent third party.[50] This prompts a (desirable) conclusion that such a bar never applied in equity.[51]

Tracing into substitutes in the context of rescission in equity appears to have received some judicial support. Authorities suggest that the defrauded party, having rescinded, obtains a trust (referred to as a 'rescission trust') over the rights that originally passed to the fraudster—now the trustee[52]—which then enables the rescinding party

[46] See M Raczynska, *The Law of Tracing in Commercial Transactions* (OUP 2018) [2.119]–[2.120].

[47] *Koenigsblatt v Sweet* [1923] 2 Ch 314, 325.

[48] MJ Hafeez-Baig and J English, *The Law of Tracing* (Federation Press 2021) [1.47]–[1.51], Raczynska, *The Law of Tracing* (n 46) [3.12] and M Raczynska, 'Subordination of the Wrongdoer in Tracing Claims' in PS Davies and H Tjio (eds), *Fraud and Risk in Commercial Law* (Hart 2024) 150; cf W Swadling, 'The Proprietary Consequences of Fraud' in PS Davies and H Tjio (eds), *Fraud and Risk in Commercial Law* (Hart 2024) 169.

[49] O'Sullivan, Elliott, and Zakrzewski (n 3) [20.23]–[20.27].

[50] See eg *Gresley v Mousley* (1859) 4 De G & J 78, 45 ER 31 (land); *New Sombrero Phosphate Co v Erlanger* (1877) 5 Ch D 73 (shares). See further authorities cited in O'Sullivan, Elliott, and Zakrzewski (n 3) [15.17]–[15.19] and see, too, *Independent Trustee Services Ltd v GP Noble Trustees Ltd* [2012] EWCA Civ 195, [2013] Ch 91 [50].

[51] O'Sullivan, Elliott, and Zakrzewski (n 3) [20.23].

[52] *Independent Trustee Services Ltd v GP Noble Trustees Ltd* [2013] Ch 91 [53]; *Shalson v Russo* [2003] EWHC 1637 (Ch), [2005] Ch 281 [122].

to trace.[53] This seems correct, but requires more precision. The analysis of tracing into the substitutes obtained by the fraudster in this context should, in principle, be similar to what was said in the context of rescission at common law. Rescission against the contracting party removes the obligation to pass property (or to create a proprietary interest), so that, as between the fraudster and the defrauded party, it is as if the rights never passed, even though in reality they did. The fraudster held those rights and disposed of them without authority from the rescinding party, so the rescinding party can now trace into the proceeds of the unauthorised disposition of those rights.

III. Rescission on Insolvency

As a matter of legal principle, there is no reason why rescission on insolvency should or should not be barred. There is no reason why the interests of the rescinding party should prevail over, or be subordinated to, the interests of the general creditors of the insolvent party.

As a matter of operation of legal doctrine, the way we view rescission is that it is generally permitted unless barred, as opposed to a doctrine that is barred unless there are reasons to make it available. Framed in this way, this section shows that there are insufficient reasons to think that the general creditors of the fraudster intervene to bar rescission of a contract between the defrauded party and the fraudster. Put in broader terms, the defrauded party is not generally precluded from rescinding the contract on the insolvency of the fraudster. As will be seen, the authorities support this line of thinking.

A. An Outline of Arguments

First, the general creditors cannot be said to intervene on insolvency of the insolvent party because they never acquire any rights in the assets of the fraudster. This is so whether the insolvent is a corporate body or an individual. Specifically, when a company goes into insolvent liquidation, a statutory (purpose) trust arises for the purpose of distribution to all creditors collectively[54] and so individual creditors do not acquire any rights that could be said to intervene. In personal bankruptcy, the title to assets vests in the trustee in bankruptcy.[55]

Second, the third-party rights bar is triggered where the effect of rescission would be to destroy or frustrate the third party's right, and mere depreciation of the rights of the third party is insufficient.[56] General creditors' rights are not destroyed on rescission,[57]

[53] See Chapter 11 of this book (L Ho, 'The Proprietary Consequences of Rescission in Equity').

[54] *Re Oriental Inland Steam Co; Ex p Scinde Railway Co* (1874) LR 9 Ch App 557, 560; *Re Yagerphone Ltd* [1935] Ch 392, 396; *Ayerst v C & K (Construction) Ltd* [1976] AC 167, 178–80.

[55] Insolvency Act 1986, s 306. See also eg *Ayerst v C & K (Construction) Ltd* [1976] AC 167.

[56] O'Sullivan, Elliott, and Zakrzewski (n 3) [20.29], citing *Scholefield v Templer* (1859) 4 De G & J 429, 45 ER 166 and *Turton v Benson* (1718) 1 P Wms 496, 24 ER 488.

[57] A creditor's right to share is converted to a right to prove on insolvency.

and in any case it would be difficult to attribute even a very serious devaluation of the general creditors' rights to the enforcement of any particular proprietary claim: it is precisely because there are many proprietary claims, typically secured by consensual security rights, that the rights of general creditors become less valuable.[58]

Third, the authorities—on balance—do not seem to support an insolvency bar to rescission. This will require some explanation below but the argument in outline is as follows. At first glance, the authorities appear to be in conflict: some authorities permit rescission while others do not. Those that do are cases of personal insolvency.[59] Those that do not involve corporate insolvency. A closer inspection suggests that there is no reason for drawing such a distinction. The authorities which disallow rescission against an insolvent company involve a special type of case, namely a contract to take up shares, in which a bar on rescission by the contributories seems justifiable. The reason for treating insolvency as a bar is such a case has little to do with the concern about prejudicing third-party rights but is instead a function of what it means to be a contributory. These authorities do not, however, justify refusing to permit other parties to rescind other kinds of contracts with the company upon insolvency.

Fourth, it is plausible that a power to rescind which is exercisable against a person pre-insolvency can also be exercised against the insolvency officer, with the attendant proprietary consequences, thus giving the rescinding party proprietary protection on the fraudster's insolvency.

This argument rests on two points. One is that insolvency officers stand in no better position than the insolvent party did pre-insolvency: they take the rights 'warts and all'. The second aspect of this argument relates to the nature of the power to rescind, which has been subject to an important debate. Some argue that the right is personal only, others that it is more than personal, constituting a limitation on the rights acquired by the fraudster. It seems difficult to understand why, prima facie, this limitation would not then bind the insolvency officer if the logic of insolvency is to facilitate the collective enforcement process by translating pre-insolvency entitlements into an insolvency forum with minimal disturbance. As Professor Thomas Jackson argued, it is unhelpful to look at whether a right is personal or proprietary, and we need instead to look at the attributes of the rights, and the relative strength of creditor's rights pre-insolvency.[60] One way to test the attributes of a pre-insolvency right is to identify its strength against an execution creditor. Clear authority is lacking, but there are some dicta which suggest that the rescinding party would be preferred over an execution creditor. Another way to look at the attributes of pre-insolvency rights is by drawing analogies with rights whose attributes are known. For example, it is known that a specific performance claim is not

[58] The Association of Business Recovery Professionals R3 found that unsecured creditors receive on average seven per cent of what they are owed, but note A Khan, 'An Empirical Snapshot of English Corporate Insolvencies' (2023) 32 Int Insolvency Rev 447, who found that in some circumstances they get about 1.5 per cent and sometimes nothing (94 per cent of creditors' voluntary liquidations).

[59] A point is sometimes made in passing that cases in which rescission was available despite insolvency are old (eg *Re Crown Holdings (London) Ltd (in liq)* [2015] EWHC 1876 (Ch), [2015] 2 P & CR DG20 [37]), presumably to undermine the strength of their authority, but twentieth-century case law is hardly old.

[60] T Jackson, 'Translating Assets and Liabilities to the Bankruptcy Form' (1985) JLS 73.

given priority on the insolvency of the person against whom it is made. On some accounts, the position of the rescinding party is similar—it is a 'right' to petition the court for 'specific unperformance'.[61] However, there is a risk in relying on analogy when it is unclear which similarities are the relevant ones for the purpose at hand, so it cannot be said that any similarities between a specific performance order and court-ordered rescission point to rescission being precluded on insolvency.[62]

The last two arguments require more explanation, which follows next.

B. Is Rescission Different on Personal and Corporate Insolvency?

The authorities do not speak with one voice when it comes to rescission against a fraudster who is insolvent. The difference, at first glance, appears to relate to whether the fraudster is an individual or a company. If the fraudster is an individual, third-party rights (unsecured creditors' rights) do not intervene to bar rescission but they do appear to intervene if the fraudster is a company that goes into insolvent liquidation. It is difficult to find a convincing reason for drawing such a distinction. It will be shown that the cases in the corporate context favouring an insolvency bar all relate to a specific type of case—a contract with contributories—and in that type of case the bar is prima facie justifiable.

1. Personal Insolvency

In *Load v Green*,[63] the Court held that title revested on rescission after the fraudster became bankrupt. In that case, the claimant (A) sold to a fraudster (B) some handkerchiefs, silk, and other fabrics, which B intended never to pay for. B went into bankruptcy, and his assignees in bankruptcy (Ts) were appointed. A brought an action for conversion against Ts asserting that he had exercised a power to rescind after B became bankrupt. The question before the Court was when the power was exercised. This was important because of the (now abolished) doctrine of reputed ownership,[64] which Ts raised to defend the conversion action by A. For the doctrine to apply, the title needed to revest at the latest by the time B went into bankruptcy. If title to goods was with A by the time B was declared bankrupt and the goods remained in B's possession, the doctrine would have deemed to pass to the bankrupt's estate all goods that were 'in the possession, order, or disposition of the bankrupt, in his trade or business, by the consent and permission of the true owner'.[65] Parke B held that the doctrine of reputed ownership did not apply because the vendor was not the 'true owner' at the time the fraudster

[61] Swadling, 'The Proprietary Consequences of Fraud' (n 48).

[62] For discussion of the issues with drawing analogies between specific performance and rescission, see Chapter 3 of this book (B McFarlane, 'Understanding Powers to Rescind: Property, Equity, and Unjust Enrichment').

[63] *Load v Green* (1846) 15 M & W 216, 153 ER 828. The doctrine did not apply to a corporate winding up.

[64] The doctrine was introduced by the bankruptcy statute of 1623, and was eventually abolished by the Insolvency Acts 1985–1986.

[65] Bankruptcy Act 1925, s 72.

became bankrupt since *he only rescinded after* the 'act of bankruptcy'.[66] This makes clear that the bankruptcy of the fraudster was not thought to be a bar to rescission. The rescinding party gains, on rescission, an equitable interest in the assets transferred under a voidable contract as against a trustee in bankruptcy, dating back to when the bankruptcy order was made.

Another authority that supports the proposition that bankruptcy is not a bar is *Tilley v Bowman*.[67] In that case, a fraudster induced a jeweller to sell him on credit a diamond brooch and six diamond rings. On the same day, the fraudster pledged all bar one ring with a pawnbroker. The fraudster paid the jeweller part of the price, but then went bankrupt. The jeweller discovered the fraud, purported to rescind the contract, paid off the pawnbroker, and took possession of the jewellery. The trustee in bankruptcy then sued the jeweller to recover the goods or their value, or, in the alternative, for the amount the jeweller was paid on the account of the purchase price. One question was whether the defrauded jeweller was able to exercise the power to rescind. Hamilton J held that the defrauded party could exercise the power to rescind in the fraudster's bankruptcy and retake possession from the fraudster. The trustee in bankruptcy could not, therefore, recover the goods or their value from the defrauded jeweller. This is because the trustee in bankruptcy acquired no better rights than the bankrupt had, and one of those rights was the interest in the goods subject to the power to rescind.[68]

2. Corporate Insolvency Prima Facie Not a Bar

The position in personal bankruptcy can be contrasted with that in corporate proceedings. The key authority associated with the proposition that it is too late to rescind a contract after the company enters insolvency is the House of Lords decision in *Oakes v Turquand*.[69] It concerned contracts to take up shares, and, as will be seen, the reasoning in this case only supports the proposition that insolvency bars rescission of a contract to take up shares; it does not support the broader proposition that insolvency of a company bars rescission generally.

In *Oakes v Turquand*, Mr Oakes and Mr Peel, in reliance on the statements in the prospectus, purchased shares in a limited liability company. Their names were put on the register of shareholders. The company went into insolvency and was ordered to wind

[66] *Load v Green* (1846) 15 M & W 216, 217, 223; 153 ER 828, 828, 831.

[67] [1910] 1 KB 745.

[68] *Re Eastgate, ex p Ward* [1905] 1 KB 465 (rescission after the act of bankruptcy but before the receiving order was made); *Tilley v Bowman* [1910] 1 KB 745, 749. The strength of authority of *Re Eastgate* has been questioned (*Re Crown Holdings (London) Ltd (in liq)* [2015] 2 P & CR DG20 [40]) based on Lord Mustill's comments in *Re Goldcorp Exchange* [1995] 1 AC 74. Lord Mustill in *Re Goldcorp* considered the position of customers claiming 'their' money back from an insolvent company if the contract could be rescinded. He said (at 102–03) that the claimants seeking to make a proprietary claim based on rescission:

> would have to contend that in every case where a purchaser is misled into buying goods he is automatically entitled upon rescinding the contract to a proprietary right superior to those of all the vendor's other creditors, exercisable against the whole of the vendor's assets . . . [which is] an extreme proposition . . . [for which] [t]he only possible [authority is] *In Re Eastgate* . . . Their Lordships doubt whether, correctly understood, the case so decides, but if it does they decline to follow it.

[69] (1867) LR 2 HL 325.

up nine months later. The statements in the prospectus, while 'literally true', omitted to mention relevant information. One issue was whether this amounted to false statements,[70] but this is not the focus here. What is of interest is that Oakes and Peel sought to have their names removed from the list of shareholders on the company's insolvency, arguing that they subscribed for shares pursuant to a contract which was voidable for fraudulent misrepresentation.

It was argued for Oakes and Peel that the register of members is not conclusive as to the liability of the members listed, so that general creditors cannot rely on this. The argument of counsel, as explained by Lord Chelmsford, was that a person who was induced by fraud to enter a contract to take up shares could rescind the contract if their name featured in the register.[71] On behalf of the liquidator, counsel argued that the purpose of the register was for the creditors to know who was liable to them.[72] Any person whose name was on the register at the time the order for winding up was made was a shareholder, and liable to contribute to pay the debts to the extent that the sums were due on their shares. The liquidator's arguments were accepted by the court but not without a qualification.

The House of Lords unanimously held that a contract for the allotment of shares may not be rescinded after the commencement of the winding up.[73] On winding up, the assets of the company must be available for distribution among the company's creditors.[74] The decision was based on the Companies Act 1862, which provided that a contributory was liable to contribute to the assets of a company when the company was wound up.[75] There was an analogy with earlier (pre-1862 Act) case law to the same effect.[76] Lord Chelmsford said that the person whose name appeared on the register was a contributory so long as they agreed to become a member.[77] Lord Cranworth was of a similar view, adding that the register of members, which shows the 'true exposition of assets' (ie possible contributories) was there for the protection of those dealing with the

[70] It did: ibid 342–43. This is a point for which *Oakes v Turquand* is often cited: *Cassa di Risparmio della Repubblica di San Marino SpA v Barclays Bank Ltd* [2011] EWHC 484 (Comm), [2011] CLC 701 [219]; *Vald Nielson Holding A/S v Baldorino* [2019] EWHC 1926 (Comm) [135]; *TMO Renewables Ltd (in liq) v Yeo* [2021] EWHC 2033 (Ch) [393].

[71] The counsel for Oakes and Peel argued that the shareholder never becomes a member if they were induced by fraud, but Lord Chelmsford said the counsel could not have meant that they never become a member as that would confuse contracts which are void with those that are voidable: *Oakes v Turquand* (1867) LR 2 HL 325, 345–46, 349–50.

[72] ibid 336.

[73] *Oakes v Turquand* (1867) LR 2 HL 325. See too cases that confirm and develop the position in *Oakes v Turquand*, eg *Kent v Freehold Land and Brick-Making Co* (1868) LR 3 Ch App 493 (the purported rescission of the contract to take up shares taking place before the winding up insufficient); *Re Scottish Petroleum Co (No 2)* (1883) 23 Ch D 413, 432–33 (Baggallay LJ) (confirming the position in *Oakes v Turquand*), 436–37 (Lindley LJ) (stating that a shareholder seeking to be discharged must rescind the contract to take up shares before the winding up, and also have 'his name taken off the register', adding that this is subject to some qualifications, eg that 'if he has before the commencement of the winding-up taken proceedings to have his name removed, that will be sufficient') and 439 (Fry LJ).

[74] *Oakes v Turquand* (1867) LR 2 HL 325, 345.

[75] Companies Act 1862, s 74. Now see Insolvency Act 1986, s 74. See also *Oakes v Turquand* (1867) LR 2 HL 325, 353, 366–67, 374–77.

[76] *Oakes v Turquand* (1867) LR 2 HL 325, 348, 361 endorsing *Henderson v Royal British Bank* (1857) 7 El & Bl 356, 364; 119 ER 1279, 1282.

[77] *Oakes v Turquand* (1867) LR 2 HL 325, 350. See too *Nuneaton Borough Association Football Club Ltd (No 1)* [1989] BCLC 454 (noting that a unilateral asset is sufficient, and a formal bilateral contract was not needed).

company, as a corollary of the company being a limited liability company.[78] Although the judges were careful not to put the decision on the ground of fairness ('which of the two innocents should suffer'), Lord Chelmsford clearly thought that barring rescission of a contract to take up shares on the company's insolvency was not unfair since those taking up shares could make themselves acquainted with the memorandum of association. This, in turn, would give a fuller picture of the health of the company. They were taken to acquiesce to the memorandum even if they only took up shares on the faith of the prospectus.[79]

The reasons identified by the House of Lords in *Oakes v Turquand* apply not only when an order for winding up is made but also on a company's liquidation event, and when the company is insolvent, if an order for winding up has not been made, barring rescission 'depend[s] upon the particular circumstances of the case'.[80]

But it is important to notice that *Oakes v Turquand* was not decided on the basis that the rights of the creditors outweighed the rights of the rescinding parties, or that rescission comes too late if it happens on the insolvency of the contracting party (a proposition for which *Oakes* is sometimes cited).[81] Therefore, it should not be seen as authority for the (broader) proposition that there is no rescission on corporate insolvency. Instead, it should only be seen as authority for the (narrower) point that a shareholder cannot rescind a contract for an allotment of shares after the company has gone into liquidation.

A more recent authority, *Re Crown Holdings (London) Ltd (in liq)*,[82] suggested that the broader proposition is true: that the power to rescind cannot be exercised when the fraudster goes insolvent because the rights of unsecured creditors intervene to prevent the recovery of the property. The case concerned two companies operating a currency exchange business that became insolvent in 2010. The liquidators made applications for clarification as to the capacity in which the companies held certain sums. Various customers raised proprietary claims based on rescission of their contracts for fraudulent misrepresentation. The question was whether the contracts could be rescinded now that the companies were in insolvent liquidation. Surprisingly, *Oakes v Turquand* was not cited. Murray Rosen QC, sitting as a deputy High Court judge, held that the defrauded customers could not rescind the contracts against the insolvent fraudster for two reasons. One was that the power to rescind was said to be personal in nature.[83] The other was a particular feature of the corporate scheme of liquidation of property that set it apart from personal bankruptcy.[84]

[78] *Oakes v Turquand* (1867) LR 2 HL 325, 366–67, 376.
[79] ibid 351.
[80] *Tennent v City of Glasgow Bank (in liq)* (1879) 4 App Cas 615, 621; L Gullifer and J Payne, *Corporate Finance Law: Principles and Policy* (3rd edn, Hart 2020) 532. But see the cases where the shareholder does take steps to be removed from the register, eg *Reese River Silver Mining Co Ltd v Smith* (1869) LR 4 HL 64, discussed below.
[81] See eg counsel in *Re Eastgate, ex p Ward* [1905] 1 KB 465, 466.
[82] [2015] 2 P & CR DG20.
[83] *Re Crown Holdings (London) Ltd (in liq)* [2015] 2 P & CR DG20 [38], citing *Bristol and West Building Society v Mothew* [1998] Ch 1, 22; *Barclays Bank plc v Boulter* [1999] 1 WLR 1919, 1925; *Twinsectra Ltd v Yardley* [1999] Ll Rep Bank 436, 461; *Shalson v Russo* [2005] Ch 281, 323.
[84] *Re Crown Holdings (London) Ltd (in liq)* [2015] 2 P & CR DG20 [41]–[43].

These reasons are unconvincing. If the power to rescind is personal in cases of contracts with a corporate body, its nature should not change merely because the contract is with an individual. If the power to rescind is personal, and therefore barred on insolvency of a corporation, it should also be personal in nature—and barred—on insolvency of an individual. But this is not, as we have seen, what the cases suggest.[85] Those cases suggest that the power is not barred, and, in that sense at least, the power is proprietary. If the power is proprietary in cases involving personal bankruptcy, it should also be proprietary in cases of corporate insolvency. Theoretically, it could be argued that the power to rescind is either personal or proprietary, but it seems odd that the nature of the power should change based on who the other contracting party is. Whatever its nature, the power to rescind might be barred on insolvency for reasons other than its nature.

It seems that the judge was looking to identify such reasons when he considered the features of the insolvency process. When a company goes into administration or liquidation, a statutory trust arises over its assets under the Insolvency Act 1986.[86] This trust captures assets subject to contingent rights of third parties but excludes present proprietary rights of third parties.[87] By contrast, a bankrupt's estate remains subject to both present as well as contingent third-party rights,[88] which means that a power to rescind may be exercised against an individual on bankruptcy. Such a rationalisation of the distinction between rescission on corporate and personal insolvency is unconvincing.[89] The liquidator stands in no better position than the company,[90] just as the trustee in bankruptcy stands in no better position than the bankrupt.[91] So, if the insolvent party (company or individual) held rights subject to certain limitations, the insolvency officer (liquidator or trustee in bankruptcy) holds the rights subject to the same limitations;[92] the statutory trust that arises on corporate insolvency is irrelevant in determining which rights bind the insolvency officer.[93] The role of the statutory trust is to ensure that company's assets are not used for the company's own benefit, and are instead held for distribution among the creditors and members of the company.[94]

[85] See the cases referred to in Section III.B.1.

[86] Insolvency Act 1986, s 107; for liquidation, see *Ayerst v C & K (Construction) Ltd* [1976] AC 167, 177. For administration, see *MK Airlines v Katz* [2012] EWHC 2764 (Ch), [2013] Bus LR 169.

[87] *Re Crown Holdings (London) Ltd (in liq)* [2015] 2 P & CR DG20 [42].

[88] ibid [43].

[89] The most comprehensive critique can be found in N Segal, 'The Impact of Insolvency on the Right to Rescind—the Flaw in the Crown' (2016) 29 Insolv Int 27, but others have also been critical. See eg C Mitchell, P Mitchell, and S Watterson (eds), *Goff & Jones: The Law of Unjust Enrichment* (10th edn, Sweet & Maxwell 2022) [40-28]; K van Zwieten, *Goode on Principles of Corporate Insolvency Law* (5th student edn, Sweet & Maxwell 2019) [6-17] fn 76.

[90] van Zwieten (n 89) [6-17]: 'The liquidator takes control of the assets of the company, including contract rights, in the condition in which he finds them, warts and all.'

[91] *McEntire v Crossley Brothers Ltd* [1895] AC 457, 461; *Madell v Thomas & Co* [1891] 2 QB 230, 234, 238.

[92] Company liquidators differ from trustees in bankruptcy in the way they generally come to hold the property: the estate of the bankrupt vests in the trustee in bankruptcy (Insolvency Act 1986, s 306), while in corporate proceedings, the property of a company does not automatically vest in the liquidator—even without the vesting order, the liquidator is empowered under the statute to deal with the property of the company (Insolvency Act 1986, Sch 4 para 6). Nothing turns on this difference for the current purposes.

[93] Segal (n 89) 28.

[94] *Ayerst v C & K (Construction) Ltd* [1976] AC 167; *Mitchell v Carter* [1997] BCC 907, 912, approved in *In re Lehman Brothers International (Europe) (in admin) (No 4)* [2017] UKSC 38, [2018] AC 465 [54].

The imposition of a statutory trust does not determine its subject matter and does not inform the question whether the power to rescind should be effective. It is also not a good reason for treating the power to rescind differently in personal and corporate insolvency.

3. Justifying the Bar to Rescission in Contracts to Take up Shares

There remains the question of why rescission of contracts to take up shares should be barred on a company's insolvency. Is it, as *Burgess's Case*[95] suggests, that the legal rights between the relevant parties change on corporate winding up, and the rights of all the company's creditors intervene? If so, this could, prima facie, be a plausible explanation why insolvency should bar rescission of all contracts, not just contracts to take up shares.[96]

In *Burgess's Case*, Jessel MR purported to rely on *Oakes v Turquand*[97] for the proposition that a defrauded party cannot rescind the contract to the prejudice of those who acquired new rights in consequence of the winding up.[98] Jessel MR in *Burgess's Case* said that 'after the company is wound up . . . rescission is impossible'.[99] He explained that winding up changes the position of creditors and shareholders: creditors can no longer look to the company for the payment of the liabilities (although they can look to the company's assets), but can look to shareholders, who become co-contributories such that 'the liabilities of the company . . . become liabilities of the shareholders'.[100] Since shareholders may be liable as co-contributories on winding up, the bar on rescission by the defrauded shareholder is thought to protect the other shareholders from having their contribution increased. The reasoning in *Burgess's Case* has been adopted in Canada and Australia.[101]

There are some problems with this analysis. First, it is difficult to see how the reasoning in *Burgess's Case* might apply where there is no basis for adjustment of the rights of the contributories[102] and where no contribution is due, as in the case of shareholders with fully paid-up shares in a limited company[103] (as is common in practice).[104]

95 *Re Hull and County Bank* (1880) 15 Ch D 507 (hereafter '*Burgess's Case*').

96 It seems that *Burgess's Case* was cited before Murray Rosen QC in *Re Crown Holdings (London) Ltd (in liq)* [2015] 2 P & CR DG20 [42], but not for such a broad point, and the judge did not consider the narrower point relevant.

97 (1867) LR 2 HL 325.

98 *Burgess's Case* (1880) 15 Ch D 507, 512.

99 ibid 509.

100 ibid 512.

101 *McAskill v Northwestern Trust Co* [1926] SCR 412, 419; *Southern British National Trust Ltd v Pither* (1937) 57 CLR 89, 114, cited with approval in *Sons of Gwalia Ltd v Margaretic* (2007) 231 CLR 160 [270]; *Cadence Asset Management Pty Ltd v Concept Sports Ltd* [2005] FCA 1280, (2005) 55 ACSR 145, 147, reversed on other grounds: *Cadence Asset Management Pty Ltd v Concept Sports Ltd* [2005] FCAFC 265, (2005) 147 FCR 434.

102 See Insolvency Act 1986, s 74.

103 See *The Matter of Direct Lending Income Feeder Fund* (Grand Court of the Cayman Islands, 13 March 2024) [145] (Segal J). I am very grateful to Steven Elliott KC for pointing me to this case.

104 *In re Lehman Brothers International (Europe) (in admin) (No 4)* [2018] AC 465 [131], citing Briggs LJ in the Court of Appeal [2015] EWCA Civ 485, [2016] Ch 50 [172] (reversed in other parts). This is so even though fully paid-up shareholders may be 'contributories' for some purposes, *Burnden Group Holdings Ltd v Hunt* [2018] EWHC 463 (Ch), [2018] BCC 404 (which concerned the meaning of (now replaced) Insolvency Rules 1986 (SI 1986/1925) r 4.79 on the inspection of documents held by a liquidator by, inter alia, a contributory).

If the reason for applying a bar on rescission is to ensure that third-party rights are not prejudiced,[105] that reason falls away in situations where the prejudice to third parties simply does not arise.

The second difficulty is that it appears to posit that general creditors' interests are more worthy of protection *in general* than those of shareholders, without providing a satisfactory reason why this should be so. *Burgess's Case* concerned a shareholder who was induced by fraudulent misrepresentation to take up shares in a company (*Oakes v Turquand* concerned a similar fact pattern). The Court held that the shareholder could not rescind the contract after the company entered winding up, even if the assets in the hands of the liquidators were sufficient to pay in full the whole liabilities of the company. This suggests that what the Court had in mind is that shareholders on winding up of a company occupy a special position because: (i) they may become liable for the company's debts,[106] and (ii) on insolvent liquidation, shareholders are paid the capital they contributed last (if there is anything left), after unsecured creditors and after certain other liabilities are paid.[107] The policy that the 'rights of members as members come last'[108] in a company's insolvency accords with the fundamental distinction between equity and debt, and the proposition that since shareholders have the most to gain when a business succeeds, they should absorb the costs when it fails—up to the full amount of their investment.[109] On this reasoning, rescission of a contract to take up shares after winding up would have the effect of elevating a shareholder to a creditor at a time where the distinction between debt and equity matters most, and would undermine the fundamental rule that shareholder funds are available for distribution to the creditors.[110]

But such reasoning is not convincing. The equity–debt divide might justify not elevating a shareholder to the status of a creditor too lightly, but it is not obvious that it

[105] Jessel MR in *Burgess's Case* (1880) 15 Ch D 507, 512 interpreted Lord Cairns in *Tennent v City of Glasgow Bank* (1879) 4 App Cas 615 (who in turn was commenting on *Oakes v Turquand* (1867) LR 2 HL 325) as saying that protection of third parties was 'a reason . . . but that does not at all affect the absolute *dictum* that it is too late [to rescind after winding up has commenced]'. If the bar on rescission on winding up is absolute there is still a need to explain why this should be so. The language of 'too late' might suggest that the reason for the bar on winding up is lapse of time rather than protection of rights of third parties. There is no shortage of dicta that generally rescission of contracts to take shares must take place 'with extreme promptness' (*Aaron's Reefs v Twiss* [1896] AC 273, 294) and 'as soon as he learns the facts' (*Sharpley v Louth and East Coast Railway* (1876) 2 Ch D 663, 685). But lapse of time is not a good reason for barring rescission on winding up. Rescission is a remedy available to those who act quickly, but there is no way of knowing when a winding up might occur. A person who was fraudulently induced to take up shares seeking to rescind the contract minutes later might be told that rescission comes too late because a winding up has been made, even though the rescinding party had no opportunity to act and rescind.

[106] In relation to limited liability companies, the extent of shareholders' liability is governed by Insolvency Act 1986, s 74. In an unlimited company, there is no limit on the liability of its members: Companies Act 2006, s 3(4).

[107] *Bloom v Pensions Regulator* [2013] UKSC 52, [2014] AC 209 [39] (shareholders are paid after unsecured provable debts, statutory interest, and non-provable liabilities are paid).

[108] *Soden v British & Commonwealth Holdings plc* [1998] AC 298.

[109] See J Slain and H Kripke, 'The Interface between Securities Regulation and Bankruptcy—Allocating the Risk of Illegal Securities Issuance between Securityholders and the Issuer's Creditors' (1973) 48 NYU L Rev 261, the premise of which was adopted in *In re Telegroup, Inc*, 281 F3d 133 (3rd Cir 2002). Note *Sons of Gwalia Ltd v Margaretic* (2007) 231 CLR 160, which allowed shareholders to rank on a par with unsecured creditors in insolvency of the company in relation to their claims for damages for misrepresentation and inadequate market disclosure. Following its criticism (for failure to give effect to the 'member comes last' policy), it was reversed by the Corporations Amendment (Sons of Gwalia) Act 2010 (Cth) (which replaced s 593A of the Corporations Act 2001 (Cth) in Australia).

[110] See O'Sullivan, Elliott, and Zakrzewski (n 3) [25.39]–[25.41].

explains a total bar to rescission on winding up. From the perspective of a shareholder, who has been induced into buying shares, eg by fraudulent representations about the financial health of the company, it is unjust to have to absorb the costs of fraud when the business fails. Arguments are sometimes made that shareholders assume the ordinary business risk of insolvency but not the risk of corporate fraud.[111]

Against this, it could be said that: (i) general creditors are in no better position to assume the risk of corporate fraud, and the effect of allowing rescission of a contract to take up shares after winding up would be to shift the risk of fraud onto general creditors; and (ii) shares have been offered to a shareholder, so the risk of a defect in a transaction of taking up shares should be with the shareholder and not the general creditors.[112] Neither argument is compelling. General creditors already share the risk of fraud (eg a defrauded creditor is still a creditor), so why should it matter that a defrauded party was subscribing for shares rather than delivering supplies?

The reason a shareholder cannot generally rescind a contract to take up shares lies, it is suggested, in the protection of reliance. The key issue to notice is that taking up shares differs from transfers of property. Third parties dealing with someone do not, generally, rely on the property transferred by others under a rescindable contract when making a decision whether to deal with them. By contrast, a person dealing with a company does rely on equity provided by the rescinding party.[113] When the law bars rescission on insolvency of a company, it does not protect the general creditor's interests; it protects general-creditor reliance.

Support for this can be gleaned from the reasoning in cases in which a shareholder was able to rescind a contract for allotment of shares when they had taken steps to have their name removed from the company register before the proceedings for winding up.[114] The reason for this, it is suggested, is the protection of the faith placed on the register. All shareholders of a company must be entered on the company's register of members,[115] and the person entered on the register is the member unless and until the register is rectified.[116] The register of members is open to inspection, and any person, on request, must be granted access unless the company obtained a no-access order from a court.[117]

[111] Gullifer and Payne (n 80) 106. It should be noted that the argument is made in relation to the Financial Services and Markets Act 2000, ss 90 and 90A, which govern liability for false prospectuses and provide for the remedy of compensation in such cases. Where the remedy under the statute is triggered the question arises whether a shareholder can claim, on the company's winding up, as a creditor, or whether they must make the claim as a shareholder, ranking beneath creditors. The reasoning by analogy can apply to the power to rescind.

[112] See Slain and Kripke (n 109) 288. cf KB Davis Jr, 'The Status of Defrauded Securityholders in Corporate Bankruptcy' [1983] Duke LJ 1.

[113] Slain and Kripke (n 109) 285.

[114] *Oakes v Turquand* (1867) LR 2 HL 325, 378; *Reese River Silver Mining Co Ltd v Smith* (1869) LR 4 HL 64, 74–75, 78, 79, 80–81. There are some exceptions to this requirement such that the shareholder will be able to rescind the contract in the usual way, without taking steps to have the name struck down from the register. One example is where there is an agreement that the shareholder will not be prejudiced by not taking proceedings pending suit by another shareholder: *Re Estates Investment Co* (1869) LR 4 Ch App 497, 500. Another is where a company forfeited shares because of the shareholder's failure to pay calls due in respect of the allotment, and ceased to be a shareholder: *Aaron's Reefs Ltd v Twiss* [1896] AC 273.

[115] Companies Act 2006, s 112.

[116] *Enviroco Ltd v Farstad Supply A/S* [2011] UKSC 16, [2011] 1 WLR 921 [37]; *Re JDK Construction Ltd* [2024] EWCA Civ 934, [2025] 3 All ER 157.

[117] Companies Act 2006, s 116(3) and (4).

Third parties (including creditors) may have dealt with the company in reliance on the shareholding recorded on the register,[118] and 'it is . . . as a matter of policy, of very great importance, in these cases, to make the register of any one of these companies as conclusive as . . . you are able to'.[119] Third parties are protected because they have acquired *or might acquire* rights in reliance on the company's share capital, recorded in a public register. Where notice of contracts is 'given to the world'[120] rescission does not happen until the notice has been removed, or the rescinding party has taken steps to have the name removed. This would explain why rescission of a contract for allotment of shares is not possible after winding up: while after winding up the register of members may be rectified by a court order,[121] general creditors may well already have relied on the register.

The analysis so far has shown that contracts to take up shares cannot generally be rescinded after the company's winding up commences in English law, and there are special reasons for this, closely related to the nature of the interest being taken up by the shareholder, and its necessary publicity. Those reasons do not translate to rescission of other contracts. For example, if a company were to mislead a supplier into selling goods to it, the company would not be able to sustain an argument that rescission on winding up is barred by drawing an analogy with contracts to take up shares.

This shows that authorities such as *Oakes v Turquand* cannot support treating rescission differently purely on the basis that the fraudster is an individual or a company, but there are special reasons to preclude rescission of contracts to take up shares when the company becomes insolvent, at least in cases where the shareholder does not take steps to rescind the contract prior to, for example, the winding-up order being made.[122]

C. Can the Power to Rescind be Exercised against the Insolvency Officer?

It is generally understood that proprietary rights translate into a priority on insolvency while personal rights mean that the creditor becomes a general creditor participating *pari passu*. It is unsurprising that there is much debate about the personal or proprietary nature of the power to rescind.[123]

Before proceeding, it is helpful to make one observations with reference to Professor Sarah Worthington's outline of four possible models of rescission, depending on the sort of interest the rescinding party has pre- and post-exercise of the power to rescind. The models identified are as follows: (i) mere equity prior to rescission, and,

[118] *Oakes v Turquand* (1867) LR 2 HL 325, 366; *Re Scottish Petroleum Co* (1883) 23 Ch D 413, 439.

[119] *Reese River Silver Mining Co Ltd v Smith* (1869) LR 4 HL 64, 80.

[120] *Re Scottish Petroleum Co* (1883) 23 Ch D 413, 438–39.

[121] See Insolvency Act 1986, s 148.

[122] See also Andrews, Tettenborn, and Virgo (n 32) [3-043] citing *Re Yorke Street Mezzanine Pty Ltd* [2007] FCA 922, (2007) 162 FCR 358 [39], esp [40], where this is suggested to be the position in English law as well.

[123] At this stage the term 'power to rescind' is treated as a shorthand for whatever entitlement the rescinding party might have.

after rescission, legal title revests or a trust arises;[124] (ii) full equitable interest in the transferred asset pre- and post-rescission; (iii) personal money claim pre- and post-rescission; and (iv) personal money claim pre- and post-rescission except where the money remedy would be inadequate (eg because the property is rare or unique) or the defendant is a fiduciary (in such exceptional cases a proprietary remedy would be available).[125] Insolvency has no effect on the power to rescind in models (ii) and (iii). If the defrauded party has a full equitable interest pre-rescission (model (ii)), this will give the defrauded party priority over unsecured creditors of the insolvent. If the defrauded party has all along only a personal money claim (as is the case in model (iii)), their claim will generally rank *pari passu* with unsecured creditors even if the defrauded party exercises the power to rescind.[126] But insolvency might affect the power to rescind in models (i) and (iv). When an exercise of a power to rescind alters the position of the rescinding party from holding a non-proprietary interest to a proprietary one (models (i) and (iv)), the question arises to what extent a fraudster's insolvency affects the power to rescind. The answer is important, not least because the first model is thought to best reflect the current law.[127]

There are two lines of thought on the nature of the power to rescind. One is that a power to rescind is a personal right exigible against the counterparty to the rescindable contract. It is not enforceable on insolvency of the fraudster. Those who take this view often emphasise that a power to rescind does not give the defrauded party any proprietary interest in the asset transferred under the contract[128] because 'the beneficial interest in any property transferred . . . remains vested in the transferee'[129] and the defrauded party 'retains no proprietary interest in the chattel'.[130] It is only when the power to rescind is exercised that the rescinding party acquires a proprietary interest in some sort of asset[131]—either the asset previously transferred under the tainted contract or its traceably linked substitute. The nature of the power to rescind is controversial, as various contributions to this book show,[132] but the preferable view is that it is more than a merely personal interest. This does not, without more, justify that it should be exercised against the insolvency officer. Another version of this reasoning is that it is not possible to rescind on insolvency of the fraudster because by then third-party rights, namely general creditors' rights, intervene. This, however, looks circular: the power to rescind is personal because the rescinding party cannot rescind as third-party rights intervene, and the reason they intervene is because the power to rescind is personal.

[124] On revesting of legal title, note Chapter 2 of this book (B Häcker, 'Explaining the Right to Rescind') (noting that if retroactivity is taken seriously, the title does not 'revest').

[125] Worthington (n 29) 35–38.

[126] The position is different in relation to claimants seeking to rescind a contract for subscription of shares because, as shareholders, they rank below unsecured creditors on liquidation of the company.

[127] Worthington (n 29) 46.

[128] *Re Crown Holdings (London) Ltd (in liq)* [2015] 2 P & CR DG20 [38]; Stevens (n 29) 194.

[129] *Bristol and West Building Society v Mothew* [1998] Ch 1, 22.

[130] *Barclays Bank plc v Boulter* [1999] 1 WLR 1919, 1925.

[131] Worthington (n 29) 35–38.

[132] Chapter 11 of this book (L Ho, 'The Proprietary Consequences of Rescission in Equity'); Chapter 3 of this book (B McFarlane, 'Understanding Powers to Rescind: Property, Equity, and Unjust Enrichment'); Chapter 2 of this book (B Häcker, 'Explaining the Right to Rescind').

The second line of thought is that a power to rescind can be exercised after the fraudster has become insolvent because the insolvency officer is in no better position than the insolvent. This is so whether the insolvent is an individual (in which case the estate of the bankrupt vests in the trustee in bankruptcy)[133] or a company (in which case the property does not generally pass to the liquidator,[134] but they have statutory powers to deal with the property of the company).[135] Either way, the insolvency officers take the insolvent's property (which in this context means not only things but also rights as well as contingent and future interests)[136] in the condition in which they find it.[137] If a power to rescind is exigible against the insolvent party, it is exigible against the liquidator and the trustee in bankruptcy too. The insolvent party holds their rights subject to a liability to have those rights defeated. This liability to defeasance is subject to a condition precedent, the condition being an exercise or a lapse of the power to rescind. When the power to rescind a contract is exercised the liability is replaced with a beneficial interest in an asset in favour of the rescinding party. It is in this sense true to say that a power to rescind is neither an interest in property nor a mere right in personam but 'rather it is an inherent limitation of the interest that has been acquired . . . an inherent qualification of the contract rights'.[138]

The effect of an exercise of a power to rescind is that, if there is a post-rescission proprietary claim, the asset is not available for distribution among the general creditors of the insolvent. This gives rise to a concern that the exercise of a power to rescind, after insolvency proceedings commenced, might appear to contravene the key principles of insolvency: the anti-deprivation rule and the rule that there is no contracting out of *pari passu*, both of which circumscribe the principle that the liquidator takes the assets in the condition in which they find them. Each is taken in turn.

First, a power to rescind is not caught by the anti-deprivation rule[139] because the condition that triggers divesting of an asset in the hands of the insolvent party is not insolvency but exercise of a power by the rescinding party.[140] This is different from a case where an owner of property contractually limits their interest by a condition taking place on insolvency.[141] In any case, the anti-deprivation rule does not affect transactions 'which do not have as their predominant purpose, or one of their main

[133] Insolvency Act 1986, s 306.

[134] *Re Oriental Inland Steam Co; Ex p Scinde Railway Co* (1874) LR 9 Ch App 557, 560; *Ayerst v C & K (Construction) Ltd* [1976] AC 167; *Tanning Research Laboratories Inc v O'Brien* (1990) 8 ACLC 248, 255.

[135] Insolvency Act 1986, Sch 4 para 6. The liquidator may apply for a vesting order (Insolvency Act 1986, s 145) but this is rarely needed given the broad statutory powers.

[136] For the purposes of insolvency law, the term 'property' is understood very broadly, see Insolvency Act 1986, s 436.

[137] In relation to trustees in bankruptcy, see *McEntire v Crossley Brothers Ltd* [1895] AC 457, 461, and see *Madell v Thomas & Co* [1891] 2 QB 230, 234, 238. In relation to liquidators, see van Zwieten (n 89) [3-05]; Segal (n 89) 28. The liquidator may be able to assert defences which the company itself could not have raised prior to liquidation, for example that a security interest granted by a company is void for lack of registration (Companies Act 2006, s 859H), or that a transaction should be set aside as a preference or at an undervalue under Insolvency Act 1986, ss 239 and 238 respectively, or a vulnerable floating charge: Insolvency Act 1986, s 245.

[138] van Zwieten (n 89) [3-05].

[139] *Belmont Park Investments Pty Ltd v BNY Corp Trustee Services Ltd* [2011] UKSC 38, [2012] 1 AC 383.

[140] A power to rescind is, therefore, different from a contractual right that is subject to a suspensive condition, where the condition is that the right terminates on insolvency.

[141] *Higinbotham v Holme* (1812) 19 Ves Jr 88, 34 ER 451.

purposes, the deprivation of the property of one of the parties on bankruptcy'.[142] Even if a contract included an express automatic rescission clause triggering rescission on the winding up of the fraudulent party, if and where a party was fraudulently induced, it would likely be considered a provision inserted bona fide and for the purpose of protecting the rescinding party, not to evade the insolvency law.[143]

Second, a power to rescind might seem to contravene the principle of no contracting out of *pari passu*. The principle is that a contract which gives one creditor more than its pro rata share under the statutory provisions for rateable distribution[144] is to that extent ineffective.[145] Rescission cases might seem to be triggered by this rule because the insolvent party's right to dispose of their own assets becomes limited when the power to rescind is exercised. In most cases, however, the power to rescind is not based on a contractual provision, and there is no contract to give one creditor more than their pro rata share. It is a remedy provided by law that places the claimant in an advantageous position—more than the pro rata share they would have received prior to rescission.

In considering the position of the rescinding party after insolvency proceedings have commenced, it is useful to reflect on the role of insolvency law. One of the goals of insolvency law is to collectivise the process by which the insolvent person's assets are distributed to the creditors. This goal can be achieved if pre-insolvency assets and liabilities are identified and replicated as closely as possible on insolvency, taking into account the pre-insolvency ranking between the claimants.[146] Jackson has explained that the entitlements of creditors must be enforced in a way that preserves their relative value when measured at the time of insolvency.[147] Relative value of a claim is understood here to mean the extent to which it binds (ie is exigible against) third parties.

Consider a claim for specific performance of a contract. Let us assume that A agrees to sell to B a particular painting for £2,000. B pays. A fails to deliver and goes insolvent. B cannot successfully assert that B should receive the painting based on a specific performance claim, ahead of the general creditors of A (B might have acquired property in the painting, which would alter B's position on A's insolvency, but we ignore this here). Jackson argues that the reason for this is that the rationale for specific performance (avoiding the undercompensation that would result from an award of damages) 'essentially describes a two-party relationship between the contracting parties'.[148] Since a claim to specific performance operates only between A and B, and not third parties, its relative value is preserved on insolvency. It does not, therefore, bind the insolvency officer.

[142] *Belmont Park Investments Pty Ltd v BNY Corp Trustee Services Ltd* [2012] 1 AC 383 [14], [79], [80]–[104].

[143] See eg *Borland's Trustee v Steel Bros & Co Ltd* [1901] 1 Ch 279 (pre-emption rights on bankruptcy inserted in the agreement bona fide, and not as a fraudulent preference).

[144] Insolvency Act 1986, s 328 (on bankruptcy), and s 107 (in liquidation in voluntary winding up), and Insolvency Rules 2016, r 14.12 (compulsory winding up and administration).

[145] *Belmont Park Investments Pty Ltd v BNY Corp Trustee Services Ltd* [2012] 1 AC 383 [1], [6]–[8].

[146] Jackson, 'Translating Assets and Liabilities' (n 60) 73. See too T Jackson, 'Bankruptcy, Non-Bankruptcy Entitlements and the Creditors' Bargain' (1982) 91 Yale LJ 857; T Jackson, *The Logic and Limits of Bankruptcy Law* (Harvard University Press 1986) ch 1.

[147] Jackson, 'Translating Assets and Liabilities' (n 60) 76. The reason for preserving the relative values of the entitlements is to minimise the risk of 'strategic gamesmanship that otherwise would hamper the smooth replacement of individual-based remedies with collective proceedings'.

[148] ibid 90.

The approach based on relative value of claims could work well in a system where all entitlements are either exigible only between two parties, or exigible against all third parties. It is impossible to apply it in cases of two-party entitlements that bind some third parties but not others. For example, in contracts for sale of unique personal property (ie contracts for which specific performance would be ordered) before title passes to the buyer, an equitable interest may well arise in favour of the buyer. This interest binds donees or transferees with notice of the interest, but not a bona fide purchaser of legal title without notice. Under English law, we know that as a matter of authority the purchaser's interest is proprietary on the seller's insolvency, meaning that it binds the seller's insolvency officer as a matter of authority, but if we wanted to arrive at an answer on the principle Jackson is proposing—the relative value of entitlements—the answer is elusive because it is impossible to know whether we should be looking at the binding effect against donees or bona fide purchasers.

Jackson's refinement of his 'relative value' approach is more promising. It is that, in assessing the relative values of rights on insolvency, it is relevant to consider how the law would treat the claimant's right against an execution creditor.[149] If a claim 'wins' against an execution creditor, it will be given priority over general creditors on the insolvency of the debtor. This refined 'relative approach' enables us to detect the legal policy on which the law is based.

In English law it is not clear whether a claimant with a power to rescind a contract and an ensuing claim for specific restitution of a particular asset could obtain an injunction to restrain execution. But there are some dicta which suggest that the rescinding party would be preferred over other creditors outside insolvency. In *Dewji v Banwaitt*,[150] Andrews J said:

> [I]n a case such as the present, where the judgment creditor is seeking to recover the money that he paid the judgment debtor under a contract that has been rescinded for fraud, together with interest, the Court might take the view when exercising its discretion that *it would not be in the interests of justice to allow the debtor's other creditors to participate in that share of his estate that was increased at the expense of the party he deceived*. That is so whether or not the original claim was a claim for damages or in restitution and regardless of the absence of any proprietary claim to trace the money into the hands of the wrongdoer. In those circumstances, given that no bankruptcy order was yet in place, the Court might consider that *it would be wrong to deprive the judgment creditor of the opportunity to recover as much of the money as he can*.[151]

If Jackson's refined 'relative value' approach is correct, it is plausible that the rescinding party should be able to rescind on insolvency if they are preferred over a judgment creditor, which they may be in English law, as *Dewji v Banwaitt* suggests. Nevertheless,

[149] ibid.
[150] [2013] EWHC 3746 (QB).
[151] ibid [29] (emphasis added).

this is relatively weak support as a matter of legal policy, so the strongest arguments rejecting insolvency as a bar on rescission remain arguments as a matter of authority.

IV. Conclusion

The third-party rights bar is more limited than generally thought. Where an innocent third party acquires a property right from someone to whom those rights passed under a contract tainted by a vitiating factor (say, fraud), the mere acquisition of a property right by the third party is not a bar to rescission of the contract *against the fraudster*. What is barred is rescission against an innocent third party, which means that the innocent third party is not, and should not be, deprived of the rights acquired. The restitution to the rescinding party in such cases is of the rights that the fraudster acquired when dealing with the third party. The reason why the rescinding party may assert such a claim to substitutes is because rescission of the contract withdraws the authority to dispose of rights that passed under the contract. On rescission, the disposition of the rights by the fraudster to the innocent party is unauthorised. It was seen in this chapter that the position is clearer in equity, but it is also arguable as a matter of principle that this could be the case at common law too, although authorities on the effect of rescission at common law would need to be revisited.

The chapter also sought to break ground in the analysis of rescission on insolvency of a fraudster, which has so far attracted very little attention. It was shown that insolvency of the fraudster does not preclude rescission of the contract, although there are some exceptions relating to particular contracts, such as contracts to take up shares.

11

The Proprietary Consequences of Rescission in Equity

*Lusina Ho**

I. Introduction

The proprietary consequences of equitable rescission for transfers made under impaired consent remain one of the most contentious issues in English private law. As the authors of *Goff & Jones on Unjust Enrichment* note, the authorities are 'in such a confused state that the law cannot be confidently stated, and a decision of the Supreme Court is needed to rationalise and restate it'.[1]

This doctrinal uncertainty stems in great part from conflicting policy imperatives, as seemingly technical questions about the nature of the equity to rescind and the timing of effective rescission mask fundamental choices between competing interests.[2] For example, in determining when rescission takes effect so that a constructive trust arises in favour of the claimant, courts are in substance deciding whether to remove the disputed asset from the general pool of creditors' assets.[3] Without a clear understanding of the normative justifications for setting aside defective transfers, it is exceedingly difficult to evaluate these doctrinal choices.

This chapter explores these justifications. My central theoretical claim is that although defective transfers are legally valid, they are liable to be unwound because the transferee contributed to, exploited, or knew of the constraints on the transferor's autonomous decision-making. Rescission serves to restore such transferors to their initial legal position. However, the transferred asset remains at risk of dissipation during the prolonged process of litigation. To protect the transferors' interests and to ensure the efficacy of the court's final order for restoration, equity confers upon them rights and powers that may be characterised as proprietary in nature.

* Harold Hsiao-Wo Lee Professor in Trust and Equity, The University of Hong Kong, Hong Kong. I have benefited from comments from Jonas Atmaz Al-Sibaie, Peter Chau, Jordan English, Eugene Fung, Joe Lau, Kelvin Low, Anselmo Reyes, Tan Weiming, and Tham Chee Ho. I am grateful to Kenneth Tsui and Jerry Zhang for research assistance.

[1] C Mitchell, P Mitchell, and S Watterson, *Goff & Jones on Unjust Enrichment* (10th edn, Sweet and Maxwell 2022) [40-12]; *Westdeutsche Landesbank Girozentrale v Islington LBC* [1996] AC 669, 681G–82, 685; *The Bell Group Ltd (in liq) v Westpac Banking Corp* [2008] WASC 329, (2008) 39 WAR 1 [4801]; A Burrows, *A Restatement of the English Law of Unjust Enrichment* (OUP 2012) 161–62; *HMRC v IGE USA Investments Ltd* [2021] EWCA Civ 534, [2021] Ch 423 [91].

[2] For the proposal to adopt a 'balance theory' in this area, see NJ McBride, 'Rescission' in G Virgo and S Worthington (eds), *Commercial Remedies: Resolving Controversies* (CUP 2017) 151.

[3] *Daly v The Sydney Stock Exchange Ltd* (1986) 160 CLR 371, 379.

Here, a useful parallel may be drawn with the vendor-purchaser constructive trust, which protects parties' interests during the typically extended process of conveyance.[4] In both contexts, the law protects the claimant's interest in specific performance (or unperformance) of the contract by granting rights and powers of increasing proprietary intensity, ultimately culminating in beneficial ownership. The key in rescission, as in a vendor-purchaser constructive trust, is calibrating the timing and intensity of such rights and powers to suit the parties' competing interests at different stages of the process of conveyance (or reconveyance).

The proposed theoretical analysis sheds light on two key debates about the proprietary consequences of equitable rescission. First, it explains why the equity to rescind is best understood as a personal power that nonetheless supports equitable tracing and binds third-party transferees. Second, it lends support to the doctrinal argument advanced by Dr Dominic O'Sullivan KC, Professor Steven Elliott KC, and Dr Rafal Zakrzewski that, in cases of fraud, equitable rescission should take effect upon the election to rescind rather than upon court order.[5] However, whilst these authors seem to leave non-fraudulent transferees who have disaffirmed in the same legal position as before, my analysis suggests that they too should receive some enhanced proprietary protection after disaffirmation.

The chapter proceeds as follows. After examining the theoretical justifications for equitable rescission and its proprietary consequences, I will examine the powers or rights of the transferor at the two main stages of rescission, before and after disaffirmation.[6]

II. Justifying the Power to Rescind and Its Proprietary Consequences

Consent is a natural starting point for understanding the normative justification for granting rescission of defective transfers,[7] because by consenting to a transfer, transferors relinquish their right and at the same time give the transferees the same right,

[4] *Lonrho plc (No 2) v Fayed* [1992] 1 WLR 1, 12; *Frenkel v LA Micro Group (UK) Ltd* [2024] UKSC 42, [2024] 2 WLR 1 [24]–[28]; J Atmaz Al-Sibaie and J English, 'The "Equitable Mechanics" of Constructive Trusts and Section 53(1)(c) of the Law of Property Act' (2025) 141 LQR 331; P Millett, 'Restitution and Constructive Trusts' (1998) 114 LQR 399, 416; W Swadling, 'The Proprietary Consequences of Fraud' in PS Davies and H Tjio (eds), *Fraud and Risk in Commercial Law* (Hart 2024) 173.

[5] D O'Sullivan, S Elliott, and R Zakrzewski, *The Law of Rescission* (3rd edn, OUP 2023) [16.39]–[16.40]. For the common law position, see *Load v Green* (1846) 15 M & W 216, 221; 153 ER 828, 830; *White v Garden* (1851) 10 CB 919, 138 ER 364; *Car and Universal Finance Co Ltd v Caldwell* [1965] 1 QB 525, 532. This approach was criticised by W Swadling, 'Rescission, Property, and the Common Law' (2005) 121 LQR 123, but defended by B Häcker, 'Rescission of Contract and Revesting of Title: A Reply to Mr Swadling' [2006] 14 RLR 106. See also B Häcker, 'Rescission and Third Party Rights' [2006] 14 RLR 21.

[6] See eg *Bainbridge v Bainbridge* [2016] EWHC 898 (Ch), [2016] WTLR 943 (a mistake case).

[7] For an account about the nature of the power to rescind and the juridical effects of its exercise, see Chapter 3 of this book (B McFarlane, 'Understanding Powers to Rescind: Property, Equity, and Unjust Enrichment'). See also Chapter 2 of this book (B Häcker, 'Explaining the Right to Rescind'): whereas Häcker's justificatory account locates the injustice of a defective transfer in its consequence—the unjust enrichment—the present chapter focuses on its source, namely the transferee's contribution to or knowledge of that defect.

which, depending on its nature, may be enforceable not only against the duty-bearer of that right, but also against third parties.[8]

A. Impaired Consent and the Remedy of Rescission

It is often argued that transfers made upon invalidating conditions (eg duress, misrepresentation, or undue influence) can be rescinded because the transferor's consent was 'impaired' or 'defective'.[9] However, it is puzzling why impairment of consent justifies rescission, because impaired consent is still consent and the transferor did perform the necessary act for a legally valid transfer.

A fuller explanation is that consent is normatively significant because it constitutes an expression of autonomy or free will. In cases of invalidating conditions, this expression has been undermined because the individual's decision-making is not free from constraints on the exercise of autonomy or free will.[10] The presence of these constraints entails that the consent given lacks normative force. HLA Hart explained the point elegantly:

> For a transaction entered into under [invalidating conditions] will not represent a real choice: the individual might have chosen one course of events and by the transaction procured another (cases of mistake, ignorance, etc.), or he might have chosen to enter the transaction without coolly and calmly thinking out what he wanted (undue influence), or he might have been subjected to the threats of another who had imposed *his* choices (coercion).[11]

If law is to track morality, as it does in these cases, then transfers made through impaired consent should not be binding as between the parties to the transfer even though these transfers may be recognised as initially valid due to countervailing policy reasons.[12] Sir Lloyd Kenyon MR summed up the law's protective stance in *Evans v Llewellin*[13] as follows: 'if the party is not a free agent, and is not equal to protecting

[8] Consent is necessary but not sufficient to justify rescission, as the transferee must also contribute to or know of the transferor's lack of consent. For a similar, relational view of rescission, see Chapter 8 of this book (R Stevens, 'The Scope of Rescission for Duress').

[9] *Swynson Ltd v Lowick Rose LLP* [2017] UKSC 32, [2018] AC 313 [22]; B Häcker, 'Proprietary Restitution After Impaired Consent Transfers: A Generalised Power Model' (2009) 68 CLJ 324. For criticism of the notion of impaired consent, see M Chen-Wishart and R Gregson, 'Impaired Intention Unjust Factors?' in E Bant, K Barker, and S Degeling (eds), *Research Handbook on Unjust Enrichment and Restitution* (Edward Elgar 2020).

[10] See J Raz, *The Morality of Freedom* (OUP 1988) 377–78, identifying coercion and manipulation as the necessary conditions of autonomy; H Frankfurt, 'Coercion and Moral Responsibility' in T Honderich (ed), *Essays on Freedom of Action* (Routledge & Kegan Paul 1973) 65, reprinted in H Frankfurt, *The Importance of What We Care About* (CUP 1988) 26.

[11] HLA Hart, *Punishment and Responsibility: Essays in the Philosophy of Law* (2nd edn, OUP 2008) 45 (emphasis in original).

[12] These reasons include, for example, protection of the interest of the original and subsequent transferees in the certainty of transaction.

[13] (1787) 1 Cox 339, 29 ER 1191.

himself, this Court will protect him.'[14] It is no small coincidence that many vitiating factors in private law also excuse criminal liability.[15]

To be sure, impaired consent alone does not render a transfer voidable save in limited circumstances.[16] The other party must contribute to the impairment,[17] exploit it, or know about it before acquiring the right.[18] Explanations of these requirements as based on unjust enrichment[19] or unconscionable advantage-taking[20] face problems. A right does not necessarily involve an enrichment in value, and treating a mere receipt of a right as enrichment begs the very question why this should be so.[21] Unconscionability, too, lacks precision, because it does not spell out what the 'morally culpable' behaviour is.[22]

A more precise explanation is that those who coerce, mislead, or knowingly exploit the constraints affecting the other party's autonomy should not be allowed to rely on the impaired consent to assert their rights against the transferors.[23] Rescission targets the integrity of the transfer *process* itself, not merely its *outcome*.[24] These exploitative acts are not attacks on the transferors' right, but on the autonomy of the right holder. The right itself is merely the prize. The purpose of rescission is therefore not simply to reverse unjust enrichment but to nullify a transaction tainted by this normative failure. This is illustrated in cases of duress and misrepresentation, where a transaction would be set aside even if made at fair value and no advantage was taken.[25] Underlying this

[14] *Evans v Llewellin* (1787) 1 Cox 339, 340; 29 ER 1191, 1194 (sale of inheritance by an improvident heir). Whilst it is unclear if the equitable jurisdiction to give relief for expectant heirs still survives, the rationale stated in this case applies equally to existing cases. See *Creswell v Potter* [1978] 1 WLR 255; *Credit Lyonnais Bank Nederland NV v Burch* [1997] 1 All ER 144, 151 (decided on the ground of undue influence); D Ibbetson, *A Historical Introduction to the Law of Obligations* (OUP 1999) 234.

[15] D Ormerod, K Laird, and M Gibson, *Smith, Hogan, & Ormerod's Criminal Law* (17th edn, OUP 2024) chs 9 and 10.

[16] These circumstances include rescission of gifts, family settlement, and unregistered conveyancing, see O'Sullivan, Elliott, and Zakrzewski (n 5) ch 29.

[17] Innocent misrepresentors contribute to the representee's misinformed decision by making a statement intended to induce the other party to enter into the contract. Undue influence can be understood as a prophylactic rule requiring the dominant party to take steps to ensure that the dependent party does not bypass their own independent assessment of options.

[18] *Royal Bank of Scotland plc v Etridge (No 2)* [2001] UKHL 44, [2002] 2 AC 773 (upon being put on inquiry of misrepresentation or undue influence of the surety by a third party, failure to take reasonable steps to ensure that the surety was properly advised); *Chwee Kin Keong v Digilandmall Pte Ltd* [2005] SGCA 2, [2005] 1 SLR 502 (notice of a unilateral mistake).

[19] P Birks and NY Chin, 'On the Nature of Undue Influence' in J Beatson and D Friedmann (eds), *Good Faith and Fault in Contract Law* (Clarendon Press 1995) 57; Häcker, 'Explaining the Right to Rescind' (n 7).

[20] *Strydom v Vendside Ltd* [2009] EWHC 2130 (QB), [2009] Costs LR 886 [36].

[21] B McFarlane, 'Unjust Enrichment, Rights and Value' in D Nolan and A Robertson (eds), *Rights and Private Law* (Hart 2011) 581, 584–85; cf Häcker, 'Explaining the Right to Rescind' (n 7) 35, observing that a personal claim based on another party's enforceable promise should be treated as an enrichment.

[22] *Strydom v Vendside Ltd* [2009] EWHC 2130 (QB), [2009] Costs LR 886 [36].

[23] Hart (n 11) 34.

[24] Contrast this with the civilian approach discussed in Häcker, 'Explaining the Right to Rescind' (n 7) 27–27, which prioritises the substantive quality of the consent (or previously *causa contractus*) over the process of its procurement.

[25] M Chen-Wishart, 'Duress, Undue Influence, and Unconscionable Dealing' in H Beale (ed), *Chitty on Contracts* (35th edn, Sweet and Maxwell 2024) [11-054], [11-094]; *Law Debenture Trust Corp plc v Ukraine* [2023] UKSC 11, [2024] AC 411 [182] (duress); H Beale, 'Misrepresentation' in H Beale (ed), *Chitty on Contracts* (35th edn, Sweet and Maxwell 2024) [10-006]; *CIBC Mortgages plc v Pitt* [1994] AC 200 (actual undue influence). While a complainant relying on presumed undue influence need not demonstrate that the transaction was manifestly disadvantageous, such a disadvantage is cogent evidence of the exercise of undue influence: M Chen-Wishart, 'Duress, Undue Influence, and Unconscionable Dealing' in H Beale (ed), *Chitty on Contracts* (35th edn, Sweet and

focus on the process is the vital interest of safeguarding the conditions necessary for the authentic exercise of autonomy when transferring rights. By policing the transfer process against fraud, coercion, and exploitation, the law ensures that the transfer of rights results from a genuine exercise of free will.[26]

B. Proprietary Consequences

Even accepting that defective transfers should be nullified, the law could have simply provided a personal remedy, such as a monetary award or a court order for reconveyance that binds the original transferee alone and only becomes effective upon issuance. Further justifications are needed for the three distinct features in the current law of rescission that produce proprietary consequences. These features are: first, ordering a reconveyance of the particular right, rather than compensation for loss or restitution of the value received; second, allowing the equity to rescind to be traceable and binding on third parties; and third, imposing a trust on the transferee at some point in time before the reconveyance.

I propose that these proprietary effects of rescission are justified both to protect transactional autonomy and to ensure the practical efficacy of the remedy of rescission. The availability of a purely personal remedy gives rise to a vulnerable period during the interval between the initial transfer and the court's final restorative order. The disputed right may be dissipated or sold to third parties, or the transferee may become insolvent. The efficacy of the court order can be easily frustrated. Whilst injunctive relief offers some protection, it too has its limits. To leave the transferor exposed to these risks, especially after they have elected to rescind, would render meaningless the fundamental interest in transactional autonomy that the law seeks to protect.

Crucially, this proprietary protection is not absolute; it is carefully calibrated to recognise the legitimate interests of the original transferees and subsequent bona fide purchasers for value without notice. This balancing framework requires an independent justification for each of the proprietary effects of rescission, namely specific reconveyance via the equity to rescind, the traceability and binding effect of that equity on third parties, and the imposition of a trust.

Before presenting the practical justification for the proprietary consequences of rescission, however, it is necessary to address competing theoretical accounts. The first of these accounts suggests that the transferor has not assumed insolvency risk. However, as Professor William Swadling persuasively demonstrates, tort victims, who similarly have not assumed such risks, are limited to compensatory liability.[27] The

Maxwell 2024) [11-083], [11-088], [11-094]; *Royal Bank of Scotland v Etridge (No 2)* [2002] 2 AC 773 [11]–[15]. See also *Strydom v Vendside Ltd* [2009] EWHC 2130 (QB), [2009] Costs LR 886 [36] (unconscionable bargains).

[26] O'Sullivan, Elliott, and Zakrzewski (n 5) [7.01]–[7.06]. This chapter will not consider payments made upon spontaneous mistakes, such as that in *Chase Manhattan NA v Israel-British Bank (London) Ltd* [1981] Ch 105. Mistaken gifts do not engage the interest in protecting the integrity of the bargaining process.

[27] W Swadling, 'Policy Arguments for Proprietary Restitution' (2008) 28 LS 506, 527–28.

second argues that unsecured creditors would otherwise receive an undeserved windfall. This argument is circular, as it presupposes that the transferor retains rights despite the transfer.[28]

Taking a different tack, Professor Charlie Webb argues that the same reasons that justify legal recognition of a transferor's interest in determining the disposition of a right also justify restitutionary liability when someone receives that right without the transferor's consent.[29] Moreover, proprietary relief gives this interest 'its fullest protection' by leaving the transferor's position 'unchanged by the fact of its receipt by the defendant'.[30] However, this conceptual argument rests on the premise that proprietary relief is inherent to property rights, and hence should always be available whenever a property right is infringed or transferred without legal basis.

This is a premise that finds little support at common law or in equity. In an action for conversion, an order for specific delivery of the goods is at the discretion of the court and may be subject to the defendant's option to pay damages.[31] Similarly, in equity, it is now established that the transfer of a full title upon a mistake or a void contract does not, by itself, trigger proprietary relief.[32] Moreover, the availability of rescission and the constructive trust in cases of defective consent is also subject to judicial discretion. Even accepting Webb's characterisation of property rights, the underlying rationale for such a property regime remains unclear. One might reasonably question whether the law must always afford transferors' interests the fullest protection in every case of non-consensual transfer.

1. Specific Relief via the Equity to Rescind

Whilst Webb refers broadly to right holders' power in determining the disposition of their rights, this chapter distinguishes between internal and external constraints on that power. Exploitative acts operate by creating an internal constraint, as they impair the right holders' consent. By contrast, theft and conversion involve an outright taking of or interference with their right without their consent.

Since the key interest at stake in the exploitation of defective consent is the right holders' autonomy in decision-making, the most appropriate remedy to vindicate their autonomy is one that permits them to reverse the consequences of the corrupted decision. This requires restoring them to their original legal (as opposed to financial) position by nullifying the transaction and ordering the return of the specific right. It would be absurd if the law were content to let fraudsters or those who exploit

[28] ibid.

[29] C Webb, *Reasons and Restitution: A Theory of Unjust Enrichment* (OUP 2016) 85, esp 178–216. For other property-based theories of unjust enrichment, see S Stoljar, *The Law of Quasi-Contract* (2nd edn, Law Book Company of Australia 1989) 5–9; P Watts, 'Restitution—A Property Principle and a Services Principle' [1995] RLR 49, 49–70; McFarlane, 'Unjust Enrichment, Rights and Value' (n 21) 602–06 (preferring a rights-based model to a property-based model); P Watts, '"Unjust Enrichment"—The Potion that Induces Well-meaning Sloppiness of Thought' (2016) 69 CLP 389; P Jaffey, *The Nature and Scope of Restitution* (OUP 2000); P Jaffey, *Justice in Private Law* (Hart 2023) ch 9; and also P Jaffey, *Private Law and Property Claims* (Hart 2007) chs 3 and 8.

[30] Webb (n 29) 178–79.

[31] Torts (Interference with Goods) Act 1977, s 3(2)(a)–(b).

[32] *Westdeutsche Landesbank Girozentrale v Islington LBC* [1996] AC 669, 709.

someone's vulnerability simply write a cheque for rights obtained by their duplicity. By contrast, since theft and the tort of conversion interfere with the owners' property rights rather than their autonomous decision-making, there is no vitiated decision by the owners to reverse. To the extent that specific recovery is available, it stems from a different legal basis than the reversal of the consequences of a corrupted decision-making process.[33]

Whilst an immediate trust would better protect transferors with defective consent than would an equity to rescind,[34] the end does not justify the means. Since transferors manifest an objective intention to make an outright transfer without restricting the transferee's power of free disposition, transferees may legitimately rely on receiving an absolute right until the time at which the transferors elect to rescind.[35] This holds true even for fraudulent transferees. Though a fraudster knows that the transferor would likely seek restitution, the absence of any restricted purpose in the initial transfer provides little basis to treat them as knowing also that they are liable to return the specific right.

The personal claim for rescission (ie the equity to rescind), therefore, adequately balances the interests of the transferor and transferee at this initial stage of the rescission process. Equity recognises that the transferee obtains a valid but defeasible right. At the same time, it grants transferors a trump card they can play subject to the bars to rescission: they can either keep the benefits of a good bargain by inaction or escape a bad one by electing to rescind. This means that, until election, the transferee continues to deal freely with the right, including dissipating it or selling it to another party.[36] The transferee may also become insolvent.[37] The allocation of all these risks to the transferor creates a strong incentive for their prompt election, which helps promote legal certainty for all parties.

[33] Specific recovery for conversion is available on a discretionary basis: Torts (Interference with Goods) Act 1977, s 3(2)(a)–(b). In *Rashid v Nasrullah* [2018] EWCA Civ 2685, [2020] Ch 37 [53], [58], the Court of Appeal held that a fraudster who obtained registered title through forgery held the bare legal estate on an immediate constructive trust for the victim. The Court distinguished this 'fraudulent taking' from voidable transfers induced by fraud, reasoning that the trust stripped the fraudster of any beneficial interest in the property. Whilst some legal systems recognise a constructive trust over stolen property, the point remains controversial in English law: *Black v S Freedman & Co* (1910) 12 CLR 105, 110; *Fistar v Riverwood Legion & Community Club Ltd* (2016) 91 NSWLR 732 [37]; *Westdeutsche Landesbank Girozentrale v Islington LBC* [1996] AC 669, 716; compare *Shalson v Russo* [2003] EWHC 1637 (Ch), [2005] Ch 281 [108]–[119].

[34] For support of this position on the ground that the transferor retains an equitable interest from the outset due to the absence of any intention to benefit the recipient, see R Chambers, *Resulting Trusts* (Clarendon Press 1987) 5, 171; P Birks, 'Restitution and Resulting Trusts' in S Goldstein (ed), *Equity and Contemporary Legal Developments* (The Hebrew University of Jerusalem 1992) 335. This notion of a distinct equitable interest nested within an absolute legal title has now been firmly rejected by Lord Browne-Wilkinson in *Westdeutsche Landesbank Girozentrale v Islington LBC* [1996] AC 669, 706. See also Swadling, 'The Proprietary Consequences of Fraud' (n 4) 180–86. Peter Birks, once a strong advocate of this view, later acknowledged that 'the battle may now have been lost': P Birks, *Unjust Enrichment* (OUP 2005) 184 fn 8.

[35] See *Barclays Bank Ltd v Quistclose Investment Ltd* [1970] AC 567, 580; *China Life Trustees Ltd v China Energy Reserve and Chemicals Group Overseas Co Ltd* [2024] HKCFA 15, (2024) 27 HKCFAR 359 [20]–[32].

[36] B Häcker, *Consequences of Impaired Consent Transfers* (Hart 2013) 351; *Basset v Nosworthy* (1673) Rep t Finch 102, 23 ER 55; *Clough v The London and North Western Railway Co* (1871) LR 7 Exch 26, 34–35 (equity to rescind defeated by a bona fide purchaser without notice); *Oakes v Turquand* (1867) LR 2 HL 325, 326 (rescission after company liquidation); *Latec Investments v Hotel Terigal Pty Ltd (in liq)* (1965) 113 CLR 265, 274 (equity to rescind enforceable against the fraudulent parties but defeated by a bona fide purchaser of the equitable interest).

[37] *Re Goldcorp Exchange Ltd* [1995] 1 AC 74; *Bailey v Angove's Pty Ltd* [2016] UKSC 47, [2016] 1 WLR 3179.

2. Third-Party Effect of the Equity to Rescind

The equity to rescind has long been recognised as capable of binding third parties.[38] Whilst Swadling finds this 'surprising',[39] such effects become more comprehensible when one examines their nature, rationale, and relatively modest impact on third parties.

O'Sullivan, Elliott, and Zakrzewski explain the binding effect of the power to rescind through the *nemo dat* principle; on their view, the power is an 'imperfection' in the original transferee's title that persists until a better title is acquired by a subsequent transferee.[40] Whilst this explains why an assignee in bankruptcy with voidable legal title cannot pass a better title (except to bona fide purchasers),[41] it is less convincing for transfers that are voidable on purely equitable grounds. In such cases, courts typically rely on the bona fide purchaser doctrine rather than *nemo dat*.[42] Furthermore, since the transfer is not voidable at common law, the transferee obtains an absolute, undivided legal title; it remains doubtful if the equity could pose a defect on such a title.[43]

The equity to rescind is better understood as a personal power that binds successors in title through conscience[44] and want of consideration,[45] just like the power of a trust beneficiary to bind successors in title.[46] Successors with notice are bound because despite being aware of the defective transfer, they acquire the right for their own benefit. As Lord Wilberforce explained in *National Provincial Bank v Ainsworth*,[47] a purchaser 'cannot claim the benefit of [a transfer] if he knows that there is a good equitable claim to reform it'.[48] The equity binds innocent volunteers because the law consistently prioritises the stability of rights and bargains over the claims of those who have not given value. In this hierarchy, the static security of a pre-existing right prevails over the claim to security for a gift.[49] Crucially, although the equity to rescind binds successors, it is not a power *in rem*. A right/power *in rem* imposes an identical duty on all parties, whereas here, the liability of a successor is different from, and arises only after, that of the original transferee.[50]

38 *Latec Investments Ltd v Hotel Terrigal Pty Ltd (in liq)* (1965) 113 CLR 265.

39 Swadling, 'The Proprietary Consequences of Fraud' (n 4) 178.

40 O'Sullivan, Elliott, and Zakrzewski (n 5) [21.29]–[21.30]; *Phillips v Phillips* (1861) 4 De G F & J 208, 215; 45 ER 1164, 1166. See also McFarlane, 'Understanding Powers to Rescind' (n 7) 61 (rejecting the *nemo dat* analysis).

41 *Re Eastgate, ex p Ward* [1905] 1 KB 465; *Tilley v Bowman Ltd* [1910] 1 KB 745, 750.

42 L Gullifer, 'Title Conflicts and Priorities' in M Bridge and others, *The Law of Personal Property* (3rd edn, Sweet & Maxwell 2022) [31-038].

43 J Wells, 'What is a Mere Equity?: An Investigation of the Nature and Function of So-called "Mere Equities"' (PhD thesis, York University 2019) 110–13.

44 *National Provincial Bank v Ainsworth* [1965] AC 1175, 1254. See also *YB* (1471) 11 Edward IV, pl 14, f 8a (equitable interest); D Fox, 'Purchase for Value Without Notice' in P Davies, S Douglas, and J Goudkamp (eds), *Defences in Equity* (Hart 2018) 57, 59–60.

45 For the plea of bona fide purchase by a legal interest-holder, see *Earl of Ardglasse v Muschamp* (1684) 1 Vern 237, 238–40; 23 ER 438, 439; *Warrick v Warrick & Kniveton* (1745) 3 Atk 291, 294–95; 26 ER 970, 972; *Kennedy v Green* (1834) 3 My & K, 718–19; 40 ER 266, 274; *Addis v Campbell* (1841) 4 Beav 401, 409; 49 ER 394, 397.

46 L Ho, 'The Nature of the Interest of an Object of Trust or Power' in J Penner and others (eds), *The Property Contract Interface: Historical and Theoretical Perspectives* (OUP 2026) (forthcoming).

47 [1965] AC 1175.

48 ibid 1254.

49 R Demogue, 'Security' in A Fouillée and others (eds), *Modern French Legal Philosophy* (The Macmillan Company 1921) 427.

50 The point is persuasively put by McFarlane, 'Understanding Powers to Rescind' (n 7) 61–62. cf Häcker, *Consequences of Impaired Consent Transfers* (n 36) 130; Mitchell, Mitchell, and Watterson (n 1) [37-34]–[37-39].

As a personal power recognised in equity, where courts have discretion to grant or withhold rescission, the equity to rescind does not give the transferor unilateral decisional control over the transferee's rights that a Hohfeldian power would entail.[51] Nonetheless, the power label remains apt because it encompasses two juridical relationships: first, between the transferor and the court, the transferor's (action) right that the court considers granting rescission (or the transferor's power to invoke the court's power to grant rescission);[52] and second, between the court and the transferee and successors, the court's power to order rescission and reconveyance.

Crucially, as a mere equity, the equity to rescind ranks lowest among equitable rights that can bind third parties, yielding to both bona fide purchasers (of legal and equitable interests) and holders of subsequent equitable interests.[53] This limited third-party effect plays an essential role in stabilising the equitable claim for rescission from being defeated by further transfers. It protects them from purchasers who did not act in good faith, or with due diligence, and volunteers. Yet this protection only preserves the transferors' equitable claim. It does not guarantee successful rescission, whether against the original or subsequent transferees, and its subordinate ranking reflects the courts' policy preference for commercial certainty over static security.[54]

3. Imposition of Trust

In determining whether and at which point to impose a trust on the transferee, one may usefully draw a parallel between orders for the specific performance of contracts of sale and orders to set aside defective transfers. Sir Peter Millett's extrajudicial characterisation of the latter as 'specific unperformance' aptly captures the mirror-image relationship of these orders.[55] In both contexts, the claimant's interest in performance (or unperformance) becomes vulnerable during the protracted process of conveyance (or reconveyance).[56] The right in question may be sold, consumed, damaged, or destroyed. The vendor or transferee might become insolvent.[57]

In relation to specifically enforceable contracts of sale, equity safeguards both the vendor's and purchaser's interests in performance by conferring various equities at different stages of the conveyancing process.[58] Once the purchase price is fully paid, the vendor-purchaser constructive trust becomes 'absolute'.[59] In rescission cases, the parties' interests evolve through two main stages. As argued above, it would be inappropriate to impose an immediate trust at the initial stage, before the election to rescind.[60]

[51] A Reilly, 'Is the "Mere Equity" to Rescind a Legal Power? Unpacking Hohfeld's Concept of "Volitional Control"' (2019) 39 OJLS 779; Swadling, 'The Proprietary Consequences of Fraud' (n 4) 176 (also arguing that it is not a Hohfeldian claim-right).

[52] S Smith, *Rights, Wrongs, and Injustices: The Structure of Remedial Law* (Oxford University Press 2019) 81.

[53] *Phillips v Phillips* (1861) 4 De G F & J 208, 45 ER 1164.

[54] M Neave and M Weinberg, 'The Nature and Function of Equities—Part II' (1979) 6 U Tas L Rev 115, 134–35.

[55] Millett (n 4) 416.

[56] In relation to the vendor-purchaser constructive trust, see S Gardner, *An Introduction to the Law of Trusts* (3rd edn, OUP 2011) 326–27.

[57] See also McFarlane, 'Understanding Powers to Rescind' (n 7) 55.

[58] P Turner, 'Understanding the Constructive Trust between Vendor and Purchaser' (2012) 128 LQR 582, 588.

[59] *Lloyds Bank plc v Carrick* [1996] 4 All ER 630, 637, 641; *Bridges v Mees* [1957] Ch 475; *Frenkel v LA Micro (UK) Ltd* [2024] 2 WLR 1.

[60] See text to nn 34–36.

The essence of a trust being to restrict right holders from using a right for their own benefit, such imposition would over-protect the transferors in the absence of their objective intention to stipulate this restriction. Instead, the transferors' claim for specific relief can be safeguarded from further transfers by giving the equity to rescind limited third-party effects.

The situation changes once the transferors communicate their election to rescind; they can also demand the return of the transferred right or take possession of the relevant property. At this point, transferees become aware of their liability to return the specific right rather than merely restore its value. They can no longer reasonably rely on the transferors' prior intention to make an outright gift. Professor Robert Stevens argues that knowledge of the defective consent upon rescission gives rise to a duty to reconvey the transferred right, and consequently a duty to not use it for personal benefit, thereby generating a trust.[61]

Critics have doubted why mere awareness of the defective consent should, without any court order, give rise to an immediate liability to make restitution.[62] They note that the transferees can contest this liability, that courts have discretion to refuse rescission, and that a personal liability to make restitution does not restrict the free disposal of the received funds—the imposition of a trust is therefore not justified.[63]

These objections carry weight if one assumes that the law's remedy for defective transfers is limited to imposing personal liability for restitution. However, since the default liability arising from defective transfers is the reconveyance of the right itself, Stevens's argument can be refined to overcome these objections. The transferees' knowledge remains crucial. It is not knowledge of a mere personal liability but knowledge that their right is insecure because it was acquired through a vitiated transfer. Once aware of the transferors' election to rescind, it would be unconscionable for the transferees to treat that right as indefeasibly their own. It would be wrong for them to freely dispose of, diminish, or destroy the right, thereby frustrating enforcement of any subsequent court order for its restoration. Such pre-emptive conduct proceeds on the basis that one is not liable to reconvey, when this very question remains contested. This behaviour is unequivocally objectionable where the transferees are responsible for, exploit, or are aware of the constraints on the transferors' autonomy.

Moreover, the risk of dissipation is particularly acute in cases involving fraud or duress, precisely where the protective function of equity is most important. This concern was recognised in *Shalson v Russo*,[64] where Rimer J observed that a personal claim would 'impose serious limitations on the remedies available to those who have been induced into such contracts', and conversely that a proprietary remedy was

[61] R Stevens, *The Laws of Restitution* (OUP 2023) 232–33. See also B McFarlane, 'Unjust Enrichment, Rights and Value' (n 21).

[62] Millett (n 4) 413; Swadling, 'The Proprietary Consequences of Fraud' (n 4) 185; W Swadling, 'Property' in J Atmaz Al-Sibaie and J English (eds), 'The Law of Restitution' [2024] LMCLQ 353, 366–67; R Leow, 'Trusts' in ibid 377–78.

[63] Swadling, 'The Proprietary Consequences of Fraud' (n 4) 185.

[64] [2005] Ch 281.

> an essential means of achieving a proper restoration of the original position if the representator has in the meantime parted with the property and is ostensibly a man of straw unable to satisfy the court's orders for restoration of the original position.[65]

In summary, proprietary relief is justified by two elements: the transferor's interest in the proper restoration of their original legal position and the unconscionability of the transferees to pre-empt reconveyance of rights. Such relief warrants, at minimum, the power to trace, injunctive protection, priority against transferees who are not bona fide purchasers, and a lien over traceable substitutes up to the value of the original right. Where fraud is involved, the case for disgorgement of profits is compelling—any legal system that provides fraudsters scope to lawfully launder or profit from their misdeeds risks undermining public confidence in the law.

III. The Unexercised Equity to Rescind and Tracing

We are now in the position to consider doctrinal debates in light of their theoretical underpinnings and practical considerations discussed above. A central contention is whether an unexercised power to rescind supports equitable tracing.[66]

A. The Classification of the Equity to Rescind

The case law, whilst not resolving this taxing question, has settled several key points. It is now well established that the equity to rescind, being merely a claim to specific relief against the transferee and thereby to obtain a property right, is distinct from an equitable interest in that right. As the Chief Baron explained in *Prosser v Edmonds*,[67] where a beneficiary had assigned his interest in a will due to fraud, the beneficiary had 'nothing but a naked right to file a bill in equity—no legal right—no equitable interest'.[68] Although Lord St Leonards LC in *Stump v Gaby*[69] suggested that a beneficiary making such a conveyance retained an equitable estate and an equity to rescind,[70] this view did

[65] ibid [122].

[66] S Elliott, 'Rescission' in S Elliott (ed), *Snell's Equity* (34th edn, Sweet & Maxwell 2019) [15-010]-[15-012], [26-013(c)], cited in *SK Shipping Europe plc v Capital VLCC 3 Corp* [2020] EWHC 3448 (Comm), [2021] 2 Lloyd's Rep 109 [242]; *Mackay v Wesley* [2020] EWHC 1215 (Ch) [165]. Another term commonly used to describe this power is 'mere equity': *Latec Investments Ltd v Hotel Terrigal Pty Ltd (in liq)* (1965) 113 CLR 265, 290; *National Crime Agency v Robb* [2014] EWHC 4384 (Ch), [2015] Ch 520 [43]-[44]; *Vale SA v Steinmetz* [2020] EWHC 3501 (Comm) [9(ii)]; *London Capital & Finance plc v Thomson* [2024] EWHC 2894 (Ch) [1976]. Note that mere equities also include claims for rectification and claims based on the doctrine of estoppel.

[67] (1835) 1 Y & C Ex 481, 160 ER 196.

[68] *Prosser v Edmonds* (1835) 1 Y & C Ex 481, 494; 160 ER 196, 201–02.

[69] (1852) 2 De M & G 623, 42 ER 1015.

[70] *Stump v Gaby* (1852) 2 De M & G 623, 630; 42 ER 1015, 1018. Applied in *Gresley v Mousley* (1859) 4 De G & J 78, 45 ER 31; *Dickinson v Burrell* (1866) LR 1 Eq 337; *Melbourne Banking Corp Ltd v Brougham* (1882) 7 App Cas 307.

not prevail. Lord Westbury LC's subsequent classification in *Phillips v Phillips*[71] of the equity to rescind as 'distinguished from an equitable estate' has become definitive.[72]

Another uncontroversial point is that whilst being fundamentally a personal claim, the equity to rescind exhibits certain features typically found in equitable interests. It can be devised[73] or assigned.[74] It is enforceable not only against the original transferee but also against successors in title who derive their interest through the original transferee, whether as volunteers or as purchasers with notice.[75] Nonetheless, the equity to rescind is more fragile than an equitable interest: it can be defeated by a bona fide purchaser of an equitable interest without notice,[76] whereas an equitable interest binds everyone except a purchaser of a legal interest without notice.[77] Further, as the equity to rescind ranks below an equitable interest, it cannot defeat subsequent equitable interests through the first in time rule. As discussed above, this hybrid character—being at once personal yet binding on third parties—finds its justification in bolstering the transferor's interest in specific restoration from further transfers during the interim stage of rescission.

B. Retroactive Constructive Trust in Fraudulent Transfers

Whilst no case law explicitly recognises that an unexercised equitable power to rescind is traceable, numerous judicial statements in fraud cases—mostly by Millett J, as he then was—suggest that when this power is exercised, the equitable interest revests retrospectively from the date of transfer, at least to the extent necessary to support tracing from that date.[78] These statements originate from *Lonrho plc v Fayed (No 2)*,[79] where, in dismissing claims for breach of fiduciary duty and profits obtained from a voidable sale of shares, Millett J observed that no constructive trust arises until election, implying that it arises upon election. He saw such a trust as taking effect retrospectively,[80] and

[71] (1861) 4 De G F & J 208, 45 ER 1164.

[72] See *Westminster Bank Ltd v Lee* [1956] 1 Ch 7, 19; *Latec Investment v Hotel Terigal Pty Ltd (in liq)* (1965) 113 CLR 265, 277, 288–89, 291; *National Provincial Bank Ltd v Ainsworth* [1965] AC 1175, 1238; *Daly v The Sydney Stock Exchange Ltd* (1986) 160 CLR 371, 389–90; *Bristol and West Building Society v Mothew* [1998] Ch 1, 22; *Independent Trustee Services Ltd v GP Noble Trustees Ltd* [2012] EWCA Civ 195, [2012] 3 WLR 597 [103]; *National Crime Agency v Robb* [2015] Ch 520; *Re Crown Holdings (London) Ltd (in liq)* [2015] EWHC 1876 (Ch), [2015] 2 P & CR DG20 [38].

[73] *Stump v Gaby* (1852) 2 De M & G 623, 42 ER 1015; Mitchell, Mitchell, and Watterson (n 1) [40-25] fn 78.

[74] *Gresley v Mousley* (1859) 4 De G & J 78, 45 ER 31; *Dickinson v Burrell* (1866) LR 1 Eq 337; *Melbourne Banking Corp Ltd v Brougham* (1882) 7 App Cas 307.

[75] O'Sullivan, Elliott, and Zakrzewski (n 5) [21.03]–[21.21]; Mitchell, Mitchell, and Watterson (n 1) [40-25] fn 80.

[76] *Ernest v Vivian* (1864) 33 LJ Ch (NS) 513, 519; *Bellamy v Sabine* (1857) 1 De G & J 566, 578; 44 ER 842, 847.

[77] Mitchell, Mitchell, and Watterson (n 1) [29-08]. This distinction is no longer maintained with respect to real property, as whether any interest is binding on a successor in title is determined by the provisions of the Land Registration Act 2002.

[78] *Lonrho plc v Fayed (No 2)* [1992] 1 WLR 1, 12, citing *Daly v Sydney Stock Exchange Ltd* (1986) 160 CLR 371, which in turn cited *Alati v Kruger* (1995) 94 CLR 216, 244; *El Ajou v Dollar Land Holdings plc (No 1)* [1993] 3 All ER 717, 734 (reversed on other grounds: [1994] 2 All ER 685); *Bristol & West Building Society v Mothew* [1998] Ch 1, 22–23; *Shalson v Russo* [2005] Ch 281 [119]–[125].

[79] [1992] 1 WLR 1.

[80] ibid 12.

later reaffirmed this view,[81] which is now endorsed by Rimer J in *Shalson v Russo*[82] and reinforced by the Court of Appeal in *Independent Trustee Services Ltd v GP Noble Trustees Ltd*.[83]

One consequence of deeming transferors as having held an equitable interest from the outset is that even if a substitution occurs *before* the transferor elects to rescind, at a time when they only hold a 'mere equity', their retroactively established interest will take priority over a subsequent bona fide purchaser of the equitable interest. It is doubtful whether this severe consequence was ever intended or justified, particularly given Lord Millett's view that it does not render unlawful an authorised application of trust funds.[84] Further, as Elliott observes, Lord Millett's approach creates an 'unfortunate lacuna' in legal protection beyond cases of fraud.[85]

C. Tracing from the Power to Rescind

There are three alternative analyses that would permit a transferor with an unexercised power to rescind to trace into substitutions.

First, instead of a retroactive constructive trust, the law could simply recognise a retroactive power to trace. The Full Court of the Federal Court of Australia effectively adopted this notion in *RnD Funding Pty Ltd v Roncane Pty Ltd*,[86] ruling that a claimant's interest after setting aside a fraudulently obtained contract is sufficient for tracing substitutions made from the date of transfer, without establishing a trust or fiduciary relationship.[87] Whilst this legal fiction avoids the invention of an interest under a trust where none is needed, it remains a conceptual artifice to achieve a result that the law could, and should, grant directly.

Second, Mr Mohammud Jaamae Hafeez-Baig and Dr Jordan English apply Professor John Gardner's continuity thesis of tort law liability to this problem.[88] They argue that since the original transferee who has disposed of the original right can no longer reconvey it, they should do the next-best thing and hold the substituted right on constructive trust. According to them, the normative reasons that justified the original duty continue and apply to the substituted right. The same logic extends to justifying liability on a knowing recipient who obtains their right from the original transferee.

Certainly, this argument avoids the legal fiction of a retroactive trust or power to trace. However, if the original right cannot be specifically restored, it is not obvious why the next best thing is a constructive trust over the substituted right, rather than a

[81] *El Ajou v Dollar Land Holdings plc (No 1)* [1993] 3 All ER 717; *Bristol & West Building Society v Mothew* [1998] Ch 1.
[82] [2005] Ch 281 [122], [127].
[83] [2013] Ch 91 [53].
[84] O'Sullivan, Elliott, and Zakrzewski (n 5) [16.42]; *Bristol & West Building Society v Mothew* [1998] Ch 1, 22.
[85] S Elliott, 'The Basic Structure of Rescission' in B McFarlane and S Elliott (eds), *Equity Today: 150 Years After the Judicature Reforms* (Hart 2023) 177.
[86] [2023] FCAFC 28, (2023) 297 FCR 91.
[87] ibid [109](i).
[88] MJ Hafeez-Baig and J English, *The Law of Tracing* (Federation Press 2021) [5.25]–[5.26].

lien securing the value of the original right. A constructive trust risks a windfall for the transferor that overreaches the rationale of next-best compliance. Further, Gardner's continuity thesis explains that the reason for a wrongdoer's original duty justifies their reparative duties; it does not extend to creating duties for unrelated third parties.[89] It is a conceptual leap to suggest that the reason for the original transferee's duty can generate a new duty on a subsequent recipient who was never a party to the voidable transaction.

The third and best solution is to simply recognise that an unexercised power to rescind constitutes a sufficient interest for tracing. This approach requires abandoning the retrospective trust analysis, which Lord Burrows has admonished in his extrajudicial writings,[90] and the supposed requirement that claimants must establish an equitable interest in the disputed right to enable tracing and proprietary protection. This purported requirement is mistaken: even in express trusts, objects of fiduciary powers who do not have any interest in the trust right can trace.[91]

Proponents of this solution have either argued that the power to trace is inherent in the power to rescind itself or that it is warranted by the same reasons that justify the tracing of equitable interests.[92] These arguments rest on sound theoretical and practical bases.[93] A transferor has a fundamental interest in the proper restoration to their legal position, and their interest lies in recovering a specific right rather than damages. In practical terms, the remedy of rescission is rendered futile if transferees, particularly fraudsters, can easily frustrate it by substituting the original right. Permitting the transferor to trace an unexercised power to rescind is a crucial step to securing their potential interest in specific recovery while the process of rescission unfolds. As Rimer J observed in *Shalson v Russo*, proprietary relief is essential to properly restore transferors to their original position, particularly where the transferee is fraudulent.[94]

IV. When Does Equitable Rescission Take Effect?

Whether equitable rescission takes effect upon election remains a deeply contested issue requiring Supreme Court guidance.[95] O'Sullivan, Elliott, and Zakrzewski suggest that only in cases of fraud should the election to rescind take immediate effect to impose a constructive trust on the defendant.[96] Whilst I agree that the imposition of a trust upon election in fraud cases is justified despite limited authority, I propose that,

[89] J Gardner, *From Personal Life to Private Law* (OUP 2018) 111–12, 116–17.
[90] Burrows (n 1) 161–62.
[91] *Lewis v Tamplin* [2018] EWHC 777 (Ch), [2018] WTLR 215; Ho (n 46).
[92] Häcker, *Consequences of Impaired Consent Transfers* (n 36) 289–94; Mitchell, Mitchell, and Watterson (n 1) [40-25] fn 76; R Nolan, 'Dispositions Involving Fiduciaries: The Equity to Rescind and the Resulting Trust' in P Birks and F Rose (eds), *Restitution and Equity*, vol 1: *Resulting Trusts and Equitable Compensation* (LLP 2000) 131.
[93] See Section II.B above.
[94] *Shalson v Russo* [2005] Ch 281 [122], [125].
[95] *IGE USA Investments Ltd v Revenue and Customs* [2021] EWCA Civ 534, [2021] Ch 423 [91].
[96] O'Sullivan, Elliott, and Zakrzewski (n 5) [16.39]–[16.49], [16.59]–[16.68].

even absent fraud, more intense proprietary protection should be available once the transferor has disaffirmed the transfer.

A. The Court's Jurisdiction to Grant Equitable Rescission

A significant body of judicial statements has established that, unlike the position at common law, equitable rescission requires a court order.[97] These statements include Lord Blackburn's oft-cited observation in *Erlanger v New Sombrero Phosphate Co*[98] that the court has power to 'do what is practically just'.[99] Lord Wright later reinforced this in *Spence v Crawford*,[100] emphasising that rescission is an equitable remedy and '[i]ts application is discretionary'.[101] Most recently, the Supreme Court observed that it is 'a discretionary form of relief available only at trial'.[102] Compared to common law rescission, which takes effect upon election but is barred if precise counter-restitution is impossible, the equitable approach allows courts to make financial adjustments to enable appropriate counter-restitution, thereby achieving practical justice in the unwinding of the transaction.

The main line of authority seemingly supporting the contrary view that equitable rescission is the act of the innocent party stems from Lord Atkinson's pronouncement in *Abram Steamship Company Ltd v Westville Shipping Co Ltd*.[103] In this decision, Lord Atkinson observed that the rescinding party's election 'terminates the contract', with the court order being 'merely the judicial determination of the fact that the expression by the plaintiff of his election to rescind was justified, was effective, and put an end to the contract'.[104] However, whilst consistent with equitable rescission *ab initio*, this dictum could also relate to rescission *in futuro* for breach.[105] Moreover, it was unclear whether his Lordship addressed common law or equitable rescission;[106] it also bears noting that although involving innocent misrepresentation, the case was decided on the basis of rescission for 'essential error' under Scottish law, a ground of rescission alien to English law.

[97] *Erlanger v New Sombrero Phosphate Co* (1878) 3 App Cas 1218, 1279; *Spence v Crawford* [1939] 3 All ER 271, 288; *Boyd & Forrest v The Glasgow & South Western Rlwy Co* 1915 SC 20, 30; *Hopcraft v Close Brothers Ltd* [2025] UKSC 33, [2025] 3 WLR 423 [77]; Elliott, 'Rescission' (n 66); Swadling, 'The Proprietary Consequences of Fraud' (n 4) 190–93; Chapter 4 of this book (W Swadling, 'Rescission—The Role of the Court') 81–88; O'Sullivan, Elliott, and Zakrzewski (n 5) [16.30]. See also the decisions cited in n 108.

[98] (1878) 3 App Cas 1218.

[99] ibid 1279.

[100] [1939] 3 All ER 271.

[101] ibid 288; *Vadasz v Pioneer Concrete (SA) Pty Ltd* (1995) 184 CLR 102, 114.

[102] *Hopcraft v Close Brothers Ltd* [2025] 3 WLR 423 [77].

[103] [1923] AC 773.

[104] ibid 781. For judicial statements citing Lord Atkinson's observation, see *Horsler v Zorro* [1975] 1 Ch 302, 310; *Drake Insurance plc v Provident Insurance plc* [2003] EWHC 109 (Comm), [2003] Lloyd's Rep IR 781 [31]–[32]; *Brotherton v Aseguradora Colseguros SA* [2003] EWCA Civ 705, [2003] 2 All ER (Comm) 298 [27], [44]–[48].

[105] D Chantler, 'Insurance and Misrepresentation: The Right to a Return of Premium' (1980) 14 UWAL Rev 237, 246; Swadling, 'The Proprietary Consequences of Fraud' (n 4) 192; cf Elliott, 'The Basic Structure of Rescission' (n 85) 174–75.

[106] O'Sullivan, Elliott, and Zakrzewski (n 5) [11.75]–[11.76].

Further, it has been argued that even accepting equitable rescission to be discretionary, it can still take effect upon election, because this discretion is not arbitrary but guided by the principle of achieving practical justice, and the court can later declare the election ineffective if it decides to deny rescission.[107] Whilst this argument may be compelling for clear-cut cases where rescission will most likely be ordered, it loses its persuasive force as a general rule. This is because, though principled, judicial discretion is inherently unpredictable.

It bears noting that the scope of judicial discretion may be very broad. A line of authority suggests that it extends beyond determining whether the bars to rescission can be overcome by the principle of practical justice, and includes the discretion to refuse rescission when it would be 'unfair and disproportionate', such as when an alternative remedy is more 'suitable'.[108] By contrast, in *Patarkatsishvili v Woodward-Fisher*,[109] a case of fraudulent misrepresentation, Fancourt J recently rejected the proposition that a court retains a residual discretion to refuse rescission.[110] In this decision, the misrepresentor who sold a valuable house for £32.5 million sought to resist rescission by arguing that he had no funds to repay the purchase price and he could not resell the house to raise the funds until title was revested in him. As Fancourt J explained: 'if counter restitution can be given and there is no bar, there is no residual discretion that the Court can exercise on the basis that it appears fairer to leave a claimant to recover damages at law.'[111] Until the Supreme Court provides guidance, these conflicting judicial opinions mean that the availability of rescission will remain unpredictable.[112]

Even if judicial discretion is confined to the bars of rescission, courts employ a multifactor approach, weighing various considerations holistically, rather than ticking off a checklist of requirements.[113] They might order discretionary adjustments of various types, such as allowances, set-offs, and accounts of profits, to achieve substantial *restitutio in integrum*.[114] They may also find that the circumstances have so changed that

[107] Elliott, 'The Basic Structure of Rescission' (n 85) 178. Even if no equitable bars apply to deny rescission, rescission may be denied under s 2(2) of the Misrepresentation Act 1967 if the courts consider it inequitable, after taking into account the nature of the misrepresentation and the respective losses on the parties. See generally Chapter 9 of this book (S Elliott, 'The Power to Prevent Disproportionate Relief').

[108] *UBS AG (London Branch) v Kommunale Wasserwerke Leipzig* [2017] EWCA Civ 1567, [2017] 2 Lloyd's Rep 621 [157], [370]–[371]; *Johnson v EBS Pensioner Trustees Ltd* [2002] EWCA Civ 164, [2002] Lloyd's Rep PN 309 [79] ('the court considers what fairness requires not only when addressing the question of the precise form of relief, but also when considering whether the remedy should be granted at all'); *Hurstanger Ltd v Wilson* [2007] EWCA Civ 299, [2007] 1 WLR 2351 [47]; *SK Shipping Europe Ltd v Capital VLCCC 3 Corp (The C Challenger)* [2021] 2 Lloyd's Rep 109 [241]; cf *SK Shipping Europe Ltd v Capital VLCCC 3 Corp (The C Challenger)* [2022] EWCA Civ 231, [2022] 2 All ER (Comm) 784 [89] preferring to defer the issue for future consideration; *ABFA Commodities Trading Ltd v Petraco Oil Company SA* [2024] EWHC 147 (Comm) [233]. For a powerful refutation of this broad discretion, see J English, 'Bribery and Secret Commissions: A Common Law–Equity Divide?' [2025] LMCLQ 158, 172–75.

[109] [2025] EWHC 265 (Ch).

[110] ibid [187]–[189]. See also *De Molestina v Ponton* [2002] 1 Lloyd's Rep 271, 287.

[111] *Patarkatsishvili v Woodward-Fisher* [2025] EWHC 265 (Ch) [187].

[112] In *Hopcraft v Close Brothers Ltd* [2025] 3 WLR 423 [77], the Supreme Court referred to the flexible approach to *restitutio in integrum* to demonstrate the discretionary nature of rescission; it did not further discuss the existence of a broad, residual discretion to refuse the remedy.

[113] Smith (n 52) 320–21.

[114] *Erlanger v New Sombrero Phosphate Co* (1878) 3 App Cas 1218, 1279; *Spence v Crawford* [1939] 3 All ER 271, 288.

no adjustment could help restore the parties substantially to their original position, and deny rescission altogether.

Crucially, this global weighing of multiple factors means that even minor differences in facts may yield different yet valid outcomes that fall inside 'the generous ambit within which a reasonable disagreement is possible'.[115] In the words of the Court of Appeal in *UBS AG (London Branch) v Kommunale Wasserwerke Leipzig GmbH*,[116] this discretion involves 'one of those multi-factorial assessments to be conducted by the trial judge, with which an appellate court will be slow to intervene, unless the judge's conclusion was clearly wrong, or based upon some evident failure of analysis'.[117]

If it is difficult to predict the outcome with any reasonable certainty—save where courts are highly likely to exercise their discretion in a particular way in certain types of cases—any commercial certainty gained through the immediate effectiveness of election proves fleeting. Indeed, complex chains of transactions made on the assumption that an election is effective may later need to be unwound. There seems little justification for maintaining as a general rule that equitable rescission takes immediate effect.

B. Special Exception for Fraud

The concern about the unpredictability of outcome carries less force in cases where courts have standardly exercised the discretion in a particular manner. In fraud cases, for instance, courts are much less likely to deny rescission against a fraudster on the ground of *restitutio in integrum*. In *Spence v Crawford*, Lord Thankerton was adamant that a fraudster 'is not entitled in bar of restitution to found on dealings with the subject purchased, which he has been enabled by his fraud to carry out'.[118] Lord Wright, after emphasising the discretionary nature of rescission, added that 'the court will be more drastic in exercising its discretionary powers in a case of fraud than in a case of innocent misrepresentation'.[119]

Patarkatsishvili v Woodward-Fisher provides a neat illustration of the courts' willingness to achieve practical justice in requiring counter-restitution in a fraud case. There, Fancourt J clarified that this bar is concerned with the ability of the claimant to make counter-restitution, not that of the defendant to make effective restitution.[120] Accordingly, the defendant vendor's lack of funds to repay the purchase price did not preclude rescission. The court ordered title to be revested in him subject to an equitable

[115] *G v G (Minors: Custody Appeal)* [1995] 1 WLR 647, 652; *Tanfern Ltd v Cameron MacDonald (Practice Note)* [2000] 1 WLR 1311 [32].
[116] [2017] 2 Lloyd's Rep 621.
[117] ibid [171].
[118] *Spence v Crawford* [1939] 3 All ER 271, 281.
[119] ibid 288.
[120] *Patarkatsishvili v Woodward-Fisher* [2025] EWHC 265 (Ch) [223].

lien to secure the repayment. As mentioned above, Fancourt J was also adamant that the courts' discretion is limited to the bars of rescission. Citing *Snell's Equity*, he observed that if rescission is not barred, the claimant is entitled to have the contract rescinded as of right.[121]

The courts' commitment to grant robust relief in cases of fraud is underscored by the *Lonrho* line of authority discussed above. In these cases, courts did not simply demonstrate a greater willingness to order rescission but took the more radical approach of treating election as immediately giving rise to a retroactive constructive trust. O'Sullivan, Elliott, and Zakrzewski attempt to reconcile the conflicting authorities by proposing that an election to rescind takes immediate effect only in cases of fraud.[122] In the absence of a comprehensive framework for proprietary relief, their proposal provides a principled and pragmatic interim solution. As a matter of principle, once transferees, particularly those who were dishonest, know of the election to rescind, it becomes unconscionable for them to deal with the transferred right in a way that would thwart a future court order against them.[123] From a practical standpoint, the proposal addresses a critical risk, namely that upon learning of the election, dishonest transferees may rush to dispose of the right, if they have not already done so. Injunctive relief may prove too slow to prevent such dissipation given the speed with which money and assets can move around in this digital world.[124]

V. Proprietary Protection beyond Fraud

As Elliott points out in separate writing, O'Sullivan, Elliott, and Zakrzewski's proposal leaves an 'unfortunate lacuna' in non-fraud cases.[125] Although the risk of dissipation is most acute in cases of fraud, it remains a material concern outside of fraud. Upon learning of the election to rescind, even honest transferees may become less diligent in preserving the transferred right, as they know they may not be entitled to keep it, or they may attempt to sell it and extract value to fund their own expenses.

A legal system must establish coherent and stable rules to protect a transferor's incipient rights throughout the protracted process of rescission. To this end, I propose a framework that defines the appropriate level of protection both before and after disaffirmation by balancing the transferor's interest against those of non-fraudulent transferees and third parties. This approach is preferable to relying on the artificial, all-or-nothing remedy of the constructive trust. Although designed for non-fraud cases, this framework can accommodate fraud cases.

[121] ibid [189]. See text to n 111.
[122] O'Sullivan, Elliott, and Zakrzewski (n 5) [16.39]–[16.49], [16.59]–[16.68].
[123] See text to nn 20–32.
[124] *Shalson v Russo* [2005] Ch 281 [127].
[125] Elliott, 'The Basic Structure of Rescission' (n 85) 177.

A. Before Disaffirmation

As argued in Section III of this chapter, transferors should be granted the power to trace their equity to rescind from the date of the transfer. This power to trace is a vital mechanism to preserve the transferor's potential interest in the transferred right by preserving its identifiability through mixing and dispositions. The equity to rescind should bind not only the original transferee but also successors in title, whose conscience is affected or who have not paid consideration. These proprietary effects would stabilise the transferor's position without impeding the legitimate interests of bona fide purchasers to deal with the property freely. Crucially, these effects could be achieved without the legal fiction of a retroactive constructive trust.

B. After Disaffirmation

Once they elect to rescind, the transferor's position becomes more vulnerable due to the heightened risk of dissipation. Correspondingly, the transferee's interest weakens, as awareness of the election makes it unconscionable for them to deal with the right in a manner that would pre-empt a future court order. This shift in balance strengthens the case for continuing to allow transferors in non-fraud cases to trace the equity to rescind, just as they could before election. Whilst the lack of a strong likelihood of the court order for rescission may not warrant treating their election as creating an immediate equitable interest under a constructive trust, they should nonetheless be afforded greater access to injunctive relief than before election.

1. Injunctions

A key relief for transferors is the proprietary injunction, which preserves assets over which a claimant asserts an *in specie* claim.[126] This relief offers stronger protection than a freezing injunction, which prevents defendants from disposing of their own assets pending judgment.[127] Courts have often emphasised their willingness to grant proprietary injunctions to prevent the claimed assets from being dissipated before trial and equity being 'invoked in vain'.[128] Furthermore, whilst a freezing injunction requires proof of both a 'good arguable case' and a 'real risk of dissipation',[129] a claimant for a proprietary injunction needs only to show 'a serious issue to be tried' and satisfy the

[126] *Republic of Haiti v Duvalier* [1990] QB 202, 214.

[127] Civil Procedure Rules 1988, r 15.1(c); S Gee, *Gee on Commercial Injunctions* (7th edn, Sweet & Maxwell 2022) [3-030]; T Grant and D Mumford (eds), *Civil Fraud: Law, Practice & Procedure* (Sweet & Maxwell 2018) [28-197]–[28-216]; *Société Générale, Singapore Branch v Inter-Pacific Group PTE Ltd* [2020] HKCFI 1508 [24]; *Zhang Yan v ASA Bullion Ltd* [2019] HKCFI 179 [11]. For details about the proprietary injunction, see P McKenna, 'What's Mine is Mine—Practical Considerations of Proprietary Injunctions' (2023) 30 CLP 67.

[128] *Raffineria Siciliana Petroli SpA v Mabanaft GmbH* (CA (Civ Div), 1 December 1978), endorsed in *Bankers Trusts Co v Shapira* [1980] 1 WLR 1274, 1281.

[129] *Convoy Collateral Ltd v Broad Idea* [2021] UKPC 24, [2023] AC 389 [101].

balance of justice and convenience tests.[130] Finally, a proprietary injunction makes no provision for the defendant's reasonable day-to-day expenses[131] and permits legal expenses only if the defendant has no other assets.[132]

Claimants seeking a proprietary injunction need to demonstrate a proprietary interest in the relevant asset. An equity to rescind is insufficient for this purpose, as the transferee has full ownership until the court orders rescission. Where transferors have disaffirmed fraudulent sales, courts have granted proprietary injunctions, citing *Shalson v Russo* to establish that the election avoids the transaction immediately and creates the necessary equitable interest retrospectively.[133] It remains unclear whether this legal fiction will also be invoked for non-fraudulent transfers.

This fiction gives the impression that the courts are merely protecting a pre-existing proprietary interest, when in fact they are protecting potential interests in property. Given the courts' readiness to order rescission for fraud, a transferor's potential interest in specific recovery is substantial; without such protection, the enforcement of the prospective court order may easily be stultified. This aligns with the approach in the parallel context of land sales, where Morritt LJ in *Chattey v Farndale Holdings Inc*[134] noted that even purchasers not yet entitled to claim specific performance (not having paid in full) have sufficient interest to secure injunctive relief.[135] These cases show that courts have considered a strong potential interest in obtaining specific relief to be sufficient for the purpose of a proprietary injunction.[136]

Should transferors in non-fraud cases also have access to proprietary injunctions? I contend they should. Whilst the prospects of obtaining specific relief may be weaker for non-fraud victims than for fraud victims, their equity to rescind nonetheless constitutes a claim for specific relief capable of binding successors, unlike a damages claim, which is typically protected by a freezing injunction. Moreover, as argued above, once a transferee knows that they may face an order for specific relief rather than mere damages, they should not retain unfettered freedom to deal with the right in a way that frustrates the enforcement of any future court order.[137] The proprietary injunction's stricter terms—particularly its prohibition on the defendant's use of assets for ordinary business dealings—better reflects this standard of conduct. Furthermore, considering the pressing need to protect the transferors' potential interest from the heightened risk of dissipation post-disaffirmation, such an interest should suffice for a proprietary injunction. Should courts nonetheless restrict transferors to a freezing

[130] *Madoff Securities v Raven* [2011] EWHC 3102 (Comm), [2012] 2 All ER (Comm) 634 [127]; *Purple Star Shipping Ltd v Fortune Shipping Ltd* (QBD (Comm Ct), 13 December 2001) (no need to establish the risk of dissipation).

[131] *Polly Peck International plc v Nadir (No 2)* [1992] 4 All ER 769, 784.

[132] *Skatteforvaltningen v Barac* [2020] EWHC 377 (Comm).

[133] *Gallahue v Tripathi* [2024] EWHC 725 (Ch); *BHSC Global LLC v Griffith* (Ch D, 27 February 2017); *Lili Hu v New Nordic Management International Ltd* [2024] HKDC 9 (proprietary injunction rejected due to lack of disaffirmation of a fraudulent contract); Gee (n 127) [7-013].

[134] (1998) 75 P & CR 298.

[135] ibid 306; Gee (n 127) [7-013].

[136] See eg *Convoy Collateral Ltd v Broad Idea* [2021] UKPC 24, [2023] AC 389 [37], [85].

[137] For the analogous position in vendor-purchaser trusts, see K Gray and S Gray, *Elements of Land Law* (5th edn, OUP 2009) [8.1.63].

injunction, such relief should be supplemented with an ancillary order imposing similar restrictions.

2. Third Parties

Even injunctive relief against original transferees may prove ineffective where they act with sufficient speed to transfer the claimed rights to third parties. In the modern commercial world, this is readily achievable. The practical reasons that justify allowing transferors to claim a proprietary injunction against the original transferee—the latter's knowledge post-disaffirmation and the risk of dissipation—also justify allowing them to make such a claim against a successor who is not a bona fide purchaser for value of the legal and equitable interest.[138]

O'Sullivan, Elliott, and Zakrzewski have argued that transferors should also be allowed to claim personal liability in dishonest assistance, the requisite trust relationship being satisfied by the imposition of a constructive trust upon disaffirmation.[139] Whilst such liability is clearly justified, the retroactive trust argument adds very little to the analysis. Given that accessory liability is not limited to fiduciary relationships but extends to inducement of breach of contract, and given that the transferors' interest in specific recovery is no weaker than a contracting party's interest in contractual performance, some form of accessory liability should be available even if we discard the trust analysis.

3. Transferees' Obligations

It remains to consider the precise nature of the transferors' interest against the transferees following disaffirmation. The analogy drawn by Millett J in *Lonrho plc (No 2) v Fayed* with specifically enforceable contracts of sale proves instructive.[140] Much like vendors in such contracts, the transferees may continue to use the property (such as driving the purchased vehicle), but must not destroy or diminish the right and undermine the efficacy of the final court order.[141] Further, vendors must maintain the property in the condition it was in at the time of contract, and are liable for any loss or damage resulting from their negligence.[142] They are no longer free to dispose of the right, as doing so would defeat any future judgment against them.[143] That said, they have no duty to enhance the value of the property.[144]

[138] Gee (n 127) [7-013], citing the *Lonrho* line of cases in support. It is beyond the scope of this chapter to discuss whether general creditors of a fraudulent transferee who has become insolvent would bar rescission. For an insightful treatment of this point, see Chapter 10 of this book (M Raczynska, 'Third-Party Rights and Insolvency as Bars to Rescission').

[139] O'Sullivan, Elliott, and Zakrzewski (n 5) [16.65]–[16.68]; Elliott, 'The Basic Structure of Rescission' (n 85) 177; cf *Naaman v Jaken Properties Australia Pty Ltd* [2025] HCA 1, (2025) 99 ALJR 295 [35]–[37] (the majority) (no liability for dishonest assistance in the absence of a fiduciary relationship).

[140] *Lonrho plc v Fayed (No 2)* [1992] 1 WLR 1 (Ch) 12.

[141] See a similar duty of a successor trustee to a former trustee's entitlement to indemnity from the trust fund, which has also been analogised to the vendor-purchaser trust: *Naaman v Jaken Properties Australia Pty Ltd* (2025) 99 ALJR 295 [28]; *Equity Trust (Jersey) Ltd v Halabi* [2022] UKPC 36, [2023] AC 877.

[142] *Englewood Properties Ltd v Patel* [2005] EWHC 188 (Ch), [2005] 1 WLR 1961 [48], [54].

[143] *Chen Con-Ling v Quay Properties Pte Ltd* [2004] SGHC 31, [2004] 2 SLR 181 [25]–[34].

[144] *Englewood Properties Ltd v Patel* [2005] 1 WLR 1961 [58].

I propose that upon disaffirmation, transferees who obtain their right through the claimant's defective consent, whether directly or indirectly, should be placed in a comparable position. In *Lonrho*, for example, Millett J noted the transferee's limited 'duty' to return the transferred right upon court order. In dismissing a vendor's claim that fraudulent purchasers of company shares held the controlling interest obtained from using the fraudulently acquired shares on trust, his Lordship was unequivocal that the obligations of the transferees 'would not extend beyond the property actually obtained by the contract and liable to be returned'.[145]

VI. Conclusion

The analysis of proprietary protection in defective transfers has long been obscured by technical debates about the timing of rescission and nature of the trust arising upon rescission. The parallel with specifically enforceable contracts of sale demonstrates that even where a constructive trust analysis is adopted, the trust operates *sub modo*, reflecting the fundamentally contractual rather than fiduciary nature of the parties' relationship.

This chapter has taken a more foundational approach by examining the theoretical foundations for setting aside defective transfers. This examination reveals the competing interests that equity must balance in unwinding such transfers. Moreover, it enables a direct assessment of the degree of protection that should be afforded to transferors in preserving the transferred right pending court order, without resort to artificial doctrinal constructs.

[145] *Lonrho plc v Fayed (No 2)* [1992] 1 WLR 1 (Ch) 12.

Index

For the benefit of digital users, indexed terms that span two pages (e.g., 52–53) may, on occasion, appear on only one of those pages.

Footnotes are indicated by n.